Overland In 1846

DIARIES AND LETTERS
OF THE CALIFORNIA-OREGON TRAIL

Overland In 1846

DIARIES AND LETTERS
OF THE CALIFORNIA-OREGON TRAIL

Volume I

EDITED BY

DALE MORGAN

University of Nebraska Press
Lincoln and London

HOUSTON PUBLIC LIBRARY

First Bison Book printing: 1993
Most recent printing indicated by the last digit below:
10   9   8   7   6   5   4   3   2   1

Library of Congress Cataloging-in-Publication Data
Overland in 1846: diaries and letters of the California-Oregon
Trail / edited by Dale Morgan.
p.   cm.
Originally published: Georgetown, CA: Talisman Press, 1963.
ISBN 0-8032-3176-8 (cloth: v. 1). — ISBN 0-8032-8200-1 (pbk.: v. 1). —
ISBN 0-8032-3178-4 (cloth: set). — ISBN 0-8032-3177-6 (cloth: v. 2). —
ISBN 0-8032-8201-X (pbk.: v. 2). — ISBN 0-8032-8202-8 (pbk.: set)
1. West (U.S.)—Description and travel—To 1848.   2. Pioneers—West
(U.S.)—Diaries.   3. Oregon Trail.   4. California Trail.   5. Overland
journeys to the Pacific.   I. Morgan, Dale Lowell, 1914–1971.
F592.094   1994
978′.02—dc20
93-8247   CIP

Reprinted from the original edition published by the Talisman Press,
Georgetown, California, in 1963. The foldout Map of T. H. Jefferson,
which was carried in a back pocket, has been divided into sections for this
Bison Book edition and inserted between pages 236 and 237.

∞

Contents

Preface   9

Introduction   14
    by DALE MORGAN

Diary of William E. Taylor,
    with a Letter by John Craig   118

Diary of Nicholas Carriger   143

Diary of Virgil Pringle   159

Journal of Thomas Holt   189

Diary of George McKinstry, with a Letter   205

Diary of James Mathers   219

The Map of T. H. Jefferson   237

Diary of Hiram Miller and J. F. Reed,
    With Letters by J. F. Reed and
    Virginia E. B. Reed   245

Diary of Patrick Breen   306

Diaries of the Donner Relief   323

Notes   369

The Jefferson Map   between pages 236–37 Vol. I

Map of the California-Oregon Trail   vi–vii Vol. II

To
Fawn McKay Brodie
for charm and grace of person, devoted friendship,
and unflinching scholarship, shared with me these
twenty years and more

Dale L. Morgan

Preface

The year 1846 is one of the most remarkable in the varied annals of overland emigration across the American West, characterized by comedy, tragedy, high adventure, achievement, and frustration as are few others in our history. Bernard DeVoto saw it as *The Year of Decision,* and under that title published a modern classic, a book which should be read by all interested in the West or our unfolding destiny as a continental nation. His purpose, he said, was to tell the story of some people who went West in 1846, and "to tell that story in such a way that the reader may realize the far western frontier experience, which is part of our cultural inheritance, as personal experience." The year 1846, DeVoto thought, "best dramatizes personal experience as national experience. Most of our characters are ordinary people, the unremarkable commoners of the young democracy." Their story nevertheless was "a decisive part of a decisive turn in the history of the United States," when for the American people the future crystallized out of the inchoate. The expansion of the United States to the Pacific, the emergence of a continental nation, in DeVoto's view may have made the Civil War inevitable, but also determined the outcome: "The past was not going to win the appeal to arms, the continental nation was not going to be Balkanized, it was going to remain an empire and dominate the future."

The Year of Decision, 1846, to repeat, is a masterpiece, and the two volumes which comprise the present work are in no sense designed to take its place. We are not here concerned with the broader history of 1846. The settlement of the Oregon question, the war with Mexico, the military campaigns on the Rio Grande, into the South-

west, and down through California, the expulsion of
the Mormons from Illinois and the commencement of
their migration into the West—these and many other
events which have given 1846 unique character are part
of the pulsing background, but do not primarily preoccupy
the people who march across our stage. They were intent,
for various reasons that will emerge from their letters and
diaries, on getting to California and Oregon. How they
got there, and what happened to them along the way, as
they themselves saw fit to record the facts, is the business
of this book.

That the pace of discovery is swift is suggested by the
fact that few of the documents here printed were available
to Bernard DeVoto for a work printed no more than
twenty years ago; some had not then been found, even.
Much else was locked up, all but inaccessibly, in contemporary newspapers. No book can undertake to print the
whole documentary record for the California and Oregon Trail in 1846, not even two volumes like these, and
the Introduction, supplemented by the notes added to the
diaries, letters, and newspaper notices, must contrive to
suggest the extent of this larger wealth of information.

Basically, the present work is a source book for overland
emigration in 1846. Many diaries too short to merit book
publication together provide the substance for Volume I.
The extent of the interrelationships among these diaries
and some related letters is brought out, I hope, in the
manner of presentation, with notes and index serving to
tie them together. This first volume, made up primarily
of diaries, but including a few letters written by the
diarists, members of their families, and others, is rather
particularistic; it invites us to share the experiences of
specific overland travelers who may or may not be making
the journey together. The second volume, fashioned from
letters and newspaper accounts, has a broader outlook,
perhaps not less personal, but exhibiting a more deliberate
purpose of communicating to others what it was like to go

West in 1846, and whether California and Oregon were worth the trouble occasioned in getting there. Together the two volumes record details of personal and universal experience which give us a better understanding of the West as well as of the emigration of this particular year, and provide a better perspective on the history of over-land emigration generally.

William E. Taylor's diary is in the collections of the Sutter's Fort Historical Monument, and is printed by the permission of his grandson, Mr. Vernon H. Taylor, Napa, California. The supplementary letter by John Craig comes from the George Boosinger Papers in the Henry E. Huntington Library, first made available to me by Mr. Leslie E. Bliss, and now printed by permission of the Librarian, Mr. Robert O. Dougan. The manuscript diaries of Nicholas Carriger, George McKinstry, Jr., and Patrick Breen are prized treasures of the Bancroft Library, and I am indebted to the Director, Dr. George P. Hammond, for permission to print them—Carriger and McKinstry for the first time. The diary of James Mathers, previously unavailable to students, and a major addition to the literature of the California trail, I have been enabled to print through the generous interest and cooperation of the owner, Miss Frances E. Campbell of San Francisco, and by permission of a descendant, Mrs. Mattie Bartol, Talent, Oregon. Virgil Pringle's diary I have resuscitated from its grave in the Oregon Pioneer Association *Transactions* for 1920, the original manu-script having disappeared; Thomas Holt's journal of the relief on the Applegate Cutoff has slumbered even longer in the 1847 files of the *Oregon Spectator*. The diary of Hiram Miller and James Frazier Reed, with other docu-ments, comes from the Reed Papers in the Sutter's Fort Historical Monument collection. This diary, with two diaries of the Donner Relief and other items of interest, was first edited by Carroll D. Hall, curator at Sutter's Fort, in *Donner Miscellany,* a 1947 publication of the

Book Club of California. All documents from the Reed Papers are reprinted with Mr. Hall's cordial cooperation and permission.

Other items, as will be seen by the notes, come from the McGlashan and other collections in the Bancroft Library, from the California State Library, the Henry E. Huntington Library, the Southwest Museum, the Yale University Library, the Oregon Historical Society, the Princeton University Library, and from newspaper files I have sought out in institutions scattered from one coast to the other of this continental nation shaped in 1846— above all, the Library of Congress, Missouri Historical Society, Newberry Library, St. Joseph Public Library, and the Bancroft Library. I have received help at different times from all those persons and institutions mentioned above; and from many of my colleagues in the Bancroft Library—especially Mrs. Julia H. Macleod, Mrs. Helen Harding Bretnor, Mrs. Elisabeth K. Gudde, Miss Estelle Rebec, Mr. Robert Becker, and Dr. John Barr Tompkins. Miss Haydée Noya in the Huntington Library, Miss Louise Barry in the Kansas State Historical Society, Miss Priscilla Knuth in the Oregon Historical Society, Mr. Archibald Hanna, Jr., in the Yale University Library, and Mrs. Frances Stadler in the Missouri Historical Society have contributed richly to this as to most of my books. Mr. Joseph G. Colgan, in association with Mr. James McConkey, son of my cherished friend, the late Darel McConkey, has prepared the general map. Others who have made material contributions include Mr. Robert Greenwood, of the Talisman Press, Dr. Charles L. Camp, Mr. Allan R. Ottley, Mr. Charles Kelly, Mr. Carl I. Wheat, the late J. Roderic Korns, Miss Madeline Reeder, my cousin Mr. T. Gerald Bleak and Mr. Dwight L. Jones, with whom (as with the regretted Rod Korns) I did much of the field research at different times, Mr. Daniel Howe and his wife Sandra, Mrs. Irene Paden, my mother Mrs. Emily H. Morgan, my brother James S.

Morgan and his wife Mary Beth, Miss Helen Sanders, Mr. James de T. Abajian, Mr. Clyde Arbuckle, Mrs. Lois C. Stone, Mr. Newton Baird, Dr. Erwin G. Gudde, Dr. Ernst Correll, Dr. George R. Stewart, and Mr. Alfred L. Bush. Many others knowingly or unknowingly over a period of twenty-five years have contributed to my education respecting overland travel, the year 1846, and the West, and whether I can name them or not, I hope they will feel that the effort has been worth while.

DALE L. MORGAN

THE BANCROFT LIBRARY
BERKELEY, CALIFORNIA
SEPTEMBER, 1963

"Crossing the Prairie"

Introduction

The origins of the emigration of the 1840's to California and Oregon may be traced as far back as one has the will to go—to the Oregon missionary crusade of the 1830's, to the opening of the unknown West by the fur hunters of preceding decades, to Lewis and Clark, to the age-long quest for a Northwest Passage and a Western Sea. But in this book we shall consider that the era of emigration began in 1840, when Joel Walker set out from Missouri for the Pacific, as the first avowed homeseeker, taking along his wife, their children, and her sister.

Brother of the redoubtable mountain man Joseph Reddeford Walker who appears and reappears in these pages, Joel Walker went to Oregon initially, but next year went south, the two women in his family the first American

14

women to reach California overland. Walker is important mainly as a symbol. John A. Sutter had similarly traveled overland to Oregon in 1838, voyaging to the Sandwich Islands and to the Russian establishment at Sitka before sailing down the coast to become in 1839, one of the most extraordinary of the early Californians. Thomas Jefferson Farnham, who had set out for Oregon in 1839 with a small party of Peorians flaunting the motto "Oregon or the Grave," had managed the happier alternative and come back to the States in 1840 to write an account of his adventures. But more momentous was the overland emigration that for no very clear reason began to shape up in the summer of 1840.

California, not Oregon, was the objective of the Western Colonization Society organized in St. Louis that summer. But the excitement attending all such movements had a way of fading out when an adverse wind began to blow, and a published letter Farnham had written from the Hawaiian Islands chilled the California fever. Comparatively few were the emigrants who put in an appearance at the rendezvous point in western Missouri in the spring of 1841. They elected John Bartleson as their captain (otherwise he would not have gone), and early in May set out into the West.[1]

The Bartleson company were greenhorns such as the West has rarely seen, and no man knows what might have become of them except that a party of Catholic missionaries under Father Pierre-Jean De Smet set out at the same time for the Flathead country, guided by the experienced mountain man Thomas Fitzpatrick. The emigrants traveled with the missionaries as far as the Bear River, in that time getting a considerable education respecting the West and trail life. At Soda Springs some of the Bartleson company thought better of striking off

---

[1]A considerable literature exists for the Bartleson Party of 1841, see Doyce B. Nunis, ed., *Josiah Belden 1841 California Overland Pioneer* (Georgetown, Calif., 1962) for a modern bibliographical summation.

into the unknown toward California, choosing to stay with
the established trail to Oregon. But 31 men, one woman,
and her infant child accepted the risks and turned down
Bear River.

That through many vicissitudes the Bartleson party
reached California is something of a miracle. They descended the Bear to the Great Salt Lake, rounded the
northern and western edge of the Salt Desert to Pilot
Peak, and succeeded in getting their wagons across Silver
Zone Pass to Gosiute Valley. At the base of the Pequop
Mountains they had to abandon the wagons — thereby
furnishing firewood for some emigrants of 1846 — and
pack the rest of the distance to California. With some
difficulty they found their way to the Humboldt. From
the sink of that desert river they rode south through the
deserts to the Walker River, and after much trouble, in
a half-starved condition, crossed the Sierra in the vicinity
of Sonora Pass. One of the party, James John, became
separated from the others, though he eventually reached
Sutter's; the rest got to the haven of Dr. John Marsh's
rancho at the foot of Mt. Diablo on November 4.

After a fashion the Bartleson party had proved that
it was possible to reach California overland. That was
the word carried back to Missouri in the summer of 1842
by a small party which included Bartleson himself—and
more to the point, since Bartleson had had his fill of far
countries, also included Joseph Chiles. This returning
party took a southern route via New Mexico, hence did
not encounter the small emigration of 1842 which had
Oregon as its destination.

That emigration left the Missouri frontier captained
by Dr. Elijah White, newly-appointed subagent for the
Oregon Indians, but characteristically the company soon
deposed White and elected in his place a 23-year-old
Ohio lawyer, Lansford W. Hastings, of whom a great
deal will be said hereafter. From Oregon Hastings traveled south to California in 1843, following the trail fur
traders had beaten out during the previous decade, then

in 1844, full of ideas, went home to write a book.

Meanwhile the trickle of emigration had become a swelling tide. In 1843 the "Great Migration" took the trail to Oregon, and among the Oregonians traveled a few professed Californians, among whom Joseph Chiles was the moving figure. West of Fort Laramie, Chiles fell in with Joseph R. Walker, who had gone to California and back as Captain Bonneville's lieutenant in 1833-1834, and Chiles engaged Walker to guide the greater part of his company to the Valley of California, hoping he could find a way across the Sierra for their wagons. Chiles himself, with a small party which notably included P. B. Reading, undertook to reconnoiter another route. He kept to the Oregon Trail as far as Fort Boise, then struck off to the west, up the Malheur River and on to the waters of the Sacramento. The route was a difficult one, never again traveled by California emigrants, but it brought Chiles safely to Sutter's the second week of November. Walker had a rough time conducting the wagons south to Walker's Pass; he finally abandoned the wagons short of the summit, and it was near the end of the year before he shepherded his charges into the settlements.

The emigration of 1844, again very large, principally had Oregon as its objective. But a small group who have come down in history as the Stephens-Townsend-Murphy party, mostly from Jackson County, Missouri, were avowed Californians. They were fortunate in having chosen Council Bluffs as their starting point, for the torrential rains of 1844 which flooded the country farther south and subjected the emigrants out of Independence and St. Joseph to interminable delay, scarcely hindered travel on the trails north of the Platte. This little company, with some emigrants making for Oregon, has the distinction of having opened across the Green River Valley what became known as the Greenwood Cutoff, named for Caleb Greenwood, traveling with his sons in the company. This cutoff, distinguished by a "dry drive" from the Big Sandy to Green River, cut across the wide bend to the south past Fort Bridger; few are the records of travel on it before 1846. Beyond Fort Hall, the Stephens-Townsend-Murphy party followed the track of 1843 up Raft River and on to Mary's River (the Humboldt), and it is their great distinction, after reaching the Sink of the Humboldt, that they opened the trail up the Truckee River and over Donner Pass which became, until 1849, the primary avenue for overland travel into and out of California.[2] Much more might be said of this emigration of 1844, as of the enlarged emigration of 1845 to Oregon and to California, but we shall focus upon the fact that the news began to spread abroad that a wagon road, however difficult, had been made all the way to California.

This news was carried back to the States by a small party of fifteen men who set out from Sutter's Fort on May 12, 1845. Caleb Greenwood and two half-breed sons were going only as far as Fort Hall, where they expected to find employment guiding the next emigration to Sutter's Fort. The others were going home. One of their number, William H. Winter, wrote of their experiences in a joint work with Overton Johnson, published at Lafayette, Indiana, in 1846 as *Route Across the Rocky Mountains, with a Description of Oregon and California.* Before discussing Winter's narrative, the only detailed account of the first eastbound journey over the California Trail, it seems appropriate to print a letter by one of Winter's fellow-travelers, E. A. Farwell, for this letter has been unknown and has some interesting things to say about the pioneering of the trail. Addressed to the New Orleans *Picayune* in late April, Farwell's communication

---

[2]The standard account of the pioneering of the California Trail up the Truckee River and over Donner Pass is that by a member of the Stephens-Townsend-Murphy party, Moses Schallenberger, edited by George R. Stewart as *The Opening of the California Trail* (Berkeley and Los Angeles, 1953). (In this work as in some others, Stewart as a matter of personal taste renders Elisha Stephens' name as Stevens, though the man himself used the form Stephens.)

was immediately picked up by the Missouri papers, notably the *Missouri Republican* of May 5, 1846, and very likely some late-departing California emigrants left the frontier comforted by his words:

Messrs. Editors:

In your paper of the 22nd I notice an article of news from California, in which Capt. Fremont is spoken of as having discovered a new and eligible route for wheeled vehicles into that country, thereby effecting a saving of sixty days in that journey.[3] Not knowing the route he may have gone, I will state for the information of those wishing to emigrate, that a very good road was discovered and traveled by a small party of emigrants who left Missouri in the spring of 1844, headed by Dr. [John] Townsend and Capt. Stevens [Elisha Stephens]. After leaving Fort Hall, they followed what is called 'Walker's Trail,' in a S. W. course, and coming upon Mary's river, followed it down to the 'Sink,'—a large lake having no apparent outlet. Finding the country to the south was barren, and destitute of water, they encamped at the Sink to explore, and having learned from an Indian that a river came down from the top of the mountain, and that on the other side was another stream that ran down into a plain in which were many cattle and horses, they concluded to try the pass, and succeeded in reaching the summit, and some of the wagons passed over; but it being winter, the snow was deep, and having built huts, some of the party proceeded down the mountain and arrived at Captain Sutter's Fort, from whence horses and provisions were sent to the mountains by Mr. P. B. Reading—who was in charge of the establishment, Capt. Sutter being absent at the time—and the women and children brought down and placed in comfortable quarters. In the spring, when the snow was gone, and the wagons were brought in, and a small party being about to return to the States, came through the same

[3]The *Picayune* of April 22 reported having had the pleasure of conversing with "a gentleman who arrived in town on Monday direct from California," who had left there by sea February 18 and come via Mazatlan and Mexico City. The most important intelligence he had brought related to Fremont, who had reached Sutter's "about the 1st of February, with a force of about sixty mounted men, and who had been so fortunate as to discover a new route, or pass, by which California can be reached by emigrants in sixty days less time than by the old route via Oregon. This new route is perfectly practicable for wheeled vehicles, and when it comes to be generally known, will give a renewed impetus to emigration to California."

pass to the Sink on the wagon trail. The distance from the Sink
on Mary's river is about 25 miles in W. S. W. direction to the
river that heads on the mountain. Dr. Townsend called this river
Turkey's [Truckee's] river, that being the name of the Indian
who gave them the information.[4] At the foot of the mountain it
bends suddenly to the north, and empties itself into a lake [Pyra-
mid Lake] abounding in fish, according to the Indians. This lake
is only known to some trappers, but probably has no outlet above
ground.

All former emigrant companies had tried to get into California
by passing round farther south, but had never been able to get
in their wagons—the scarcity of grass and water causing their
cattle to give out, and some of them had suffered much for the
want of provisions. The better route is to follow down Bear
river, leaving the Oregon trail at the Soda Springs. One party
[the Bartleson company] followed down that river to the Great
Salt Lake, into which it empties itself, and thence crossed over
on to Mary's river. Capt. Fremont will probably be able to improve the route from the Soda springs, as it is lost distance to
keep on to Fort Hall, unless out of provisions, in which case it
is well to go there, provisions being for sale there, and no game
to depend upon from the Soda Springs to California.

William H. Winter's narrative, not less than Farwell's
letter, must have interested intending California emigrants. Besides describing California generally, with
incidental information concerning the 1844 emigrants
who had first got wagons over the Sierra, he provided a
general account of how his party crossed the mountains
and went down "Truckies River," over to "Marie's River"

---

[4]The Paiute chief Truckee has had less attention in connection with
the opening of the California Trail than he merits, though Moses
Schallenberger and Edwin Bryant, like Farwell, have shown clearly
that it was he who guided the Stephens-Townsend-Murphy party up
the Truckee and over Donner Pass. Truckee and two of his sons
were members of Fremont's California Battalion in 1846-1847, their
names appearing in the muster rolls as Jose, Juan, and Philip
"Trucky." According to his granddaughter, Sarah Winnemucca Hopkins (*Life Among the Piutes,* Boston, 1883, p. 9), "Truckee is an
Indian word, it means *all right,* or *very well.*" Mrs. Hopkins relates
much of interest respecting her grandfather, including his death in
1860.

and up that stream, past the "Hot Pools" soon to be known as Thousand Springs, and then on to Raft River and the Snake. Winter reached Fort Hall June 20, "forty days having elapsed since we left Capt. Sutter's, in California." Soon after, the Californians joined an Oregon contingent which had left Oregon City April 19 and arrived at Fort Hall June 17. That twelve-man party from Oregon, which included John M. Shively as well as Overton Johnson, swelled the whole number of homeward-bound travelers to twenty-four. However, after encountering the westbound emigration the second week of July, the party split up. Seven went ahead, Shively included, to arrive at Independence just prior to August 16. The other seventeen kept together as far as Fort Laramie, then they in turn split up. Ten, including Farwell, accompanied a fur company caravan to Fort Pierre on the Missouri, thence descending by water to St. Louis. The remaining seven, including Overton Johnson and William H. Winter, made it through to Westport on August 29, reaching the settlements about a month ahead of those who came via Fort Pierre.[5]

We have seen what Farwell had to say about the Western trails. Shively went on to Washington, D. C., where next year he published one of the rarest, as also one of the earliest, guides to Oregon and California. So interesting is this guide, and so pointed in its remarks, that it is reprinted in its entirety as an appendix to the present work. But it was not nearly so influential in shaping the emigration of 1846 as the *Emigrants' Guide to Oregon and California* which had resulted from the travels of Lansford W. Hastings, published at Cincinnati in the

[5]The arrival on the frontier of the three detachments of the eastbound companies of 1845 is recorded in *Niles' National Register*, August 30, 1845, vol. 68, p. 416; *Jefferson Inquirer*, August 21, 1845; *South Dakota Historical Collections* (1918), vol. 9, p. 205 (specifically mentioning Farwell's arrival at Fort Pierre); and Overton Johnson and William Winter, *Route Across the Rocky Mountains. . .* (Lafayette, Ind., 1846, pp. 120-132.

spring of 1845.

In the preface to this book, which Hastings hoped "might prove useful to all those, who contemplate emigrating to Oregon or California, and interesting, at least, if not useful also, to the general reader," the man who was in process of becoming "the celebrated traveler Hastings" told of letters he had received from nearly every portion of the Union, far more than he had been able to answer, propounding questions about California and Oregon. "The above, and innumerable other manifestations, indicative of the extraordinary avidity with which all information of this nature is every where sought, have been strong incentives to the present undertaking. But the fact, that among all the various works now extant, which treat of Oregon and California, there are none which contain that practical information, which is so much desired by the enquiring emigrant: and the fact, of the utter destitution, of all information in reference to the different routes to those countries, the equipments, supplies, and the method of traveling, have been the chief inducements to its early [publication]."

Hastings made quite a tale of his travels in Oregon and California, particularly the favored land under Mexican rule, closing his book with a soaring pulpit eloquence: "In view of their increasing population, accumulating wealth, and growing prosperity, I can not but believe, that the time is not distant, when those wild forests, trackless plains, untrodden valleys, and the unbounded ocean, will present one grand scene, of continuous improvements, universal enterprise, and unparalleled commerce: when those vast forests, shall have disappeared, before the hardy pioneer; those extensive plains, shall abound with innumerable herds, of domestic animals; those fertile valleys shall groan under the immense weight of their abundant products: when those numerous rivers, shall team with countless steam-boats, steam-ships, ships, barques and brigs; when the entire country, will be everywhere intersected, with turnpike roads, rail-roads and canals; and when, all the vastly numerous, and rich resources, of that now, almost unknown region, will be fully and advantageously developed."

He bade his readers "contemplate the time, as fast approaching, when the supreme darkness of ignorance, superstition, and despotism, which now, so entirely pervade many portions of those remote regions, will have fled forever, before the march of civilization, and the blazing light, of civil and religious liberty; when genuine *republicanism,* and unsophisticated *democracy,* shall be reared up, and tower aloft, even upon the now wild shores, of the great Pacific; where they shall forever stand forth, as enduring monuments, to the increasing wisdom of *man,* and the infinite kindness and protection, of an all-wise, and over-ruling *Providence.*"

Hastings was really not very helpful in his advice to those who might yield themselves to the gospel he was preaching. To California emigrants he was able to say only: "Those who go to California, travel from Fort Hall, west southwest about fifteen days, to the northern pass, in the California mountains; thence, three days, to the Sacramento; and thence, seven days, down the Sacramento, to the bay of St. Francisco, in California. . . . Wagons can be as readily taken from Fort Hall to the bay of St. Francisco, as they can, from the States to Fort Hall; and, in fact, the latter part of the route, is found much more eligible for a wagon way, than the former. The most direct route, for the California emigrants, would be to leave the Oregon route, about two hundred miles east of Fort Hall; thence bearing west southwest, to the Salt Lake; and thence continuing down to the bay of St. Francisco, by the route just described. The emigrants, up to this time, however, have traveled together, as far as Fort Hall, because of this being the only settlement, in that vicinity, at which they are enabled to procure horses, and provisions. The soda springs, however, will, undoubtedly, be found to be the point, at which the routes will most advantageously diverge. . . . The entire distance by this route, from Independence, either to Oregon or California, is about twenty-one hundred miles; and the usual time required in performing the journey, to either of those countries, will be found to be about one hundred and twenty days, exclusive of delays. . . ."

Hastings had no later information than the experience of the emigration of 1843, so this was not a very factual discussion. He was mainly interested in expounding what you found after getting to California or Oregon; getting there was a mere detail, if a detail that would matter much in 1846.

What were Hastings' motives in publishing this book? John Bidwell, who had come to California as a member of the Bartleson party in 1841, asserted in after years on the basis of admittedly hearsay information that Hastings originally came from Oregon with the purpose of instigating a revolution that would wrest California from Mexico and establish an independent republic of which he might be president. "Seeing the country not ready for such a movement, he entertained the idea of obtaining a grant of land from Mexico on the west side of the Sacramento River in what would be now [1877] Yolo and Colusa Counties and went so far as to have the same mapped out. The want of population was needed whether an independent republic was organized or annexation carried out. And to accomplish that purpose—the bringing of a large immigration from the United States, Hastings determined to return and write a book giving a glowing account of California and its resources and have it published as soon as possible. He went through Mexico in order to reach Texas and confer with the Pres. of that Republic in regard to his plans. The book was in due time published and extensively read, especially in the West, and created a considerable furor. In addition to writing the book both previous and after Hastings availed himself of the opportunity to deliver lectures on the subject setting forth the wonder of the California Paradise.... The book was well written and set forth things in the brightest light. This was published by the summer or spring of 1845, it having been delayed on account of Hastings' want of means. It did much to attract settlers to Cal. for the publication of this book and perhaps other causes, during the next year set on foot the great immigration to Cal. about six hundred persons crossing the plains that season."[6]

2.

Hastings' lecture tour in the interests of California, his book, or his own pressing needs—no one can now be sure how much weight to give these various factors — brought him to New York in the late spring of 1845. There he fell in with that kindred spirit, Thomas Jefferson Farnham, whose book of 1841, mainly devoted to

[6]Bidwell dictated two reminiscences concerning his early life in California, a still-unpublished MS. in the Bancroft Library, California 1841-8, and a somewhat similar narrative published in *The Century Magazine* in 1890-1891. The portion printed in the *Century* for December, 1890, makes it clear that Bidwell had only hearsay information respecting Hastings' alleged filibustering ambitions, though a somewhat similar story was carried north to Oregon in the spring of 1846, as seen in Volume II. A pleasant touch in Bidwell's *Century* articles (which were posthumously reprinted in pamphlet form as *Echoes of the Past*) is the recollection that Hastings "labored hard to get money to publish his book, and went about lecturing on temperance in Ohio, where he became intimate with a fellow by the name of McDonald, who was acting the Methodist preacher and pretending, with considerable success, to raise funds for missionary purposes. At last they separated, McDonald preceding Hastings to San Francisco, where he became bartender for a man named Vioget, who owned a saloon and a billiard table—the first, I think, on the Pacific coast. Hastings returned later, and, reaching San Francisco in a cold rain, went up to Vioget's and called for brandy. He poured out a glassful and was about to drink it, when McDonald, recognizing him, leaned over the bar, extended his hand, and said, 'My good temperance friend, how are you?' Hastings in great surprise looked him in the eyes, recognized him, and said, 'My dear Methodist brother, how do you do?' "

Oregon, had been followed up with a work, *Travels in the Californias, and Scenes in the Pacific Ocean.* Farnham had a filibustering spirit; he felt that California must be wrested from the faltering hand of Mexico — the only question was proper timing. Like Hastings, he intended to return to California, and did so next year.[7]

More important, Hastings fell in with a devious New York merchant, A. G. Benson, who had or professed to have access to high authority in Washington. Though Benson kept other irons in the fire, he had begun to talk with the Mormon authorities in the Eastern States. Joseph Smith had died at the hands of an Illinois mob the previous year, but the death of their prophet had not had the effect many had anticipated, of scattering the Saints into the world. It would appear that Hastings' and Benson's conversations mainly involved Samuel Brannan, publisher of the Mormon paper in New York. That these conversations went rather far is shown by things Hastings had to say after reaching California, when he had been some months beyond the reach of written communication. The general idea was not formally outlined by Brannan to Brigham Young and his brethren at Nauvoo until late January, 1846, by which time the Mormons not only had

[7]Farnham's two books were titled *Travels in the Great Western Prairies, the Anahuac and Rocky Mountains, and in the Oregon Territory* (Poughkeepsie, 1841), and *Travels in the Californias, and Scenes in the Pacific Ocean* (New York, 1844, but with Part 4 dated 1845). How and when Farnham reached California has not been established. He was still in the States as late as October 20, 1845, when he wrote Brigham Young from New York recommending that the Mormons move to California (Brigham H. Roberts, ed., *History of the Church of Jesus Christ of Latter-day Saints,* Salt Lake City, 1922, vol. 7, p. 510). As seen in our Volume II, *The Californian* of October 17, 1846, supposed him to be coming overland in the Leavitt company from Arkansas. However he managed it, Farnham was in San Francisco next year, his presence at a public meeting in San Francisco June 15, 1847, recorded in the *California Star* four days later. His death in San Francisco of intermittent fever, September 13, 1848, was noticed in *The Californian,* September 16, 1848.

made up their minds to move west but had sanctioned the departure of one company to go by water under Brannan's direction. (This was the contingent which in the *Brooklyn* sailed from New York February 4, 1846, and after the long passage around Cape Horn anchored off Yerba Buena July 31.) The contract Brannan drew up with Benson declared that the latter had it in his power "to correct any misrepresentations which may be made to the president of the United States, and prevent any authorized interference with them on their journey, and also to extend to them facilities for emigration, especially by sea, and afford them great commercial facilities and advantages at their new homes." In appreciation the Saints were to agree that if they reached their new homes unmolested by the government, they would convey to Benson, his associates, or heirs and assigns, one half of any lands they might acquire "from the said United States or from any other source," including alternate lots in any cities they might lay out.[8]

The power behind the scenes, Brannan revealed, was A. G. Kendall of Kentucky, Postmaster General from 1835 to 1840; it was intimated that unless the Saints went along with this agreement, to which the President of the United States was termed a silent party, the government would not permit the Saints to go west. Brigham Young denounced the proposed contract as soon as he heard about it, but clearly Hastings thought something of the sort was in the wind when he departed New York on July 6, 1845; and it is not just coincidental that weekly from July 12 to September 6, 1845, Brannan published in his *New York Messenger,* extracts from Hastings' book, with the initial explanation: "Mr. Hastings has recently been lecturing in this city, upon the advantages of emigrating to [California]. The principle indorsements held out, is a grant of land from the Mexican Gov-

[8]For the intrigues involving Benson and Brannan, see Roberts, *op. cit.,* pp. 577, 587-591.

ernment, not less than one square league nor over nine to every emigrant. The climate is never so cold as to freeze—and an instance of death on the coast by a fever, has never been known. The soil produces the fruit and vegetation of every climate in the world. Its commercial advantages and natural resources are the greatest in the known world." And editorially on August 2: "Some of our readers may enquire why we have so much to say about California. We would say that our religion is to acquire all the intelligence possible concerning every country. History is a matter of great interest to the elders that are called to go to the nations of the earth, and as California is a portion of the new world, so called, yea, a portion of that which God made choice above all others, we deem it sufficiently worthy of our attention."

Not only in New York, or among the Mormons, had Hastings made an impression. Even before he left the eastern seaboard, on July 2, 1845, the St. Louis *Missouri Reporter* was saying:

A number of our citizens propose forming a company to emigrate to California. A meeting in reference to the subject was held at the Court House on Monday evening last. Several persons started from this city to California a few months ago, and from the enterprising spirit of those familiar with the life of pioneers, of whom we have a large number in this neighborhood, it may be safely inferred that large additions will be made in a few years to the American population south of Oregon. The fertility of that country and its commercial advantages will attract future emigrants, and we doubt not that Mexico will find it for her interest to establish there a separate Republic, or leave it entirely to the control of the adventurous spirits already preparing to settle it.

And on July 24, Hastings having reached St. Louis, the *Reporter* advised:

A meeting of the friends of Oregon and California will be held at the Court House to-morrow evening. Mr. Hastings who has visited Oregon, and is about returning thither, will address the meeting.

A company will start from Independence for California on the 10th of August next.

The company referred to Hastings himself proposed to captain. It got under way more slowly than had been forecast, but on August 9 the Independence *Western Expositor* reported:

> We understand that Mr. Hastings, the author of the Emigrant's Guide to Oregon and California, is now in our town on his way with a company to California. He leaves here on the 15th inst. and expects to complete the trip in 70 or 80 days. The outfit for each is no more than can be conveniently taken on pack animals, as he is determined not to be burdened with many if any waggons. The opportunity thus offered for any one to accompany him (who is desirous of making such a trip) is the best imaginable at this season of the year. He assures us there can be no possible danger of delay and the difficulties which presents themselves to the minds of many about such a journey, are easily removed. Respecting the practicability of the route, none need fear for a moment—it is his intention to show to the world that the plains can be crossed at any and every season of the year. His camp is in the neighborhood of Fitzhugh's on the Santa Fe road—where any inquirer for settling any doubts that may arise in the mind may find his company.

A week later the *Expositor* announced that Hastings' company had set out the previous day.[9]

> They seem to be men of the right stamp for such an undertaking, and leave right willingly for the plains. Apparently regardless of all dangers, they venture forward buoyed up with hopes of success, and stimulated by deeds of daring, by the desire of bettering their condition and that of their friends who have gone before them. The season of the year for such a jaunt, *is* unusually late; *they* seem to think not, and appear determined to show to the world, that nothing need prove an obstacle to our crossing the plains. We give the names of the company and their late residences:
>
> Lansford W. Hastings, Captain, San Francisco, California.
> Dr. R. Semple, Alton, Illinois [6 feet 8 inches high].

---

[9]The report from the *Western Expositor* of August 16 is derived from *Niles' National Register,* September 6, 1845, vol. 69, p. 7, which erroneously gives the source as "Independence Mission Expositor of the 6th July." (The latter date is that of Hastings' departure from New York.) This error may be corrected by reference to the Jefferson *Inquirer,* August 21, 1845.

O. S. Burnham, Cincinnati, Ohio. J. H. Nash, South Alabama.
Missouri—A. H. Crosby, Lexington, W. N. Loker, St. Louis;
T. Merange, do. T. E. Robbins, St. Chas.
New York city—J. Bristol.
Hagerstown, Maryland—C. Venerable.
Springfield, Illinois—J. W. Ward, R. Rankin.
St. Josephs, Michigan—N. B. Smith, H. Downing, J. B. [Ira]
Stebbins, P. Mendenhall, H. C. Smith.
Iowa—J. A. Simpson, C. Carroll, S. Bancroft, P. S. Philips,
A. Little, T. F. Waters.

This company underwent a mighty shrinkage; only
Hastings, Semple, Nash, Crosby, Loker, the Smith
brothers, Downing, Stebbins, and Mendenhall reached
journey's end. The other thirteen must have had serious
second thoughts. Such an attempt at a late crossing of
the continent was in fact a foolhardy undertaking, sum-
ming up Hastings' extensive ignorance. That the endeavor was nevertheless entirely successful, that he was
able to cross the Sierra in mid-December without the
slightest difficulty, is one of many evidences that the Lord
sometimes has a forbearing eye for fools and children.

One of Hastings' party, Napoleon B. Smith, in 1875
gave John C. McPherson an account of their experiences,
and in view of Hastings' central role in the events of
1846, it seems desirable to quote this hitherto unpublished
narrative.[10] By "Bony's" recollection, the Hastings company left Independence August 17, 1845, consisting of
ten men.

Nothing of interest occurred until their arrival at Fort Laramie. Prior to this they had met with many Indians, but were not
interfered with. Reaching Fort Laramie, they were told by the
Chief in authority there, that the Sioux and Shians had united
against the Snake Indians and were then out on the Warpath and
were not expected to return for 10 or 15 days. The former tribes
had vowed death to every person white or black they should meet

[10]The Napoleon B. Smith narrative, entitled by John C. McPherson
"Biographical Sketch of an Early Pioneer" (Bancroft Library, MS.,
C-E 64:33) was mistakenly attributed by H. H. Bancroft to John
A. Swan.

and Bony and party were advised to remain at the Fort for a while At Laramie, they met Bridger of Bridger's Fort who was there for goods with 2 Frenchmen, trappers in his employ— They had been there for some days, detained in consequence of the Indian War and Bridger was very desirous to return to his Fort.[11] He proposed to Bony and party that if they would accompany him, he would take them by a trail through the Wind River Mountains to Fort Bridger, by which the Country of the hostile Indians would be avoided. The proposition was accepted, so, after a stay of 10 days in Laramie, Bony and his Companions left and guided by Bridger and the Frenchmen resumed their journey by the trail through the Wind River mountains. This trail was so rugged and wild that Bony believes to this day it is the worst on the American Continent. Sometimes climbing precipitous mountains—then down, down to a wild chasm—then assisting their animals with ropes over a precipice they would find themselves in a canion where sunlight never penetrated—but on —on they went and after 20 days travel at length reached Fort Bridger.—They had barely escaped Encountering the Sioux & Shians who on returning from the Warpath had divided—one party travelling on the South Side of Sweetwater mountain and the other on the North side—

After a stay of 2 days at Bridger's to recruit, our party of 10 started for Fort Hall. Before they had reached there, they became very short of provisions and suffered not a little. One of the party—no matter as to the name, for he has for many years been slumbering in the grave, succeeded one Evening in Shooting a very lean and apparently Superannuated Coyote, which he broiled and before morning, ate all the carcass, minus bones and Entrails himself. At length, weary and hungry the party reached Fort Hall.—They had but very little money but Major Grant, the Factor at the Fort for the Hudson Bay Company was induced to supply them with some provisions, payment for which they promised to make by sending the money on their arrival in California to Doctor M Laughlin Chief Factor for the

[11]Bridger had made a trapping foray to California in the fall of 1844. His return from thence, and arrival at Fort Laramie on September 2, 1845, is reported in a letter from A. R. Bouis at Fort Pierre to P. Chouteau Jr. & Co., September 17, 1845, printed in *South Dakota Historical Collections* (1918), vol. 9, pp. 209-210. The N. B. Smith account is the only source showing how and when Bridger returned to Fort Bridger; it is not very explicit as to the route he took through the Wind River Mountains, north of South Pass.

H. Bay Co. in Oregon.[12]—The promise we believe was fulfilled.
—After a 2 days stay at Fort Hall, the party resumed their
journey.—Travelling past the Snake River Falls a few miles
beyond the Fort in a northerly [westerly] direction, on they went
until they reached Cajeux Creek [Raft River]—27 miles from
Fort Hall—Here the road for California diverged to the South—
that northward [westward] being the Emigrant highway for
Oregon.—They now proceeded on the trail for some distance and
at length struck Mary's River now known as the Humboldt.—
They continued down the River for several days and at length
reached the 'Sink'—Their travel now was over the Truckee desert
—48 miles and then arrived at the transparent rocky, fast-flowing
Truckee.—Pushing on, by crossing & recrossing this river no less
than 27 times in a distance of 18 miles, they at last Emerged
into the Truckee Meadows. . . . They soon began the ascent of
the Sierra Nevada and when near Donner Lake they stopped
and consulted as to their future course. — For the previous 14
days they had been on Very short rations and it was determined
that the flour, and that was about all they had to sustain life
should be given to 4 men who would travel as they best could
while the remaining 6 of the party would proceed in advance
& rely on finding game.—The 6 men, (Bony and his Brother
Henry being of the number) went ahead — For 2 days they
travelled without seeing even a 'chickadee' and had nothing to
eat during that time, so it was determined to stop for a day to
hunt.—Bony hunted diligently about in vain and was about to
return dejected to Camp when after Sundown, he beheld a noble
Buck looking over his Shoulder and wistfully at him—Bony had
not the 'Buck fever'—but he fairly trembled with anxiety as

---

[12]Some incidental intelligence respecting the westward journey of
Hastings appears in the *Oregon Spectator,* February 5, 1846: "We
are informed by a respectable gentleman, who, a short time since,
received a letter from Captain Grant of Fort Hall, stating that Doctor White, Indian agent for Oregon territory, and his whole party,
had been cut off by the Sioux Indians, between Fort Bridger and
Fort Larramie. Capt. Grant writes in the positive. His information
was from Mr. Hastings, who left New York on the 6th of July last,
and must have passed the scene of massacre in October." This rumor
as to a massacre of Dr. Elijah White's eastbound party was un-
founded, as White arrived safely at Fort Laramie from Fort Hall
on October 15, and with his three fellow travelers made it through
to Independence. The *Expositor's* Extra of November 17, announcing
his arrival, is reprinted in *Times and Seasons,* December 1, 1845,
vol. 6, pp. 1046-1049.

he placed the rifle to his Shoulder—He Endeavored to quiet his nerves and take steady aim but could not and fearful that the animal would speed away he pulled the trigger and to his joy the Buck tumbled over—In a minute he was up again & ran over a ridge for perhaps 50 yards.—when Bony gained Sight of him he appeared to be sick & swayed to & fro as though trying to lay down—Bony had reloaded his rifle by this time and now taking steady aim, fired and the Buck fell dead! What a prize! Running up, Bony cut the animals throat and giving a loud yell 2 of his companions soon appeared for they had heard the 2 shots by Bony and they said that his yell could have been heard 5 miles distant—Taking out the entrails, the deer was placed on the back of a horse and in triumph thus brought to Camp. . . .

Bony & his 5 Companions determined to camp there & hunt during the afternoon but saw no game, so the following morning they continued their journey.—It were needless to follow them in their travel, hungry enough frequently,—it is sufficient to say that they at length reached Johnson's Ranch on Bear River, California.—Procuring provisions here, Bony and Helms Downing the succeeding morning returned on the trail to meet the Travellers behind.—Just about sunset they were descried and the hills fairly rang with shouts of joy.—From Johnson's the whole party now proceeded to Sutters Fort where they arrived on Christmas day. . . .

Sutter's New Helvetia Diary has only an incommunicative entry for December 25, 1845, "Arr*d* Capt. Hastings from the U. S. . . .," and a similar notation next day, "arr*d* M*r* Nash (Lawyer) one of Capt. Hastings party—" Some ten years later, in the narrative that has become known as his "diary," Sutter provided a more elaborate entry for December 25: "Arrived Capt. W. L. Hastings direct from the U. States crossing the Mountains with 11 men, among them was Doctor Semple, if they arrived one day later they would have been cut of by the immense quantity of Snow. I keept the whole party over winter, some of them I employed." At the time he was content to write General Mariano Vallejo, under date of December 26, advising of the arrival of a little party of ten men, namely Guiller*mo* Locker, Comerciante, ———— Simple, Doctor, A. Crosby, Carpenter, N. Smith, H. Smith, H. Mendenhall, H. Downing, and

I. Stebbins, Rancheros, and J. H. Nash and L. N. Hastings, Abogardos; they had come from Missouri with the intention of remaining permanently in the country.[13]

What may have been in Hastings' heart and mind at the time of his return to California is far from clear, may not even have been clear to himself though obviously he felt that increased emigration to California from the States offered him more scope than an easy acceptance of the existing order. His extant letters show Hastings pulled this way and that; it was far from certain as 1846 wore on that he would go east on the trail and seek to divert the emigration into California.

Sutter had first taken note of Hastings' activities in a letter written to Thomas O. Larkin from New Helvetia on July 15, 1845: "I send you a Newspaper from St. Louis send to me over the Rockey Mountains, with a somewhat exaggerated Description of California. . . . A little later will arrive here direct from the U. S. a very large Company more as 1000 Souls, familys from Kentucky and Ohio and a good many young enterprising Gentlemen with some Capital to improve the Country under lead of L. W. Hastings Esq.re of whom I received some letters which informed me of this Arrival, I am looking for them in about 8 or 10 weeks from now, I am very glad that they meet with some good Pilots at fort Hall [the Greenwoods], people who went over there from here, to pilot Emigrants the new Wagon road which was found right Down on Bear creek on my farm."[14]

Sutter again wrote Larkin on October 8, after the emigration had begun to come in, some weeks before Hastings himself appeared: "To Oregon was a powerful

---

[13]See *New Helvetia Diary* (San Francisco, 1939), p. 19; Douglas S. Watson, ed., *The Diary of Johann August Sutter* (San Francisco, 1932), p. 29; Sutter to Vallejo, December 26, 1845, Vallejo Papers, Bancroft Library.

[14]Sutter to Larkin, July 15, 1845, Bancroft Library; printed in George P. Hammond, ed., *The Larkin Papers* (Berkeley and Los Angeles, 1952), vol. 3, pp. 270-273.

Emigration this year consisting out about 3000 Souls
with 800 Wagons and 6000 Cows, no Doubt the next
Month of July we will have a great Number of them
here, and the next year in this Month we shall have 1000
and thousands of Emigrants here, the best what the Government could do would be to give these Emigrants the
San Joaquin and the whole tular Valley, and they would
no more losse their Horses by the Horsethiefs [Indians].
Nothing can stop this Emigration, in Case of Opposition
they would fight like Lyons, they are all well armed,
better as all the former Emigrants the have all Superior
Rifles and Pistols etc."[15]

The New Helvetia Diary records on January 22,
"Capts. Sutter & Hastings went to the river." Then in
explanation, on February 7, "Capt. Hastings & Bidwell
finished laying out the town." The town in question was
Sutterville, just below the future Sacramento; Hastings
is said to have been one of the proprietors, with Sutter;
it is evident that both men had a speculative eye on the
emigration Hastings was predicting, and for which he
could take full credit.

Meanwhile all sorts of rumors were going abroad.
Jacob P. Leese wrote Larkin from Sonoma on January
12: "Capt Hastings has jest arived at Sutters, from the
U. S. by land with 10 men. He says he has found a road
through the Stoney Mountains 400 miles shorter than
has ever been traveled. A Larg Emigration will be
through this summer. A Company has been formed in
New York Called the Califa. Agriculturing Co/a. Two
Shipps sailed in August last for this with all Kinds of
cultavating implements & Seeds. For this purpose Capt
H. has Came a head to enter the Shipps and make arrangements. I should think that they are at Monterey
by this time. I do not giv you this as a fact. You do get
it as I do by report. I shall wright up to Capt H. to-

---

[15]Sutter to Larkin, October 8, 1845, Bancroft Library, printed in *The
Larkin Papers* (Berkeley and Los Angeles, 1953), vol. 4, pp. 10-11.

morow. I hav not the least doubt he will come down this weigh. . . ."[16]

How Fremont influenced Hastings, and the Leese view of events, we shall remark hereafter. For the moment observe Sutter writing Dr. John Marsh on January 31: "Capt. Fremont arrived and left by water for Yerba Buena and from there to Monterey to see Mr. Larkin, he remains here until Capt. Walker arrives wich is the Guide of his other party which he had dispatched to explore the southern pass etc. Capt. Fremont like Capt. Hastings which arrived the last month here with 8 men, both of these Gentlemen bring us the news that it is a great excitement through the whole of the U. States to emigrate to Oregon and California, and that we could expect several thousands of them here, and a good many of wealth and Capital, and some rich merchants from New York, Steamboats will be here in the month of April, a Printing press, and thousands of other articles."[17]

Hastings himself wrote William A. Leidesdorff from New Helvetia on February 25:

> As the ship of the Hudson's Bay Company has not, as yet, arrived, and as there is no probability of its arriving in time for my purpose, I have determined to make an overland tour to Oregon, as early as the weather will permit, Upon this excurtion, I shall, in all probability, be absent from this country, until the first of August, next, and, perhaps longer, If, in the interim, either of the ships, of the house of Benson, of New York, should arrive, and any thing shall be consigned to me, will you have the goodness to receive, pay charges, and keep such property until I shall have returned? I shall address the supercargo of those ships, upon this subject, previous to my departure, which letters, I shall be much obliged to you, if you will have the kindness to deliver with promptitude. The letters alluded to, I shall write previous to my departure, and will forward them to you, in due time, In procuring an outfit for my contemplated excurtion, I find that there are several articles, which I shall require, that can not

---

[16]Leese to Larkin, January 12, 1846, *ibid.*, pp. 160-161.
[17]Sutter to Marsh, January 31, 1846, Marsh Papers, California State Library.

be procured at this place, If you will, therefore, be so kind as to forward to me, by the return of the launch [from Yerba Buena], the following articles, you will confer a favor which will be duly appreciated. The articles of supplies, which I shall need, are, 15 lbs. of coffee; 30 lbs. sugar; 1, 6 or 8 quart camp kettle, and 1, coffee pot, of common size.

Hastings was engaged in making the news, as we look back to 1846 from a later vantage point, so a further passage of this letter reads oddly: "As this is not the source of news, I can not, of course, communicate any thing to you, other than that of which you are already apprised." He added that he would settle for 10 pounds of coffee and 20 of sugar.[18]

Six days later Hastings wrote to Larkin in Monterey, and this letter of March 3 sounds much more like the expansive author of the *Emigrants' Guide*:

I, gladly avail myself of this opportunity of addressing you, but did circumstances admit, I would much prefer to communicate to you *personally,* To see you at this particular cricis, and converse with you, in your own *propari personi,* I assure you, would afford me the greatest pleasure; but as I have determined to make another inland tour, I shall not find it convenient, until I shall have returned, I design to set out for Oregon, by land, early in the month of April, and shall not return to this country until August or September next, when I shall endeavour to visit your place at the earliest opportunity.

The tide of emigration to both, this country and Oregon, is unparalleled in the annals of history, The eyes of the American people are now turned westward, and thousands are gazing with the most intense interest and anxiety upon the Pacific shores, with a full determination to make one more, one last move more, to the *"far West,"* then to make a final & permanent location, The emigration of this year to this country and Oregon will not consist of less than *twenty thousand* human souls, a large majority of whom, are destined to this country. Our friend Farnham and many other highly respectable and intelligent gentlemen will accompany the emigration of this year among them are also, many wealthy gentlemen and capitalists, who design to make

---

[18]Hastings to Leidesdorff, February 25, 1846, Leidesdorff Papers, Henry E. Huntington Library.

large investments in California, in both agricultural and commercial pursuits, The house of Bensons & Co. is about to establish an extensive commercial house, in some portion of the country, One of the ships of that house is expected in a few weeks, and another will arrive in the Month of May or June both of which, are bringing out large cargoes of merchandise, suitable to the trade of the country. Such arrangements are now made, by that house, that its ships will sale annually, for this country, one in June, and another in November of each year, By these ships also, thousands of emigrants will find their way thither especially, as that house proposes to bring all emigrants to this country, and to bring free of charges, they furnishing their own provisions, Here I will remark, (that I wish it to be understood that it is confidential,) that this latter arrangement is a confidential, governmental arrangement, The expense, thus incurred, is not borne by that house, but by our government, for the promotion of what object, you will readily perceive.

Thus Sir, you can not but observe, that a new era in the affairs of California, is about to arise; these now wild and desolate plains must soon abound with all the busy and interesting scenes of highly civilized life, And what a change, what a scene, to behold such a vast amount of dormant intelligence, inert energy, and dead and buried enterprise, as the Mexicans and Californians here possess, bursting forth in a day, as it were, into brilliant intelligence, commendable activity, and unbounded enterprise!

I am not aware that I am in possession any news, which you have not received from other sources, you will, therefore, allow me to conclud, by requesting you to present my compliments to your Lady, and Mr. Spence and Lady,

With the highest respect,
I remain Dear Sir,
Yours truly
L. W. Hastings[19]

Larkin was not impressed; the U. S. Consul wrote the Secretary of State on April 2 that according to a rumor "L. W. Hastings (Author of the History of California) is laying off a Town at New Helvetia for the Mormons. ... As a general thing Hastings Book is very untrue and absurd. He brought a number to this Country, which do his country no good and perhaps injures them. No gen-

---

[19]Hastings to Larkin, March 3, 1846, *The Larkin Papers,* vol. 4, pp. 220-221.

eral English reader will read one quarter of the Book."[20]

Hastings told both Leidesdorff and Larkin of his intention of revisiting Oregon. This was not just a loose way of referring to a journey east to meet the overland emigration; it was his purpose to work out a wagon road between California and Oregon—perhaps to facilitate the evacuation of Oregon.[21] But he had changed his mind by March 26, when he wrote Dr. John Marsh from New Helvetia:

> Although an entire stranger to you, personally, yet i have had the honor of knowing you by reputation, during the last several years, which fact I hope Sir, you will have the goodness to receive as sufficient apology for my thus addressing you, without the ordinary preliminary of a formal introduction, Nothing, I assure you sir, could afford me greater pleasure, than to see you personally, and to have the honor of making your valuable acquaintance; but existing circumstances appear to deny me that honor,
>
> As you may, perhaps, have learned, I arrived in this country, in December last, with a view of visiting Oregon by the earliest opportunity; but as no opportunity has, thus far, presented, I have now changed my purpose, and determined to go as far back, as Green river or Bridger's Fort, with the view of conducting the emigrants to this country, by a better and more direct route, than that usually travelled. The change of purpose, above alluded to, will prevent my visiting any portion of the lower country, until my return, which will be sometime in the month of August or September next, when Sir, you can rely upon an accession of six or seven thousand human souls to our foreign population in California, This is the very least estimate that can be made; for, judging from the universal excitement, which pervaded almost every portion of the Union, the emigration will be much more likely to amount to fifteen or twenty thousand, And

---

[20]Larkin to Secretary of State, April 2, 1846, *ibid.*, pp. 275-277.

[21]Sutter wrote P. B. Reading from New Helvetia on February 8, 1846: "Capt. Hastings intends to be here back again in the first days of July with about 100 pack Animals loaded with Goods, and he will examine this time well if even not Wagons could be brought in here, Doctor McLaughlin (his great friend) do all, what lays in his power to assist him. I let him have Vaqueros, I build a Store and dwelling house for him in the New City . . ." (Reading Papers, California State Library).

the emigration of this year, is only a prelude to what is to follow in succeeding years, for California is now looked upon, among a large majority of our people, as the *garden of the earth,*

No one will doubt but that this is perfectly right; for our people have, undoubtedly, the same right that other foreigners, or even the Californians themselves have, to locate in, and enjoy this delightful country, conforming always, to the established, and existing laws.

I brought a letter, which I discover, among others, for you, from your old friend, T. J. Farnham Esq., but as I have had no opportunity of forwarding it directly to you, I have thought proper to defer sending it until now, as the presumption is, that it contains facts and statements, which are not designed for the public eye, and which should not be placed into the hands, or under the control of strangers or enemies to the cause of *freedom,*

Friend Farnham is doing everything in his power, to increase the emigration to this far-famed region, and he is of the opinion that he will be able to bring, at least, three or four thousand, from the State of New York alone, But there are many other states, which will do much more than the State of N. York, Ohio, my native state, will send her thousands annually, and Kentucky, Indiana, Illinois, Michigan, Missouri, Tennessee and Arkansas, will not be far in the rear, As to the natural, the inevitable result, of this unprecedented emigration to the Western World, I need not trouble you with my own speculations, for the result must have been, long since, anticipated by yourself.

I hope Sir, the false impression, that our people design to wrest this country forcibly from the Californians, will not be promulgated, and if promulgated, I sincerely hope, that it will not be credited by either the Californians or others, for it is not true. But on the contrary, they design to emigrate to this country, with a settled purpose, to comply with all just laws, and reasonable governmental requirements, And above all things as far as I am able to learn, they come with a settled purpose also, to cooperate with the Californians, in their opposition to any foreign encroachment upon their rights, whether that encroachment be by Mexico or any other power. In return for this cooperative aid, they expect protection of both person and property, and they also expect, equal rights, privileges and immunities. But they can not be expelled from the country, nor must their expulsion be attempted What consummate folly it is, for the natives of the Californias, to attempt to check the emigration to this country; they might just as well, attempt to arrest thundering wheels of time, to restrain the mighty waters flow, or to

extinguish the blazing light of civil and religious liberty!²²
In much haste, allow me to conclude by subscribing myself,
Your most ob. and humble Servt.
L. W. Hastings²³

The Farnham letter Hastings had borne across the continent had been dated in New York July 6, 1845, the day Hastings left there for the West:

Doctor Marsh,

My dear friend, I have thought of you almost daily since I left you at Monterey [in 1840], & have strongly desired to write you; but fear that by so doing I should subject you again to the tyranical suspicions of the Spaniards: for I can write to no person in California, without expressing the strongest desire of my heart, to wit, that the "Republic of California" should arise— exist— & shed the blessings of Freedom over that delightful land.

Will you pardon me for a suggestion—Neither Europe or the States are yet prepared for the event.

The excitement consequent on the admission of Texas into the Union must have time to abate. The winter of 46 will do. Next year will see me & my family—God willing, at your house.

From 10 to 20 thousand emigrants will enter California next summer. There will then be population enough to *authorize* the step; & we shall have force enough for any Contingency.

Excuse the haste with which I write, and believe me your fellow citizen of California, & your sincere friend.
Thomas J. Farnham²⁴

Sutter was less than happy with Hastings, for he in turn wrote Dr. Marsh from New Helvetia on April 3: "Capt. Hastings is leaving this place in a few days, to cross the mountains again, with the party which is going from here out to the U. States, if he is going to the U. S.

---

²²A good deal of apprehension existed in California during the winter of 1845-1846 over measures the Mexican government was reportedly making to check American emigration to California and to establish firm administrative control over California affairs. *The Larkin Papers* amply reflect these doubts and fears, and the accompanying rumors that intermittently washed over California.

²³Hastings to Marsh, March 26, 1846, Marsh Papers, California State Library.

²⁴Farnham to Marsh, July 6, 1845, Marsh Papers, California State Library.

or not, or go, and meet the Emigrants, nobody knows for certain, perhaps nobody will see him here again, as his life will be in danger about his book, making out California a paridise, even some of the Emigrants in the Valley, threatened his life, and by his imprudent writing, he made himself the Country people to his ennemy I like to be hospitable, but I am very glad when Capt. Hastings is gone, because he make me a disagreeable situation, and I dont like to tell him to leave, paticular as it is only a few days longer."[25] It must have been with satisfaction that Sutter read the entry for April 11 in the New Helvetia Diary: "Departed Hastings and Heudspeth for the Valley above." Hastings was at Johnson's Ranch when, five days later, the homeward-bound James Clyman reached that point. As Clyman says in his diary,[26] "arived at Mr Hastings camp on Bear creek a small river Running into Feather River about noon Mr Hastings welcomed us to his cam[p] in a warm and Polite manner and we unpacked under the shade of a spreading oak tree...."

Clyman remained in Hastings' camp, making preparations for the journey, until April 23, when with five other men he started in advance of the main company. They considered themselves "two weak to venture to drive our way through," so they halted on the 25th to wait for the laggards. These fellow-travelers, doubtless including Hastings, came up on the afternoon of April 27.

Despite Sutter's testy remarks, before Hastings set out he gave the expansive master of New Helvetia some notion of his plans, for with Hastings two months gone

---

[25]Sutter to Marsh, April 3, 1846, Marsh Papers, California State Library.

[26]The Clyman diaries comprise one of the great documents of Western history. They were originally edited by Charles L. Camp in California Historical Society *Quarterly,* 1925-1928, separately reprinted as *James Clyman, American Frontiersman* (San Francisco, 1928), and reprinted by Camp in a "definitive edition" containing additional material (Portland, 1960).

Sutter wrote Leidesdorff on June 28: "The Emigrants from the U. States will be here this time in the Month of August, because Capt. Hastings is gone so far as fort Pritcher to bring them a new route Discovered by Capt fremont which is about 3 or 400 Miles shorter as the old route over fort Hall, the foreigners will be very strong this fall. . . ."[27]

3.

Before we follow Hastings and Clyman eastward, we must turn back to bring upon the stage another of the year's prime actors, John Charles Fremont. This dashing young topographical engineer in 1842 had reconnoitered the emigrant road as far west as South Pass, then in 1843 had gone all the way to the Columbia, with a side excursion to Great Salt Lake. After a period of hesitation, Fremont made his way south into California, skirting the eastern edge of the Sierra, coming upon and naming Pyramid Lake, and finally crossing the Sierra into the Valley of California. He re-outfitted at Sutters, rode south through the San Joaquin Valley, crossed the Tehachapis to strike the Spanish Trail, then traveled east and north to Utah Lake, thus within nine months accomplishing nearly a complete circuit of what he soon afterward named the Great Basin. Fremont continued east through the mountains to Bent's Fort and reached the Missouri frontier on the last day of July, 1844. Scarcely pausing, he made his way back to Washington and got to work on his report. His report of his first expedition had created a national sensation, even being stolen out of the libraries, so anxious were people to read it, and the new narrative was received with the same enthusiasm.

Fremont's father-in-law, the orotund Thomas Hart Benton, had more than enough influence to assure that funds would be forthcoming for a third exploring expedi-

---

[27]Sutter to Leidesdorff, June 28, 1846, Leidesdorff Papers, Henry E. Huntington Library.

tion in 1845. It was afterwards said that deeper motives were at work, that in the expansionist frenzy taking hold of the Nation, many advantages were seen in having a military force operating in the West, that Fremont carried secret instructions from President Polk in relation to certain contingencies that might arise. Less than a convincing case has been made for this view of Fremont and his Third Expedition, but we need not debate this matter. We are primarily interested in the influence of Fremont on the emigration of 1846.

When he set out from Westport on June 26, 1845, the Independence *Western Expositor* published its understanding of what Fremont's party was about in making this new exploring tour:

> The main division under Captain Fremont, will cross the Colorado, complete the survey of the great Salt Lake, and penetrate by the waters of Mary's river, (which flows westwardly through Upper California) in the vicinity of the 42d deg. parallel of latitude, and is lost in a lake at the eastern base of the California mountains. It is believed that from a point on Mary's river, some days journey from its mouth, the head of the Sacrimento may be reached in two day's travel. The Sacrimento penetrates the main chain of the California mountains and forms a practical pass directly to the Bay of San Francisco. This is already known. It is also known that a practical route exists from the head of the Sacrimento, in a northerly direction, by the heads of the Klamet, Chuttes and Wallamette rivers on the Columbia. The route then by which Capt. Fremont proposes to penetrate to the Pacific is the shortest and most direct from the lower Missouri—about 650 miles in distance—is as yet unexplored by the white man and generally designated as the great 'California desert.' None of its waters, excepting the Colorado, reach the ocean—they are absorbed or disappear by evaporations.
>
> After passing the winter among the American settlements of Upper California, the exploring party will, if the country be found practicable, pass round by the lower route from California, crossing the Colorado below the 'great Kennion,' and return to the Arkansas by the waters of the Gila and St. Juan, large tributaries of the lower Colorado, which have their sources west of the mountains of New Mexico. This sketch contemplates a route of five or six thousand miles. It will probably eventuate

in the discovery of a new and straight road both to Oregon and California, passing for the most part through our own territory, diminishing the distance some three or four hundred miles and the time two months. The country to the right and left will be examined and its geography, at present a blank, somewhat understood. The importance of these contemplated explorations is very great—every confidence is reposed in the energy and ability of the commanding officer. We shall hope for their success and look anxiously for their safe return towards the close of the year 1846.[28]

Fremont rode rapidly west to Bent's Fort, arriving August 3. There detaching young Lieutenant James Abert for a separate reconnaissance, with the main party he struck west into the central Rocky Mountains. He reached Utah Lake the second week of October, and rode on north to encamp on the site of the future Salt Lake City. After exploring the vicinity, and splashing through the shallow brine of Great Salt Lake for a horseback reconnaissance of Antelope Island, Fremont continued on around the south shore of Great Salt Lake to confront the forbidding Salt Desert.

Fur hunters had frequented the Great Salt Lake country for twenty years, but none had crossed the Salt Desert centrally. Guided by several of the greatest of the mountain men, including Kit Carson and Joe Walker, Fremont now accomplished this feat, a hard drive which cost him several mules and horses bringing him to the springs at the base of the tall mountain he named Pilot Peak. After resting a few days, he continued west across several small ranges to what he called Whitton's Springs, now known as Mound Springs, west of the Pequop Mountains. Here Fremont divided his party. One detachment, commanded by young Theodore Talbot, guided by Walker, and including the promising cartographer Edward M. Kern, he started off nearly west to intersect the known emigrant road somewhere on the desert stream

[28]The information from the *Western Expositor* is derived from the St. Louis *Missouri Reporter,* July 21, 1845, no files of the *Expositor* being known.

known as Mary's or Ogden's River. He himself took a more southerly course across the future Nevada, having agreed to meet Talbot's party at Walker Lake, near the west edge of the Great Basin.

Fremont's own route has no further significance here, but that taken by Talbot and Walker is of the highest importance, for it led directly to the opening of the Hastings Cutoff. Walker guided Talbot's detachment across the Ruby Mountains by Secret Pass, and thus on November 8 reached the desert river Fremont would soon rename the Humboldt. The expedition rode west on the emigrant road, hearing from the Indians that three separate companies of emigrants had passed during the fall (the party led by Hastings had yet to make its appearance); and having reached the Sink of the Humboldt, on November 24 struck south through the deserts to the Walker River. On the 28th Talbot's party reached the rendezvous point to find that Fremont's detachment had got there four days earlier.[29]

Well satisfied with what had been accomplished thus far, Fremont ordered Walker to conduct the main party to the San Joaquin by the route employed in guiding the emigrant company of 1843—that is, by way of Walker Pass—while he himself with what he called "a selected party of fifteen, among whom were some of my best

---

[29]The principal sources for Fremont's Third Expedition have been his *Geographical Memoir upon Upper California* (Washington, 1848); De Witt C. Peters, *The Life and Adventures of Kit Carson . . .* (first published at New York in 1858); and John Charles Fremont, *Memoirs of My Life* (Chicago, 1887)—these Memoirs based upon the first two sources, Fremont's memory having failed him to a marked degree by 1887. Edward M. Kern's journal of his experiences with Talbot's detachment, commencing November 5, 1846, when he separated from Fremont at Whitton's (Mound) Spring was printed as Appendix Q in James H. Simpson's *Report of Explorations across the Great Basin of the Territory of Utah . . .* (Washington, 1876). A full journal by Kern having been discovered, some extracts were printed in *Life Magazine,* April 6, 1959. Unpublished letters by Theodore Talbot are in the Library of Congress.

men," rode north in an attempt to reach Sutter's by way of the new emigrant trail. Fremont had struck upon the lower Truckee in the course of his Second Expedition, in January, 1844, naming it the Salmon Trout River. He had then made no effort to ascend this stream, and it had been left for the Stephens-Townsend-Murphy party to establish it as a means of approach to the high Sierra. In his *Memoirs* Fremont wrote forty years later that on December 1 he struck the Truckee "above the lower canon, and on the evening of the 4th camped at its head on the east side of the pass in the Sierra Nevada. Our effort had been to reach the pass before a heavy fall of snow, and we had succeeded. All night we watched the sky, ready to attempt the passage with the first indication of falling snow; but the sky continued clear. On our way up, the fine weather which we had left at the foot of the mountain continued to favor us, and when we reached the pass the only snow showing was on the peaks of the mountains." He rode on down the western slope and on December 10 the New Helvetia Diary took note of his arrival.

Sutter gave the young officer a characteristically cordial reception, and on the 13th "Started Capt. Fremont to meet Capt Walker to the South." A rendezvous point had been agreed upon, but there had been some mistake about the place, so that on January 15, 1846, the New Helvetia Diary noted: "Arr*d* Capt. Fremont [from] below not having been able to find Capt. Walker . . . fired a salute for Capt Fremont." By this time Lansford W. Hastings had reached Sutter's, and he had four days to exchange experiences before Fremont started off for Yerba Buena by water.

It was from Yerba Buena, on January 24, that Fremont wrote a letter to his wife which Jessie and her father promptly released to the newspapers:

I crossed the Rocky Mountains on the main Arkansas, passing out at its very head-water; explored the southern shore of the

Great Salt Lake, and visited one of its islands. You know that on every extant map, manuscript or printed, the whole of the Great Basin is represented as a sandy plain, barren, without water, and without grass. Tell your father that, with a volunteer party of fifteen men, I crossed it between the parallels of 38° and 39°. Instead of a plain, I found it, throughout its whole length, traversed by parallel ranges of lofty mountains, their summits white with snow (October); while below, the valleys had none. Instead of a barren country, the mountains were covered with grasses of the best quality, wooded with several varieties of trees, and containing more deer and mountain sheep than we had seen in any previous part of our voyage. So utterly at variance with every description, from authentic sources, or from rumor or report, it is fair to consider this country as hitherto wholly unexplored, and never before visited by a white man. I met my party at the rendezvous, a lake southeast of the Pyramid Lake; and again separated, sending them along the eastern side of the Great Sierra, three or four hundred miles in a southerly direction, where they were to cross into the valley of the San Joaquin, near its head. ... The eleventh day after leaving them I reached Captain Sutter's, crossing the Sierra on the 4th December, before the snow had fallen there. Now, the Sierra is absolutely impassable, and the place of our passage two years ago is luminous with snow. By the route I have explored I can ride in thirty-five days from the *Fontaine qui Bouit* River to Captain Sutter's; and, for wagons, the road is decidedly better.

Some of this was vainglory; it verged upon dangerous nonsense if Fremont similarly expressed himself in conversation with Hastings. Fremont continued possibly showing that his plans had changed since leaving the States:

I shall make a short journey up the eastern branch of the Sacramento, and go from the Tlamath Lake into the Wahlahmath valley, through a pass alluded to in my report; in this way making the road into Oregon far shorter, and a *good* road in place of the present very bad one down the Columbia. When I shall have made this short exploration, I shall have explored from beginning to end *this road to Oregon. ...*

I am now going on business to see some gentlemen on the coast, and will then join my people, and complete our survey in this part of the world as rapidly as possible. ... So soon as the proper season comes, and my animals are rested, we turn our faces homeward, and be sure that grass will not grow under our feet.

All our people are well, and we have had no sickness of any kind among us; so that I hope to be able to bring back with me all that I carried out. Many months of hardships, close trials, and anxieties have tried me severely, and my hair is turning gray before its time. [He was just three days past his thirty-third birthday.] But all this passes, *et le bon temps viendra*.[30]

With Fremont's further experiences in California we are not much concerned, and they must be dismissed in brief. He rejoined his men in mid-February, near Pueblo de San Jose, and rode south toward Monterey. His continued presence in the country was challenged by the authorities, and he was ordered out of California. After a period of defiance, he realized he had no alternative and rode north to the Klamath country. There, he was overtaken by Lieutenant Archibald Gillespie of the U. S. Marine Corps, who had come to California across Mexico with dispatches for Larkin, and at least some private word for Fremont about anticipated war with Mexico. Whatever the news Gillespie brought into camp on May 8, it induced Fremont to turn back into California and by May 24 he had reached Lassen's Rancho on the upper Sacramento. Doubtless his return encouraged the American settlers who raised the Bear Flag standard at Sonoma a few weeks later. Although by then war between the United States and Mexico had broken out on the Rio Grande, no one in California knew the fact, and as Bernard DeVoto has observed, the Bear Flag Rebellion almost died of second thoughts. Encouraged by U. S. Navy officers on the coast, who feared that Britain might be preparing to seize California, Fremont eventually abandoned an attitude of benevolent neutrality and organized a California Battalion, absorbed into the U. S. military establishment when news of hostilities arrived in

---

[30]Fremont's letter to Jessie, January 24, 1846, as contemporaneously published, may be seen in *Niles' National Register*, May 16, 1846, vol. 70, p. 161, as also in St. Joseph *Gazette*, July 10, 1846; he reprinted the letter in *Memoirs of My Life*, pp. 452-453.

July. In the autumn Fremont recruited more men from the incoming emigration and marched south to conquer southern California, as described in the letters printed in Volume II of this work.

4.

We must now return to Hastings and Clyman, whom we left at their camp in the Sierra foothills, April 27, 1846. There was considerable doubt whether it was yet possible to cross the mountains, but several of the party were "verry anxious to try and assertain that fact," as Clyman observed, and on the 29th the matter was put to the test. Though the going was slow, on May 1 the party reached the summit over snow from three to eight feet deep: "here we commenced the desent over step Pricipices rough granite Rock covered in many places through the chasms with snow 15 or 20 feet deep and luckily for us we lost no horses although we had to force them down several perpendicular cliffs afer about 3 hours unpacking and repacking we succeeded in clearing the steepest pitches of the whole length of which is not one mile you may imagine that we felt a happy relief to find ourselves on bear ground one more which we found at the head of truckys [Donner] lake a small sheet of water about two miles in length and half a mile wide the N hill sides being intirely clear of snow but verry little green vegitation."

The party moved on down "Truckee^s River," astonished that the nearly naked Washoe Indians they encountered should not complain of the cold, although the whites could scarcely get enough clothes on to keep themselves comfortable. Reaching the bend of the Truckee on May 8, the following morning they struck out into the desert toward "the sink of Marys river." Midway of the desert, having reached the present Bradys Hot Springs, Clyman had a tragedy to record, for into one of the muddy boiling springs went his little water spaniel Lucky: "poor fellow not knowing that it was Boiling hot he deliberately walked in to the caldron to slake his thirst and cool his limbs when to his sad disappointment and my sorrow he scalded himself allmost insantly to death I felt more for his loss than any other animal I ever lost in my life as he had been my constant companion in all my wanderings since I Left Milwawkee and I vainly hoped to see him return to his master in his native village." As we shall see in Volume II, this was one of the passages in Clyman's diary which attracted the attention of a newspaper reporter when Clyman reached St. Louis in July.

Clyman and Hastings reached the Sink of the Humboldt next day, then in a continuous dust cloud of their own making moved up the river. On the 13th, approaching the great bend of the Humboldt, Clyman noted that their company consisted of "19 men and boys 3 women and 2 children and about 150 mules and Horses too many for this rout at so early a season of the year as the grass has Just began to shoot and is yet young and short and we will probably devide our company in a few days." This division came on June 16, Clyman going ahead with Hastings, Hudspeth, their Indian vaquero, and some others; he says "8 men and 37 animals" made up the party, besides one woman, the wife of Owen Sumner, Jr., and a boy who may or may not have been included as one of the men. The detachment behind, which went by way of Fort Hall, was evidently guided by Old Greenwood and two of his sons, again seeking employment as emigrant guides.

The Clyman-Hastings party encamped on May 21 at "the point whare Mr Freemant [meaning Talbot and Walker] intersected the wagon Trail last fall on his way to california." Clyman observed that "Mr Hastings our pilot was anxious to try this rout but my beleef is that it [is] verry little nearer and not so good a road as that by fort Hall." On May 22, "after long consultation and many arguments for and against the two different routs one leading Northward by fort Hall and the other by the Salt Lake we all finally tooke Fremonts Trail by the way of the Salt Lake Late in thee day"—and thus Clyman recorded the fateful decision which meant that there

would be a Hastings Cutoff . . . and a Donner tragedy.[31]
The little company, following the Walker-Fremont trail
with occasional difficulty, reached the water at the base
of Pilot Peak on May 27, somewhat daunted by the look
of the salt desert stretching before them: "To the S. s. E.
and East you have a boundless salt plain without vegitation except here and there a cliff of bare rocks standing
like monumental pillars to commemorate the distinction
of this portion of the Earth."

The following morning Clyman's party "Left our
camp at the Snowy or more properly the spring Bute
for this Bute affords several fine Brooks and took the
Trail East and soon entered on the greate salt plain the
first plain is 6 or 7 miles wide and covered in many places
three inches deep in pure white salt passed an Island of
rocks [Silver Island] in this great plain and entered the
greate plain over which we went in a bold trot untill dusk
when we Bowoiked for the night without grass or water
and not much was said in fact all filt incouraged as we
had been enformed that if we could follow Mr Fremonts
trail we would not have more than 20 miles without fresh
water In fact this is the [most] desolate country perhaps
on the whole globe there not being one spear of vegitation and of course no kind of animal can subsist and it is
not yet assertained to what extent this immince salt and
sand plan can be south of whare we [are] now our travel
to day was 40 miles.

"29 As soon as light begin to shew in the East we
ware again under way crossed one more plain and then

---

[31]Clyman's travel from the Humboldt to Pilot Peak is not described
in detail here; those interested should refer to the 1960 edition of
the diaries or to the notes of J. Roderic Korns in *West from Fort
Bridger* (Salt Lake City, 1951, published as *Utah Historical Quarterly,* vol. 19). In one respect the Clyman-Hastings route varied
from the wagon route Hastings worked out later in the summer;
the eastbound party traveled by way of Secret Pass, between the
East Humboldt and Ruby mountains, whereas Hastings took the
wagons south around the Rubies, correctly judging Secret Pass to
be impassable for wagons.

assended a rough low mountain [Cedar Mountains] still
no water and our hopes ware again disapointed Commenced our desent down a ravine made 14 miles and at
length found a small spring of Brackish water [Redlum
Spring in Skull Valley] which did not run more than
four rods before it all disappeared in the thirsty earth but
mean and poor as the water was we and our animals
Quenched our burning thirst and unpacked for the day
after our rapid travel of about 20 hours and 30 hours
without water"

On May 30 the party crossed to the eastern side of
Skull Valley, then rode north around the rugged Stansbury Mountains, reaching on the afternoon of the 31st
"some holes of fresh water" soon to be known to emigrants as Hastings Wells or Twenty Wells (at present
Grantsville in Tooele Valley). On June 1 Clyman makes
one of the most interesting entries in his diary, harking
back to twenty years before, when he had first seen this
country as a mountain man: "proceeded nearly east to
the point of a high mountain [Oquirrh Mountains] that
Bounds the Southern part of the greate salt lake I observed that this lake like all the rest of this wide spread
Sterility has nearly wasted away one half of its surface
since 1825 [1826] when I floated around it in my Bull
Boate and we crossed a large Bay of this Lake with our
horses which is now dry . . ." The little party camped
near the northeastern extremity of the Oquirrh Mountains. They saw a few Indians around, and after "considerable signing and exertion" got them to camp. "These
Ewtaws as well as we could understand informed us that
the snakes and whites ware now at war and that the
snakes had killed two white men this news was not the
most pleasant as we have to pass through a portion of the
snake country."

Next morning, June 2, the "Eutaw guide" appeared
"and conducted us to the ford on thee Eutaw [Jordan]
river which we found Quite full and wetting several packs

on our low mules but we all got safely over and out to
the rising ground whare we found a fine spring brook
and unpacked to dry our wet baggage." Clyman was
favorably impressed by Salt Lake Valley, where the Mormons would settle next year, "a wide vally in some places
well set in an excelent kind of grass But I should think
that it would not be moist Enough for grain the mountains that surround this vally are pictureesque and many
places beautifull being high and near the base smoothe
and well set in a short nutericious grass. . . ." In the afternoon the party moved on into the Wasatch a few miles,
camping in Parleys Canyon, then on June 3 rode "N. E.
up the Brook into a high ruged mountain [Big Moun-
tain] not verry rocky but awfully brushy with some
dificulty we reached the summit and commenced our dis-
sent which was not so steep nor Quite so brushy." They
descended to what Clyman called "the South branch of
Weebers rivir," now East Canyon Creek, and followed
it down "untill it entered a rough Looking Kenyon when
we bore away to the East up a small Brook [Dixie
Creek] and encamped at the head springs . . . ." On June
4 they went north 4 miles down a ravine (the present
Main or Little East Canyon) to the Weber River, striking it "a short distance above the Junction of the N. and
S. Branches and immideately above whare it enters the
second Kenyon above its mouth [present Henefer]."

All this detail has been quoted from Clyman's diary
because it has a crucial bearing on Hastings' thinking
when he returned from Fort Bridger a few weeks later,
guiding emigrants. In preference to taking the route
across the Wasatch just described, Hastings conducted
wagons down the canyons of the Weber. He had serious
second-thoughts about that, and recommended to the
Donner Party that they cut a road across the Wasatch,
following much the same route he had traveled with Clyman eastbound; Hastings even rode back upon the trail
with James Frazier Reed as far as Big Mountain to point

out the proper route, as we shall see hereafter. And Hudspeth, guiding the mounted William H. Russell party in advance of the emigrant trains, returned in July to this very locality above the canyons of the Weber, eventually taking his charges back on this trail as far as East Canyon, thence along the mountainside down to the open valley where East Canyon Creek reaches the Weber. More will be said of this on a later page, in reviewing Edwin Bryant's journal of the Russell party.

Now, however, let us go on with Clyman and Hastings, who on June 5 traveled up Echo Canyon ("several summer songsters ware warbling their loves or chirping amongst the small willows which skirted the little Brook as we passed along") and crossed the divide to reach Bear River at present Evanston. The following day a northeast course across the sage hills brought them to "the wagon trail leading from Bridgers Trading house to Bear River." Turning southeast on this plainly marked trail, on the morning of June 7 the little party reached Bridger's fort. "Judge of our chagrin and disapointment on finding this spot so long and so anxiously saught for standing solitary and alone without the appearance of a human being having visited it for at least a month and what the caus conjectur was rife but could [not] be certain except that Bridger and his whole company had taken the road N. W. Toward the Lower part of Bear River." (Bridger may have set off in that direction, but he soon changed his course, making for Fort Laramie, as we shall learn in Volume II.) "In our weak and deffenceless state it was not easy to fix on any safe plan of procedure some proposed to return to Bear River and risk the hostility of the snake Indians others proposed to take the trail Travel slowly and risk the Siouxs. which ware supposed to be on our rout to Fort Larrimie so that the day was taken up in discussing what would be the most safe way of disposing ourselves a sufficient time to await the company from oregon to the states which was generally supposed would be Quite large this season . . . . nothing can be mor desolate and discouraging than a deserted fort whare you expect relief in a dangerous Indian country and every imaginary Idea was started as to what had been the caus of Bridgers leaving his establishment But nothing satisfactory could possibly be started and we ware still as far in the dark as ever."

Next day, after long deliberation, it was agreed to part. "Mr Hastings his man [Hudspeth] and Indian servant wished to go some 50 or 60 miles N. stop and await the arival of the company from Oregon 4 men of us one woman and one boy ware detirmined to go back to Bear River there being two trails from green river to bear rever it was uncertain which the oregon company might take if allready not passed so wa all started togather once more and after comeing to the seperating place we all continued on for the day and encamped in a small vally whare we encamped in Augt 2 yare ago [when en route to Oregon]."

This is Clyman's last mention of Hastings. His language is sufficiently ambiguous that we are unable to determine whether Hastings separated from the returning Californians a few miles below Fort Bridger or kept on with them for a time; he is next heard from on July 2 in William E. Taylor's diary, just west of South Pass. Clyman and the others went back to the Bear River valley, disappointed to find on arriving at the Oregon Trail (probably where the Greenwood Cutoff came in, south of Smiths Fork) "that a large party of horses and mules had passed appearantly some 5 or 10 days previous so our hopes ware to all appearances Blasted for this season." (These returning Oregonians were the party with which Joel Palmer traveled, discussed a little farther along; they had come along about May 19, some three weeks earlier.) On the 11th Clyman's little party "Packed up and concluded to move down Bear River to Bridgers camp [probably the site near present Dingle, Idaho, afterward frequented by Pegleg Smith] and await a few days for more company after Traveling 4 or 5 miles down

the wagon trail we met our old companions from california who had come by the way of Fort Hall and as we
ware informed that all the company from Oregon had
probably passed we turned our course to the East again."

The route taken swung a little south of the Greenwood
Cutoff, bringing the party to Green River by way of
La Barge Creek. With considerable labor, on June 14-15
they rafted across the Green, and on the 18th crossed
South Pass to the Sweetwater: "it gave Quite a cheering
statisfactory Idea allthough at so greate a distance to
think that I was once more on the waters of the Missisippi
and its ripling waters sounded in Idea like sweet home."
At Independence Rock on June 21 "our party small as
it was split-and about half of us concluded to remain over
night the others went ahead late in the afternoon." Clyman's group camped next night at the Willow Spring.
Near sunset two trappers arrived with information that
the advance party of emigrants were over the North
Platte, and on June 23 "we met the advance company
of oregon Emigration consisting of Eleven wagons nearly
oposite the red Butes." Thus Clyman met the William
J. Martin company with which Taylor, Craig, and Stanley were then traveling. Clyman continues: "when we
came in sight of N. Platte we had the Pleasant sight of
Beholding the valy to a greate distance dotted with Peopl
Horses cattle wagons and Tents their being 30 wagons
all Buisily engaged in crossing the River which was found
not to be fordable and with the poor material they had
to make rafts of it took two trips to carry over one waggon with its lading." He and his fellows made small ceremony of crossing, throwing their baggage on the returning rafts and swimming their animals over to encamp
"onc more in the Buisy humm of our own Language."

On the 24th, descending the North Platte, Clyman
tells of passing three small companies, some for Oregon
and some for California: "It is remarkable how anxious
thes people are to hear from the Pacific country and
strange that so many of all kinds and classes of People

should sell out comfortable homes in Missouri and Elsewhere pack up and start across such an emmence Barren
waste to settle in some new Place of which they have at
most so uncertain information but this is the character
of my countrymen." On the 25th, when Clyman and his
fellows turned away from the river into the Laramie
Mountains "on account of the Rocky Kenyons that bind
the stream on its passage through the Black Hills mountains," he noted: "To day we met all most one continual
stream of Emigrants wending their long and Tedious
march to oregon & california and I found it allmost impossible to pass these honest looking open harted people
without giving them some slight discription of what they
might Expect in their newly adopted and anxious sought
for new home but necessity only could compel us on-
ward." They encamped that night just as some emigrants
were making camp; "they came to us with Pails full of
good new milk which to us was a treat of greate rarity
after so many long tiresome days travel."

This chronicle continues on the 26th: "South across
the hills and to day as yestarday we passed several small
Brooks and met 117 teams in six different squads all
bound for oregon and california in the evening we again
had the pleasur of encamping with a company for california and they kept us in conversation untill near midnight." And on the 27th: "we met numerous squads of
emigrants untill we reached fort Larrimie whare we met
Ex govornor Boggs and party from Jackson county
Miourie Bound for California and we camped with them
several of us continued the conversation untill a late
hour."

Clyman remembered many years later that the Donners were with Boggs at Fort Laramie. "We camped one
night with them at Laramie. I knew Gov. Boggs, had
got acquainted with him at St. Louis. Had known mr
Reed previously in the Sauk war . . . . Mr Reed, while
we were encamped at Laramie was enquiring about the
route. I told him to 'take the regular wagon track and

never leave it—it is barely possible to get through if you follow it—and it may be impossible if you don't.' Reed replied, 'There is a nigher route, and it is of no use to take so much of a roundabout course.' I admitted the fact, but told him about the great desert and the roughness of the Sierras, and that a straight route might turn out to be impracticable."[32] Clyman's warning proved to be more than warranted.

In his diary Clyman remarks further that this night he "again obtained a cup of excellent coffee at Judge Morins camp the first I had tasted since in the early part of last winter and I fear that during our long conversation I changed the purposes of Govornor and the Judge for next morning they both told me they inteded to go to Oregon." (Boggs changed his mind later.)

Late on the morning of June 28 Clyman got on the road again "and met another party of emigrants cnsisting of 24 Wagons and they told us that so far as they knew they ware the last on the road about noon we passed Bisinnett^s. Trading house [Fort Bernard] and a few miles further on we met Bissinette [Joseph Bissonette] himself returning from Missouri with a small supply of goods for the trade and from him we ware informed that thier ware 40 Teams yet on the road and that the Pawnees had killed one man We had previously heard that they had stolen a number of horses and one company had lost 120 head of cattle either Strayed or Stolen"

Clyman concludes this part of his chronicle as follows:
"29 Parted with some of my old acquaintances who ware on thier way some for Oregon and some for california . . . Passed a small trading house on the River a few miles Below the old Larrimee establishments and one more company of emigrants [he may have been repeating here the information set down in his diary the previous day] most of the Emigrants we have met seemed

---

[32]Clyman's recollections of the encounter with James Frazier Reed at Fort Laramie were set down by Ivan Petroff in 1878, with an abstract of the Clyman diaries now in the Bancroft Library.

to be in good health and fine spirits But some are much discouraged and a few have turned back about noon we passed the sumit of Scotts Bluffs and took a drink of good cool spring water in the evening we met a nother party of waggon and with a larger company at night which ware supposed to be the last we should meet on the way . . . .

"30 Passed the chimney rock and at noon overtook a party of 12 or 15 men some from oregon [stragglers from Palmer's party] and a few that had turned back to Missouri at Laramie in the evening we encamped on the River within about one mile of those a head of us

"July the 1th 1846 A heavy dew last night and a clear cool morning in the afternoon met Mr. J. M. Wair with a small party of six wagons Mr Wair risidid in Oregon some yares and had went to the states last summer and was now on his return to Oregon again . . . .

"2 Rapid Thunder & Lightnin last night with a light shower of rain this morning is extremely warm we traveled S of East down the River untill about noon when we arived at the ash Hallow whare we found a company of Mormon Emigrants Encamped consisting of nineteen wagons these people are on their way to Oregon and informed us that the Pawnees had followed them and stole three horses last night They keeping a strick guard and the animals haveing been Tied to their wagons."

Clyman had encountered the Mississippi Saints, the sole Mormon company to get so far west in 1846. More will be said of this company hereafter. As one of a party which now consisted of eight men, two women, and one boy Clyman pushed rapidly ahead, to get through the Pawnee country as quickly as possible, and on the 4th "overtook a small prarty of Emigrants that ware ahead consisting of sevn men 2 young Ladies and one verry sick man some of thier company haveing left them an hour before our arival on account of their slow traveling The eight men that had parted from these in their defenceless state intended to make a rapid Push and travel

day and night untill they passed the Pawnee Teritory."
This philosophy of devil take the hindmost was popular
on the emigrant trails of this decade. Clyman and his
fellows nevertheless adjusted their pace to that of the
afflicted and did not suffer for it. On July 10 he writes:
"a Mr McKizack was left Behind last night being himself nearly Blinde and his horses verry poor his messmate
Mr. Stump went back this morning to assist him to come
up . . . . Mr stump returned about noon and could find
nothing of Mr McKissick we moved on in the afternoon
to the west fork of Blue river [Little Blue] and encamped early for the purpose of making a more thorough
search for the lost man But in a few minutes after stopping the old man hove in sight to the mutual satisfaction
of all parties."

This was the last worrisome incident of the journey.
On July 15, after crossing the Big Blue, Clyman observed "the grave of Mrs Sarak Keys agead 70 yares
who had departed this life in may last." (As we shall
see, she was the mother-in-law of James Frazier Reed.)
"This stone shews us that all ages and all sects are found
to undertake this long tedious and even dangerous Journy
for some unknown object never to be realized even by
those the most fortunate and why because the human
mind can never be satisfied never at rest allways on the
strech for something new some strange novelty." These
reflections brought Old Greenwood to his mind: "on our
Return from California a Mr Greenwood and his two
sons made a part of our company this man the Elder
is now from his best recollection 80 years of age and has
made the trip 4 times in 2 yares in part."

Clyman crossed the Kansas River on July 19 and three
days later reached Independence, so that on the morning
of the 23rd he found himself "surrounded by civilization
and had to answer numerous [questions] about the country we had visited and many more conserning acquaintances that ware in Oregon and California disposed of

my mules and mad my appearance at Mr [Smallwood] Nolands Tavern and a Rough appearance it was But such things are not atall strang in Independence as it [is] the first place all the Parties rach from the Mountains from St A Fee California and Oregon." On an end page of Clyman's diary is his record of the emigrant wagons encountered on the journey eastward:

[June]	23	W	11
	24	"	50
	25	"	66—17
	26	"	26 . . 91
	27		104 . . 24
	28		28 . . 24
	29		15 one Party of Packers
	30		22
[July]	1		6 " " " Packers
[July	2		19 Mormon wagons]

Clyman went on to St. Louis for the interview in the *Missouri Republican* of July 30, reprinted in Volume II. We have followed his account at length, for it is the lone diary yet found written by one who traveled against the current in 1846. Clyman came home as a member of the only party to leave California this year by the northern route, though Solomon Sublette with others came up through the southern deserts from Pueblo de los Angeles to reach the main trail at Fort Bridger, follow that trail east to Fort Laramie, then swing south to Bent's Fort on the Arkansas. Clyman's diary is, besides, a trail document of paramount importance, for through it we are enabled to travel the Hastings Cutoff while Hastings himself was first passing over it. As we read, Hastings is rarely absent from our thoughts.

5.

Now we must turn north to Oregon and review developments on that frontier. In contrast to California, several parties left Oregon for the States in the spring of 1846. We are fortunate that Joel Palmer, who had gone out to Oregon in 1845, accompanied the first of these returning parties and published a narrative of his experiences in 1847.[33] Although Palmer wrote only a condensed account of his return journey of 1846, like Clyman's diary, Palmer's narrative is a unique document. Before we take it up, let us remark the diary of the Rev. George Gary, who had reached Oregon in the spring of 1844 as a representative of the Mission Board of the Methodist Episcopal Church. Gary established his residence at Oregon City, where he made the first of the entries we shall quote.

"Wednesday, [February] 25 [1846]. Today I hand to Mr. Redshirt [*i.e.*, Hiram] Smith three letters for the states . . . . Mr. Smith is about starting over the mountains for the states [with Palmer] . . . .

"Monday, March 2. This day I close my letter to the board to be sent over the mountains . . . .

"Tuesday, April 28 [now visiting the mission establishment at The Dalles] This day I seal the letters for the states; in hopes of an opportunity to send them to the states . . . .

"Thursday, 30 . . . . Send by Mr. Bonney letters to J. L. P[arrish]., D. Leslie, J. Force, and G. Abernethy . . . . This Bonny is supposed to be a dreadful man.

"Friday, May 1. This day we give to the returning emigrants the letters above mentioned for the states, entrusted with Mr. Hockerman. We hope our friends will receive them by about the first of September . . . .

"Sunday, 3. Bonny returned from his effort to go to Williamette . . . .

"Tuesday, 5. We are annoyed with the company of a Mr. Bonny, a real hanger-on; strong reason to fear he is a murderer; it is supposed he murdered a man on his way to this territory in 1845; he never has ventured to

[33]Joel Palmer's much respected book was published as *Journal of Travels over the Rocky Mountains, to the Mouth of the Columbia River; made during the Years 1845 and 1846* . . . (Cincinnati, 1847).

show himself in the Williamette portion of this country; now talks of returning to the states; has in company with him a Spaniard; I wish they were far away from this mission. It is not easy to calculate the depravity of many of the emigrants to this country. I give Mr. Bonney rather of a plain talk about the emigrants hanging about this mission and tell him our business as a mission is with the natives and we do not want any traffic with the whites; he leaves with his Spaniard; but I fear he will be back again.

"Mr. Galligher is also here after cattle which were left by the emigrants last year; he is afraid to leave with his herds lest Bonny and his Spaniard should pursue him and rob him; but as Bonny is now gone, possibly Mr. G. may conclude to go soon . . . . At night Mr. Burn appears . . . .[34]

"Monday, 11. A beautiful fine morning; while nature is smiling in her lovliness, lo, Mr. Bonny appears in sight; the more we hear and see of this man, the more we are convinced that wherever he appears, depravity in some of its aggravated forms may be feared.

"Tuesday, 12. We are having pleasant, warm weather. Ther. in the shade, 76. These families are annoyed with

---

[34]The *Oregon Spectator,* February 19, 1846, contains a paragraph: "Hugh Burns, Esq., informs us that himself and party will leave early in March next, for the United States. Their route will be across the Rocky mountains by way of the South Pass. Persons wishing to send east by the party, would do well to avail themselves of this opportunity." It would seem that Burns did not make the trip, for the *Spectator* of November 26 reports a meeting Burns attended in his own home on October 3. At the time of the original story, the *Spectator* explained that the Postmaster General had contracted with Burns to carry the mail for one trip only, from Oregon City to Weston, Missouri, he to receive 25 per cent on the amount of postage the department received for the letters. Since only fifty cents could be charged for a single sheet, it may be that there was no money in such transport of the mail. Burns gave up the project or he hired someone in his place: postal historians may be interested to inquire into the details.

Mr. Bonny.

"Wednesday, 13. Most beautiful weather. Thermometer in shade 80. Poor Bonny has just started for the states. Doubtful! Doubtful!"[35]

To say the least, Gary gave Wales B. Bonney a bad press! But this was a view from the Columbia of the three separate parties which started homeward from Oregon this spring; developments in connection with the Applegate Cutoff, a new southern road to Oregon, are to be considered hereafter.

The first party to leave was that whose fortunes are described by Joel Palmer. A second company is known to us mostly from mentions in the diaries of those westbound on the trail, its arrival on the frontier noted in the Missouri newspapers, as seen in Volume II; this party seemingly left Oregon City April 18 and The Dalles about May 1, reaching St. Joseph August 1. The name of only one of the party, B. Genois, has been ascertained unless Gary's "Mr. Hockerman" was among their number. Bonney made a much greater impression upon the emigrants who kept diaries or wrote letters home. He left The Dalles on May 13, as Gary recorded, and after remarkable adventures reached Independence on September 30. Much more will be said of him in these pages.

Joel Palmer declares that he himself set out for the States from Oregon City on March 5, 1846, a week after a party of seven which he and his companions expected to overtake at Whitman's missionary station. He reached the Dalles on March 14, finding five of the party in advance, and on the 28th arrived at Waiilatpu. After a visit to Henry Harmon Spalding's missionary station on the Clearwater, on April 17 Palmer's party got under way, consisting of 18 persons having 51 horses and mules.

[35]These extracts come from Charles Henry Carey, ed., *"Diary of Reverend George Gary,"* Oregon Historical Society *Quarterly,* September, 1923, vol. 24, pp. 302-311.

Not without adventures en route, the party reached Fort Boise April 29 and Fort Hall May 14. On the 16th, Palmer relates, they arrived at the Soda Springs, and two days later they met about 600 lodges of Snake Indians moving from Bear River to the Snake. On the 23rd the party reached Green River, "taking the northern route." Crossing Green River on May 24 and South Pass on the 26th, they moved on down the Sweetwater to camp about four miles east of Independence Rock on May 30. "Soon after encamping it commenced raining, which turned to snow, and in the morning we had about five inches of snow upon us. We were uncomfortably situated, as we could procure but little fuel, and had no means of sheltering ourselves from the 'peltings of the pitiless storm.' Our horses too fared poorly." On the 31st they remained in camp. "By noon the snow had disappeared, and we succeeded in finding a few dry cedar trees, built a fire, and dried our effects. We had an abundance of buffalo marrow-bones, tongues, and other choice pieces, on which we feasted. We saw large droves of mountain sheep, or big-horn, and thousands of antlope."

June 2 brought the returning Oregonians to the North Platte, found too high to cross. Next day they succeeded in finding a ford, and on June 4 the party went on to Deer Creek, some thirty miles. "On the way we saw a band of Indians whom we supposed to be of the Crow nation, and as they are generally for fight, we prepared to give them a warm reception; but it seemed that they were as fearful of us, as we were of them. They were soon out of sight. After traveling about five miles, we saw them drawn up into line two miles from the road. As they were at a respectful distance, we did not molest them. We however kept a sharp look out, and at night were cautious in selecting camp ground." On June 5 Palmer's party "traveled about fifteen miles and encamped on Mike's-head creek [probably a corruption of Mark Head's Creek, now La Prele Creek]. Here we found two trappers, who had been out about three weeks. They accompanied us to Fort Laramie, which we reached on the 8th of June. In the morning H. Smith, one of our party, in catching a mule was thrown, and his shoulder dislocated. We attempted to set it, but could not succeed. He traveled on to the fort, but in great misery. We remained here until the afternoon of the 10th. Mr. Smith's shoulder was so much injured that he could not travel. He concluded to remain at the fort a few days; three men were to stay with him, and the rest of us had made arrangements for starting, when a company of Oregon emigrants came in sight. We awaited their arrival, and had the gratification of hearing from the States, it being the first news we had received since leaving our homes. A part of us remained a few hours to give them opportunity of writing to their friends; while five of the party took the road . . . .

"We continued for a distance of two hundred miles meeting companies of from six to forty wagons, until the number reached five hundred and forty-one wagons, and averaging about five souls to each wagon. They were generally in good health and fine spirits. Two hundred and twelve wagons were bound for California; but I have since learned that many of those who had designed to go to California had changed their destination and were going to Oregon.

"At Ash hollow we met a company who had lost many of their cattle and horses; but they were still going on. A short distance below the forks of Platte, we met a company of forty-one wagons, under the command of a Mr. Smith, which company had lost about one hundred and fifty head of cattle; they were encamped, and parties were out hunting cattle. We remained with them a short time, and then passed on. This was on the 18th of June."

Palmer goes on to relate the killing by the Pawnees of Edward Trimble, one of Smith's company, as recounted in greater detail in Volume II. Here we shall note that Palmer goes on to say:

"Mr. Trimble had left a wife and four children. She had sent by the party a request that we might come back, and allow her and family to travel with us to the U. States. We accordingly all took the road to the company's camp, (driving the cattle) which we reached at day-break on the morning of the 20th June. Here we remained until the afternoon. By the persuasion of her friends, Mrs. Trimble concluded to continue her journey to Oregon. But there were four families who had lost so many of their cattle, that they were unable to proceed on their journey. They had four wagons, and only five yoke of cattle, and some of them were very small. They wished us to travel with them through the Pawnee country, as the Pawnees were the perpetrators of the act which had caused them so much difficulty. We accordingly traveled with them until the 30th, when we left them, and resumed our journey towards home.

"On the morning of the 21st we were joined by Mr. Smith, and the three men who had been left at the fort. We traveled on rapidly day and night, barely giving our animals time to rest. The weather was becoming warm; the flies and musquitoes were very annoying. We arrived at the Mission or Agency [for the Iowa, Sac', and Fox Indians] on the morning of the 6th of July. Here are extensive farms, and a most delightful country. The first view of cultivated fields, and marks of civilization, brought simultaneous shouts from the whole party. Our troubles and toils were all forgotten."

Next morning Joel Palmer, Hiram Smith, and their companions reached St. Joseph, where their arrival created the splash in the newspapers reflected in Volume II. In his narrative Palmer says: "We had been so long among savages, that we resembled them much in appearance; but when attired in new apparel, and shaved as became white men, we hardly knew each other. We had been long in each other's company; had undergone hardships and privations together; had passed through many dangers, relying upon each other for aid and protection. Attachments had grown up, which when we were about to separate were sensibly felt; but as we were yet separated from our families, where still stronger ties were felt, each one took his course, and in a few hours our party was scattered, and each traveling in a different direction."

6.

Prior to 1845 the Cascade Mountains had been for Oregon emigrants almost as much of a barrier as the Sierra Nevada farther south. Wagons were brought over the Blue Mountains to the Columbia as early as 1840, but they could be taken no further down the river than The Dalles; it was necessary to carry them the rest of the way by water, which was slow, hazardous, and often expensive. These conditions were discussed by Jesse Applegate in a series of contributions to the *Oregon Spectator* published over the signature "X" between January and April, 1847. Applegate embarked upon this literary labor, as he wrote his brother Lisbon the following October, in consequence of the furious abuse and injurious slanders occasioned by the disasters on the Applegate Cutoff in the fall of 1846 to which we will soon be giving attention.

In the first of these articles, printed in the *Spectator* for January 21, Applegate discussed the history of earlier emigrations, disregarding anything that happened before he himself migrated to the Willamette. The emigrants of 1843, he wrote:

> were the first who traveled with wagons below Fort Hall—of these a part reached the Dalles of the Columbia in the month of November—others left their wagons and animals at Wallawalla, and a few remained at Dr. Whitman's Mission through the winter.
>
> When we consider the scarcity of grass and water along most of the route, the dangerous crossings of Snake river, and the making of the road for so great a distance, over wide plains of sage and sand, and almost impassable mountains, that they

arrived on the Columbia at all, is a proof of energy and perserverance not often equalled by those who have followed them.

The obstacles so formidable had not been surmounted without much labor and loss, both of life and property; yet, though so near the end of their journey, they experienced by far, more losses, hardship and sufferings in descending from the Dalles to the Willamette, than in all the rest of the journey together; and almost in sight of the great object of their wishes, many were relieved from perishing by the benevolence of the Hudson's Bay Company, and the timely and gratuitous assistance of Capt. James Waters, a fellow emigrant.

The emigrants of 1844 fared even worse than those of the preceding year; arriving late in the season, when, by reason of the snow, the trail by Mount Hood was thought to be impassable; the greater part of their worn-down animals were swum to the north side of the Columbia, which is nearly a mile wide, driven down on that side and re-crossed in boats at Vancouver; a route of great danger, fatigue and exposure to the owners, and in which more than half the animals were lost. The rear of this emigration also, got no further than Dr. Whitman's Mission. Most of the citizens having experienced these calamities, and seeing their friends arrive in this distant country, shorn of the means of their comfort, or of becoming useful citizens, a desire to remedy these evils became universal.

Hopes were entertained that this could be effected by finding a nearer and better road into the Willamette valley, by a route formerly traveled by the Hudson's Bay Company, leaving the present road in the Malheur, or Powder river valley, and crossing the Cascade mountains by a pass near mount Jefferson. This was attempted by a party under the patronage of Dr. E. White, late Indian Agent of this Territory, in the summer of 1845. This party, after spending about a month in exploring the Cascade mountains up the Santiam river, and south of it, returned without accomplishing their object. As by this enterprise, Dr. White had been at considerable expense, the Legislature of Oregon passed a resolution recommending his claims to remuneration, 'to the favorable consideration' of the Federal Government.

Two attempts have since been made to penetrate the Cascade mountains from the Willamette valley; and, as on one occasion, in case of success, the guide was to receive one thousand dollars, we have reason to believe they have been prosecuted, with due energy.[36] Yet, I think these attempts should not be taken as

---

[36]The efforts to penetrate the Cascades made after Elijah White's in the summer of 1845 (described in White's undated letter to "the

final evidence that no pass can be found. . . .

The failure of Dr. White's enterprise left the large emigration of 1845, to find their way into the Willamette valley by the usual means; the supply of boats being wholly inadequate to their speedy conveyance down the Columbia, and the stock of provisions failing at the Dalles, famine, and a malignant disease at the same time raging amongst them, a scene of human misery ensued which scarcely has a parallel in history—the loss of life and property was enormous. . . .

The whole community were again aroused to the necessity of finding a remedy for an evil so distressing and calamitous. Two road companies were chartered by the Legislature, and a large amount raised by subscription, to encourage individual enterprise; and the year 1846 is not more an epoch to be remembered in the history of Oregon, for the quiet settlement of its boundary, than for the arrival of emigrants from the United States with their wagons, at both ends of the Willamette valley. . . .[37]

In his second article, printed in the *Spectator* of February 4, 1847, Applegate continued:

From the Dalles, horse trails cross the Cascade mountains on both sides of Mount Hood—the northern route is the most direct,

Hon. The House of Representatives of Oregon Assembled," in a Bancroft Library MS., Oregon Archives, P-A 55, pp. 87-94) are reflected in the columns of the *Oregon Spectator* for March 19, April 2, and June 25, 1846, reprinted in Volume II. In addition, a correspondent, "Oregonian," in the *Oregon Spectator,* March 18, 1847, recalls in some detail how in the summer of 1846 a small company of men including Neal Gilliam, guided by Joseph Gervais, "undertook to explore and survey a wagon route leading from the settlements upon the Santiam river, and following that river up to its head waters, and from thence striking the waters of Crooked river near their conjunction with those of DeChutes or Falls river, and following up the waters of Crooked river in the direction that would ultimately strike on the banks of the Malheur river . . . ."

[37]The Oregon legislature on December 17, 1845, passed a bill authorizing Samuel K. Barlow to construct a road across the Cascade Mountains, but a bill giving similar authorization to Stephen H. L. Meek, after having passed its second reading, was tabled. See Lafayette Grover, *The Oregon Archives* (Salem, 1853), pp. 125-151. Another project that failed of passage was a petition from Thomas McKay for a charter "to construct a road from Fort Boise across the Blue, and Cascade Mountains, to the Willamette Valley."

but the southern is less difficult, and better supplied with grass.
Though these paths run over very steep and rugged mountains,
and were still more difficult from the great quantity of fallen
timber, and the thickness of the undergrowth, yet emigrants
arriving before the snow was too deep on the mountains, usually
drove their animals by one of these trails in preference to twice
crossing the Columbia river.

To avoid the danger and heavy expense of descending the
Columbia by water, a party of emigrants of 1845, under the
direction of Samuel K. Barlow, undertook to open a road for their
wagons along the southern trail.

They succeeded in penetrating the mountains to within a few
miles of the main ridge, but the increasing snow, and the scarcity
of pasturage and provisions forced them to leave their wagons
and hasten with their animals to the valley. To encourage Mr.
Barlow to complete his road, as it would be of great benefit to
future emigrants, a considerable sum was raised by subscription
for his benefit, and the privilege granted him by the Legislature
to collect a toll of $5 on each wagon, and 10 cents a head for
horses and cattle that passed his road; and to its completion it is
evident the van of the emigrants of 1846, owe their early and less
expensive arrival at the Willamette valley.

Some little improvements to Mr. Barlow's road over the Cascade mountains will complete the northern route to Oregon, and
no material improvements upon the ground can hereafter be
effected. . . . [38]

---

[38]Applegate's articles in the *Spectator* aroused a rejoinder by "Oregonian," who in the *Spectator* of February 18, 1847, said that he
could not persuade himself "that it is consummate wisdom to dis-
parage and underrate the old road so excessively as this writer has
done, until a better one can be found. 'Praise the bridge that carries you safely over,' is an old adage, and worthy of consideration
in this case; for thousands of immigrants now resident in the Willamette valley, have been safely carried over this old road, and that
too, when various attempts have been made to obtain a nearer and
better route, but without success.

" 'Z' says, that 'a considerable sum was raised by subscription
for Mr. Barlow's benefit,' to enable him to complete his road. I understand, from an authentic source, that Mr. Barlow has received
the enormous sum of thirty dollars on this subscription for opening
and improving this great thoroughfare . . . . When 'Z' will discover
a shorter, better, and more practicable road, which will admit of
'material improvement,' than the old one, and Mr. Barlow's, then
will I advocate his claims to a share out of the enormous sum which

On March 18, 1847, the *Spectator* printed Applegate's third communication now having reference to the country traversed by the cutoff he had found in the summer of 1846:

The three streams forming the Willamette river unite about the 44th degree of north latitude, to which point the settlements now extend. It will probably be found less expensive to make the Willamette river the channel of trade as high up as the forks, than to build a railroad; the navigation of the river will have the further advantage of being convenient to both sides of the valley. The fine water power on the river, the natural beauty of the site, and broad and fertile valleys which follow up the three rivers which here unite, seem to mark this place as the center of trade for the upper Willamette; and should a branch of the expected railroad from the U. States to the Pacific be extended to this country, it will most likely here find its northern terminus.

Capt. Fremont (on the 27th Dec. 1843,) crossed the Siera Nevada directly on the 42d parallel; as the wagon road over the Calapooia mountain bears about the same relative position to the forks of the Willamette, that the wagon pass over the Siera Nevada does to the pass of Capt. Fremont, the distance in both cases (according to Mitchell's late Map) on a right line, is about 225 miles. But as the road makes but very little easting until it crosses Rogue river, and is forced from a direct line in crossing the mountains and meandering the lakes, it is according to the way bills, about 335 miles to the top of the Siera Nevada. About 280 miles of this distance lies in the valleys of the Umpqua, Rogue river, Clamet and Sacramento; the remainder in the Calapooia, Umpqua, and Siskiu or Cascade mountains.

Of the road in the valleys, it is only necessary to state that the grass is every where plenty, and water at convenient distances— the road crosses a few hills in the different valleys, and some rocky country in the valley of the Sacramento; with these exceptions, it is over firm, level plains—the streams are crossed at good rocky fords, and at the proper season are, from their size, of little impediment. The mountains require a more particular description.

---

was 'raised by subscription for Mr. Barlow's benefit;' but until this is accomplished, I think Mr. Barlow is entitled to all the profits arising from this subscription, and in addition to this, a considerable amount of approbation and credit, for the victory he has achieved in finding a wagon road leading into the Willamette valley . . . ."

More is said of the Barlow Road in Volume II.

The ridge dividing the waters of the Willamette and Umpqua rivers, is called the Calapooia mountains; it is narrow and of no great hight, and may be crossed in many places; the wagon road crosses it by a ridge way about 10 miles in length from prairie to prairie, and is not complained of by the immigrants; but chasms similar to the pass of the Umpqua mountains, may be found through the Calapooia, by which a railroad will meet but slight ascents or descents.

The Umpqua mountain divides the waters of the Rogue river and Umpqua, and is much more formidable than the Calapooia, being a much higher, rockier ridge, and over it, it is impracticable to make a wagon road.

The road passes through a chasm which cuts the mountain from side to side to its very base. As this pass has been a place of much disaster to some of the immigrants, and is of itself a natural curiosity, it requires a minute description. A good pool of water about 15 feet in diameter, occupies the dividing ground between the waters of the Rogue river and Umpqua; there is from east to west about 30 yards of level land between the mountains which rises abruptly to the hight of about 1500 feet—the descent each way from this point is very gentle—that to the south is about three miles—conducts by a good way to the open country: that to the north is about 12 miles in length—for three or four miles there is sufficient level ground, and but little work required to make a good road; but below this, the stream increasing in size by the entrance of affluents, and the mountains closing in upon it, the road must descend in its rocky bed, made more difficult by some large stones and short falls, or be graded along the side of the mountain, which being loose soil, or decomposed basalt, can be done with the greatest facility these last two or three miles, when the hills recede and leave, by frequently crossing the creek, a bottom wide enough for a road the remainder of the distance. The party employed in opening the road, being in want of the necessary tools, and scarce of provisions, were unable to make this road properly, and attempted only to make it passable with as little labor as possible. On the level ground it is made crooked in going round logs and trees, and the banks at the crossings of the creek are left too steep, and at that part of the pass properly called the kanyon, the road is taken along the side of the hill, about a mile, when it descends into the creek by a hill so steep as to require the greatest care to prevent wagons from upsetting. The difficulties of the road were much increased by the rains commencing about the time the first wagons were crossing the mountain. The failure of some of the weaker teams so discouraged others, that several wagons were left on the south side of the mountain, their owners thinking it impossible to take them through the pass. But nearly a month after the commencement of the rains, and at a time when they were falling, one of the largest wagons on the road, with 800 or 1000 lbs. in it was drawn through the pass, and could easily have reached the prairie on this side on the second day, had not the heavy rains which fell during its passage so swollen the little creek that runs down from the pass, as to endanger the wetting the goods at one of the last crossings. As it was, the wagon was brought over all the bad road, and within a mile and a half of the prairie where Mr. P. arrived with his team before night. From which it is evident that with a little additional labor, heavily laden wagons may pass either way through this formidable mountain in dry weather in a day: and through it a railroad may be constructed as cheap, and with as little labor as the same distance over a level plain.

By a gradual ascent of several miles through open country, the road reaches the summit of a high plain, or rather broad mountain, the western run here being a ridge rising considerably above the general level. This plain is timbered with a variety of pine, (by far the finest tree I have seen of that family,) with occasional small prairies, well stocked with grass and water; the road runs upon this plain about 27 miles and descends to the Clamet, at a prairie about 5 miles below the lake. The road is generally good, there being two short steeps to ascend, and two to descend to the little streams which afford the camps.

This mountain is usually called the Siskiu, but it is my opinion the Cascade range, as this broad plain runs directly south of the foot of a mighty pile glittering in eternal snow, and surmounted by a peak by far the highest in the range called Mount Shaste. Though the Clamet river cuts its way through this plain, it makes no opening, and is generally in kanyons of great depth.

The Siera Nevada is a continuation of the Blue mountains, and here is a high, narrow ridge, capped with snow. The road runs through a good, open pass, and the only hill to cross is on the east side of the range; fine grass runs up to the top of the mountain, and fine springs break out on both sides, which, though the ascent of the hill is long and laborious, the fine grass and water, and abundant wild fruits, make this a pleasant part of the road. Goose Lake lies on the west, and Plum Lake on the east side of this mountain; they are probably fifteen miles apart. From the hights west of Goose Lake, the pass through which Capt. Fremont crossed this mountain is in plain view, and is about 25 miles north of the wagon route. That the road may be made shorter and better, as an immigrant route in this division, there is no doubt. . . .

The last of Applegate's articles over his pen name "Z" appeared in the *Spectator* for April 15, 1847; now he looked at the country farther east:

From the crossing of the Siera Nevada to the entrance of the most direct immigrant route into Bear river valley (called Greenwood's cut off,) is on a straight line according to Mitchell's late map, about 445 miles. The immigrant route is south of a right line to about the head of the Cajeux or Raft river, where it crosses to the north and remains on that side of the remainder of the distance. To the head of the Raft river, it is on a straight line 350 miles—and by the way bills of the road 160 miles. The road from the pass of the Siera runs in a southeasterly direction to Ogden's river about 140 miles; the first 70 miles of this distance, which reaches a large grassy plain, is a good road, and well supplied with grass and water the remainder of the distance to Ogden's river, which includes all the long camps on the route, is as follows:

From the grassy plain above alluded to, it is 3 miles to a fine spring with sufficient grass for a camp. From this it is 17 miles over a level, but in places a heavy road to the hot springs at the foot of the Black Rock; these springs extend along the foot of the mountain about 5 miles and the extensive fields of grass produced by the spreading of their waters over the plain makes this a good recruiting place after the privations suffered in arriving here from Ogden's river. From the Black Rock to Ogden's river, it is about 45 miles; there are along the road two springs at convenient distances for camps, but owing to the extreme drouth of the last season, but one of these afforded sufficient grass and water for a camp, and at the other some of the immigrants could only get a small supply of water for their teams, making the distance of 35 miles over a level, but in places a heavy road without camping. To avoid this long stretch, the country north of Ogden's river, was examined for about 50 miles above the leaving point, but no grass or water could be found to supply the necessary camps.

The remainder of the road to the head of Raft river, a distance of about 320 miles, is in a northeasterly direction. The grass and water is plenty and at convenient distances, and the road is good, lying most of the distance in the level green valleys along the streams. As this part of the country is broken into detached mountains and level sandy plains, in the season of floods, the water collects in larger or smaller basins, but dry up as the summer advances; the little brooks which collect in the mountains, mostly sink in a short distance from their sources. It is doubtful whether an immigrant route can be made much shorter than the present, as Ogden's river alone affords a connected chain of verdant plains supplied with water through this arid region: but a trail road may be taken over the level plains on nearly a straight line. . . .

The curve made in the road by following down Ogden's river to the 41st parallel, as it necessarily increases its length but 25 or 30 miles, is more compensated by the fine traveling and pasturage on that stream, and a good camp being at any time to be had, is of great advantage to caravans.

Though the southern route to Oregon, so far as traveling is concerned, is much superior to the northern route, yet under present circumstances, I should hesitate to advise immigrants to travel it, particularly if their destination be to northern portions of the territory. The Indians along the route not being dependent upon any trading establishment, have nothing to restrain them from the exercise of their natural disposition to plunder, and as they are at present, from causes which it is unnecessary to mention, but illy disposed towards us, it requires vigilance to prevent their depredations.

Though so far from being formidable that parties of 5 and even 4 men have traversed their country in its whole extent in safety and without the loss of a single article, and have remained stationary for weeks in the midst of them without being molested, yet large parties of immigrants were not equally successful.

Immigrants may embody for the protection of their property— but from the natural repugnance with which a free people submit to any kind of discipline or controll, the duty of guarding it, which is its only security, will be negligently performed or wholly neglected. And besides failing in the object to which they unite, they will be subjected to all the tardiness and dissensions of a large undisciplined and discordant mass. The diligent will be withheld from prosecuting the journey, by the slothful and indolent, more inert from the knowledge that they will not be left behind.

Thus Jesse Applegate, writing after the fact, but nearly thirty years before his brother Lindsay wrote the primary account of the pioneering of the Applegate Cutoff. We may suppose that Lindsay had a diary to fall back upon, for the journal he published in the Portland

West Shore between June and September, 1877, has the
immediacy of a contemporary trail record as well as the
wisdom of hindsight.[39] He relates that Levi and John
Scott, Lindsay and Jesse Applegate, Henry Boygus,
Benjamin Burch, John Owens, John Jones, Robert
Smith, Samuel Goodhue, Moses Harris, David Goff,
Benit Osborn, William Sportsman, and William Parker,
with a caballada consisting of thirty animals, gathered on
June 20, 1846 "on the La Creole, near where Dallas now
stands," and promptly commenced their journey south.
On the 21st they reached the foothills of the Calapooia
Mountains, and on the 22nd passed the peak later called
Spencers Butte, crossing the summit of the main chain
to encamp on a small tributary of the Umpqua River,
with good grass for the horses and superb strawberries
for the men. The company arrived at the "north Umpqua
river" on June 23 and next day at the south branch, up
which they traveled "almost to the place where the old
trail [used by early pack parties going to and from Cali-
fornia] crosses the Umpqua mountains."

On June 25 the company entered the Umpqua Canyon; they "followed up the little stream that runs through
the defile for four or five miles, crossing the creek a great
many times, but the canyon becoming more obstructed
with brush and fallen timber, the little trail we were following turned up the side of the ridge where the woods
were more open, and wound its way to the top of the
mountain. It then bore south along a narrow back-bone
of the mountain, the dense thickets and the rocks on either

---

[39]Lindsay Applegate's narrative is more accessible as reprinted in Oregon Historical Society *Quarterly,* March, 1921, vol. 22, pp. 12-45,
and from that source in Maude Applegate Rucker, *The Oregon Trail
and Some of Its Blazers* (New York, 1930), pp. 248-288. For lack
of a parallel record, it is impossible to verify the dates Lindsay
Applegate gives us on the outbound journey. All his dates after
Jesse Applegate rode on to Fort Hall are more or less incorrect,
but we are obliged to use the earlier dates for lack of anything
better.

side affording splendid opportunities for ambush. A short time before this, a party coming from California had been attacked on this summit ridge by the Indians and one of them had been severely wounded. Several of the horses had also been shot with arrows. Along this trail we picked up a number of broken and shattered arrows. We could see that a large party of Indians had passed over the trail traveling southward only a few days before. At dark we reached a small opening on a little stream at the foot of the mountain on the south, and encamped for the night." Next morning the road company divided, part going back to explore the canyon while the others stayed to guard the camp. "The exploring party went back to where we left the canyon on the little trail the day before, and returning through the canyon, came into camp after night, reporting that wagons could be taken through."

The explorers went on cautiously on the 27th, for Indians were hovering around, frightening the horses. "Whenever the trail passed through the cuts we dismounted and led our horses, having our guns in hand ready at any moment to use them in self-defense, for we had adopted this rule, never to be the aggressor. Traveling through a very broken country the sharp hills separated by little streams upon which there were small openings, we came out at about noon into a large creek, a branch of Rogue river, now called Grave Creek. . . . " Great precautions were exercised, approaching the Rogue that afternoon, as in crossing the river on the 28th.

After crossing, we turned up the river, and the Indians in large numbers came out of the thickets on the opposite side and tried in every way to provoke us. Our course was for some distance southwest along the bank of the river, and the Indians, some mounted and some on foot, passed on rapidly on the other side. There appeared to be a great commotion among them. A party had left the French settlement some three or four weeks before us, consisting of French, half-breeds, Columbia Indians and a few Americans; probably about eighty in all. Passing one of their encampments we could see by the signs that they were were only a short distance ahead of us. We afterwards learned

that the Rogue Rivers had stolen some of their horses, and that
an effort to recover them had caused the delay. At about three
o'clock, we left the river and bore southward up a little stream
for four or five miles and encamped. From our camp we could
see numerous signal fires on the mountains to the eastward. We
saw no Indians in the vicinity of our camp, and no evidence of
their having been there lately. They had evidently given us up,
and followed the other company which the same night encamped
in the main valley above. Under the circumstances, we enjoyed
a good night's sleep, keeping only two guards at a time.

On June 29 the road company passed over a low range
of hills which afforded a magnificent view of the Rogue
River Valley, and that night "encamped near the other
party on the stream now known as Emigrant creek, near
the foot of the Siskiyou mountains. This night, the
Indians having gone to the mountains to ambush the
French party as we afterwards learned, we were not disturbed. Here our course diverged from that of the other
company, they following the old California trail across the
Siskiyou while our route was eastward through an unexplored region several hundred miles in extent."

Next day they climbed the mountains to the east, "examining the hills above the stream now called Keene creek,
near the summit of the Siskiyou ridge," and encamped "in
a little valley, now known as Round prairie," some ten
or twelve miles farther on. Several days the party spent
searching for a practicable pass, and succeeded on July 3,
when they encamped in a valley afterward called Long
Prairie.

On the morning of July 4th, our route bore along a ridge
trending considerably towards the north. The route was good, not
rocky, and the ascent very gradual. After crossing the summit of
the Cascade ridge, the descent was, in Places, very rapid. At
noon we came out into a glade where there was water and grass
and from which we could see the Klamath river. After noon we
moved down through an immense forest, particularly of yellow
pine, to the river, and then traveled up the north bank, still
through yellow pine forests, for about six miles, when all at once
we came out in full view of the Klamath country, extending

eastward as far as the eye could reach. It was an exciting moment, after the many days spent in the dense forests and among the mountains, and the whole party broke forth in cheer after cheer. . . . Following the river up to where it leaves the Lower Klamath Lake, we came to a riffle where it seemed possible to cross. William Parker waded in and explored the ford. It was deep, rocky and rapid, but we all passed over safely, and then proceeding along the river and lake shore for a mile or so when we came into the main valley of the Lower Klamath Lake. We could see columns of smoke rising in every direction, for our presence was already known to the Modocs and the signal fire telegraph was in active operation. Moving southward along the shore we came to a little stream coming in from the southward, and there found pieces of newspaper and other unmistakable evidences of civilized people having camped there a short time before.

Afterward they concluded that here Fremont had been overtaken by Gillespie on May 8, the camp from which he had turned back to find his destiny in California.

On the morning of July 5 the road company left the camp on Hot Creek to ride southward along the shore of Lower Klamath Lake. Not until evening did they reach the eastern side of the lake. Next day they climbed a high, rocky ridge to the east. "Near the base of the ridge, on the east, was a large lake, perhaps twenty miles in length. Beyond it, to the eastward, we could see a timbered butte, apparently thirty miles distant, at the base of which there appeared to be a low pass through the mountain range which seemed to encircle the lake basin." Making for that pass through the lava beds, they were surprised to come upon a large stream afterward called Lost River, which seemed too deep to ford. However, they surprised an Indian crouching under the bank. "By signs, we indicated to him that we wanted to cross the river. By marking on his legs and pointing up the river, he gave us to understand that there was a place above where we could easily cross. Motioning to him to advance, he led the way up the river about a mile and pointed out a place where an immense rock crossed the river. The sheet

of water running over the rock was about fifteen inches
deep, while the principal part of the river seemed to flow
under. This was the famous Stone Bridge on Lost river,
so often mentioned after this by travelers. . . . After crossing the bridge we made our pilot some presents, and all
shaking hands with him, left him standing on the river
bank." Lost River flowed into Tule Lake, along the
northern shore of which they rode for a few miles. Next
day they struck off to the east, "over a rocky table land,
among scattering juniper trees. We still observed the
timbered butte as our landmark, and traveled as directly
toward it as the shape of the country would admit. This
butte is near the State line, between Clear lake and Goose
lake, and probably fifty miles from the lava ridge west
of Lost river, from which we first observed it, and supposing it to be about thirty miles away. On pursuing our
course we passed through the hilly, juniper country between Langell valley and Clear lake without seeing either
the valley or lake, and at noon arrived at the bed of a
stream where there was but little water. The course of the
stream was north or northwest. . . . This was evidently the
bed of Lost river, a few miles north of where this singular
stream leaves the Clear river marsh." They kept on to
camp on the 7th near the base of the timbered hill.

On the morning of July 8th, we passed our landmark and
traveled nearly eastward, over a comparatively level but extremely
rocky country, and nooned in the channel of another stream,
where there was a little water standing in holes. On leaving this
place we found the country quite level, but exceedingly rocky;
for eight or ten miles almost like pavement. Late in the afternoon we came out into the basin of a lake (Goose lake), apparently forty or fifty miles in length. Traversing the valley about
five miles along the south end of the lake, we came to a little
stream coming in from the mountains to the eastward. The grass
and water being good, we encamped here for the night. . . . A
little southeast of our camp there appeared to be a gap in the
mountain wall, and we decided to try it on the succeeding day.

Across the ridge toward the gap, they went on July 9,

soon entering a handsome vale afterward called Surprise Valley, where emigrants on the Applegate road (and after 1848 the Lassen Cutoff to California) would recruit stock, having won through the deserts to the east.

Exploration the following morning disclosed a means of access to the plains, a remarkable chasm afterward called High Rock Canyon. This brought them on the afternoon of the 11th down to desert playa, Mud Lake. "The country eastward had a very forbidding appearance. Rising from a barren plain, perhaps fifteen miles away, was a rough, rocky ridge, extending as far as the eye could reach towards the north, but apparently terminating perhaps fifteen miles south of our course." They thought it circumspect to travel south to the point of this ridge before heading into the desert. The party did not get far by nightfall. Next morning, July 12, "we observed vast columns of smoke or steam rising at the extremity of the black ridge. Reaching the ridge a few miles north of its extremity, we traveled along its base, passing a number of springs, some cold and others boiling hot. At the end of the ridge we found an immense boiling spring from whence the steam was rising like smoke from a furnace. [Clearly this phenomenon led Jesse Applegate to speak of volcanoes in his letter of August 10 printed in Volume II.] A large volume of water issued from this spring which irrigated several hundred acres of meadow. Although the water was strongly impregnated with alkali, it was fit for use when cooled, and the spot was, on the whole, a very good camping place for the desert. The cliffs, at the extremity of the ridge, were formed of immense masses of black volcanic rock and all about were vast piles of cinders, resembling those from a blacksmith's forge. This place has ever since been known as 'Black Rock,' and is one of the most noted landmarks on the Humboldt desert. At this place we rested a day and consulted as to the best course to pursue in order to reach the Humboldt, or, as it was then called, Ogden's river.

The result of the council was that we agreed to separate, one party to travel eastward and the other to pursue a more southerly direction."

Accordingly, on the 14th, eight men started off to the south while the other seven, including Lindsay Applegate, rode east, across desolate country that had the appearance of a bleached lake bed. After traveling about 15 miles, Lindsay says:

> We began to discover dim rabbit trails running in the same direction in which we were traveling. As we advanced the trails became more plain, and there were others constantly coming in, all pointing in the general direction toward a ledge of granite boulders which we could see before us. Approaching the ledge, which was the first granite we had seen since leaving Rogue river valley, we could see a green mound where all the trails seemed to enter, and on examining the place closely we found a small hole in the top of the mound, in which a little puddle of water stood within a few inches of the surface. This was a happy discovery for we were already suffering considerably for want of water and our horses were well nigh exhausted. The day had been an exceedingly hot one and the heat reflected from the shining beds of alkali, had been very oppressive. The alkali water at Black Rock had given us temporary relief—our thirst was really more intense from having used it. Unpacking our horses, we staked them in the bunch grass about the granite ledge, and began digging down after the little vein of water which formed the puddle in the rabbit hole. . . Digging down . . . we made a basin large enough to hold several gallons and by dark we had quite a supply of good pure water. We then began issuing it to our horses, a little at a time, and by morning men and horses were considerably refreshed. Great numbers of rabbits came around us and we killed all we wanted of them. This is the place always since known as the Rabbit Hole Springs.

So much smoke obscured the landscape that the explorers did not venture to strike directly east toward the hoped-for river, instead riding southeasterly along the granite ridge, where there was a prospect of finding water. Late in the morning of the 15th more rabbit tracks disclosed the existence of a small spring, but it took until late in the evening to get water enough for men and horses. Another four or five miles along the ridge on the morning of the 16th brought the party to a large spring, but so strongly impregnated with alkali that it could be used only for coffee. "At this spring our granite ridge terminated, and before us was a vast desert plain, without a spear of vegetation, and covered with an alkaline efflorescense which glittered beneath the scorching rays of the sun." Into this forbidding expanse the company rode to make a dry camp.

As we started out on the morning of July 17th to the eastward we could see only a short distance on account of the dense clouds of smoke which enveloped the country. We spent much of the day in searching in various places for water and at about four o'clock in the afternoon we came to some ledges of rock. They afforded a shelter from the scorching rays of the sun, and we halted to rest for a while as some of the party were now so exhausted that they could scarcely ride. From the top of the rocks we could discern a small greenish spot on the desert, five or six miles distant, and, hoping to find water there, we decided to ride towards it. Robert Smith was now suffering severely from a pain in the head, and, as he was not able to ride, we were compelled to leave him under the rocks, with the understanding that he would follow us as soon as he felt able to ride. After going four or five miles, we beheld a horseman approaching us. This soon proved to be John Jones, one of the party who left us at Black Hole on the morning of the 14th. He had found water at the place we were making for, and, in searching for the rest of his party, had accidentally fallen in with us. We of course made a 'stampede' for the water. On our arrival there two of the party, filling a large horn with water, started on their return with it to Smith. They met him on the way, hanging on to the horn of his saddle, while his horse was following our trail. By the time they returned the other party also survived, so that, at about six P. M., we found ourselves all together again. The other party had fared almost as badly as we had, not having had any water since ten o'clock in the forenoon of the day before.

The water found, though a Godsend, was foul beyond description, warm but nauseating; but with the reeds and grasses growing roundabout, it greatly restored the horses. Next morning, July 18, Lindsay says, they rode nearly southeast "along the edge of a vast level plain to our right. Immense columns of smoke were still rising in front of us, and at about ten or eleven o'clock we came to places where peat bogs were on fire. These fires extended for miles along the valley of the Humboldt river, for we were now in the near vicinity of the stream, and at noon had the great satisfaction of encamping upon its banks. We found this sluggish stream about thirty feet wide, and the water strongly alkaline and of a milky hue. Along its banks were clumps of willows, affording us an abundance of fuel, and as there was plenty of grass for our horses, our camp was a good one."

Since leaving Rabbit Hole Springs they had traveled much too far south to suit them, so the explorers moved up the Humboldt some forty miles, and at noon on the 21st "came to a point where the river bottom widened out into quite an extensive meadow district." From this area, later called Lassen's Meadows, they could see a low pass through which ran a dry channel of a Humboldt tributary, so it was decided to encamp and send a party to examine the country towards Black Rock.

> We had nothing in which to carry water but a large powder horn, so we thought it best not to risk sending out too large a party. On the morning of the 22nd of July, Levi Scott and William Parker left us, and, following the dry channel of the stream for about fifteen miles, they came to a beautiful spring of pure spring water. Here they passed the night, and the next day, July 23rd, they ascended by a very gradual route to the table lands to the westward, and within about fifteen miles of their camp of the previous night, they entered quite a grassy district from which they could plainly see Black Hole. Exploring the country about them carefully they found the Rabbit Hole Springs. The line of our road was now complete. We had succeeded in finding a route across the desert and on to the Oregon settlements, with camping places at suitable distances, and, since we knew the source of the Humboldt river was near Fort Hall, we felt that our enterprise was already a success, and that immigrants could be able to reach Oregon late in the season with far less danger of being snowed in than on the California route. . . .

This pioneering of the Applegate Cutoff was one of the

great achievements of 1846, fully warranting the space we have given it, and placing in better perspective events of the ensuing fall. Little more will be said here of the further fortunes of the road company, though some details are brought out in Volume II. Lindsay Applegate relates that as their stock of provisions was almost exhausted, they decided to send a party, with the strongest animals, to Fort Hall for supplies, while the rest moved along slowly, "making such improvements on the road as seemed necessary, and perhaps reaching the head of the river in time to meet the Fort Hall party on its return. Accordingly, on the morning of the 25th of July, Jesse Applegate, Moses Harris, Henry Boygus, David Goff and John Owens, left us for Fort Hall. The place decided on for the reunion of the party was known as Hot Spring or Thousand Spring Valley. . . ." Lindsay says that with those behind, he himself reached Hot Spring Valley on August 5. Five days later the Fort Hall party returned with a supply of provisions, and on the 11th "we turned our faces towards our homes, which we judged to be eight or nine hundred miles distant." These dates do not check out, for Edwin Bryant met the rear party on the Humboldt August 8; they may not have reached Thousand Springs Valley before the 9th; and Jesse Applegate, who had reached Fort Hall August 8, did not leave there until the 11th; it was about six days later that he rejoined his party. Lindsay gives only a brief account of the return journey; with a note that the party arrived home October 3.[40] In Volume II we shall see how the *Oregon Spectator* remarked the completion of this historic job of road-finding. Nearly all of the emigration which reached Fort Hall after Jesse Applegate's arrival there took the new road; those earlier on the trail and bound for Oregon had

---

[40]According to the British botanist Joseph Burke, who accompanied them from Fort Hall, the Applegates got home September 26, a week earlier than Lindsay remembered. Compare the story in *Oregon Spectator,* October 1, 1846, in Volume II.

gone on to the Columbia by the old road, gratified to find that Samuel K. Barlow had succeeded in locating a wagon road through the Cascades, up over the shoulder of Mount Hood, by which they reached the Willamette earlier than any previous immigration.

7.

After our long preoccupation with backgrounds, and with the commandingly important developments in California and Oregon, we now turn to the Missouri frontier and to the emigration itself. The newspaper reports reprinted in Volume II display how the distinguishing characteristics of the 1846 emigration emerged early and unmistakably. There would be a substantial Oregon emigration, but for the first time since 1841 California was the primary goal. Lansford Hastings must have been responsible; he had focused attention upon California as no one had before.

Although the war with Mexico would break out before the emigration left the frontier, with somewhat mixed effect upon those bound for the Pacific, during the first four months of 1846, Oregon more than California had seemed a likely bone of contention. The Polk administration had come to power with the war cry "54 40 or Fight," and though the United States in settling the dispute with Great Britain would neither win all of Oregon nor come to blows over that far land, it was not clear until summer that the joint occupation stipulated in 1818 would end with a peaceful division of the country along the 49th parallel: there was plenty of fight talk in the newspapers and in the bar rooms as the snows of 1846 melted in the fields and along the roads.

There was much more fight talk in the south, where the annexation of Texas was now an accomplished fact despite the hostile attitude of Mexico, which had never acknowledged the independence of the Lone Star Republic. Mexico let it be known that war would come if United States forces occupied the "neutral ground" between the Nueces River and the Rio Grande, and war came soon after Zachary Taylor in accordance with orders moved his "Army of Occupation" across the Nueces in March; hostilities began April 25.

With all these wars and rumors of wars, violence stirred within the Republic itself. In the fall of 1845 the anti-Mormons in Illinois roused themselves to expel the Saints, following the example of Missouri seven years earlier. The Mormons agreed to begin evacuating Illinois next spring, as soon as grass should grow and water run. They actually began crossing the Mississippi River at Nauvoo early in February—on the same day, as chance would have it, that Sam Brannan sailed from New York with his contingent of California-bound Saints. Attended by hardship and suffering, the advance companies of the Mormon migration dragged west across Iowa all through the rainy, muddy spring of 1846. No one knew where they were going—California, Oregon, Vancouver Island were among the destinations proposed—nor were the Saints themselves entirely sure, though Fremont's reports had directed their attention to Bear River or the Valley of the Great Salt Lake.

This westward movement of the Mormons in the spring of 1846 had a direct effect upon the general emigration. Everybody was disposed to give them elbow room, so that for the first time since 1843 no California or Oregon-bound company undertook to cross the Missouri at the Council Bluffs and go west by the trail north of the Platte. A fruitful topic of speculation was what might be the fate of an unlucky emigrant, especially from Missouri, who might fall in with embittered Mormons in the immensities of the west.

Blue apprehension and rosy hopes together colored the thoughts of all who went overland in 1846. Opportunity seemed real, the chance to acquire land in Oregon or California for a pittance or for nothing at all. Even more impelling, perhaps was the hope of finding a healthy country. Malaria had always been endemic in the Mississippi Valley. What it might mean if a man need not drag through half of every year, alternately pinched with the chills or dizzy with fever, while the burying ground was continually enlarged by levies made upon his family, is now beyond our comprehension, though the diaries and letters printed in these two volumes are more than eloquent.

In these circumstances the emigration of 1846 began its movement toward the frontier. We see in Volume II how Independence and St. Joseph, in particular, argued their superior facilities to emigrants who must equip themselves before launching out upon the trail. We also see in Volume I, through the diaries written by specific emigrants, how preparations advanced.

The overland travelers of 1846 best tell their own story, and it is not proposed to deprive them of the privilege. But because only a few diaries have yet come to light, and because these report the overland emigration in rather spotty fashion, some gaps must be filled in. Especially do these gaps exist in relation to the front-running emigration to Oregon.

William E. Taylor, traveling with Larkin Stanley and John Craig, ended up in California; but in a measure his diary reflects the westward advance of those who left the frontier bound for Oregon. These advance companies constituted almost half of the emigration to the Columbia and most of them passed Fort Hall before Jesse Applegate arrived with news of his southern road, so that they reached Oregon City over the new Barlow Road across the Cascades. No diary by a member of this portion of the Oregon emigration has yet come to light—hopefully, publication of this book will bring to view just such a document. But in the library of the Oregon Historical Society are some reminiscences by John R. McBride

[41]The Thomas R. McBride MS. in the Oregon Historical Society collections is in three parts, typewritten and with handwritten emenda-

which greatly enlarge our understanding of the 1846 emigration.[41]

McBride relates that on April 16 his father's party, consisting of about 22 wagons conveying a dozen families and employees, crossed the Missouri at St. Joseph, intending to go forward "some eighty miles into the Indian Territory to a point where we should strike the old wagon road made by the fur traders from Independence, Missouri, to the West." On reaching the common meeting ground, about April 20, they found on hand about 100 wagons, including their own. "These were joined in a short time by a number of men who had passed the River at Iowa Point in Andrew County, Missouri, with numbers from Holt and Andrew counties, so that before we reached the Big Blue. . . . our train comprised one hundred and thirty wagons and teams, moved by oxen, with large herds of horned cattle and horses, and one small flock of sheep."

This train organized, McBride says, by choosing as its captain "John Brown, a prominent citizen residing for many years in Platte County, Missouri"—probably a mistaken reference to Elam Brown.[42] Several candidates were suggested for the command, "among them one Jonathan Keeney, who had once been a mountaineer in the employment of the American Fur Company. His experience with the Indians was thought to qualify him for the duties of the command, and he was strongly urged for the choice by his friends. William J. Martin, of Platte County, had made the entire trip to Oregon and California in 1843, and returned. . . in 1844. His friends strongly supported him. But he had had some experience with the fickleness of emigrants on the plains, and declined, knowing full well that it entailed much responsibility and little honor."

At the Big Blue, McBride recalled, the company was

tions; it was written after the completion of the Pacific Railroad, but the exact date of composition is not clear.

[42]For Elam Brown consult the Index.

"overtaken by a storm of extraordinary proportions. The rain poured down in torrents; the wind howled dismally; while thunder and lightning rent the air. Just as night closed down we reached the West bank of the rapidly rising river, and went into camp. During the following night the storm went on with unceasing fury, soaking our wagon covers, tearing down the tents and filling the encampment with confusion and misery. . . . Such was the demoralization caused by the storm during the night, and the condition of the weather the following day, that no effort was made to move."

As will be seen from William E. Taylor's diary, this storm more probably occurred at the crossing of the South Platte, on May 30-31. However that may have been, McBride relates that while his company was on the "Republican Fork of the Kansas" (the Little Blue), the heavens opened up again, doing considerable damage as well as fraying tempers. "A proposition was made to divide into something like equal numbers, and by traveling a short distance apart, facilitate the movements of both parties. The caravan had altogether more than a thousand head of stock; two thirds of them were oxen to draw the wagons, the remainder loose cattle, cows, calves, horses and sheep. The proposal was carried by consent, and the next day about fifty teams, embracing those of Captain Martin and his friends, and Captain Burnett and his friends, of which we were a part, drew out of camp and passed on in advance. We continued together along the valley of the Republican for several days, when the Martin train again seceded from us, taking about thirty teams, and struck out ahead, continuing this relation to us nearly the entire distance to Oregon. Thenceforth our camp or train embraced twenty-eight teams with about sixteen families. We remained together until we reached the Willamette Valley in the last days of September. . . . "

McBride recounts many incidents of the journey, more than we have space for, including encounters with Army deserters. On the Platte a Mrs. Cromwell died after a day's illness. Her husband, aged about sixty, two "young lady daughters," and a 12-year-old son continued on to Fort Laramie, there disposed of wagons and team, bought riding and pack mules, and set out for home—doubtless in company with Palmer or Clyman at some stage of the journey. McBride speaks of meeting Palmer, but at Chimney Rock; a young man of his party, Miles Carey, overcome with homesickness, stole a horse and joined the eastbound travelers. (Later Carey's family paid $125 to the McBrides to legitimize the acquisition.) After a brief pause at Fort Laramie, the McBride company moved along, crossing the North Platte and rolling on to the Sweetwater.

> Near the end of the Sweetwater we came upon the camp of three men; the leader was Lansford W. Hastings, his comrade was a man by the name of Hudspeth and a California vaquero (herder). Hasting's name was familiar to us from his journal of the journey in 1842, which had been published in Cincinnati, I think, and was in the hands of our party. It had been used as a guide book, and seeing the author of it was like meeting a friend. . . . . He painted the attractions of California in glowing colors; and as he was a man of plausible manners and fine address, he made some impression, and finally a portion of our train changed their destination further on.[43] It was in the morn-

[43]In an article, "Pioneer Days in the Mountains," *Tullidge's Quarterly Magazine*, July, 1884, vol. 3, pp. 311-320, McBride provided a few other details of interest, saying that "on the morning of the 3d of July, 1846, we met about twenty miles east of the summit of the South Pass, Lansford W. Hastings," who "had come all the distance from Sutter's Fort on the Sacramento River, California to meet the emigrant trains and pilot them by a new route, discovered by himself, to the paradise of the Pacific—as he insisted California was. He had but a single companion, and a Mexican vaquero. His companion's name was Hedspeth, and he was about as repulsive in manner as Hastings was attractive. He was a coarse, profane creature, who seemed to feel that loud swearing was the best title to public favor." In contrast, McBride described Hastings as "a tall, fine-looking man, with light brown hair and beard, dressed in a suit of elegant pattern made of buckskin, handsomely embroidered and

ing that we passed Hastings, who was waiting to gather a train for his promised land. We obtained considerable information from him as to routes, proper places to rest and recruit our teams, the particular drives that were long and waterless, etc. At one O'clock in the afternoon we descended a gradual slope for a mile, and in a flat basin in an almost level plain found ourselves at Pacific Springs, and had crossed the backbone of the American Continent. . . . In the private manuscript journal of my father was this story: 'July 4th:—Pacific Springs. Here, hail Oregon!'

By McBride's recollection, it was at Pacific Springs this same afternoon that Wales Bonney rode into camp:

As the day closed, two men with one pack horse carrying blankets and supplies, came into camp from the West. One who had gone to Oregon the year before and spent the winter there, as he said, was of the name of Bonney; the other was a trapper who left Jackson County, Missouri, about five years before, named Hawkins. He had joined Bonney at Fort Bridger, about one hundred miles West, and intended to go to Fort Laramie. Hawkins left his home in Missouri an invalid, seeking the mountain climate for his health. He was now thirty years of age, and a perfect specimen of health and vigor. He was dressed in buckskin throughout except a heavy drill cotton shirt. He was an acquaintance of G. O. and G. W. Burnett, of our camp, and regaled us with interesting accounts of his life as a mountaineer. Bonney had traveled so, except the last one hundred miles, the entire distance from the Willamette, as he stated, alone. He said after he should arrive at Fort Laramie, if he found no other company, he should 'cache' himself in the daytime, and travel only at night, so as to avoid the Sioux and Pawnees. He said he intended to return to Oregon the following year. He took some letters in charge for delivery to our friends in the States, which arrived at their destination; so we had reason to believe, however he may have made the journey, he did it in safety. On our arrival in Oregon we found ugly rumors about this man afloat, to the effect that a companion of his had disappeared the winter he was in Oregon, and that he was believed to have left

---

trimmed at the collar and openings, with plucked beaver fur . . . an ideal representative of the mountaineer."

Since William E. Taylor met Hastings on the Big Sandy on July 2, two days' travel west of where McBride places him on the morning of the 3rd, there would seem to be an error of place or date in the McBride reminiscences.

money, which was never found; also that Bonney instead of wintering the Willamette Valley, had lived in a camp in the heart of the Cascade Range near the base of Mount Hood, where some wagons had been left, until a road should be completed to the valley to take them through. It was believed that Bonney would never return to Oregon, and he never did to my knowledge.

Several trappers named Hawkins are known, and so far McBride may have been correct. But Bonney was traveling alone when he met various diarists and letter-writers six days later. It is possible that when Bonney came up with Hastings at the last crossing of the Sweetwater, presumably on July 5, Hawkins decided to join Hastings and Hudspeth, and with them drifted back to Fort Bridger. The rest of what McBride says is verifiable.

McBride tells of going on two days' travel to the Big Sandy. "Here the famous Greenwood cut-off branched from the main road as a shorter route, and it was said that from this point to Green River by that route was 50 miles of sand and desert. All the mountain-men warned us against taking this route, and tales of suffering and disaster were released to us by those who had gone that way. It shortened the distance many miles, but was perilous to slow moving ox teams of emigrants. Here we saw the last buffalo on the journey. A herd was seen a few miles up the stream from camp, but we saw none after this. . . ."

Green River, crossed near the mouth of the Big Sandy three days later, was "a bold, clear stream, about two hundred and fifty feet wide, with broad bottoms, fine groves of cottonwoods on its banks, filled with fish, trout and other varieties. We succeeded in fording it, but it was deep and dangerous, the water running into the wagon-boxes and wetting their contents in many instances. The day we crossed this stream we met another party of mountaineers on their way to St. Louis. One of the number was Milton [*i.e.,* Solomon] Sublette, . . . He was recently from California, and was quite outspoken in his criticism of Hastings' scheme of a new route to California.

He said it was an impracticable route for teams, and if they attempted it, would lead to disaster. His predictions, however, were erroneous; for Hastings, having induced some sixty wagons to follow his leadership, piloted them safely through on his proposed route to California. Pursuing our journey in three days more we arrived at Fort Bridger, so-called by courtesy. It was only a camp where some fifty trappers were living in lodges (Indian tents). A single cabin of logs, with a roof composed of willow brush, covered with earth composed the fort. . . . There was a large village of Indians of the Snake Tribe encamped here, and a brisk traffic in dressed deer skins, buffalo robes and moccasins went on during our stay with them, which was for the half of a day and the following night. The mountaineers and the Indians alike wanted to buy whisky or brandy; but were were not provided with this kind of merchandise. The next most desirable articles were coffee, sugar, soap, and flour. . . ."

By McBride's chronology, he reached Fort Bridger July 9, the same day as William E. Taylor, but more probably he got there about noon of the 10th; like Taylor, he may have started on again July 11. He has another interesting incident to relate on arrival at the Bear River Valley:

> Just as we had reached the level of the valley by a long descent, a horseman came into view. Without halting when he came to the head of the train, which he did in dashing mountaineer syle, with his horse at nearly full run, he rode fiercely on. Every one wondered at his singular behavior, but we soon received an explanation. A jolly man about fifty years old came up from the same direction on horseback and saluted our party. Whilst he was making some excited inquiries as to whether we had seen a man, describing the recent horseman, one of our party, Mr. John M. Wilson, an ex Santa Fe trapper, walked up to our visitor and called out, 'Why, Peg Leg, how do you do!' The stranger turned and recognized him, and there was a joyful handshaking between the two. The man thus addressed was J. [*i.e.,* Thomas] L. Smith, one of the most noted mountaineers in all the West, who had been nearly twenty years a trapper and fur

hunter, and was known from the Mexican settlements on the South to the Hudson Bay Company's stations on the North. He had fought Apaches in Mexico, had 'captured' the horses of the Spanish Dons in California, lived among the Sioux and Crows, had a Snake Indian wife, and was as notorious for his lawlessness as for his success in all the walks of a trapper's life. He had been compelled by misfortune to part with one of his legs just below the knee in order to save his life; and had long been known by the name of 'Peg Leg Smith.' The man who had gone so unceremoniously past us in advance of him had been an employe of Smith; they had disagreed on the question of wages, and the employe, possessing himself of a sufficient quantity of beaver skins, the recognized money of the region, to satisfy his demand, had undertaken to decamp with little ceremony. Smith started in pursuit and ordered him to halt; and failing to secure obedience he fired some shots at the flying fugitive, which no doubt accelerated his rate of speed, as he passed our train on his way to the trappers' rendezvous at Bridger. Smith gave up the pursuit, and spent an hour with us at noon, and then returned to his own lodge, which stood in sight a short distance up the stream, here called after him Smith's Fork, a name it still bears.[44]

With his friends and family McBride passed on to Soda Springs, where time has brought its many changes. "The hills and the valley in the vicinity were scatteringly clothed with juniper trees, making a handsome shade. These have since been cut down by the settler and firewood vandal. . . . and the spot, when I saw it again, in midsummer a few years ago [during the 1870's] had a barren and desolate appearance, though when I first saw it it was a charmingly shaded and inviting locality.[45]

At Fort Hall McBride again has interesting things to say:

---

[44]Smiths Fork appears to have been named not for Pegleg but for Jedediah Smith, who penetrated to this area in 1824-1825. The remarkable Thomas L. Smith became "Pegleg" in the winter of 1827-1828 while trapping with Ceran St. Vrain on Green River waters. He frequented the country where McBride met him throughout the 1840's, but then moved along to California, where he died in 1866.

[45]In his article in *Tullidge's Quarterly Magazine* cited in Note 43, McBride has a puzzling account of a reconnaissance made by mem-

Captain [Richard] Grant was now in charge, and his man of affairs was one [Archibald] McDonald. Both were Scotchmen and gentlemen. They treated our party with great courtesy, and we visited the post without any restrictions. They furnished us with a written guide for the journey westward, with all the camping places specified; the distance from each to the next, with information as to wood, water, and grass, good and bad roads, which was of exceeding value. Captain Grant had an Indian wife, and two of his children appeared in his office. The older was a daughter of fifteen. She wore the Indian frock of dressed deer skin, but it was scrupulously clean and neat, and she was strikingly beautiful, with her long dark hair falling around her bare neck and shoulders. She had sewing materials at the time in her hands, and seemed to be engaged in embroidering some garment of deer skin. The boy [Johnny] was evidently the pride of the Captain. He was about ten years old, spoke good English, and took me all over the quarters and was full of fire and energy as live boys are. . . . The Fort was a square adobe structure, with walls about twenty feet in height, with a heavy wooden door entrance, which was so constructed as to be secure from any savage attack. Water was supplied by a well in the center of the Fort, while the quarters were of adobe built to the main walls. The Captain's business office was reached by a stairway to the second floor. . . .

On the day the McBride party left Fort Hall, they were overtaken by Passed Midshipman Selim E. Woodworth, carrying dispatches to Oregon, and since Woodworth afterward figured so prominently in the Donner Relief, McBride's impression of him is instructive.

He wore an immense black beard, in which his diminutive head and visage was shrouded. He rode around the camp for quite a time before he could find a spot to his taste upon which to pitch his tent, and generally acted, as one of his men remarked, 'like a lost puppy in tall rye.' In everything but energy

---

bers of his party after reaching Soda Springs, a reconnaissance down the Bear River extended as far south as the site of Salt Lake City. Nothing in the literature supports such a reconnaissance and there is no mention of it in the Oregon Historical Society MS. Since some details are scarcely believable, it may be that as one of Utah's "Gentile" community, McBride was needling the Mormons with suggestions that many men had scrutinized the Rockies ahead of the excessively lauded Mormon Pioneers.

he seemed wanting in the qualities of a Western traveler. He could not saddle his own horse, and did not know how to ride when he was saddled and mounted. He was assuming to direct his men how to do things which they perfectly understood, and of which he knew nothing. Because he was in command of the party he seemed to think it his duty to exercise his authority on all subjects, even if he were ignorant of them. A ludicrous description of his performances when he concluded to abandon his ambulance at Laramie and travel on horseback was given by one of his guard at our camp fire that night. He knew no more how to fasten a pack on a horse than a Bedouin would know to set the rigging of a ship; but as ropes have much to do with both, the gentleman of the United States Navy assumed that he understood one because he did the other. He not only directed his men how to pack his train, but he enforced his commands. The results were very like a shipwreck on a rough coast. The pack train, loaded according to the Navy regulations, got into confusion before it was fairly under way. The cargoes were scattered for miles along the road, and it took two full days, so the humorous narrator said, to repair damages and restore the rigging of the overland fleet. The Lieutenant was, however, very kind in furnishing us with newspapers giving accounts of the opening scenes of the Mexican War. . . . [and] while silent about his trip to the West coast, was very affable on other matters. It transpired afterward that he bore orders from Washington to the United States Naval Squadron in the Pacific, and he hastened on to Oregon, took ship for the Sandwich Islands, then Squadron headquarters, without delay. A Canadian half-breed, whom I always heard called 'Quebec,' was his guide on the journey....

At Raft River, McBride relates, two women and eight men of their party separated to pursue their way to California, including several men named Rhodes [Rhoads?], and Alvis and Thomas Kimsey. Those bound for Oregon went on to cross the Snake at the Three Islands, 30 miles below the Salmon Falls, then made north for the Boise River and down the stream to Fort Boise, near its mouth. The Snake was then recrossed here, not without some difficulty and danger, after which the company journeyed up over the Blue Mountains to reach the Columbia and descend that river to The Dalles. Here they met "Thomas J. Brown, a young man about twenty-five years old, a son of Captain [Elam] Brown, whose company had lost their stock on the South Platte. He had gone to Oregon the year before, and was on his way to meet his father [who, however, took the Applegate route by way of the Humboldt, changed his mind, and went on to California]. . . . Young Brown ascertained this, and went on to California, never returning to Oregon. The gratifying news was brought us by him that the [Barlow] wagon road which had been partially constructed the previous autumn across the Cascades, South of Mount Hood, had been completed, and that the first party bound for the Willamette on that route was now about forty miles in advance of our company. This would save us the perils of the trip by canoes down the Columbia River, which had been heretofore taken by all emigrants and required that stock should be driven over the mountains by trail. The history of this river navigation was one that recorded many a watery tragedy, and was always one of peril, and had been the dread of the latter portion of our journey." By the Barlow Road the McBrides and those with them arrived safely in Oregon City some days later, having received help in the way of fresh oxen and provisions from friends in the Willamette Valley; J. J. Hembree and C. B. Gray brought out this welcome aid. McBride does not date the arrival in Oregon City, evidently the latter part of September.

8.

We have followed the McBride narrative at great length, for it is relatively inaccessible and deals with a portion of the emigration about which little has been published. We cannot devote comparable space to some better-known narratives of the 1846 emigration to Oregon and California, the contemporaneously published books by Edwin Bryant and J. Quinn Thornton, and the reminiscent account, based upon a diary, by Heinrich Lienhard, which only very recently has been translated and published in full.

Bryant's book was issued in New York late in 1848 with the title, *What I Saw in California.* Thornton's appeared a few months later, early in 1849, without so much as a bow in Bryant's direction, though there are obvious borrowings on the first stage of the journey; Thornton's narrative markedly changes character after he and Bryant went their separate ways. This narrative, *Oregon and California in 1848,* appeared like Francis Parkman's *The California and Oregon Trail,* during the early excitement occasioned by news of the California gold discoveries; indeed, the "California" in Parkman's title was added by his publisher, eager to cash in on the demand for California publications.[46]

Although he was no emigrant, having gone out to Fort Laramie in the summer of 1846 to acquaint himself with wild Indians as an essential preliminary for writing books on the French and Indian wars, Parkman requires attention here, for in recent years his diaries and letters have been found, documents which not only give a new cohesion and solidity to his narrative but also fill in our understanding of a part of the Oregon emigration not well reported in the literature.[47]

Parkman rendezvoused at St. Louis in April with a fellow Bostonian, Quincy Adams Shaw, who would be his

---

[46]Parkman's book was originally serialized in the *Knickerbocker Magazine,* February, 1847—February, 1849, with the title, "The Oregon Trail, A Summer's Journey out of Bounds." When George Palmer Putnam published the narrative in book form in February, 1849, he retitled it *The California and Oregon Trail,* but Parkman restored the original title for a revised edition issued in 1892. Mason Wade, who discovered the lost Parkman diaries while engaged in research for a biography, used these diaries and also restored some of the Knickerbocker text in editing *The Oregon Trail* for the Heritage Press in 1943.

[47]Mason Wade edited *The Journals of Francis Parkman* (New York, 1952), 2 vols., and Wilbur R. Jacobs edited *The Letters of Francis Parkman* (Norman, 1960), 2 vols., the 1846 manuscripts in each case coming from the Parkman Papers in the Massachusetts Historical Society.

trail companion, and immediately began to make notes
we are glad to have. On April 16: "Passed Midshipman
Woodward is here (St. Louis), on his way with dispatches
to Columbia River. He has a wild plan of raising a body
of men, and *taking Santa Fe.*" Again, on April 25: "I
have seen a strange variety of characters—Dixon, the non-
entity—Ewing, the impulsive, unobserving ardent Ken-
tuckian, who lays open his character to everyone, and sees
nothing of those about him—the quiet, sedate, and manly
Jacob(s), his companion. These two are going to California." (They were then in company with Edwin
Bryant.) Parkman boarded the steamer *Radnor* on April
28, and next was observing, "On board the boat are a
party of Baltimoreans [also observed by Bryant],—flash
genteel—very showily attired in 'genteel undress,' though
bound for California. They make a great noise at table,
and are waited on by the Negroes with great attention
and admiration. Also a vulgar New Yorker, with the
moustache and the air of a Frenchman, bound for Santa
Fe. . . . A young man on board from St. Louis, bound for
Santa Fe, has one brother on the Atlantic and another on
the Pacific, and a third on the Mississippi, while he is going to the [Rio Grande] del Norte. So much for American wandering." On May 2, in cameo: "The landing at
Independence—the storehouses—the Santa Fe waggons—
the groups of piratical-looking Mexicans, employees of the
Santa Fe traders, with their broad, peaked hats—the men
with their rifles seated on a log, ready for Oregon. Among
the waggons behind, some of the Mexicans were encamped.
The Baltimoreans got shamefully drunk, and one of them,
an exquisite in full dress, tumbled into the water." On
May 5: "The emigrants, encamped at some distance, are
choosing officers. W.[oodworth] seems to be making a
fool of himself. We have joined Chandler's party.
Bought an excellent horse, for which I paid too much."

In his published narrative Parkman elaborated all these
notes, saying for example, "I rode to Westport with that

singular character, Lieutenant Woodworth, who is a great busybody, and ambitious of taking command among the emigrants. He told me that great dissensions prevailed in their camp—that no organization had taken place, no regular meetings had been held, though this was to be done on Saturday and Sunday [May 8-9], and the column to get under way on Monday.

"Woodworth paraded a revolver in his belt, which he insisted was necessary—and it may have been a prudent precaution, for this place seemed full of desperadoes—all arms were loaded, as I had occasion to observe. Life is held in little esteem. This place, Westport, is the extreme frontier, and bears all its characteristics.

"As we rode home we met a man itching for Oregon but restrained by his wife. At McGee's at Westport there was a restless fellow who had wandered westwards from New York in search of work, which he had not found; and now he was for Oregon, working his passage as he could not supply himself with provisions."

Parkman also elaborated upon his diary concerning his own traveling arrangements with "Captain Chandler of the British army, who with his brother and Mr. Romaine, an English gentleman, was bound on a hunting expedition across the continent. I had seen the captain and his companions at St. Louis. They had now been for some time at Westport, making preparations for their departure and waiting for a reinforcement, since they were too few in number to attempt it alone. They might, it is true, have joined some of the parties of emigrants who were on the point of setting out for Oregon and California; but they professed great disinclination to have any connection with the 'Kentucky fellows.'

"The captain now urged it upon us that we should join forces and proceed to the mountains in company. Feeling no greater partiality for the society of the emigrants than they did, we thought the arrangement a good one and consented to it. . . . " These companions had a hunter named

Sorel, a surly-looking Canadian, and a muleteer Wright, "an American ruffian from St. Louis," while Parkman and Shaw had employed a mountain man of experience and distinction, Henry Chatillon, and also one Deslouriers.

Parkman left Westport on May 9, not taking the trail out the Kansas River followed by the emigrants leaving from Independence or Westport; he soon crossed the river to ride north to Fort Leavenworth, where his "English friends" were waiting. It was from Fort Leavenworth that he wrote his mother on May 12: "We arrived at this place day before yesterday, riding up, with our whole equipment from Westport. Our tent is pitched under the fort close by that of our English friends. We are a little in advance of the main body of the caravan, which will shortly arrive and follow on our track. Our companions are Captain Chaunley, of the British army, and his brother and Mr. Romain. They are all men most excellently fitted for companions on such a journey, as they have all travelled very extensively and Romain has been on this route before—in 1841 [when he went as far as Green River with Father De Smet and the Bartleson party]. We find them exceedingly intelligent and agreeable and consider ourselves very fortunate in meeting with such a party, and so avoiding the necessity of too close contact with a very different sort of men who compose the trading parties. Our own *engages,* Henry Chatillon and Delorier are as good as can be found anywhere on the frontier. Chatillon, in particular, is everything that could be wished. . . . I hear that two or three men intend to accompany the Oregon emigrants—with whom we do not come at all in contact—part of the way on their route, and then return. If this is true, we may have an opportunity of sending letters."

Parkman and Chandler broke up camp at Fort Leavenworth on May 13, and after some difficulty made their way to the emigrant road west from St. Joseph. They had been taken in by prevalent rumor that a vast body of Mormons had crossed the Missouri at St. Joseph, and Parkman's diary for some days referred to the encampments of these Mormons, until it dawned on him that the emigrants ahead were simply the St. Joseph division of the emigration—with which William E. Taylor and John R. McBride were traveling. A few wagons would leave St. Joseph later on the trail, but the greater part of the emigration now was thronging out of Independence. Not until late on May 23 did Parkman see emigrant wagons. Next day his diary says (and it should be compared with Virgil Pringle's diary):

"We have struck upon the old Oregon Trail, just beyond the Big Blue, about seven days from the Platte. The waggons we saw were part of an emigrant party, under a man named Keatley [Keithley]. They encamped about a mile from us behind a swell in the prairie. The Capt. paid them a visit, and reported that the women were damned ugly. Kearsley and another man came to see us in the morning. We had advanced a few miles when we saw a long line of specks upon the level edge of the prairie; and when we approached, we discerned about twenty waggons, followed by a crowd of cattle. This was the advance party—the rest were at the Big Blue, where they were delayed by a woman in child-bed. They stopped a few miles farther to breakfast, where we passed them. They were from the western states. Kearsley had complained of want of subordination among his party, who were not very amenable to discipline or the regulations they themselves had made. Romaine stayed behind to get his horse shod, and witnessed a grand break-up among them. The Capt. threw up his authority, such was the hurly-burly— women crying—men disputing—some for delay—some for hurry—some afraid of the Inds. Four waggons joined us—Romaine urged them, and thereby offended us. Kearsley is of the party."

In his book, which has a much lengthier account of these events, Parkman says that ten men, one woman, and one small child made up the "go-ahead" faction which had joined them. Both book and diary have occasional allusions to the emigrants out of Independence during the following days: thus the day he reached the Platte, May 30, Parkman recorded that "Robinson's party," referred to by Virgil Pringle, "were encamped three miles off." Two days later Parkman wrote: "There are plenty of emigrants ahead. Among the different bands that we have passed, there is considerable hostility and jealousy, on account of camping places, etc." On June 4 Parkman came upon the eleven boats bound down the Platte from Fort Laramie under D. D. Papin, referred to by so many other travelers of 1846, and improved the opportunity to send letters home. He "found the boats lashed to the bank waiting—flat-bottomed—with 110 packs each—one month from Laramie—aground every day, for the Platte is now low, and is very shallow and swift at best. The crews were a wild-looking set—the oarsmen were Spaniards— with them were traders, F.[rench] and American, some attired in buckskin, fancifully slashed and garnished, and with hair glued up in Ind. fashion. Papin a rough-looking fellow, reclining on the leather covering that was thrown over the packs." Here Parkman again saw Woodworth, his party reported close behind.

On June 7, ascending the South Fork of the Platte, Parkman wrote in his diary: "The lagging pace of the emigrants—the folly of Romaine—and the old womanism of the Capt. combine to disgust us. We are resolved to push on alone, as soon as we have crossed the South Fork, which will probably be tomorrow." Next day at the crossing of the South Platte Parkman remarked the distressed condition of the company we know to have been Elam Brown's, which had lost so many horses and cattle—"they have not enough cattle to carry them on, and are in great trouble." He thought the emigrants here "rather mean-looking fellows, much less respectable than those with us," which indicates that the dispositions of Brown's company may have suffered. It was not until the 10th, just before reaching Ash Hollow, that Parkman and Shaw rode on ahead toward Fort Laramie. Two days later, in site of Chimney Rock, he "Overtook a company of emigrants, Americans and foreigners, encamped with whom were five men from Laramie, going down." The five had come from Oregon in Joel Palmer's party, for Parkman also refers to them as "Oregon men returning to the settlements." Passing various emigrant companies, Parkman at length reached Fort Laramie on the afternoon of June 15, five days behind the advance companies of the emigration with which William E. Taylor traveled.

Parkman has much of interest to say about the fort in his book and his diary. And also in the letter he wrote his mother on June 19:

The Oregon emigrants are arriving in large parties every day, and remain for several days to refit, buy supplies, etc.; and the Indians are coming in from all quarters to meet them, and get presents, so that the whole fort is surrounded by wagons, tents, and Indian lodges. As for us, we are well lodged in the fort itself, and though the fire is none of the most luxurious, the bourgeois, Mr. Bordeau, takes the greatest pains to make us comfortable. The traders and trappers are daily coming in from the mountains, so that the area of the forest is crowded with them and their men—all in half-Indian dress—besides a swarm of Indians, squaws, and children. Every moment a group of rough looking fellows from the emigrant camps, escorting a bevy of scraggy-necked women, appears at the gate. They go peering about in every direction, without scruple or reserve—no place is sacred from them—twenty times a day a crowd of women, with prying curious eyes, come pressing into our apartment, which generally contains, besides, half a dozen or more Indians smoking on the floor. . . . We have passed on the road eight or ten large companies. . . . bound for Oregon or California, and most of them ignorant of the country they are going to, and the journey to it. They have immense droves of cattle and horses, which they turn loose at night, range their waggons in a circle, and build their fires around it. Sometimes a thunder-storm will come up, and frighten their cattle, or the wolves will make a noise and startle them, and the whole body will break off and [*torn*: run] for fifteen or twenty miles upon the prairie. [*Torn*: It] takes a day or

two to collect and drive them back, and meanwhile the women
will get impatient and cry to go home again, and the men will
quarrel and complain, till the party splits up into two or three
divisions that in future travel separately. This is a specimen of
their vexations upon the easiest part of their journey—what they
will do when they get beyond the Mountains, lord knows. Here
at the fort, they are very suspicious and mistrustful, and seem to
think the traders their natural enemies. We are invariably taken
for traders in disguise, and find the most effectual way to persuade them to do anything, is to advise them to something directly
the contrary.

After spending a few days some miles away at a camp
on the Chugwater, Parkman rode back to the fort on June
25 to note the presence of plenty of Illinois and Michigan
emigrants, perhaps a reference to the Harlan party. Next
day he wrote in his diary: "Emigrants crossing the [Lar-
amie] river, and thronging into the fort—a part of Russel's
comp'y, which becoming dissatisfied with their pragmatic,
stump-orator leader, has split itself into half a dozen
pieces. Passed along the line of waggons, conversing with
the women, etc. These people are very ignorant, and suspicious for this reason—no wonder—they are grossly imposed on at the store. . . . The emigrants had a ball in the
fort—in this room—the other night. Such belles! One
woman, of more than suspected chastity, is left at the Fort;
and Bordeaux is fool enough to receive her."

On June 28 Parkman rode down to Fort Bernard.
"Found there Russel's or Boggs' comp'y, engaged in
drinking and refitting, and a host of Canadians besides.
Russel drunk as a pigeon—some fine-looking Kentucky
men — some of D Boone's grandchildren — Ewing,
Jacob(s), and others with them—altogether more educated
men than any I have seen. A motley crew assembled in
Richard's rooms, squaws, children, Spaniards, French, and
emigrants. Emigrants mean to sell liquor to the Mini-
conques, who will be up here tomorrow, and after having
come all the way from the Missouri to go to the war, will
no doubt break up if this is done. . . . Returning to the

Fort, met a party going to the settlements—to whom Montalon *had not given my letters*. Sent them by that good fellow Tucker."

This party going to the settlements was Clyman's, of whom Parkman had nothing to say. But in a letter written that same day to his father he wrote, "hearing of a party of homesick emigrants on the return, I have just despatched a man with the letter. . . . I rode in this morning [from "Laramie Creek," 18 miles distant] to get the news, and see the fresh arrivals of emigrants. I found a party of the latter; from Kentucky, chiefly drunk, at a little trading fort not far from this. They were busy in exchanging horses for mules, and were being handsomely imposed on by the *bourgeois* of the fort and the trappers and hunters. Their captain was the most drunk of the party, and, taking me by button, he began a long rigmarole about his 'moral influence' over his men. But, in fact, they have no leader—each man follows his own whim, and the result is endless quarrels and divisions, and all sorts of misfortunes in consequence. A party that passed yesterday, left at the Fort a woman, who it seems, had become a scandal to them, and, what had probably much greater weight, caused them trouble to feed and take care of her. She is now lodged among the traders—in a most pitiful situation; for it is quite impossible that she will be able to get to the settlements before many months at least, and, meanwhile, she is left alone among the Indian women, and the half-savage retainers of the Company—for there are no white women, and very few civilized white men in the country. . . . "48

48The woman left at Fort Laramie, twice referred to by Parkman, had traveled from Missouri in the same company with Heinrich Lienhard. As translated by Erwin G. and Elisabeth K. Gudde, his *From St. Louis to Sutter's Fort, 1846* (Norman, 1961), pp. 54-55, 68, describes her as "a skinny widow with two children. She owned a small wagon drawn by a light oxen team, which at the beginning of the journey was driven by a man of about forty, whom we considered to be the woman's husband . . . ." The man found it more

It is impossible here to do justice to Parkman's Western chronicle—book, diaries, and letters. In these pages it has been possible only to excerpt some of his remarks concerning the emigration. At the end of June he anticipated that he would go home via Fort Pierre on the Missouri, thus getting back to the States around the first of October, but after spending some weeks in the Black Hills, with ample opportunity to observe the Sioux, he came back to Fort Laramie on August 3 and the following day turned homeward via Bent's Fort.

He reached Pueblo on August 20, and Bent's on August 25. There he, Shaw, Chatillon, and Deslauriers found a reinforcement, a sick soldier, "two men from California, Munro and the sailor Ben," and a homesick Missourian apparently named Ellis who had turned back from Fort Bridger—all having come this far in company with Joe Walker and his horse herd. On September 21, within a few miles of the frontier, Parkman reported a characteristic meeting with a waggoner: " 'Whar are ye from? CaliforAny?' 'No.' 'Santy Fee?' 'No, the Mountains.' 'What yer been doing thar? Tradin'?' 'No.' 'Huntin'?' 'No.' 'Emigratin'?' 'No.' 'What *have* ye been doing then, God damn ye?' (Very loud, as we were by this time almost out of hearing.") The incident could as well have happened on the emigrant road. Five days later Parkman was back in Westport, having been absent a little over four months and leaving us greatly in his debt.

---

than flesh could bear to drive all day and satisfy the widow by night, so he departed the company, leaving her to drive the wagon herself. On arrival at Fort Laramie "the notorious widow declared that she had decided to stay in the Fort if no man would take care of her," and the women of the party saw to it that no one volunteered. In all probability the widow was espoused by a prominent mountain man, but for lack of definite evidence, I forbear naming the husband.

9.

Francis Parkman's experiences were shared to a certain extent by the only party of Mormons to reach the Fort Laramie area, the Mississippi Saints encountered by Clyman at Ash Hollow on July 2. A narrative of their adventures was written by John Brown sometime after the event. Their leaders, largely from the Southern States, had been instructed by Brigham Young early in 1846 to "take these families that were ready and go west with them through Missouri and fall in with the companies from Nauvoo, in the Indian countries." "We started out some fourteen families," John Brown says.

"I left home on the 8th of April. William Crosby, D. M. Thomas, William Lay, James Harmon, Geo. W. Bankhead and myself formed a mess. We had one wagon, calculating to return in the fall [for their own families]. We crossed the Mississippi River at the Iron Banks and traveled up through the state of Missouri to Independence, where we arrived on the 26th of May, a distance from home of 640 miles. There was great excitement here. Rumor said Ex-Governor Boggs had started to California and the Mormons had intercepted him on the way and killed and robbed several companies, etc. They tried to persuade us not to go on the plains on account of these Mormons, but we told them we were not afraid.

"Brothers Crow from Perry County, Illinois, Wm. Kartchner and some Oregon emigrants joined us here. We had in all 25 wagons. Wm. Crosby was chosen captain of the company; Robert Crow and John D. Holladay, his counsellors. When we got into the Indian country, our Oregon friends found out that they were in company with a lot of Mormons. They were a little uneasy and somewhat frightened, and began to think that we did not travel fast enough for them. They left us and the next day we passed and left them in the rear. They were a little afraid to go on not being strong enough. This repeated again. At length they traveled with us till we got to the Platte River where we met a company of six men from Oregon and when they saw six men who had traveled the road alone, they took courage, having 13 or 14 men in company. So they left us again and we rested a day for repairs, so we saw them no more.

"We had nineteen wagons left and twenty-four men. The Fox Indians stole one yoke of oxen belonging to Geo. Therlkill. We traveled the Oregon Road from Independence and expected when we got to the Platte River to have fallen in with the company from Nauvoo or find their trail, but we found neither, and could hear nothing of them. We supposed they had gone up the north side, so we continued our journey up the river though some of the company were very loath to go.

"On the 25th of June, we got among the buffalo and laid in some meat. We were very much delighted with buffalo hunting. Our eyes never had beheld such a sight—the whole country was covered with them. On the 27th, a buffalo calf came running into the train of wagons. The dogs, teamsters and everyone else took after it, running through the train several times and it finally got into the loose herd, and the dogs driven out, it became contented.

"A Spaniard whom we had taken in a few days before, caught it with a lasso and tied it up but it killed itself in a few minutes. It made good veal. This Spaniard, whose name was Hosea [Jose], had started down the river in a boat with some traders. The river being low, they lodged on the sand. He was afraid to stop in the Pawnee Country and turned back with us to the mountains. He was of great service to me in camp life and helping to care for the animals; also taught us how to approach the buffalo.

"At the crossing of the South Fork of the Platt, we encountered a severe storm in the night. There were five of us sleeping in a tent which blew down. We tried in vain to pitch it again. The wind was so violent that we had to find shelter in the wagon, seven of us together, and when morning came, we were almost frozen. This was the 29th of June.

"Next day we crossed the river, and July 1st we reached Ash Hollow. This day my Spaniard was bitten by a rattle snake and was laid up a week or more. We camped near the brush in the hollow after dark, not knowing we were so near the North Fork of the Platte. I came on second watch that night. The first guard told us to keep a sharp lookout. The mules were very uneasy. One man discovered something near where a mule was staked and threw a bone at it, supposing it to be a dog, but it ran off like a man half bent. About this time I discovered a horse going loose across the corral. I went and examined the rope which was about six feet long. I felt the end of it and pronounced it cut, and immediately alarmed the camp and turned out all hands. We found several horses cut loose and one mare and two colts missing. We then kept everything close till morning, when search was made and a trail up the hollow in the sand where the three animals had been driven off, and nine pairs of mocassin tracks in the trail were found. We moved down to the river and six men followed the trail that day but could see nothing. We here met a company from California [Clyman's party, as seen above], by whom we learned there were no Mormons on the route ahead of us.

"There was considerable dissatisfaction in the camp. Some were in favor of turning back. However, we went on. On the 6th day of July, we came to Chimney Rock. We stopped one day at Horse Creek and repaired wagons. Here an alarm of Indians was made but none could be found.

"One circumstance I have passed over. Opposite Grand Island one night, our cattle being corralled close, took a stampede, and the horses staked close by, all broke loose and of all the running and bellowing and rattling of bells I never before heard the like. Men, women and children were almost frightened to death. We supposed the Pawnees were upon us and one man was so certain of it he fired a rifle in the midst of the fuss. Orders were given immediately not to fire. Men were running in every direction to catch their horses. There was no damage done, excepting the breaking of a cow's leg and knocking a provision box off the hind end of a wagon.

"A few miles below Laramie, we met with Mr. John Reshaw [Richard]. He had some robes to trade and was camped in Goshen Hole. Said that he heard the Mormons were going up the South Fork of the Platte. We held a council and concluded to go no further west but find a place for the company to winter on the east side of the mountains. Mr. Reshaw said that the head of Arkansas River was the best place, as there was some corn growing there and it was near the Spanish country where the company could get supplies. He was going to Pueblo in a few days with two ox teams, there being no road and as he was acquainted with the route, we concluded to stop and go with him."

Thus it happened, Brigham Young and the main body of Mormons having failed to advance beyond the Missouri River, that the Mississippi Saints wintered in the mountains at Pueblo. (There they were joined by the "Sick Detachment" of the Mormon Battalion, enlisted by the U. S. government for service in the war with Mexico, and marched to California by way of Santa Fe.) Brown says that the Saints moved over to Richard's camp, and on July 10 started with him south along the east front of the Rockies. On reaching the South Fork of the Platte, they "searched in vain for the trail of the Mormons, not knowing anything of their moves. We crossed the South Fork on the 27th of July, a few miles below St. Vrains Fort. Here, we struck a wagon trail that led to Pueblo, made by the traders. We reached Pueblo on the 7th of August. We found some six or eight mountaineers in the fort with their families. They had Indian and Spanish women for wives. We were received very kindly and they seemed pleased to see us. . . . News had reached this place that the Mormons had stopped at the Missouri River and 500 of them had joined the army and were on their way to New Mexico."

> We counseled the brethren to prepare for winter to build them some cabins in the form of a fort. The mountaineers said they would let them have their supplies, corn for their labor, etc. Those of us who had left our families stopped here until the 1st of September. We organized the company into a branch and gave them such instructions and counsel as the spirit dictated, telling them to tarry here until they got word from headquarters where to go. They were much disappointed as they expected to get with the main body of the Church. We comforted them all we could and left our blessing with them.

The Saints left on the Arkansas next spring returned north to Fort Laramie, arriving there a few days before the Mormon Party of 1847 came up the Platte under Brigham Young, and with those pioneers they opened the way to the Valley of the Great Salt Lake. But we are primarily interested to note that other travelers from California and Oregon had been passing Pueblo on their way to Bent's Fort, including Joe Walker and Solomon Sublette. Moreover, when Brown and six fellow Saints set out from home on September 1, with them went "a man by the name of Wales Bonny, who had been to Oregon." They reached Bent's on September 3 and Independence the last day of the month: "Here, Mr. Bonny left us."

It is worth returning to Francis Parkman in this context, for when he departed Fort Laramie for Bent's on August 4, he followed the wagon track made by the Mississippi Saints. At Pueblo on August 20 he remarked in his diary: "The Mormons that came across with [Richard] are on the other side [of the Arkansas, across from the trading post] encamped for the winter, and perhaps longer, and on the 21st we rode over to see them. Found them at work upon their log-houses, but they suspended their labors to talk with us. Some of them completely imbued with the true fanatic spirit—ripe for anything—a very dangerous body of men. [Rather, as Bernard DeVoto has remarked, just some devout Mormons far from home, but with manners too rude for Francis Parkman.] . . . . A great many more are said to be on their way up the Arkansas." (Apropos of nothing, Parkman also wrote in his diary this day: "The barefaced rascal, Bonny." Wales Bonney's eventual arrival on the frontier, marked by his faithful delivery to the postoffice of many of the letters printed herein, is reported in Volume II.)

The staggering complexity of the overland emigration to California and Oregon in the year 1846 has now, perhaps, been fully reflected in this Introduction, as in the letters, diaries, and newspaper reports that follow. This emigration was unlike any earlier one, breaking all bounds of precept and practice, and there has been no disposition in these pages to give it an order, simplicity, and tautness it did not have; what should emerge is a sense of magnificent spectacle, with human nature on the loose. The emigration of 1846 was in some respects representative of all overland migrations, but the terrible climax in the Sierra Nevada also makes it unique. Necessarily we read some of the letters with a point of view stabbingly different from that of the writers, as when a friend innocently tells James Frazier Reed before starting that "the Journey is nothing in Comparison to what our forefathers went thru

but dont forget to take plenty to eat," or when Tamsen
Donner serenely writes her sister as she prepares to leave
Independence, "I am willing to go & have no doubt it will
be an advantage to our children & to us." But these same
letters correct ideas we may have entertained that the
1846 emigration is a thing apart, shadowed from the beginning by the wings of disaster.

How many people went West in 1846? Even with all
the contemporary records gathered into these pages, no
one can be sure. The usual reckoning was in terms of
wagons, of which the most authoritative account doubtless was that supplied to the St. Louis *Gazette* by Joel
Palmer arriving on the frontier in August; he gave the
total as 541, and since the rule of thumb was five emigrants to the wagon, a total Oregon and California emigration of some 2,700 souls is indicated. Not all those
wagons got through; four at least came back to the
States; the 19 wagons of the Mississippi Saints rolled
south to Pueblo; and others were traded or abandoned.
The only exact count is for travel over the Barlow Road,
which totaled 152 wagons. A few emigrants who took the
old Oregon Trail wintered at Whitman's missionary station in preference to crossing the Cascades, five families
in all. From 90 to 100 wagons seem to have traveled
the Applegate Cutoff. Altogether, the Oregon emigration of 1846 may have totaled 1,100 to 1,200 souls. The
California emigration in the end may not have been very
much larger, say 1,500 men, women, and children. We
learn that 256 wagons crossed the Missouri at St. Joseph
or points higher up. Most of these left early in the season, save for the 40 wagons (more or less) of the Smith
company in which Edward Trimble was killed. The emigration out of Independence and Westport was evidently
larger, though not very much so—perhaps 280 wagons in
all.

This latter emigration has been reported in the literature down to the present; the Taylor and Carriger diaries

printed herein help to correct the imbalance. Although it has not been possible to incorporate into the present work full summaries of the separately published narratives by such travelers out of Independence as Edwin Bryant, J. Quinn Thornton, and Heinrich Lienhard, pertinent material being extracted primarily in the form of notes, Bryant and Thornton traveled a good part of the time with our diarists George McKinstry, Hiram Miller, and James Frazier Reed, and we are not deprived of their point of view. Lienhard, originally a member of the George Harlan train captained by Josiah Morin, afterward of the G. D. Dickenson company, and finally of the Jacob D. Hoppe party, was in the same sector of the emigration at the beginning, and later he traveled in the same dust cloud with our diarist James Mathers, and our mapmaker T. H. Jefferson. All who find the present work interesting are urged, nevertheless, to read Bryant, Thornton, and Lienhard. They will come back to the diaries and letters which make up these two volumes with a lively new appreciation, and surely will join in the hope that discoveries are yet to be made, opening up further frontiers in the world of 1846.

DALE L. MORGAN

"The California Trail"

Diary of William E. Taylor

With a Letter by John Craig

It is rare good fortune that we should have two different accounts of the first company to bring wagons across the Sierra in 1846. The eight-man Craig & Stanley party was overtaken near the Sink of the Humboldt by the William H. Russell pack party which has Edwin Bryant as its chronicler, and was preceded over the mountains by those packers. But these eight men have a place all their own in the 1846 emigration.

Since John Craig himself describes the circumstances which led him, with Larkin Stanley, to embark upon the western trails in the spring of 1846, and since the Introduction has set the stage generally, we shall note here only that the Craig & Stanley party always was at the forefront of the emigration, from the time it left the frontier—originally as members of the company under

William J. Martin which started from the St. Joseph area and for the most part ended up in Oregon. The names of only four of the eight men are known—Craig and Stanley, W. E. Taylor, and Israel Brockman. The name of the latter is preserved solely in a document found in the Jacob R. Snyder Collection, Society of California Pioneers. (On March 15, 1847 at City of Angeles, Brockman addressed His Excellency Col. J C Fremont to explain that he was under the necessity of applying for his discharge from the California Battalion; he hoped this discharge would be granted for the reason that Mr. Stanley, deceased, and himself owned a wagon and team and other property, which Mr. Craig, Stanley's administrator, could not dispose of without his consent; as Mr. Craig was going to the States the ensuing season and wanted to take the proceeds of Stanley's estate to his family, Brockman thought it necessary that he should repair to the upper country to dispose of Stanley's property.)

The circumstances of Stanley's death are brought out on a later page. Concerning his partner, John Craig, little more is known than he himself records in the letter to George Boosinger here printed in association with W. E. Taylor's diary. The *California Star,* April 10, 1847, contains a notice: "We are requested by Mr. John Craig to state, that he is now forming a company to return to the United States this Spring by the overland route. The company will rendezvous at Fort Sacramento, and start as soon as the mountains can be crossed. An invitation is extended to all who wish to return to the United States by land, to join the company. They will probably start about the first of May." Craig's passage eastward—at first in company with the mountain man Miles Goodyear—is recorded in a variety of contemporary records quoted in the Notes. His letter shows that he safely arrived at his home in Ray County, Missouri, with his diary in his pocket. But thereafter he and his diary vanish from history. It is to be hoped that this publication of Craig's letter respecting his two-year odyssey in the West may serve to bring to light more information about him.

W. E. Taylor remained in California, and to this fact we owe both the preservation of his diary—ultimately given by a descendant to Sutter's Fort Historical Monument—and a biographical record. An obituary printed in the Downieville *Mountain Messenger,* July 29, 1905, relates that he was a native of Tennessee, aged 85 years, 1 month and 6 days at the time of his death on July 26, 1905; he was therefore born on June 20, 1820. He must have removed to Missouri at a comparatively early age, for among his papers is a certificate signed by Garret McDowell, Colonel of the 84th Regiment, 2nd Brigade, 7th Division, Missouri Militia: "Know ye that I . . . Have appointed William E. Taylor, Marshall of said Regiment hereby authorizing & empowering him to discharge the duties of Said office according to Laws Given under my hand the 20th Sept., 1844."

Taylor's laconic diary carries on the chronicle of his life as he traveled from Missouri to California. This record ends on reaching Johnson's Ranch on September 13, but several notations among the end pages of the diary reveal that he went on to Sonoma (he was in fact, one of the Sonoma garrison the ensuing fall and winter):

"Oct the 14 1846 Sonoma
   Doct Edward Bail Dr to
   Mr [?] Ed Guy[?] money Loaned $600
Oct 15 Samuel Kelsey To Dr
   money Loaned   2.00
   W H Scott Dr to one pea Jacket $10 00
   To 1 dollar Cash Loaned   1 00
       The above acct is paid
       Dec the 2 1846

Two letters are preserved, addressed to Taylor at Sonoma. The first is dated Yerba Buena, March 15th 1847:

Dear Sir.

I have received your note by which I am informed that nothing new has happened at home. Mr Scott had told me at his arrival here that new attempts had been made by the instigations of Green and Berreyesa to attack again my house and property. So I was somewhat frightened on account of the diffidence that inspires to me the ill intention of Green and weakness of Nash. All persons of some respectability learned with surprise and indignation the slanderous act attempted by the tou latter to stirp me of my house and property, and I have no doubt that I will obtain an order from General Karny to arrest so horrible transgression.

I thank you for your good care and efficacy and pray you to continue them until my return which will be about 3 or 4 weeks.

Do me the favor write to me by every opportunity, and let me know the state of things. I place my property under your care, and my servants under your orders.

I am very sorry for the death of Refugio, I did not believe that the could heal.

Excuse my bad English, present my best respects to Madame Taylor and believe me your truly friend and obed^t Servt

VR PRUDON.

P. S. American Store Shop Hiland from Sandwitch Iland anchored yesterday evening 19 days navagation no news.—We shall leave for Monterrey to morrrow on board Ship Vandalia.

* * *

The second of these letters, addressed "Mr W^m E Taylor Sonoma U. C.," is of special interest in that it refers to another of our diarists, Nicholas Carriger:

U S Ship Warren
Monterey Mar: 28th 1847

Dear Sir

I am Sorry to inform you that there is no prospect of

Gaylords getting his discharge at present. All those men whose times have expired were transferred to the Savannah & consequently our complement is shut.

We expect to sail tomorrow for San Pedro to bring up some of Col Fremonts men & will probably take them to San Francisco when we return perhaps the period of our departure for home will be known Gaylord may then either get his discharge or be transferred to some other vessel to be discharged when his time expires

If we return to San Francisco I shall be pleased to see you on board

Be pleased to present my respects to Mrs Tayler Mr Griffiths family Mr Carrager & Powell & others,

Your Friend & Obt Servt
WM L MAURY

These letters have been quoted in full, among other reasons because they complete the slender record of Taylor's life afforded by his papers. Both, it will be noted, refer to a Mrs. Taylor. According to an obituary reprinted in the Downieville *Mountain Messenger,* February 6, 1904, from the *Nevada County Morning Miner,* she died at Downieville on January 30, 1904, of "asthma and la grippe." "Her maiden name was Nancy Griffiths and she was born in North Carolina seventy-three years ago [on June 15, 1830]. When a mere child she removed with her parents to Missouri, where they resided for about eight years. In 1845 the family came to California and settled in Sonoma County. On December 13, 1846, she was united in marriage to W. E. Taylor. After a few years in Sonoma they removed to Napa Valley and later to Indian Valley, where they resided until nine years ago, when Mr. and Mrs. Taylor took up their residence in Downieville. On December 13, 1896, they celebrated their golden wedding in Downieville. She leaves to mourn her death an aged husband, six sons, George F., Ross L. and John Taylor of Downieville; Dr. R. L. Taylor of San Francisco; James Taylor of this city and William Taylor of Idaho; two daughters, Mrs. M. E. Gott of Goodyear Bar and Mrs. William Mawer of Lassen county, besides a number of grandchildren, among whom is Mrs. W. R. Sharkey of this Nevada, and a wide circle of friends . . . She was highly esteemed for her many noble qualities and was possessed of a kindly and generous disposition . . ."

Taylor's own obituary, previously mentioned, adds that he died after an illness of several weeks, from old age and other infirmities. "His first residence in the State was in Sonoma county, and after residing there a great many years he removed to Plumas county, where [he] lived until about ten years ago when he came to Downieville. . . . During his residence in Sonoma county Mr. Taylor held several public offices, one being the first superintendent of public schools of that county. He also served as under sheriff for several years of Napa county."

Thus the record of William E. Taylor's life in the long perspective provided by his death. But in taking up his diary, we turn back through the years to find him a young man, three months short of his twenty-sixth birthday, with the great experiences of life yet before him.

❀ ❀ ❀

THE TAYLOR DIARY

Monday April the 20th 1846 We this day lef home for Oregon and proceeded 5 [15?] miles to Elk horn[1] whare we got some work done on our waggon Our company consisting of Craig Shreve and myself

Tuesday, the 21. We Left at 10 O'clock and Standlly's wagon Broak 2 miles from Elk horn whare we continued [?] all night

Wed. 22. Left at 12 O'clock after having finished [?] all the repares our waggon proceeded about 3 [?] miles This day one of our Crowd (Shreve) took his [*illegible*: leave?] Mr Lad Joined us.[2]

Th. 23. went 12 miles

Friday 24. passed plattsburg travailed 12 miles

Sat. 25. traveled 20 miles

Sund. 26. got to St. Josephs, traveled 3 miles

Monday 27 Tuesday 28 we remained at St. Josephs

Wen. 29 we Left St. Josephs went to parrots ferry 5 miles above town.[3] Weather fair wind high

Th 30 Remained in Camp Wind prevents us from Crossing

May 1 Crossed over the river which was very hig for the season we find an abundance of grass for the oxen

2 Remained in camp

3. Struck our tents and proceeded to wolf River whare we had some difficulty in getting over went 14 mils

4. Started Early passed the Iowa Agency,[4] distance 25 [miles]

5 Left camp Early travled 15 miles

6 We overtook 18 waggons at the Nemihaw River crossed over found [*deleted*: 7] 6 wagons encamped making 27 waggons and 50 men.[5] A view from the prairie hills of this Little River is very sublime and beautiful it Surpasses any thing I have yet seen

7 we traveled about 20 miles the road verry undulating and the Land of the Richest kind Scarcely any timber or Water Some symptoms of discord in camp owing to all not being preasent at the Election of officers[6]

8 we traveld over Level wet prairie 18 ms

9 we traveld 2½ miles Crossed one fork of the Blue.[7] Staid all day found we were wrong

10 Changed our course Crossed over the other fork of Blue came to Independence trail[8] we are ahead of all distance 16 miles

11 traveled 14 miles Camped in a small grove on a tributary of Blue

12 Camped on Horse Creek[9] 7 miles

13 Travailed 7 miles Camped on Blue

14 Camped on Sandy a tributary of the Blue after travling 20 miles

15 Camped on the blue 16 miles verry warm The Mercury stands 76 at noon in the shade

16 traveld up Blue 16 miles Stanley killed a deer Mercury Stood at 86 at noon in the shade

17 traveled 4 miles

18 we went But 2 miles owing to the indisposition of Mrs Munkerass who brough an increase in to the emigration

19 travailed 8 miles

20 traveled 16 up Blue

21 arrived at the Nebraska,[10] travailed 17 miles

22 to day we saw a party of pawnees some hunters quite friendly distance 18 miles

23 traveld 8 miles

24 traveld 20 miles Saw and killed some Buffalo

25 traveled 18 miles thousands of Buffalo

26 Traveled 18 A sevier h[a]il storm in the Evning.

27 "   16 miles quite Cool Mercury at 57

28 "   23 another hail Storm Reached the South fork of platt

the 29 travaled 16 miles first used the excrement of the Buffalo for fuel

30 Crossed the South fork which is one mill wide with an average depth of 18 inches[11] dis. 12 miles this evening we had the most sevier storm I ever saw

31 Lay by all day owing to incessant Rain and intense Cold with Some Snow Tem. 48 Fah[renheit]

June the first today there was quit a snow storm passed over to the Ash hollow[12] distance 25 miles Tem. 38 deg. Fah.

2nd Staid here all day

3 went 10 miles Camped out of the Rain Tem. 57 deg

4 travelled 20 miles Saw wild horses

5 travaled 20 miles. Came in sight of Castle Rock also the Chimney Rock Crossed Sandy[13]

6 passed the Chimney Rock dist. 25 miles

7 passed Scotts Bluff[14] Beautiful Scenry dist 18 miles

8 Company divided[15] distance 19 miles

9 Travelled 15 miles Temp. 90 deg of Fah.

10 Went 7 miles came to Laramie.[16] Tem. 100 deg of Fah.

11 Lay By. mercury at 100 Fah.

12 travelled 20 miles through the Black hills Camped on the Bitter Cotton Wood a Smal Stream[17]

13 Came 20 miles camped on horse Shoe Creek[18]

14 camped on Butte creek[19] distance 20 miles

15 camped on Black Creek dist 20 miles Red Rock[20]

16 travelled 18 miles camped on deer creek[21]

17 traveled 16 miles Tem 90 deg of Fah.

18 Came to the Crossing of platt not fordable met some Return emigrants[22] Tem. 81 deg. of Fah.

19 Remained trying to cross our Cattle

20 Do Do 16 more waggons Came up

21 got all over Rafted the waggons Swam the Cattle

22 passed the Red Butt[e]s dist 12 miles a good Spring[23]

23 Came to the Willow Spring[24] distance 20 miles

24 20 miles Braught us to the Rock Independence[25]

25 Passed the Kenion on Sweet water[26] saw mountain sheep travelled 16 miles

26 Went 18 miles, passed a party of men.[27]

27 traveled 25 miles Thousands of buffalo

28 Lay By all day

29 Traveled 20 miles a plain view of the wind River mountains Covered with snow Bad roads Some Sick

30 Came to the South Pass at 16 miles

July the 1 23 [*deleted*: 16] miles Braught us to Little Sandy extremely sterile country in sight of eternal snow on the Bear River mountan[28]

2 Broak a waggon a man sick dist 10 miles Camped on Big Seany [Sandy] Mr L W Hastings visited our camp[29]

3rd travelled 18 miles Tem. 29 deg. of Fah.

4 crossed the colorado of the west a stream of 40 Rods wide 2 feet deep[30] dis. 16 miles

5 traveled 15 miles camped on Blacks Fork[31] near half the company confined by sickness[32]

6 traveled 2 miles Lay By on account of the sick Tem 90 deg. of Fah.

7 Lay By Sick get worse Mr. S Sublett & three others staid with us they ware from California[33] Wrote home By them. Tem. 105

8 We Left the main croud with 7 waggons travelled 16 miles some Rain

9 16 miles Braught us to Bridger Shoshone in abundane Mr Joseph Walker et al from California[34]

10 Lay By Indians visited us in great numbers

11 traveled 18 miles Cam[p]ed on muddy[35] a bad camp

12 traveled 18 miles Camped at a good Spring

13 Crossed the Bear River mountain Rain 25 miles

14 16 miles Brought us to Smiths fork[36]

15 traveled 22 verr[y] Bad Roads hard Rain

16 traveled 14 miles more Rain

17 21 Braught us to the Soda Spring[37]

18 Lay By Rain thunder and Lightning

19 Left our company with our 2 waggons alon never shall I forget the deep Regret at a Leaving our friends[38] passed the old Crater travaled 12 miles

20 our oxen sensable of the impropriety of Leaving their as well as our friends Left camp and ware overtaken 3 miles from the Soda Spring so that we only got to portneif River[39] 7 miles

21 traveled 22 miles Crossed divers streams

22 traveled 21 to the Blue Spring 5 miles from fort Hall[40]

23 passed Ft hall traveled 14 miles to portneiffe River.

24 traveled 18 mils passed the American falls of Snake or Saptin River.[41]

25 travelled 18 miles to Casua[42] Bad Road

26 Left the Oregon Road traveled 22 miles up the casua or Raft River good Road

27 traveled up casua 18 miles Rain Lightning and thunder

28 20 miles Braught us to a good Spring Road Bad Crossed over to goose creek[43] [*deleted*: 10 miles]

29 we came 10 miles

30 travelled 15 miles

31 we came 18 miles Tem. 30 deg. Fah. morning

August the 1 traveled 17 miles

2 passed a verry hot Spring 20 miles Struck the head of Marys River[44]

3 met Black harriis and applegate who had Been to view a new Road to oregon and designed meeting the emigrants to turn them into it[45] travelled 20 miles Tem 88 of Fah.

4 Traveled 17 miles down Marys Rive. Tem 90

5 This day we came 20 miles sevral diggers[46]

6 passed sevral Remarkabley hot Springs[47] 20 miles

7 Came 14 miles

8 " 17 " hot Springs[48]

9 " 16 "

10 " 20 miles quit steril[e]

11 " 23 miles " "

12 " 18 miles Natural Soap[49]

13 " 18 miles Salaeratus visited by Large party of Indians

14 Travelled 22 miles (Rain Lightning

15 " 20 miles. divergence of new oregon road[50]

16 " 20 " Extreme Sterility

17. " 25 " to day we Suffered for water as the Road Left the River for 14 miles[51] Rain

18 Lay By Joined By Col. Russell of Mo. & 8 others packing[52] Tem. 42 morning 96 noon

19. 20 miles Braught us to the Sink of Marys Riv[53] Vegetation entirely disappear water verry bad

20 traveled all day and all night passed some Boiling Springs quite salt distance 40 miles making 60 miles that 8 of us had 12 gallons of Water Extreme suffering Reached Trucky[54]

21 Lay by all day Tem 100 of Fah.

22 Entered the Siera Nevada or Cascade mts up Trucky vally 15 miles[55] Tem 87 deg of Fah.

23 Traveled 18 miles Bad Road

24 " 10 miles came to timber Tem 94 deg Fah

25 Crossed a spur of the mts[56] 12 miles Tem 84.

26 travelled 12 miles good Road Tem 32.

27 " 8 miles Trucky Lake[57] Tem 30

28 travelled 1 mile up the worst mountain that waggons ever crossed[58] sevier frost Tem 28

29 got up the mts. Distance 2 miles

30 travelled 3 miles Lay by the Ballance of day

31 " 15 miles on top of the mt. Bad Road Tem 22 at day Light & 60 at Sun down

Sept 1 travelled 7 miles Bad Bad Road Bear sign Tem. 40 deg morn

2 traveled 7 miles of distressing Road

3rd " 8 miles ove if possable worse Road.

4 Lay by to Rest our oxen

5 travled 16 miles principally upon the top of a high Spur of the mountain our Oxen are worn nearly out we have but three that are able to Render service and we have as steep a hill befor us as we have Left behind us Heaven only knows how we are to get Along Our Oxen are almost perishing for food and nothing grows in this hateful valley that will sustain life.[59]

6 Lay by to day as yestardys Long drive has well nigh done for the oxen. We cut down Oak Bushes and trees, for them to Brows on, or such of them, as are able to Stand on their feet.

7 the indians drove off two of Mr. Stanley's ablest Oxen; tho' we succeeded in Recapturing one of them We unloaded our waggons and packed the Load near a mile on our horses We then took four of the best yoaks of Oxen and put to the empty waggons with a man at each wheel and by such exertions as I have seldom saw used we got the wagons up one at a time and proceeded about 5 miles[60] grass verry Scarce and dry Our oxen are as

near gone as I ever saw oxen to be driven at all

8 This morning we found that the Indians had taken off another one of Stanley's oxen, it was seen by following the trail that they had taken him up a steep hill and carfully Covered Evry track for the distance of a mile he was taken probably whilst I was on guard. I do not know how he managed to affect this Roguery it must have been very Sly W[e] travelled 11 miles and Stoped at a Small patch of dry grass and no water for the Cattle or horses

9 we traveled 3 miles and Stoped for the day at a Little grass and a hole of water one of Mr. Craigs Best oxen has gave out; the hills have got much Smaller and the Rocks are not so much in the way as on any part of the Road Since we Struck the waters of Trucky River

10 Lay by all day our oxen are so near worn out and our provisions are getting scarce

11 Started on slow went about 6 miles today we had to Leave an ox on the Road

12 we traveled 7 miles and Stopt we are in five miles of the first settlement today we left another ox we have but two oxen to our waggon

13 We this morning got into the Valley and stoped at Cap. W^m. Johnsons Whare we ware Recieved in the most Kind and hospitable manner[61] We made several trades Bought a beef swaped our broak down oxen for fresh ons this day our company Lay by and so for several days distance 5 miles

So Ends my Diary

The Roads from St Joseph to Nimahaw is over Extensive prairies high dry rolling hills with an abundance of wood on the Little Streams (which are numers) for all purposes There are some deer on the Nimehaw tho they are quite scarce; the grass on this part of the Road is good any whare.

From Nimahaw to Blue is some thing like that part Back to the States the timber is not so plenty nor the

water so good tho there is quite a sufficiency of Both I
saw some Antelopes on the Little Blue. The Road up
Blue is generally on the Second Bottom through a most
luxurient growth of Grass and Rushes togather with
other vegetation common in the States Over this part of
the Road there is the greatest abundance of timber and
water any place for all ordinary purposes from Blue to
platt a distance of 20 miles you pass over high dry prairie
neither wood or water Upon arrivin on the Nebraska
things ware quite a different appearance   the Road
Strikes the River about the middle of the grand Island
which is sixty miles Long and thickly covered with Cotton wood and willows; on the Banks of the stream you
some times find willow in quantaties quite sufficient for
fuel when this is not the cass the traveler is obliged as a
substitute to use the dried Excrement of Buffaloes which
By the by is no bad makeshift At about 4 or 5 days
travel up the River the travler usually finds Buffalo in
great quantaties I hav saw thousands at a Sight however easily others may have taken them I found that it
cost us a great deal of trouble

Antelopes are verry numerous and whare they have
not been much hunted are easily killed; the best way is
to extend your hankerchief on your gun rod and Remain
as still as you can This seems to excite their curiosity
they will aproach near enough for you to kill them with
a pistol I knew them to be shot by men from their tent
doors; they are found in greater or Less quantaties on
all portion of the road after you strike the prairies; the
hungry traveler may rely more certainly upon them for
a supply than any other game that meets with. Deer are
scarce on any part of this Rout. we have killed only two
on the entire Journey Black tailed deer are verry numerous on the Cascade Mountains tho they are verry wild
Wolvs are also numerous they are of all colours and
sizes from the size of the Largest Mastiffs down to the
smalles Fiste dog they have frequently been known to
attack and kill the Lagargest Buffalo I Saw fifteen

wolves after one Bull They run him directly to whare
we ware encamped Some of the Comompany killed the
buffalo and compelled them to abandon the chase we
found that they had verry nearly succeeded in cutting his
ham strings they had eat his tail entirely off he was
nearly exhausted and the probability is that his Race was
nearly Run even if he had not passed our camp he was
verry fat and the best meat of the kind that we had yet
been able to procure as the buffaloes that we had hitherto
killed were verry poor

The Rocky Mountain Sheep are now verry scarce and
hard to catch I did not see but one flock and that was
on a cliff of the Kenion on Sweetwater near Independence Rock I had no gun consequently I did not kill any
of them they are a verry active and beautiful Little animal and Some what Resemble the deer in the blue Season
but much smaller the male wearing a pondrous head of
horns much Larger than; but in Evry other Respect Like
the domestick Rams their flesh is preferred to any other
by the Indians and Mountaineers I found them domes-
tickated at the forts they are said to be quit docile

Mountain hairs are numerous but verry wild they are
Large and have the Largest Ears in proportion to their
size of any other animal being 7 or 8 inches in Length
they are also good when no other meat can be obtained

Bear are said to be plenty on the Cascade Mountain
tho I have not been able to get a sight of one there is as
much Sign in pla[c]es on the mountain as therr is of
hogs Round the oaks of a good mast year in Tennessee.

The Road crosses South Platt some distance above its
Junction with the north Branch; the ford is verry good
the Road then Leads over hills 20 miles Rather South of
West to the ash hollow here is wood grass and water of
the best quality Keep up the North fork [*blank*] miles to
fort Larima a good Road

here the Road Leaves the River and takes through
the Black hills this part of the Road is not verry good
tho when it is compaired with some other parts of the

Road it is excellent   it is [*blank*] miles before the Road
Comes to the River again after which the Road is good
again to the crossing of the North Fork of platt this
generally has to be Rafted over a process which is teadi-
ous Laborious and dangerous

JOHN CRAIG TO GEORGE BOOSINGER, RAY COUNTY,
MISSOURI, OCTOBER 4, 1847

Dear Sir

After my respects to you and family I will inform
you that we are all injoying much better health this
Season that we have for a number of years Your children have arived in our neighborhood and have called on
us and from them we heard of the health of yourself and
family. Your Son Wesly is of the opinion that you had
not recived my letters in which I informed you of the
insolvency of the Rickets estate and of the imposibility
of me colecting your money out of the administraton
And all that I colected from Mr Brasheres of your money
I sent you with the exception of what I Spent on your
buisness in going several trips to Far west[62] feeing a Lawyer and paying Clerks fees to get you the transcrip All
of thos matters I informed you of by letter years ago
when every thing was fresh in my memory and when I
had all the vouchers aroud me to show. You can then
Judge my Surprise and regret after Such a long laps
of time to be informed that you was yet in the dark
concerning what disposition I had made of your affairs
intrust to me[63] . . . Having Just returned home from a
long Jurney and not having time to examine through
my numerous old papers and receipt at the present it
will be a pleashure to me at a more convenient time and
having the proper notice to give you a full and Satisfactory acount of what disposition I made of what little
funds that was in my hands heretofore belonging to you.
. . . [In 1844] the great Overflow took place of all our
watercourses[64] and a General Sickness prevailed over our
county amongst the rest my own family Suffred Severely

and one youg man an aprentice died This together with
my own bad health disqualifyed me from attending to my
own buisness So that I eventuly rented out the tanyard
and bottom place and concluded to take a trip to the
Paciffic Oacean for the benefit of my health and to See
if I could find a health county to remove my family. . . .

On the 3th of may 1846 I in company with Mr Larken
Standley Started to visit Oregon and if posible California
intending to be absent Some 18 mounths. We each took
a good waggon and Ox team I had three good yoke to
my waggon we each had two young men that drove for
us before Starting we layed in two hundred pounds of
flour to each person Some 60 or more lb of bacon fifteen
lb of coffe as much Shuger Some rice and dryed fruit
Salt peper &c Each mess had a frying pan a small bake
oven a teakettle coffee pot and each person a tin plate
and cup and a tent to each waggon Mr Standly and
myself had each a horse Saddle and bridle a good Set
of holster pistols and a good rifle and one or two of the
youg men had horses all good rifles and Some pistols and
all plenty of amunetion. Thus equiped we Started on our
long and (Some what perilous Journey) I have not time
to tell you of the immense herds of Buffel I Seen what
Sport we had in runing them on horse back over theas
vast plains the number we Shot the vast amount of antelope we Seen the mountain Sheep &c Neither have I
time to tell you of the thousands of the red Sons and
daughters (not of the forrest) but of the great American
desert that we Seen as we traveled Slowly along through
thair chery Country At times those Sons of natue would
through our camp or party into quite a flurry by aproach-
ing us on horse back at full Speed thundering and dashing over the plains towards us thair robes and blankets
Streaming in the air behind them which with thair painted
faces and other indian equipage made them have quite a
warlike apearance

On the road we altered our plan of travel in place of
going first to oregon we concluded to first go into Cali-

fornia Sell our teams and waggons and Some Store goods
that I had take a look round the Bay of San Francisco
then take shiping go to Oregon and Spend the winter
and return home from thair the following Summer.[65] Our
two waggons having ondly Eight men in all traveld
from fort Hall to California alone (being a distance of
Seven hundred miles) We arived at the frontier Settlements on the 13th day of Sept being four months and
ten days from One frontier to the other the distan'e
acording to my calculation being near two thousand miles.
The last hundred miles was ovr the most lofty chain of
mountains in north america and part of the road as bad
as can well be immagined runing through external [*i.e.*
extensive?] groves of the largest and loftiest pine and
ceder I ever beheld or even heard of. The ballance of the
road from the confines of the State of missouri to the
eastern foot of the California range of mountains is equal
if not Superiour to any road of equal distane in the States
that I have aney knowledge of. On reaching that county
we arived in the great Sacramento valley on Bear river
we foud the grass and vegetation in Jeneral dryed up
and the groud parched and dry on acout of the draught.
But close on the runing Streams and low bottoms was
green grass in abundance And the dry grass was equel
to our hay of the States as no rain and but little dew
had fallen on it. The consequence was that cattle in general was beef fat and Stock of all discriptions was in good
order.

About the time we arived in the county the Spanyards
made an effort to drive off and conquer or kill all the
americans in the county in consequens we had as a matter
of necesity to colect together for thair was no regular
troops of the United States in the county and although
those of us that had no familys mite have gone to Oregon
on the first Ship yet as the majority had familys thay were
bound to conquer or be killed. The consequens was that
all our little company voluntered ourselves for Six months
under Comedore Stockton as Govnor and C Freemont as

our commander. We was put on board of boats, which
conveyed us across the Bay (the distane of fifty miles)
Whare a Ship was ready to carry us to the main Seat
of war in the South part of the teritory. We was fifteen
days on the great Pacific Oacean the greater part of the
time out of Sight of land and after our Sea Sickness was
over we beguiled our tedious houers in looking at the
numerous·whales porpesis Seal Shark, and other inhabitants of the mighty deep. But after Sailing till near the
lower part of Alta California we was ordered back to
Monteray the former Seat of Govrmet for the teritory
and within two hundred miles or less of whare we first
took Shiping. Here we was landed and furnished with
horses and traveled by land to the lower part of the county. Small party of our Batalion was at times atacked
and Severel of our men was killed and wounded and we
frequently marched for days in the order of battle but
the enemy never atacked us and would at no point make
a final Stand although we marched five or six hundred
miles through the hart of their county. The at last sur-
rendered to our Batalion and give up thair arms And
on the 2th of June last when I left that county the Stars
and Stips waved tryumphant over all the coutry and
Americans for the first time felt Secure in thair persons
and property[66]

Upper Calefornia is a long narrow coutry (I Speak
of the part fit for cultivation) being probebly a thousand
miles in lenth and varying from one to two hundred in
breanth, But after crosing the California range and getting in to the County fit for the habitation of civilized
man even then I consider that two thirds of the county
is mountains so far as I traveled over it (which was a
distane of at least Seven hundred miles up and down
the Coast) A good proporion of the valleys is rich the
Soil in places being equeal (in my opinion) to the best
Missouri bottom. But in other places more thin and in
Some valleys poor Sandy and gravely. The county in
Jeneral is lacking good valuable timber. But in places

particularly aroud and north of the Bay of San Fransisco thair is extensive groves of pine and red wood (The red wood is a Species of ceder) Aroud the harbour of Monterey both north and South is large bodys of the before mentioned timber. But this timber in Jeneral groes on the mountain Sides and top and it is mostly difficult to get roads to and from it. The county to be a mountenious region is lacking good spring water but in Some Sections thair is Spings in abundane

The climate is mild and delightfull with no Snow in the valleys in the winter and but little frost and the thickest ice I seen was not the fourth of an inch thick and that was on thin Sheets of Standing water and never on runing Streams Yet the Summers is cool and plesent and up to the time I left (the 2th of last June) I mostly foud it more cumfortable to ware a Janes coat morning and eavening and found it nessery for cumfort to Sleep under one and frequently two blankets. And from information this is the case through the entire Sumer mounths. But in the large valleys Such as the Sacremento and San Jauquin where the Sea breases is obstructed by a coast range of mountains the heat of the noon day Sun is greater than in our western States but even here the nights (As I have been informed is plesantly cool. For grasing this county cannot be exceled. As every family has more or less Stock varying from fifty to five thousand head of Cattle each besides large quantityes of horses and Some have large droves of Spanish Sheep and hogs But jenerally but few of the latter. And as long as I was in that County which was over eight mounths and nearly all the time traveling over the county in various directions Yet I Seldom ever Seen a poor animal excepting horses which ware rode down in the War

And the Batalion principally Subsisted on beef Slaughtered off the grass and that all through the winter mounths (or rainey Season) and frequently we had nothing to eat but beef for fifteen and twenty days at a time. And yet done well. For with but few exceptions better tasted or

fatter beef I never eat. As to health I think but few
countrys can excel upper Calefornia For let the wind
blow from aney point of the cumpass it will be from a
healthy quarter. If from the west it is from of the
Oacean from any other point is from off high and frequently Snow caped mountains. But in the center of the
two large valleys (before mentioned) and close on theas
large Stteams thair is in Autumn a few cases of chills
and fever. But even thair I consider it more healthier
than in Illinois or Missouri. But any whare, in reach of
the breeze from off the Bay or Ocean chills is unknown.
But the glory of this County lays in its Superiour advantages of trade and Commerce It is a common Saying
that all the navyes of the wourld mite ride at Safety in
the Bay of San Fransisco. At the town of Yerba buena
I mostly Seen laying from fifteen to 20 Ships of vareous
tonage besides numerous boats and Launches. And every
day thair is more or less vessels ariveing and departing
from the Bay

And yet every thing is in its infancy. Thair is a constant and fair demand for all that a farmer raises. Wheat
one dollar per bushel —Onions about four dollars fresh
butter fifty cents per lb chickens Six dollars per dozen
All kinds of vegetables and fresh provisions is verry high
excepting beef which is verry cheap. Thus you See I
ondly recommend the county for four or five things. first
a delightfull climate 2 a good grazing county 3 and
above all as a healthy county 4 as a county having Superior advantages of Commerce. And fifthly from what
I Seen of the prospect of wheat crops in 1846 as when
we arived in the county a numbers was yet imployed
getting out thair wheat which mostly looked well and
from apearence had yiealded from fifteen to thirty bushels
for every one Sowed. And when I left better crops I
never Seen grown in any part of the States than was
growing aroud the Bay and all throug the Sacremento
vally up to the western foot of the Mountains. I have
rode for half a day at a time through plains of Oats of

a Montanious groth varying from one up to five foot high and frequently as well Set as any cultivated in our fields. I have counted Six kinds of clover that groes Spontanious in that county frequently growing as tall and rank as when we cultivate it

This is but a poor corn county the nights is rather cold and the dry Season Sets in before corn makes its Self. And all vegetables that are late coming to meturity in order to do well must be airigated. This is truly the land of the vine and olive. Vineyards is numerous in the old Settled parts of this county and they at present make considerable of Wine. The grapes is of the most delicious kind often as large as our fox grape. I have seen hudreds of large olive trees loded with fruit besides quantitys of fig trees but the time of figs was over before I got to where the grew. The palmn tree is here and I Seen one kind of the coconut tree. And in Short most of the tropical fruits do well perticularly in the South of the teritory. Wild game is here in abundance Such as Elk the black tailed deer antelope the brown and grisley Bear and vast quantityes of wolves. The water courses abound with fish of the best quality Perticularly Salmon and Several other Salt fish run up and are caught in the Streams of this country. The rainy Season set in the year I was thair on the 29th of Oct and continued to rain at intervals up to the last of May in a few instances it rained five and Six days and night with out intermition but Generally it rained two and three days and nights and then cleared off with as butifull weather as I ever beheld and by a refference to my Jurnal I find that near two thirds of the winter was clear pleasant weather And as regards this country the prediction is literally fulfiled that December is as pleasant as May (I mean May in the States) I Seen roses and wild flowers in full bloom all through the winder mounths and in January I on Severel Ocasions Seen butterflyes aroud our camp. And in Short as Soon as the rain commences falling grass and all kinds of vegetation commences growing Slow but Stedily all

though the winter mounths. Whilst at the Same time the
tops of the high mountains is covered deep in Snow. Thus
winter is looking down on plains of eternal verdure.

I will here informe you of the death of my old neigh-
bour Standly as he was a diseased person and like myself undertook the Jurney for his health he unfortunately,
on acount of the war was too much exposed being frequently wet for days which brought on a return of his
old complaint (a disease of the lungs) which terminated
his existance on the 11th of December and his remains
reposes in a lovely valley Some twenty five hundred miles
from his old home and family. You can imagine but rest
ashured that I am unable to discribe to you my feelings
at his death. To meet death at home serounded by Wife
family, and friends is at all times a Solemn thing. But to
see it in reality you must be Seperated far from family
and friends be Serounded by Dells and bleak barren
mountains your ondly music the Srill Sound of the bugel
or war trumpet with the wickedness and confusion of a
camp around You and the person deprived of all most
every nessery cumfort And this O this is death in deed.[67]

On my return home I Suplyed myself with Seven
Mules with packs and all things nessery and in company
with Seven others we Started for home on the 2th of
June. On the fifth day we crosed the peak of the California mountain and had to travel about thirty five miles
over Snow varying from five to twenty foot deep and rode
over numerous mountain Streams on arches of Snow
whilst we could hear the water running and dashing under
our feet. My curiosity prompted me to return a Somewhat
different road from that we went out For the war and
the death of Mr Standly prevented me going to Oregon.
So I returned by the way of the great Salt lake runing
South of it and not far from the Utah lake.[68] And with
a few exceptions a more dry Sandy and barren county
doze not (in my opinion) exist on Gods footstool. Ex-
ceptng the great african desert. The intire county having a Streaking and volcanic apearance and aboundng

with hot and even boiling Springs. And if the different parts of our continent is cursed in proportion to the Sins of the inhabitants that formerly dwelt on them Then indeed must those ancient inhabitants have been awfully wicked for this is truly a land that the Lord has cursed. On one ocasion we traveled over a vast Sandy and Salt plane a distance of at least Seventy five miles without either grass or water and lost four head of horses that perished for want of water. We was 22 houers constantly travelng before we got to water And when we did arive at a Spring the great Salt lake lay off in full view having a number of high rocky barren Isilands all through it.[69] But close aroud the lake between the beach and high mountains that Seroud it is considerable of rich land with abundance of good Spring water and occasionally Salt Spings But even here the country is nearly destitute of timber ondly here and thair a patch of willow and cotten wood on the Streams and a little ceeder and pine on the mountains aroud. And the fourth and fifth of July I Seen these mountains white in places with Snow close aroud the lake. But mountain traders have wintered thair animals here on the grass and rushes and I Seen at a trading post a Small garden where the vegetables looked well but had to be watered and I think by airagation wheat could be raised here.[70]

About Seventy five miles this Side the Lake on the 11th of July we met 83 waggons being an advance party of the Mormons on thair way to the lake intending (as they informed us to Sow Buckwheat and establish a coleny aroud this and the Uataw Lake intending to Sow a large quantity of wheat. The having all kinds of Seeds with them together with implements of husbandry. The party numbered about two hundred men with Eight or ten females.[71] The informed us that thair was about Six hundred more waggons on thair way from the Councill Bluffs that expected to reach these Lakes and thair Spend the winter and in the Spring Such as could not be Suited here would proceed on to California proper.[72] On the 30th we

Seen Severel hundred waggons belonging to the last mentioned people but as thay was traveling up the north Side of Platt river and we down the South with a wide river having quick Sand in its bed between us. We of course had no conversation with them. But this I know that they will be compeld to winter at the lake no odds how much they may dislike the country as when I Seen them on platt they had yet Six hundred miles to travel before they would reach the lake and nine hundred miles from the Lake to the valley of California. So that before they could [*Here the extant letter breaks off.*]

"Antelope"

Diary of Nicholas Carriger

Nicholas Carriger provides the best possible introduction to his diary, with an autobiography written for H. H. Bancroft in 1874 and some biographical information furnished for the *History of Sonoma County* published at San Francisco by Alley, Bowen & Co. in 1880. He was born March 30, 1816, on the Walnut Grove farm in Carter County, Tennessee. After being educated in the town of Elizabeth, on June 26, 1835, he enlisted in the First Tennessee Mounted Volunteers for a year's service. Most of the regiment was engaged in the Seminole War, but he himself was stationed the greater part of the time on "the ground occupied by the Charekee nation."

After receiving his honorable discharge, Carriger returned home to engage in milling and distilling, then was associated with his father in manufacturing iron and hardware. In November, 1840, he emigrated to Warren

County, Missouri, but soon moved to Jackson County. After a year in that quarter, Carriger moved to St. Joseph, or Robidoux Landing, as it was then called, then settled in Holt County. But this was "a place too gloomy for my taste; therefore I left without delay and settled definitively in Andrew county Miss. where I purchased *one hundred and Sixty acres of land.* I fenced my land, built a house upon it; and when I had already cleared many an acre; the rumor of the fertility of California, brought on the wings of fame, made me feel displeased with my farm; and without consulting with any person; I sold it to a broker for the paltry sum of *five hundred* Dollars, less than the amount I had invested in lumber for my house—"

In later life Carriger remembered that he had set out for California, but his diary is titled, "Journal of an Orrigon Trip," which indicates that he had another destination in mind on leaving Missouri. The 1880 sketch says that he had been occupied in cultivating hemp, tobacco, and cereals, but on April 27, 1846, "started from Round Prairie for California, and was joined at Oregon City, Holt county, by Captain Grieg, their number being further augmented on the journey by the addition of Major Cooper, the Indian agent at Council Bluffs." The 1874 autobiography relates: "Having sold my house on the 24th of April 1846 on the 27th day of same month I started for California, crossed the Missouri river at Thompson and Hayman's ferry, the last settlement of the white people the other side of the Rocky Mountains; myself and party employed ten days in crossing over our wagons and stock—Our little party left Missouri under command of Captn Gregg, but we were afterwards joined by a large party under command of major Steven [Stephen] Cooper, (afterwards one of the framers of the constitution of the state of California) . . ."

On September 29, 1842, in Andrew County, Carriger had married Mary Ann Wardlow, a native of Highland County, Ohio, and they had two young children, one born in July, 1843, the other in January, 1845; a third would be born along the way. Also members of the overland party were his father, Christian Carriger, and his mother, his brother-in-law, John Lewis, and others. A list of "Names" preserved with Carriger's diary presumably lists the male adults of the party: Samuel Davis, Samuel Cook, John B. Davis, Redwood Easton, Frederick De Rooche, Mahlon Brock, Joseph Davis, Isaac Wilson, William Taylor, Abijah Carey, [   ] Milburn, Christian Carriger, Daniel Carriger, David W. Cook, Nicholas Carriger, Thomas Spriggs, Joseph O'Donnell, John Lewis, John L. Tanner, Burlington Acres, Ezekiel Stewart, Charles Stewart, and Joseph Wardlow.

As is brought out in the Notes, Carriger records travel by a somewhat different route from the Missouri River to the head of Grand Island on the Platte—the general route, in fact, which came to be known a year or two afterward as the "Old Fort Kearny" road. If this route had been used by emigrants prior to 1846, no records have come to light, which makes the Carriger diary so much the more interesting. The road was used by many from 1849, but in 1846 wagons may have been attempting it for the first time.

In his autobiography Carriger writes: "in company with Cooper and his party we passed the Pawnees villages, where fifty Pawnees chiefs, mounted on splendid horses came forward to meet us, and had a long talk with Captn Gregg and major Cooper; the words that passed between our chiefs and Pawnees warriors I cannot repeat, for while the talk was taking place, I was standing by my team talking to my young wife. This much however I know, that on the ending of the conference, major Cooper gave Pawnees chiefs several presents of dry goods and a fat steer which the indians killed on the spot, and eat after broiling it over the fire—After travelling several days, one of our party, a brother in law of mine, lost three of his oxens and in the morning could not resume his march at the bidding of major Cooper; who devoid of humane feel-

ings, started, leaving Mr Lewis behind; however Lewis
was not left alltogether alone, for nine wagons stood by
him, and with the assistance of his friends was enabled to
rig his team and keep on travelling; as Lewis and his
friends travelled faster that [than] the party under major
Cooper we overtook him again at Soda Sp[r]ings, and
travelled in his company until we reached fort Hall—We
crossed Mary's river (now Humboldt) which at that season was entirely dry, and water was to be had only in deep
pools—at the sink of Mary's river the digger Indians
drove away six of our oxen; we immediatly the loss was
discovered, armed ourselves to the teeth and gave pursuit,
but all to no purpose, for we failed to overtake our vily
foe, and recovered only the hides of two oxen which we
found slaughtered in the reeds: while we were pursuing
the cattle thieves, some indians that had watched our movements stole three of our best horses; a loss which we felt
most seriously and regretted very sincerly.

"After the loss of our stock, with down cast countenances, we kept on travelling, keeping a sharp look out at
night, fearing another visit of the red men, who while
professing friendship towards 'melican man' is still more
friendly to his goods and chattels which he never hesitated
to appropriate to his own use whenever he could do so
without incurring the risk of being detected.

"After a week of painful travelling we came to the
river Truckee, which we had to cross thirty eight times
before we arrived at the base of the eastern slope of the
Sierra Nevada—the Sierra Nevada being very steep and
our cattle very poor our pilot Mr Greenwood, who had
already informed us that we had arrived in California;
advised us to follow the counsel of our fellow traveller M^r
Judson Green, who had proposed to make a roller, and
fasten chains to the wagons, and pull them over the mountain with the help of twelve yokes of oxen: I consider it
needless to say that Mr Green's plan worked admirably,
and in a few days the whole of our party was safely placed
on top on the mountain—After climbing the steep moun-

tain we kept on travelling without meeting any accidents, till the evening of the 26th of september 1846 when I had the misfortune of loosing my father and sister in law, both having been called to their long home about at the same hour; and strange at [as] it may seem the same hour in which my respected father expired, my beloved wife gave birth to a lively little girl—may could I have exclaimed with the french poet Labure

un âme montant dans la celeste esfere
un autre on y descendit—

yet unabated by so sad a calamity I placed the dead bodies of my relatives in a wagon, handsomely decorated with black crape, and at night having reached the fords of the Yuba river I there dug two graves and consigned their beloved remains to mother earth—while I was engaged in paying the last tribute to the dead, that I held so dear, my oxen strayed and ate poisoned weed; such unheard of piece of gluttonry cost my oxen their lives, and deprived me of their services; and were it not that my cows did their work; and nobly and with a good will pulled the teams, I would have been compelled to travel on foot; but a kind and benign Providence had her eyes on me and mine, and with her assistance I reached Joh[n]son's ranch situated in Bear river; where by trading I again rigged my team; and kept on on my journey.

"After leaving Missouri I never found a stream requiring ferrying, until I reached Sacramento River, at a place now called Fremont; where, we, being then worn out and weary, stopped at a ranch belonging to William Gordon; who also owned a mill in which he ground wheat and corn by means of stones turned by hand; in justice to Mr Gordon I will here state that he treated me and my party with great kindness, did everything in his power so as to make us feel at home, and abstained from driving any hard bargains, a thing quite unusual in those days, except with the natives Californians that were always ready to extend a friendly hand to the needy emigrant—Having recruited our strength at Gordon's, we proceeded to Woolscale's

[William Wolfskill's] ranch where we got everything we paid for at a good round sum: from Woolscale's farm we went to Napa Valley where we stopped at the flour mill of Mr Yont [George Yount]; said mill was run with an over-shot wheel and turned out excellent flour, by way of remark I will observe that Mr Yont is or was an excellent man, a good citizien, kind to every body, well liked by white men and indians, and always ready to extend the hand of friendship to the new comers; in fact he was, what may be called a kind father to every poor man; from Napa we camped west of Sonoma creek—

"Shortly after camping, and while our women were preparing our evening meal, ladies Vallejo and Leese, desirous of forming our acquaintance paid us a visit, in which they displayed the liveliest interest in everything that concerned us; as neither of the ladies spoke the american tongue; and none of our party understood the Spanish lenguage; I cannot, with any degree of certainty, repeat the conversation which took place between us; yet judging by the affectionate manner in which they petted and caressed our children, and the quantity of sweet meats they gave them, I may, without fear of being contradicted, state, that, the interview was quite agreable to both parties —After camping two days in Sonoma, one fine morning, as we were about bidding adieu to our fellow travellers, (kind and affectionate friends that during four months had shared our pleasures and our sorrows, had helped us to hurrah when a stately buffalo fell under the unerring shot of Mr Lewis, and had mourned with us when the vily digger stole Brandywine, Gerry, Pike, Brindle, John, and Wash (name of our six oxen stolen from us by the digger indians at the sink of Mary's river) our journey was ended, and part we must: The men stood side by side with roeful countenances feeling kind queer at the prospective separation; while the women holding one corner of their aprons in close proximity to their eyes, wept tears of sorrow, that taken together with the loud cries of our children presented a scene of real and unfeigned voe) capitain Salvador Vallejo, in his undressed uniform came to us followed by three stalwart indians, one groaning under a heavy load of flour, one carrying a basket of sugar, and the other holding a basket of chocolate; the Capitain, by means of an interpreter asked us if we were in need of any of the articles his servants carried; and expressed his willingness and readiness to serve us to the full extent of his ability: on taking farewell from us, he added 'near by I have thousand cows, if any of you wishes fresh meat, go and kill as many animals [as] you need for your daily support' Captain Salvador Vallejo observed the same conduct towards every other emigrants camped in the vicinity of Sonoma; years have gone by since then, the then gallant captain is now a worn out old man, stricken by sorrow and grief; his many miles of pasture land have passed into strange hands; his then loving and beautiful bride miss Luz Carrillo a descendant of the noble race of the Carrillos, that have filled Peru, Mexico and California with their noble deeds, has been called to her long home, his children have married and settled in far off counties; his moveable property sold to defray the expenses of many law suits, that were decided against him, yet his dauntless spirit is unabated, even if his bodily strength has decayed; and is now living [h]is young days over again, in the person of his beautiful and intelligent niece, miss Lulu Vallejo a lively brunette of seventeen springs, daughter of General Mariano Vallejo, a girl of refined taste, that reciprocates the tender caresses of her fond uncle. . . ."

Carriger's later experiences must be passed over briefly. Lieutenant Revere persuaded him to enter into service with the U. S. Navy; for six months he carried the mails between Sonoma and San Rafael, and occasionally he was sent to the site of Benicia with other marines "to watch the movements of the Spaniards and keep them from crossing over to the north side of the bay." The Sonoma garrison, he relates, "kept up a defiant demeanor, and upheld with dignity the name of citizens of the United

States: as a proof of my assertion I will here state that a[s] soon as we heard that the Bonner [Donner] party had been frozen on the east side of the Sierra Nevada, we started to relieve the sufferers and I am most happy to record, that a few of the victims were saved [by] the arrival of our party."

He settled in Sonoma, after the discovery of gold mined successfully at Kelsey's Diggings, then with his gold dust bought a farm from General Vallejo, on which he settled in July, 1849. His farm eventually became one of the showplaces of Sonoma County, of which he in turn became one of the prominent citizens. Carriger died on June 30, 1885.

❁ ❁ ❁

THE CARRIGER DIARY

Set out from Andrew County Round prairie[1] Monday 27th April 1846 Crossed the Noddiway and strake [?] Tent

28th Travelled to Davises Creek[2]

29th reached Thompsons; Hameys Ferry[3] about 5 miles

30 rested boat not ready

May 1 rested boat not ready but brought up

2nd & 3rd got ready and Crossed one Waggon

4th & 5th Crossed 12 Waggons & Teams and 40 head loose Cattle

6th We lay at Camp fare well at the base of the bluffs waiting for the Company to Cross

7th 8th 9th & 10th Still waiting for Company

11th set out across the bluffs into the Prairie about 3 miles where we again encamped and lay by the 12th[4]

12th our numbers have increased to 31 Waggons and are still Waiting for more to Cross

13th and 14th this day Joseph Blanton died and his family went bak set out with fifty Waggons from our Camp on Honey Creek and Travelled about 12 miles to a Water of the big Ome Haw [Great Nemaha][5]

15 Travelled about 5 miles and encamped on Water of the Big Ome haw

16th travelled about 6 miles and Camped on a Water of the big Omehaw

[17th] 8 miles and Camped on big O [*this entry interlined*]

17th [18th] Traveled 20 miles & Camped [*word or two eroded from bottom of page*] travelling

May 19 [*corrected from* 18] Traveled 10 miles & Camped on the head of little Nimmihaw

20th [*corrected from* 19th] lay by on account of rain

21st travelled to [*deleted*: big Nemihaw]- a branch of the saline [Salt Creek] 8 miles

22nd Crossed by a bridge 15 miles to the head of [*deleted*: big nimihaw] of Saline[6]

23 traveled 8 miles to a branch of the blue Earth [Big Blue]

24 lay by on account of storm and rain and had two horses stolen by the Indians

[*Torn*: 25] Joined by Major Cooper[7] & Traveled 10 miles

26 Travveled 15 miles to a water of the saline

27 Travelled 12 miles to a Water of the Saline

28 Cooper separated from us and six of our Waggons With him

29 Travelled 20 miles to big platt

30 Travelled 10 miles up platt

June 1 travelled 15 miles to near the Pawney Village[8]

2 travelled 10 [?] miles

3 Cooper again joined us and passed by the Pawny Villge where we were met by about 50 Warriors who held a talk with Cooper & Gregg We travelled 10 miles and in the evening gave the Indians some triffling presents and an ox which they killed and ate[9]

4th Travelled up platt 20 miles and Cooper again left us in the evening and nine [*torn*: more?] Waggons with him this reduced our numbers to 37 Waggons on this day We overset one Waggon with a family some of which were slightly hurt and one lady fell and the Wheels run over her legs hurt her badly and had a marriage at night Parson Stewart officiating

5th This day travelled 15 miles to the Independence road[10]

6 this day travelled 9 miles one boy fell and two wheels run over one leg and the other foot and ancle nearly Cutting the leg off breaking the bone, so it injuring the other foot and Ancle and We encamped for the day

7 lay in Camp and mr [?] Ellis Cow ran away

8 Travelled this day 20 miles

9 Traveled 16 Miles and Killed one Antelope

10 Traveled 15 Miles

11 traveled 15 miles

12 Travled 12 miles found 9 Work steers and have them in the Teams and left my Bell Cow on the Road this day seven Waggons left us leaving us With 30 Wag this day we killed 2 Buffaloes

13 Traveled 12 miles

14 this Day lay in Camp and Cut off the thigh of the boy and he died in the hands of the Operator Frederic Derusha[11] were overtaken by an Oregon Company of 20 Waggons and our Company again split up and left our Company 26 Waggons strong this Company kept up the south side of River and we had [have?] heard nothing more of them since there are two Companies Close behind us and three before us not far ahead[12]

15th this day traveled 15 miles

16th this day travelled 25 miles to the Crossing of plat[13]

17th Crossed plat and travelled up the River 10 miles to where the road turns over the bluffs

18 Crossed the bluffs part of this road passes over a high table land We found the road Very heavy traveling through the sand and Bluff hills for near five miles when We reached the River in all 18 miles This day Eli Grig- gery [?] died in sight of the spring[14]

19th this day We are detained in burrying him on the

right side of the road on a bench of the bluff near a rock near four feet high at the Cedar Creek[15]

20th this day We travelled 25 Miles passed Col Russels & Boggses biag [?] Company of 40 Waggons[16] after a hard run of half a day

21 this day [Redwood] Easton's Wife died after We encamped and had Travelled 25 miles and [*torn: word or two lost*] now in sight of the Chimney

22nd We burried Mrs Easton on the West side of our encampment and north side of the road on the second bank of the river not far from Castle rock from this we Travelled 10 [18?] miles passing the Chimney Rock about 3 miles where we Camped

23rd Travelled this day 18 miles in the Valley along the scotts bluffs and encamped in 2 mile of the uper end of the Valey

24th this day We Traveled 25 miles Crossing horse Creek[17] at 14 miles Easton lost his work oxen from our encampment

25th this day stokes one of our Company broke one wheel of his Waggon near a Trading house[18] & brought it to the fort and sold the Waggon for 4 pair Moccasons and the Owners Came for the 9 Oxen and we Travelled 20 miles that was 8 miles to the fort Crossing the River at the fort[19]

26th Travelled 12 miles to bitter Water

27 Travelled 12 miles to a large Creek

28 travelled 15 miles over a bad road to a large Creek

29th [*corrected from* 30th] [*deleted*: lay by] travelled 12 miles to a large Creek

30 lay by

July 1st travelled 15 miles

2 travelled 9 miles to a Creek and Davisvisses [?] left us with 9 Waggons and we have 18 left

3 July this day We travelled 12 miles Crossing a big Creek and Camped on Platt River & Stuart left his black oxen and Campbells & Crabtrees California Company[20] We left Camped 4 miles[s] behind on the Creek

4 We reached the Crossing of platt 15 miles and found three Companies encamped above us[21]

5 We Crossed the river and traveled 6 miles passing the three Companies

6th We traveled 12 miles to the muddy Spring and three Companies passed us at the Spring[22]

7 We travelled to the Willow Spring 15 miles

8 We travelled to the Sweet Water near Independance Rock 18 miles

9 We travelled 18 miles up sweet Water.

10th We travelled 18 miles over a sandy road up sweet Water

11th We travelled 18 miles up sweet Water

12th We travelled 7 miles up sweet Water

13th we travelled 20 Crossing sweet Water

14 We travelled 20 miles Crossing a mountain to a Creek of sweet water[23]

15 we travelled [*deleted*: 7] 6 miles to Sweetwater

16 We travelled 20 miles Crossing the divide to a dry Creek of sandy[24]

17 We travelled 15 miles Crossing little sandy at 8 miles thence to Big Sandy 7 miles

July 18th We lay by preparing to Crossing the Cut off to Green river a distance of 40 miles Without Wood or Water[25] set out on the Journey at 3 A m and landed on Green River the distance aforesaid at 3 O'clock of the 19th it being 24 hours drive

20th We Travelled 8 miles down Green River over a Very bad road to black Creek[26]

21 from thence 17 miles Crossing a mountain to a small Creek[27]

22 from thence across a mountain spur 6 miles to a large Creek[28]

from thence 23rd 19 [9?] miles to a small stream Crossing a Very bad mountain[29]

24 [*corrected from* 23rd] from thence 8 miles Crossing a mountain to Bear river [*deleted*: 25 thence 4 miles to bear]

25 [*corrected from* 26] from thence 12 miles to a trad-ing house on bear River near a large Creek[30]

26th [*corrected from* 27] from thence down the river 17 miles to a Creek in a Valley passing a Trading house on the river[31]

27th [*corrected from* 28] thence up [down] the Valley and Crossing a spur of the mountain 20 miles to the river[32]

28th To the soda springs 6 miles

29th To a Creek in the Valley 7 [?] miles[33]

30th from thence 15 miles Crossing a mountain to a Creek in a Valley[34] and lost Jerry one of my steers & Wardlaw lost one of his

31st from thence down the Valley 10 miles on a Creek and Camped by ourselves[35]

August 1st from thence down the Valley 15 miles passing Fort Hall to a sulphur spring[36]

2nd from thence down the plains 6 miles to Lewises [Snake] River

3 & 4th We rested at the river

5 from thence 6 miles Crossing the River to a lake [slough]

6th from thence down Snake River 14 miles to a small Creek

7th from thence 10 miles over a Very bad road Cross-ing 2 Creeks to the river

8th from thence up the [*deleted*: Creek] Crossing the Cassia Creek 10 [?] miles to the Creek a very good road[37]

9th from thence 15 miles up the Creek a very good Road to the Creek again

10th from thence up and across the Creek 15 miles to a Very good spring and good road[38]

11th from thence up the Creek Crossing a divide to another Creek 12 miles near some warm springs[39] a good road

12th from thence 18 miles Crossing 3 divides to a small Creek a branch of Goose Creek[40] bad road

August 13th from thence Crossing the divide to Goose Creek 10 miles[41] a good road

14th from thence up Goose Creek 15 miles this day John Lewises son William Died and We buried him in the road near the Creek[42]

15th from thence up the Creek and Crossing a Very rough divide of Iron Ore & stone 25 miles to a Cold spring in a Valley[43]

16th from thence up the Valley Crossing a divide to the horse spring[44] 13 miles a good road

17th from thence up the Valley passing the hot springs at 10 miles these are situated in a beautiful Valley 40 miles long and from 3 to five Wide and near the head of the Valley[45] in all this day 18 miles

18th Crossing a divide into a Valley on a Creek a water of St. Marys river[46] 10 miles

19th Down the Creek Crossing it 9 times and passing through a gorge of the mountain a very rough road passing some hot springs 6 miles to a good spring[47]

20th from thence down the Creek a good road 16 miles to where the Creek was dry[48]

21st from thence down the Creek 15 miles a good road but Very dusty & frost for three mornings

22nd from thence down the St Marys Crossing 2 ridges and the sal a ratus fork 17 miles[49] this morning John [*deleted*: Lewises] Chisman son [*deleted*: William] Martin died of [*deleted*: Worms or Croop] and we buried him in the road at the foot of the second ridge on the west side of the saint Marys[50] a dusty road

23rd from thence down the river 17 miles Crossing the river[51] road Very Dusty

24 from thence down the river 10 miles

25th from thence across the mountain 20 miles a Very rough road[52]

26th from thence down the river 12 miles Very Dusty road and passed part of Van der pools Company[53] they have three in Camps sick and not expected to live they also informed us of Beechams death who had been one of Greggs Company and passed on in his pack Company till his death[54]

27th from thence down the river 8 miles

28th from thence down the river 16 miles

29th from thence down the river 8 miles

August 30 from thence down the river 12 miles a good road

31st from thence down the river and over a Very bad ridge 18 miles—[55]

Sept 1 from thence down the river 16 miles passing some hot springs that were near the Camp[56]

2nd from thence down the river and over a Very bad sand hill 18 miles passing Scotts and Dearborns battle Ground with the diggers[57]

3rd frome thence Down the river 16 miles

4th from thence down the river 12 miles to the forks of the road[58] & from thence Down the river 8 miles in all 20

5th from thence down the river over a [*deleted*: high] Table land heavy road 15 miles

6 from thence down the river 10 miles

7th from thence Down the river a sandy road to near the lake[59] 14 miles

8th from thence to the Sinks 16 miles a sandy road here the Indians drove off 6 head of our Work Oxen and We gave Chaes and found two of them Killed in a reed & rush patch and suppose the rest were used like wise[60]

9th from thence We set out at one O Cl over a sandy route 20 miles to the boiling springs at 2 O'Clock from thence 20 miles to Truckeys river 8 miles Very heavy sand no grass or good water

10th We reached the river in the evening our Work Cattle much tired and several gave out from fatigue Hunger and thirst and We lost three horses in the night through Carelessness of the drivers[61]

11th we lay on the banks of the rivers to rest ourselves & recruit our Cattle [*deleted*: after C] Crossing the [desert]

12 thence up the river crossing the river 5 times [in] 13 miles a sandy road

13th　thence up the river 8 miles Crossing it 6 times this day a Very rough road

14th　lay by on account of the sickness of Mrs. Wardlaw

15th　thence up the river 8 miles Crossing it 6 times a Very rough road.

16th　thence up the river 9 miles　this morning Mrs. Wardlaw had a son born who died in a few minutes after birth[62] We Crossed the river 4 times and had a Very bad road

17　thence Crossing the river 4 times then up the river 16 miles　verry bad road

18　thence crossing the river and mountain 16 miles to wind river[63]

19　thence to John Greenwoods Creek[64] 9 miles　verry good road

20　crossing a small hill thence a goo[d] [road] to the foot of the mountain 12 miles[65]

21　up the mountain distressing bad 8 miles to the foot of the high California mountain and got 8 waggons

22　we we made a roller and fasened chans to gether and pulled [?] the wagons up withe 12 yoke oxen on the top and the same at the bottom[66]

23　halling wag[on]s

24　we traviled 8 miles to the lake[67] distrissing bad road

25　laid by

26　Christain Carriger died of Slow fever　on the same day Joseph wordlaws wife died　the same day[68]

"Crossing the Platte"

Diary of Virgil Pringle

Through the diaries of William E. Taylor and Nicholas Carriger we have shared the experiences of those who chose northerly points of departure from the Missouri River. Now, with the diary of Virgil K. Pringle, we turn farther south to observe the earliest departures from the Independence area.

The Oregon-bound emigrants, of whom Pringle was one, have had much less attention than those with California as their destination, except as J. Quinn Thornton has laid siege to scholars. Thornton traveled with one of the rearmost Oregon companies, most of the time in rather close proximity to the company in which the Donner Party traveled. Virgil Pringle's diary is consequently all the more welcome in documenting the experiences of those who were ahead of Thornton on the trail. Like Thornton,

159

he took the new Applegate Cutoff, giving us a vivid picture of the hardships of those who traveled that route.

An account of Pringle, based upon information from his daughter, Ella Pringle Young, is published in Sarah Hunt Steeves, *Book of Remembrance of Marion County, Oregon, Pioneers 1840-1860,* (Portland, 1927) accompanied by the reminiscences of his youngest son, Octavius, "An Immigrant Boy in 1846-47." (These reminiscences have been separately published in O. M. Pringle, *Magic River Deschutes,* n. p., n. d.) Further information about the experiences of the family is provided by a letter written in August, 1854, by Pringle's mother-in-law, Mrs. Tabitha Brown, as cited hereafter in the Notes.

From these various sources we learn that Virgil K. Pringle was the son of Norman and Sarah (Kellogg) Pringle, born at Harrington, Connecticut, in 1804. In 1825 the family moved to Missouri, engaging in business at St. Charles, establishing a library, and starting a literary society—incidental facts which help to explain the literacy and fluency of Pringle's diary. In 1827 Pringle married Phernie (or Phernia, or Pherne) Tabitha Brown, daughter of Rev. Clark Brown, and they had six children who accompanied them to Oregon—Virgilia, Clark, Alero, Sarelia, Emma, and Octavius. Mrs. Pringle's brother, Orus Brown, had been a member of the Great Migration to Oregon in 1843, so pleased with the country that he returned in 1845 to persuade the rest of the family to migrate to the Willamette Valley, whence he was taking his own wife and eight children.

So eloquent was Orus Brown, that in April, 1846, the Pringle family left their farm, "Hickory Grove," near St. Charles to seek out this healthy land beyond the Rocky Mountains. With them went the indomitable Mrs. Tabitha Brown, then 66 years old, who as she says "provided for myself a good ox wagon-team,[and] a good supply of what was requisite for the comfort of myself, Captain Brown [John Brown, her aged brother-in-law] and my driver. Uncle John insisted on coming, and crossed the plains on horseback." Pringle's nephew, Charles Fullerton, also made one of the company. Octavius Pringle remembered many years later that the company numbered 16 wagons on setting out, but he may have been thinking of the total after crossing the Big Blue River of Kansas.

Since Pringle himself describes the journey across Missouri—the only daily record we have of a land passage by emigrants across the State this year, little need be said of the first stage of the trek. The Pringle company scarcely paused on reaching Independence May 7, launching out immediately into the prairies beyond. Pringle does not mention the emigration as a whole until reaching the Wakarusa River on May 11, but he was probably not out of sight of other wagons after crossing the Missouri line into Indian territory.

He performs his first signal service to history in saying on May 11 that he "came into Carel with the whole emigration in sight," adding immediately, "Divided into two parties. Our party organized with William Keithly for Captain, and O. Brown for pilot for both parties. The other party chose a Mr. Robinson from Illinois for Captain." The two divisions evidently consisted of about 20 wagons each. Robinson is more fully identified hereafter, but except for Pringle we would not have known of his special place in the 1846 emigration. His company stayed ahead the whole distance, and reached the Willamette Valley via the Barlow Road in September, Orus Brown remaining with this division.

We are further indebted to Pringle for identifying William Keithly. Francis Parkman encountered the man on May 24, shortly after the erstwhile captain separated from Pringle; patently uncertain how to write his name, Parkman rendered it Keatley, Kearsley, Keathley, and Keathly in his trail diary, and standardized it as Kearsley in his *California and Oregon Trail*. Pringle and Parkman unite in bringing out the circumstances under which Keithly threw up his command, as we shall see.

On leaving the Big Blue, the truncated Pringle company traveled in proximity to another company of 13 wagons, probably the Dickenson-Gordon party discussed on a later page; and at the crossing of the South Platte they fell in with Elam Brown's unlucky company. Near Courthouse Rock on June 18 Pringle writes, "Divided our company into three parties for the greater convenience of traveling," but how many then comprised the company is not stated. Octavius Pringle recalled long afterward that the company along the way was enlarged from an initial 16 to 69 wagons, "manned by one hundred and fifty men," and it may be that he was remembering the total at the time of this division on June 18. Virgil Pringle himself provides no more information on the composition of the company until after entering upon the Applegate Cutoff; we might infer from his remark of September 29 that the Pringle company numbered 31 wagons.

Pringle overtook the earliest emigrants who attempted the Applegate Cutoff and became one of these at the forefront of the emigration on this new southern road, which adds much to the interest and value of his diary. After reaching Oregon, he took up land near Stayton, but later settled just south of Salem, on what became known as Pringle Creek. His son Clark participated in the Cayuse War and eventually married Catherine Sagers, one of the survivors of the Whitman Massacre. The remarkable Tabitha Brown settled at Forest Grove and became one of the principal founders of the educational institution ultimately named Pacific University. It is related by Sarah Hunt Steeves that "Mr. and Mrs. Pringle lived to a ripe old age and died at their home near Salem [shortly after celebrating] their sixtieth wedding anniversary, surrounded by children, grandchildren and great-grand-children."

THE PRINGLE DIARY

Wednesday, April 15, 1846—Left Hickory Grove [farm] this day with my family for Oregon. Went seven miles. Stopped for more company[1]— 7 —

Thursday, April 16—Absalom Faulkner and Jas. Brown and their families joined us and we went ahead 17 miles to J. Wheeler's. Parted this day with Octavius, having bid adieu to my other brothers and sisters the day before. Went along well, teams and everything doing to my satisfaction.

Friday, April 17—Went this day 15 miles. Virgilia [Pringle] has the ague. We gave her Champion pills. The rest all well.

Saturday, April 18—All well. Made 18 miles and camped on Harrison's branch of Auvaux.[2] All things in good order and agreeable.

Sunday, April 19—Travel 12 miles. Well pleased with teams and company. Three families from Georgia overtook us. They left their homes on the 10th of March. Camped at the house of Mr. Schock, Audrain County, Grand Prairie,[3] on Harrison's branch of Auvaux. All well and teams first rate and everything agreeable.

Sunday, April 19 [4] —Went 12 miles and camped. Well pleased with teams and company. This day 3 families from Georgia overtook us on their way to Oregon; they started 10th March from home. Camped in Audrain County at the house of Mr. Schock in Grand Prairie.

Monday, April 20. Started in fine season and traveled on fine road generally on Grand Prairie. Went 20 miles and camped at a Mr. Palmer's near Grand Prairie, Boons's Lick.[5] Teams and all things in good order. Find our cows a great help to our living. 20 miles.

Tuesday, April 21—This day went 18 miles over good road generally on Grand Prairie and camped at Mr. Austin's in Randolph County. Well pleased with wagons and teams. Weather good so far and health of all improving with the exception of Mrs. Brown who complains with a bad cold. This evening Clark [Pringle] shot a gr— and pheasant.

Wednesday, April 22—Passed this day through Huntsville, county seat of Randolph. Traveled 13 miles and encamped near the line of Chariton. Detained by Brown and Faulkner buying more stock. Roads good and all things in fine order. 13 miles.

Thursday, April 23—Traveled 14 miles over a fine farming country. The land good but too many lakes for health, and camped two miles from Chariton River; roads good but travel slow. 14 miles.

Friday, April 24—Crossed the Chariton this morning, found the bottom very muddy, but [*i.e.* had?] difficulty in getting through, the river having been off bottom but a few days. Passed through Keytesville, the county seat of Chariton County, a location similar to Cotterville[6] on the Muscle fork of Chariton [Muscle Creek]. Went 14 miles and camped 1½ miles from Brunswick. 14 miles.

Saturday, April 25—Passed through Brunswick on Missouri River near the junction of Grand River, a place of considerable business, located on bottom land. Crossed Grand River at Crosses ferry.[7] Paid the extravagant price of $2.50 for two teams and 5 head of loose stock. Traveled 13 miles and camped 11 miles from Carrolton. All in good health, roads in good order over a rich country thinly settled but low and of unhealthy appearance. 13 miles—161 miles.

Sunday, April 26—Left encampment in good season, passed through Carrolton, located on Wakendah Creek and traveled up Moss Creek, a branch of the Wakendah running through Wakendah prairie, which is Missouri bottom, and was the greatest curiosity we had met, there being a mill about two miles from timber, and propelled by a stream running through level prairie and not a stick of timber on its banks. Went 9 miles on the prairie and camped 2 miles from Pilot Grove on the banks of Moss Creek without any wood but drift we found on the prairie that was left by the flood of 1844.[8] 20 miles. 181.

Monday, April 27—Last night had a thunder storm and continued to rain this morning. Left camp in the rain, the first we had since we started. Tried our new recents [*i.e.* recruits?] but they stood it well. Went 16 miles and crossed Crooked River and camped on wet ground. Rained all night in Ray County. 16 miles.

Tuesday, April 28—Left our muddy camp as soon as possible and made sail for Camden. Cool and cloudy. Roads good. Passed Camden in the evening and arrived at Manthano Brown's,[9] having traveled 13 miles. All well and teams in good order. Broke the tongue of the first wagon I bought, about a hundred yards from Brown's house.

Wednesday, April 29, 30 and 1st of May—Remained at M. Brown's and put new tongues in both wagons and made two new yoke and employed ourselves at other arrangements for our trip.

Saturday, May 2—Left M. Brown's and went about 6 miles and encamped in Missouri bottom about one mile from the ferry. 6 miles.

Sunday, May 3—Came to the ferry soon in the morning and found the crossing slow.[10] Occupied the day in getting our wagons across. The day showery. Encamped at a vacant house on the south bank.

Monday, May 4—Completed ferrying our stock and went 3 miles and camped in Jackson County. Make slow headway. Got my bacon this day for which I paid $3.75 per hundred. Fine country of land. All well. No loss of property. 3—219 miles.

Tuesday, May 5—Got under headway for Blue Mills.[11] Went ahead with my wagons and commenced loading in my flour for which I pay $2.00 for S[uper]. fine and $1.75 for fine. The first accident happened this day that has befallen us on our trip. The wagon in which Mrs. James Brown and family were, was overturned and Mrs. B. badly hurt and one of the children slightly. The oxen taking fright by a drove of mules. All much alarmed for Mrs. Brown. 12 miles.

Wednesday, May 6—Laid by this day on account of Mrs. Brown. Completed taking in our flour. The weather still showery. The Blue Mills the best water mills I have seen in the state. Make flour that passes the Boston market, to which place they often freight. 231 miles.

Thursday, May 7 (1846)—Set sail for Independence, 8 miles from our encampment, at which place we arrived at 2 o'clock. Finished our outfit and encamped 4 miles beyond Independence. All things in good order, our teams doing well and not overloaded. 12 miles.

Friday, May 8—This day the weather was fine, the first for nearly a week. Went 12 miles to the Blue[12] and encamped, it being too high to cross. Another wagon capsized at the encampment, a family from Pennsylvania. No injury to persons or property. The country today is very different from any I have ever seen, it being prairie, quite rolling or broken, and rocks in ledges. The soil good, interspersed with springs and patches of small timber. 12—255 miles.

Saturday, May 9—This day the weather fine. Crossed the Blue soon in the morning. Went 16 miles over prairie, that is rich and beautiful but no timber or water, and encamped at the lone tree,[13] no wood but green willows such as are common on prairie branches. Made better fire for cooking than we expected. Plenty of branch water. 16 miles.

Sunday, May 10—Fine weather. Went about 9 miles and dined. Then left the Santa Fe road,[14] traveled about six miles over beautiful prairie and camped on a fine branch of running water, with its banks well wooded with oak, walnut, Linn and ash, timber generally scarce. 15 miles.

Monday, May 11—Rolled about 10 miles to the Wakarusa, a fine stream of clear water, between a creek and a river in size with fine timber on its banks.[15] About half of the emigration missed the road and crossed about 4 miles above. Traveled about six miles in the evening and came into Carel with the whole emigration in sight. Divided into two parties. Our party organized with William Keithly for Captain, and O. Brown for pilot for both parties. The other party chose a Mr. [John] Robinson from Illinois for captain.[16] Our encampment to right on a high ridge of prairie. 16 miles.

Tuesday, May 12—This day lost some cattle. Delayed some time to find them. Traveled only 9 miles and on same prairie as last night. 9 miles.

Wednesday, May 13—A fine, cool day. Traveled 20 miles to Kanzas and camped on prairie near its banks. A shower in the evening and night. Cool. Saw Indians plenty about. 20—309 miles.

Thursday, May 14—The foremost [Robinson's] company crossed the Kanzas and a part of the other, myself of the number, and encamped on the bank for the night.

Friday, May 15—The remainder of the company crossed the ferry, which consists of two flat boats owned by a Shawnee Indian whose name is Fish.[17] Went 4 miles and encamped. 4 miles.

Saturday, May 16—A fine day and a good road the most of the way. In the evening crossed a creek with very steep banks; had to double teams, which delayed much time.[18] Rolled 16 miles. 339 miles.

Sunday, May 17—Our course this day was on hills running parallel with the Kanzas. The morning cool. Drove ahead till after two o'clock, it became very hot. Several oxen overcome with the heat. Stopped about three hours on a branch at the edge of the Kanzas bottom. Country still very fertile and handsome, timber scarce. Encamped this night near a Caw Village.[19] Mr. Barnard while on guard caught one attempting to steal our stock. Made, by our reckoning, 20 miles—20.

Monday, May 18—Delayed this day crossing creeks and branches, traveled about ten miles over broken prairie and encamped on a handsome branch with some cottonwood and elm. 10—369 miles.

Tuesday, May 19—Traveled over broken prairie and made good progress, passed some branches, but generally on the high lands between Kanzas and the Blue. The land generally good with plenty of rocks and springs. Camped at the branch where White and Brown ate their turkey.[20] Make 18 miles. This night Mr. and Mrs. Brown came up, the first of our seeing them since Mrs. B. was hurt [on May 5]. A shower this night. 18 miles.

Wednesday, May 20—Pushed ahead for Blue River, the foremost of the caravan reached in time to cross; found it rising fast. 20 wagons crossed, the remainder detained by the water Thursday and Friday, which was much to our advantage, our teams recruiting, more overhauling provisions and fine. 15—402 miles.

Saturday, May 23—Occupied this day in crossing the Blue River by fording; raised our wagons by placing blocks between the beds and bolsters and went over dry. Camped on a beautiful spring branch on the right bank of the river. A child born in the camp this night, it being an addition to the family of Aaron Richardson. This is the most beautiful and convenient spot for a farm I have seen. Our company burst asunder this day, leaving 27 with us, the captain and others taking the lead, the sickness of Mrs. Richardson and the detention being the cause.[21]

Sunday, May 24—Traveled this day 12 miles and camped on a handsome branch. Found 8 of our runaway wagons waiting to join us. Three went ahead, viz., Keithly and Barnard with a company of hunters, ten in number. Price and four families from Illinois going, they knew not how but headway was the word.[22]

Monday, May 25—Our course today was over the highlands between the [Big] Blue and Blue Earth [Little Blue] rivers. Road good. About 3 o'clock the most violent hurricane overtook us I ever experienced. The wind blew from every point of the compass with utmost violence but principally from the southwest, and the rain fell in torrents. Its severity was such as to blind a man and take his breath to face the storm. It continued about 45 miles [sic] when it abated and every prairie branch was a river. Went 12 miles and camped. Everything in our wagons appeared wet. Went to bed tonight in wet beds. 12 miles.

Tuesday, May 26—Examined our wagons and put our clothing to dry. Find our provisions generally dry and in good order and but little damaged by the storm. A fine day for the purpose; spent the day in drying and repairs. In the evening a company of 13 wagons overtook us.[23]

Wednesday, May 27—Left camp about 8 o'clock, made about 12 miles headway and camped on a high prairie. Hauled wood about half mile. Grass good—day showery. In sight of our new company all day and at camp. 12—438 miles.

Thursday, May 28—Made sail at 8 o'clock and traveled about 8 miles over broken country to noon. Passed a stream with a sandy bed. The country more sandy. In the evening more level than for some days. Crossed and camped on another sandy stream 8 miles from place of dinner. 16 miles.

Friday, May 29—Left camp at 9 o'clock, not finding teams to start sooner. Arrived at another sandy stream at 12 o'clock and dined. Find the country less rolling and the sand increasing. Arrived at the Blue Earth [Little Blue] River at six and encamped on its banks. Find the river up and over the low bottoms. This stream is generally known as the Republican Fork.[24] Traveled 15 miles. The health of all generally good. Charles [Fullerton] complains of bowel complaint and some others of our company. 15—469 miles.

Saturday, May 30—469. A fine day for our teams and road good. Traveled 18 miles. Begin to find some antelope and elk and other game. The country still good but more sandy and thin soil than before. Grass short but good quality and more level country, the uplands being but little above the bottoms. 18 miles.

Sunday, May 31—A cold, unpleasant morning and very cold rain in the evening, cold enough for November with high wind from N. E. Traveled 10 miles. Our course up Blue with sometimes over the high lands but generally on the bottoms. 10 miles.

Monday, June 1—Continued our course up the river, a cold, disagreeable day. Showers in the evening with hard and high wind. 15—512 miles.

Tuesday, June 2—A fine day for travel. Leave the Blue Earth early in the day and shape our course for the Platte, over ridges of level land of slight elevation. Travel 15 miles and camp without wood. Antelope been in sight for two or three days, the first one killed today. 15 miles.

Wednesday, June 3—The weather disagreeably cool. Started in fine season and came in sight of the sand hills of Platte in about 3 miles and arrived on the borders of the bottom about ten o'clock.[25] This is the most romantic view I have ever seen. Make 18 miles and encamped by some willows on the banks, the sluice [sloughs?] of Grand Island. Mr. Shelton, from Franklin, had a daughter [die] in this night from a swelling on her throat occasioned by the scarlet fever before they left the State, having lost another child since they left home, which they buried in Jackson County.

Thursday, June 4—The weather still cold and disagreeable. Went ahead till 12 o'clock and made preparation to bury Mr. Shelton's child, which was done in a decent manner considering the circumstances, in an elevation of the prairie bottom near the head of Grand Island. Camped this night on the bank of the river which looks very majestic, but in fact is nothing but a broad vale of sand with banks about 3 feet high, which are full at high water and the sand dry in a dry time. There is now just water enough to barely cover the bars, leaving them sometimes in sight. 14—559 miles.

Friday, June 5—The morning cool but the day pleasant for traveling and the roads of the best order, being level bottom and firm. Met two Pawnee Indians returning to the north from a hunt, their horses heavy packed with skins. Understand from them that about 30 lodges are a short distance ahead coming down the river, and that we will find buffalo plenty in two days. Made 16 miles and camped with plenty of timber. Antelope plenty. 16 miles.

Saturday, June 6—A fine, pleasant day. Pass thirteen boats for St. Louis from Fort Laramie, all loaded with peltry and furs.[26] They draw about a foot of water and seldom float clear. Made 20 miles this day. 20—595 miles.

Sunday, June 7—A fine day for travel. The scenery of the country very similar since we came on the river, although there is enough of change to render it agreeable. The breadth of the river, the numerous islands and the variety of shape in the sand hills all keep the mind relieved from sameness. Buffalo sign is now plenty and we see occasionally a dead one in the bottom, but they are all on the highland plains beyond the sand hills at this season. In the fall they come in the bottom for water. The appearance of their range is like an old field closely grazed. Have seen some dog-towns for the last few days.[27] Made 17 miles. Use buffalo chips for wood. 17—612 miles.

Monday, June 8—A good day and cool. The sand hills, the most romantic of any day yet, rising into high, irregular peaks, resembling majestic snow drifts in form. Camped near the junction of the two forks, traveling 22 miles—22.

Tuesday, June 9—Another pleasant day and a great day for hunters. Buffalo plenty, two being killed and several wounded and prairie dogs and antelopes also plenty. The appearance of the country different, the sand hills disappearing on this side of the river, and the highlands but slightly rolling and the elevation but little above the bottom. Made this day 18 miles—18.

Wednesday, June 10—The weather fine for traveling but too cool for farming. The country destitute of timber. Water plenty but not good, it being in standing pools and warm and bad tasting, the alkaline efflorescence plenty, intermixed with saltpeter. Buffalo in sight almost constantly. Traveled 20 miles and camped near the hills which are still low, by some standing ponds of water, warm and bad tasting. 20 miles.

Thursday, June 11—This morning bids fair to be a hot, sultry day, but the wind raised from southeast and rendered it very pleasant. Went in sight of the ford for dinner. After dinner went on to the ford and found ourselves too late to cross and camped on the right bank. Found a company of thirty-three wagons from St. Joseph on the other bank, having been there a week hunting cattle, a hundred head strayed from them last Thursday.[28] 13—685 miles.

Friday, June 12—Crossed the river in the morning. Found the water in no place over our forward axle, seldom that deep; the pulling hard through the sand; put double teams to our wagons; the difficulty nothing compared to the appearance. The distance with the angle we took being about one and a half miles. Traveled up the south fork to the place of leaving for the N. fork, it being 12 miles.[29] The day fine, wind from the east. 12 miles.

Saturday, June 13.—Our encampment last night was with the company that lost stock and our travel today with them, which was all the chance excepting laying by, there being no chance for water till we arrived at the mouth of Ash Hollow on the north fork. The road down Ash Creek bad for three or four miles. Arrived at the north fork at 7 o'clock. Found currants and choke-cherries plenty, and a fine spring near the mouth of Ash Creek, and a cabin called Ash Grove Hotel. Inside at the bar we found the cards of all the companies that had preceded us, which was quite a treat.[30] The distance from one fork to the other 15 miles. Day fine. Road dry and dusty. 15 miles.

Sunday, June 14—Left Ash Hollow and traveled up the river about ten miles and camped early, the day being warm. The hills on the fork are more rugged and rocky than any we have seen 10 miles.

Monday, June 15—This and yesterday were very warm days; proceeded on our journey 15 miles. The country poor and sandy and has the appearance of being formed by the wind blowing out the sand in basins, some of which are forty feet deep. Camped on the river. Feed good. 15 miles.

Tuesday, June 16—Laid by to recruit.

Wednesday, June 17—This also another warm day. Proceeded ahead 15 miles. The sand not as heavy for our teams as the two last. No other alteration in the country. Camped at a fine spring. A thunder shower after sunset. 15 miles.

Thursday, June 18—The day pleasantly cool. Visited Parker's castle, a most beautiful location on the meadows of a tributary of Platte.[31] The castle bearing strong resemblance to a real castle of ancient date. Came in view of the chimney early in the morning, which was 20 miles distant. Divided our company into three parties for the greater convenience of traveling. Proceeded ahead 20 miles and camped on the river. 20 miles.

Friday, June 19—Passed the chimney in the fore part of the day and the formation of the bluffs have a tendency to fill the mind with awe and grandeur. The chimney might pass for one of the foundries in St. Louis, were it blackened by burning stone coal.[32] There is a nearby bluff near it, that reminds me of prints that I have seen of the capitol at Washington. Made 20 miles and camped near Scott's Bluffs. 792 miles.

Saturday, June 20—Passed the Scott's Bluffs through a beautiful valley, near the head of which we found a cold spring[33] at which we took dinner, then drove on to Horse Creek and encamped. Traveled 22 miles. A fine shower in the evening. 22 miles.

Sunday, June 21—Drove ahead over rolling uplands and came again to the Plate in about 8 miles and a handsome spring branch. Took our nooning and remained in our position for a shower to pass which was very heavy ahead of us. The grass the poorest we have found. Made this day 15 miles.

Monday, June 22—Came early in the day in sight [of] a Sioux encampment of about 20 lodges. They were putting up and moving on to the fort Laramie, where we arrived at about 4 o'clock and found about 200 lodges of Sioux. This was a disagreeable day, the wind blowing a tornado and the sand filling the air which continued to increase till midnight, when it abated. Camped one mile from the fort, which was 15 miles from last encampment. 844 miles.

Tuesday, June 23—Camped last night with about 70 wagons. This morning all united in giving our Sioux brethren a feast with which they appeared highly pleased. It was conducted with considerable order and regularity on their part, smoking the pipe of peace and a friendly address from their chief and a present of powder, lead and tobacco on our part.[34] This done, we went ahead about six miles and encamped on the river with fine feed. 6— 850 miles.

Wednesday, June 24—We deviated the usual route on leaving the fort which is over the highlands between Platte and Laramie fork. Ours was up the Platte. Traveled about 9 miles and intersected the old road at the spring which is very bold and rather warm.[35] We now enter the Black Hills. Rose from a valley onto high rolling prairie. Went 6 miles from the spring and encamped on the banks of a clear mountain stream.[36] Grass tolerable. 15 miles.

Thursday, June 25—Our course in the fore part of the day was up the aforesaid creek. Passed a large, fine spring about 10 o'clock, and timber plenty on the creek consisting of cottonwood, box, willow, choke-cherry and ash. Passed over the highlands towards another creek. Camped at a small spring 14 miles [from] last encampment. 14 miles.

Friday, June 26—Detained this morning hunting cattle till 10 o'clock. Went to a bold running creek to dinner. Met two companies returning from California dissatisfied with the country.[37] Passed over the hardest pulling hill we have had on our route to a small branch of spring water and camped. 8 miles.

Saturday, June 27—Traveled this day 12 miles over

hilly and rocky road. An axletree broke in one of Mr. Shaw's wagons, which was replaced and ready for a start in the morning. 12 miles.

Sunday, June 28—The weather still continues fine, cool in the morning and evening and warm in the middle of the day. The country well watered with springs. Traveled 20 miles and camped in sight of the Platte at a spring branch. 20—919 miles.

Monday, June 29—Came to the N. fork in about 10 miles from camp after passing a stream with fine grass, water and timber. Went up the river five miles and camped on another of these handsome mountain streams, the road good. 15 miles.

Tuesday, June 30—Our route this day was up the river, generally on the bottom. Traveled 12 miles and camped on the river, the weather dry, roads dusty and sandy. 12 miles.

Wednesday, July 1—The day fine with considerable wind in the evening. Found three trappers at the ford where we arrived at noon. They had been quite successful in catching beaver; this spring had been on ground that had not been trapped for fifteen years.[38] Crossed the ford, went up the river two miles and camped.[39] Traveled today 12 miles.

Thursday, July 2—Left the N. fork and took to the mountain desert, the first time we have seen land that appears perfectly sterile. Saw plenty of buffalo. The wind blew very severe and moved the sand in clouds all day. Traveled 15 miles to a plentiful spring and encamped, the grass flourishing but closely grazed.[40] 15 miles.

Friday, July 3—Traveled 18 miles, dined at a place of very irregular, miry wells. Two of our cattle got mired before we discovered them. They show no appearance until I placed my foot on them, then there was no more resistance than water. Camped tonight at a fine bold spring.[41] A buffalo killed after we encamped. 18 miles.

Saturday, July 4—Encamped about one mile above In-

dependence Rock after traveling 18 miles over hard pulling sand on the banks of the Sweetwater. We begin to
discover that we are in a high region, there being frost both
this and yesterday mornings and the days pleasant for
the season, but the 5th and 6th laid by to recruit our
teams.[42]

Tuesday, July 7—Our lame oxen being much better
we made sail and traveled about 12 miles and encamped
on the banks of Sweetwater. The boys took a ramble on
the mountains and saw plenty of mountain sheep.[43] 12
miles.

Wednesday, July 8—Laid by.

Thursday, July 9—Traveled 15 miles.

Friday, July 10—Our route up the river generally on
its banks, passed a narrow defile of the mountains.[44]
Made 15 miles—15.

Saturday, July 11—Left the river on our left and
traveled a country of barren, rolling plains for 15 miles
and came onto the Sweetwater and encamped. 15 miles.

Sunday, July 12—This morning Mr. Townsend had
a daughter born, which detained us this day. My health
for the last two days has been bad, being threatened with
an attack of fever.[45] 1,066 miles.

Monday, July 13—Our route in the fore part of the
day was up the Sweetwater, everything bearing the appearance of a high altitude, the Wind River Mountains
having been in sight at times for several days. After
dinner we ascended the high lands to the right of the
river, the highest ground we have been on. Made about
17 miles and encamped on a branch with fine grass.
Passed several fine springs on the high lands. 17 miles.

Tuesday, July 14—Our road this morning more level
and pretty good. Twelve miles brought us to the last
crossing of Sweetwater where we made our halt for noon.
Our road in the evening was equally good. Traveled six
miles and camped on the Sweetwater one mile north of
the road and between Table Rock[46] and the Wind River
Mountains. 18—1,101 miles.

Wednesday, July 15—Passed the divide [South Pass] about two miles from camp. Traveled twenty-six miles over level country, without water or grass. Had a hard shower in the evening and a light one yesterday. Camp on Sandy.[47] 26 miles.

Thursday, July 16—Traveled 15 miles to Big Sandy. The weather cold and disagreeable. 15 miles.

Friday, July 17—Our route was down Big Sandy. Traveled 15 miles and camped on its banks; road level, weather cool. 15 miles.

Saturday, July 18—Reached Green River in about 8 or 9 miles, crossed at a good ford, went down the river about 7 miles and camped on the right bank.[48] Road good. 15 miles.

Sunday, July 19—Left Green River in the morning and traveled 18 miles over high, broken and desert country to Black Fork of Green River, and camped at a place of good grass. 18—1,190 miles.

July 20—Laid by.

Tuesday, July 21—Traveled 15 miles over tolerable road and camped on Ham's Fork, a clear stream.

Wednesday, July 22—Still travel up Ham's Fork. Went 18 miles to Fort Bridger;[49] found grass plenty. 18 miles.

Thursday, July 23—Left Ham's Fork and traveled in a more northerly direction. Went 8 miles and camped at a small stream of salt water.[50] 8 miles.

Friday, July 24—The morning and evening cool. Travel 22 miles and find very little water or grass. Camped out of our course up the Muddy. 22 miles.

Saturday, July 25—Find water and grass plenty. Travel 7 miles and camped.

Sunday, July 26—Passed over the divide between the waters of Green River and Bear River. Found the road good for a mountain pass. Traveled 22 miles and camped on Bear River. 22—1,281 miles.

Monday, July 27—Travel down Bear River 10 miles and camp, grass good and willows plenty for fire. 10

miles.

Tuesday, July 28—Met this day a village of Shoshone Indians, 600, traveling up the river. Took dinner on South Fork.[51] Found plenty of yellow currants nearly ripe. Traveled 15 miles.

Wednesday, July 29—Traveled 7 miles and camp to recruit teams on Thomas Fork.

Thursday, July 30—Passed over 12 miles of mountain that shoots into the river and camp again on the river. 12 miles.

Friday, July 31—Travel 12 miles of good road and camp at a fine spring with good grass for teams. 12 miles.

Saturday, August 1—Pass through a gap in the mountains with a good road and reach the river bottom in 8 miles from camp, the . . . . . high and rolling; travel 18 miles and camp 2½ miles from Soda Springs. 18—1,348 miles.

Sunday, August 2—Travel 2½ miles to Soda Springs and camp to enjoy the novelties of the place which are many and interesting.[52] 2½ miles.

Monday, August 3—Made an early start from the springs intending to go to Port Neuf, but was stopped by an awful calamity in 3½ miles. Mr. Collins' son George, about 6 years old, fell from the wagon and the wheels ran over his head, killing him instantly; the remainder of the day occupied in burying him at the place where leave the river. 3½ miles.

Tuesday, August 4—Leave Bear River and travel up a plain, covered in places with volcanic rock, and camp on Port Neuf, a branch of Columbia. Made 18 miles—18.

Wednesday, August 5—Travel up Port Neuf to its head and passed through the mountains to another branch of Snake River[53] and camped. Traveled 17 miles. 17—1,389 miles.

Thursday, August 6—Our travel today down the branch on which we camped last night 12 miles and camp, 4 miles from Fort Hall. 12 miles.

Friday, August 7—Pass the fort and camp four miles

below on Port Neuf. Find the fort located on a rich, fertile plain, well watered with springs and creeks and some scattering timber. 8 miles.

Saturday, August 8—Traveled 14 miles and crossed the Port Neuf and Pannack at good fords. The road good. Camp at some springs on the edge of Snake River bottom. 14 miles.

Sunday, August 9—Passed the American Falls about 2 miles from camp, and some interesting springs half a mile above. Traveled today 16 miles of bad road and camped on the river bank with indifferent grass. Met Mr. Applegate from Oregon who had viewed a new route.[54] 16—1,439 miles.

Monday, August 10—Went ten miles to the Casue or Raft River and took our nooning; at this place the Oregon and California road fork. We took the California road, intending to follow it about 300 miles and then to take the new viewed route. Went up the river four miles and camped. 14 miles.

Tuesday, August 11—Traveled over a level ridge to save a bend in the creek and dined on the creek 10 miles from camp. Went 2 miles in the evening and camped. 12 miles.

Wednesday, August 12—Ran out the Casue to the gap where the road crosses the mountain to Goose Creek and camped on the head of the stream. 14 miles.

Thursday, August 13—Crossed a low ridge by a gentle ascent of a branch and camped by a spring that arose among some broken rocky knobs 2 miles above our camp. 10—1,489 miles.

Friday, August 14—Traveled today 16 miles, some part of the way bad road through ridges of Snake River Mountains, and camped at a spring in a narrow gap of the mountains with knobs ahead of various shapes and forms.[55] 16 miles.

Saturday, August 15—Traveled 7 miles over very broken ground and road rough to Goose Creek and dined and went up the creek 8 miles in the evening on good road and camped on the creek. 15 miles.

Sunday, August 16—Traveled to the head of the creek and camped at the last crossing. 12 miles.

Monday, August 17—Passed over a chain of low, broken ridges to the head of Hot Spring Valley, 12 miles.[56] Went down the valley 6 miles and camped by some singular springs that rise in the level bottom, forming little wells of various depths. The road good with the exception of some rocks. 18—1,550 miles.

Tuesday, August 18—Traveled today 20 miles in Hot Spring Valley and camped by the branch of a hot spring that is quite large and the water warm. 20 miles.

Wednesday, August 19—Took our nooning 8 miles from our last night's camp at the place where the road leaves the valley. Passed over a ridge in the evening to the first spring of Mary's River, 9 miles, and camped.[57] 17 miles.

Thursday, August 20—Traveled 17 miles down the valley on good road and camped near the river. Water and grass fine. 17 miles.

Friday, August 21—Rolled down stream today 13 miles, the river generally dry. 13 miles.

Saturday, August 22—14 miles.

Sunday, August 23—13 miles.

Monday, August 24—16 miles.

Tuesday, August 25—Made our camp on a mountain at a spring 8 miles from the place we left the river and 19 miles from camp of last night.[58] 19 miles.

Wednesday, August 26—Found the river again in 9 miles—road rough. Went 2 miles down the river and camped. 11—1,690 miles.

Thursday, August 27—13 miles down the river.

Friday, August 28—14 miles.

Saturday, August 29—15 miles.

Sunday, August 30—Traveled 17 miles.

Monday, August 31—16 miles. 16.

Tuesday, September 1—15 miles.

Wednesday, September 2—15 miles.

Thursday, September 3—16 miles.

Friday, September 4—2 sand points—12 miles.

Saturday, September 5—Arrived at the place where the Oregon road leaves the California road and Mary's River[59]—6—1,831 miles.

Sunday, September 6—The new road takes immediately to the desert of fifty-five miles extent with two weak springs on the route. We arrived at the first spring[60]— 15 miles—at four o'clock in the evening, took our supper and gave our teams what water we could get and started for the second,[61] where we arrived at four in the morning. Found the spring weaker than the first. 10 miles. Slept and rested till nine—1,865—of the 7th, then started the last stage of the desert [Black Rock Desert]. Our stock weak and working badly, getting very little water and nothing to eat. Arrived at Black Rock at 8:15 in the evening. Left 2 steers belonging to Collins on the road, they being too weak to come in, several others barely getting through. Found a large, hot spring[62] and plenty of first-rate grass. This desert is perfectly sterile, producing nothing but grease-wood and sage, and some of it perfectly barren and the ground very salt. The road good and level and generally firm. The mountains barren and dark looking rocks. 21 miles.

Tuesday, September 8—Laid by for the benefit of stock.

Wednesday, September 9—Traveled 8 miles to another good camp with several hot springs, some of them very hot and one cold in 10 yards of a hot one.[63] The country barren with the exception of the places watered by the spring. 8—1,894 miles.

Thursday, September 10—Traveled 20 miles of heavy pulling road and camp at a grassy flat[64] with plenty of water but bad for drinking. 20 miles.

Friday, September 11—Moved across the flat and camped, our teams being badly jaded and the desert country still continuing. 2 miles.

Saturday, September 12—Our first six miles was rocky,

bad road, with a steep hill to go down into a canon.[65] We then pass a flat into another beautiful, grassy canon with plenty of springs, road good. 12 miles.

Sunday, September 13—Travel up the canon 5 miles, the road good but crooked and narrow in places. The branch dry except where springs break out. 5 miles.

Monday, September 14—Eight miles from our last camp, the mountains recede and a grassy flat opens,[66] offering us a good camp to recruit our jaded teams. The weather cool and clouds look like snow. Yesterday and today roads dusty. 29 wagons ahead.[67] 8—1,941.

Tuesday, September 15—The first 4 miles through a narrow, rocky canon, road bad.[68] The rest of the day's travel the road good but rolling. Camp at a spring at a gap of a hill. Little grass. 10 miles.

Wednesday, September 16—Travel today 17 miles. Road slightly rolling but heavy pulling. The country improving in appearance. The sage mixed with grass in the plains and small cedar and grass on the hills. Camp at some springs at a high elevation. Plenty of grass but dry and yellow. 17 miles.

Thursday, September 17—Move our camp 3 miles over a ridge to another spring.[69] Nights and mornings quite cool.

Friday, September 18—Pass out of the mountains by a good road into a plain and camp at a warm spring, 14 miles from our last camp.[70] 14 miles.

Saturday, September 19—Found one of my oxen shot with an arrow and two cows belonging to the company also shot; one soon died and another was driven off our trail.[71] Today was 10 miles, 8 of desert and 2 of fine, rich soil. Our camp was at a pretty mountain stream with plenty of pine timber. This is very pleasant after traveling so long through desert country. 10 miles.

Sunday, September 20—Cross over a mountain, the ascent about 2 miles and quite steep. Travel 9 miles and camp in a beautiful plain surrounded by stately pine and cedar.[72] Excellent feed for our stock. 9 miles.

Monday, September 21—Travel today 8 miles, principally through large, lofty pine timber, and camp on Goose Lake.[73] 8 miles.

Tuesday, September 22—Travel 14 miles on the beach of the lake, road good. 14 miles.

Wednesday, September 23—Our road today was over a high plain and very stony and well timbered with pine and cedar. Camp at some holes of water at the head of a creek.[74] Grass good. The country generally less mountainous than before. 12—2,030 miles.

Thursday, September 24—Travel today 8 miles down Pool Creek. Road tolerable.

Friday, September 25—Traveled 14 miles of rolling road and very rocky. Camp at a good spring. 14 miles.

Saturday, September 26—Travel 8 miles of stony road but generally level; but little timber today. Good camp. 8 miles.

Sunday, September 27—We are now in the range of country of lakes of which the Klamath Lake is the largest known. Make 9 miles and camp by a pretty lake.[75] Road good and level. Weather fine. 9 miles.

Monday, September 28—Our route for 9 or 10 miles over a rocky ridge,[76] the balance of the day's travel level bottom and quite extensive. Make 22 miles. 22 miles.

Tuesday, September 29—Overtook the foremost company last night, which makes our company 50 wagons strong.[77] Found some cattle missing this morning owing to the inefficiency of our guard. They were driven off by Indians. The day spent trying to recover them. 2,081.

Wednesday, September 30—Found all our cattle but ten head that the Indians succeeded in getting off. Went ahead 12 miles and camped on the Klamath Lake. Crossed the Sacramento River on a singular rock which made a good shallow ford, the river generally swimming.[78] Road good except one steep point which was bad. 12 miles.

Thursday, October 1—Made 12 miles on the coast of the lake and camp on a creek that enters the lake. Road good. 12 miles.

Friday, October 2—Still crooking round the inlets of the lake, make 8 miles and camp at a fine bold spring but not cold. 8 miles.

Saturday, October 3—Make our last drive on the lake. Travel 12 miles and camp near the outlet of Klamath River.[79] Road good. 12 miles.

Saturday [Sunday], October 3—Cross the Klamath River four miles from camp at a very rocky ford and cross a ridge four miles and camp on the river.[80] 8 miles.

Monday, October 5—Cross a spur of the Sis-que Mountains[81] and camp without water or grass. Road bad and rough. 10—2,133 miles.

Tuesday, October 6—Move six miles to a tolerable camp. Road fair. 6 miles.

Wednesday, October 7—Cross another spur of the mountain and camp at a high flat—good grass and water.[82] Road tolerable except a steep hill to go down. Our teams very weak.

Thursday, October 8—Rest our teams and improve the road.

Friday, October 9—Travel ten miles of tolerable road and camp on the head of a branch of Rogue River.[83] Timber heavy and fine and the land good but very rough and broken between this and Klamath River. 10 miles.

Saturday, October 10—Engaged all day in making 3 miles, the branch so near impassable. Found a tolerable route at last.[84] 3—2,158 miles.

Sunday, October 11—The valley opens and we pass some very pretty locations. Timber in a great many varieties, some entirely new to me. Make 10 miles and camp at a considerable sized creek, the best camp we have had for several. Road very good. High mountains around.[85] 10 miles.

Monday, October 12—Travel 15 miles of very pretty mountain country and camp in a fine prairie without water. 15 miles.

Tuesday, October 13—Move about one mile to a spring and spend the day to explore ahead, the road not being marked. 1 mile.

Wednesday, October 14—Travel 12 miles of good road and camp on Rogue River, a beautiful, pure stream about fifty yards wide, but shut in by mountains.[86] 12 miles.

Thursday, October 15—Move down the river 10 miles and camp. Plenty of Indians about, but none come near. Lose some cattle by them. 10 miles.

Friday, October 16—Cross Rogue River about 4 miles from last camp. Ford good. Camp on the right bank.[87]

Saturday, October 17—Travel 8 miles, road good and a good camp which is not common, the country being mostly burnt. 8—2,218 miles.

Sunday, October 18—Have some bad road that takes till after dark to go 6 miles. 6 miles.

Monday, October 19—Move one mile to a camp, having none last night, and spent the day burying Mr. Crowley's daughter, who died yesterday evening, age about 14 years. 1 mile.[88]

Tuesday, October 20—Our route continues over spurs of mountains, with steep pulls and thick timber and underbrush. Make 6 miles.

Wednesday, October 21—The time from this to Monday, 25th, we were occupied in making 5 miles to the foot of Umpqua Mountain and working the road through the pass, which is nearly impassable. Started through on Monday morning and reached the opposite plain on Friday night after a series of hardships, break-downs and being constantly wet and laboring hard and very little to eat, the provisions being exhausted in the whole company. We ate our last the evening we got through. The wet season commenced the second day after we started through the mountains and continued until the first of November, which was a partially fair day.[89] The distance through: 16 miles. There is great loss of property and suffering, no bread, live altogether on beef. Leave one wagon.[90]

Sunday, November 1—Moved 3 miles. Find our oxen very stiff and sore from scrambling over rocks with wagons. 3 miles.

Monday, November 2—No rain today but partially cloudy. Make 5 miles. 5 miles.

Tuesday, November 3—Clear in the morning. Rains hard from ten in the morning to midnight. Make 7 miles. Octavius goes ahead for provisions to the other side of the Callipoa Mountains, forty miles distance.[91] 7 miles.

Wednesday, November 4—Make 4 miles and cross a steep hill. Oxen very weak. The new grass is no support. Very rainy. 4 miles.

Thursday, November 5—3 miles today. Rains all day. Pherne and the girls obliged to walk the oxen so weak. 3—2,274 miles.

Friday, November 6—Go to the Umpqua River, 6 miles to the upper ford.[92] Find no chance to cross, the river too high.

Saturday, November 7—Go to the lower ford and commence crossing in canoe, get all over but the wagons. No rain. 5 miles.

Sunday, November 8—Cross the wagons, and go 1 mile. Had nothing to eat yesterday for supper. A beef killed in camp and we got the paunch and upper part of the head, which did us till Monday for breakfast. Rains all day. 1 mile.

Monday, November 9—Ate the last of our tripe. Start with heavy hearts. Meet some Indians and get six venison hams, a great relief to our minds. Go one mile further and meet Octavius with half a bushel of peas and forty pounds of flour, which gives us joy.[93] No rain today. The happiest day to us for many. 4—2,284 miles.

Tuesday, November 10—Travel 5 miles and cross Elk Creek[94] and camp in first-rate feed. A rainy, cold day. 5 miles.

Wednesday, Thursday and Friday, November 11, 12, 13—Lay by to repair shoes and lay in a stock of meat; get 3 deer and a salmon from the Indians and our teams much improved and ourselves rested.

Saturday, November 14—A fine day but cool. Travel

6 miles of hilly road and camp on the head of a branch.[95]
Bury Mrs. Bounds, who died the day before, wife of J. B.
Bounds. 6 miles.

Sunday, November 15—Travel 4 miles, find a good
camp and stay 1 day for the benefit of the teams. Road
muddy and heavy. 4 miles.

Tuesday, November 17—Make four miles to the foot
of Callipoa Mountains.[96] 4 miles.

Wednesday, November 18—Go over one ridge of the
mountains and make 2 miles. 2 miles.

Thursday, November 19—Climb another ridge with
double teams and make 3 miles headway and camp with
little feed. 3—2,308 miles.

Friday, November 20—Move forward to the top of the
mountain on gently rising ground and camp with the
foremost wagons 4 miles from last camp. One steer dies
at this camp. 4 miles.

Saturday, November 21—Make 2 miles headway and
camp. Rains yesterday and today. 2 miles.

Sunday, November 22—Help finish the road and complete the pass of the mountains and camp 2 miles from
the foot in the Willamette Valley. My wagons and one
other the first that entered the valley.[97] All in good
health and well pleased with the appearance of the country. Headway, 5 miles—5.

Monday and Tuesday, November 23 and 24—Rest and
feed our teams and move one mile and make arrangements for a small supply of provisions. About seventy
miles from settlement. 1—2,318 miles.

Wednesday, November 25—Travel down the valley 6
miles and passed over some spurs of the mountains and
camp on the Willamette River, the handsomest valley I
ever beheld. All charmed with the prospects and think
they will be well paid for their sufferings. 6 miles.

Thursday, November 26—A very cold, rainy day.
Went 3 miles and camped this day and the next. Lost 2
steers by the cold. 3 miles.

Saturday, November 28—Traveled 6 miles—6.

Sunday, November 29—Traveled 4 miles and made a halt near where I intend to make a location.[98]

Monday, November 30—Commenced making a canoe for the purpose of going to settlement for supplies in company with Robert Lancefield and Isaac Leabo,[99] and continue our work until Thursday, December 3. I then start ahead for beef, on horseback, leaving the others to finish the canoe, and go down the river for flour, etc. I arrived at Long Tom Bath on the 4th, found it swimming, was detained until Sunday, 6th, in making a canoe and crossing in the evening met Orus Brown in company with some others coming back with pack horses to bring in those behind.[100] I returned with them, and was from this to the twenty-fifth of the month getting my family to Salem, the weather all the time rainy and swailes of water to wade every day. Left my wagon and cattle at the forks of the river.[101]

I would conclude this journal by saying that I was well pleased with the society and location of Salem; was kindly received and besides much indulgence granted me as I needed, but our living is poor. Can obtain nothing but bread and meat, vegetables being very scarce and we nothing but labor to give.

"Swimming the River"

Journal of Thomas Holt

Virgil Pringle having introduced us to the hardships experienced by those who traveled the Applegate Cutoff in the autumn of 1846, we are better able to appreciate Thomas Holt's record of the relief efforts made by Oregon settlers that fall and winter on the new Southern Road. Holt was not himself an 1846 emigrant, but so valuable is his journal and so inaccessible—never reprinted in its entirety since first published in the *Oregon Spectator* of March 4, 1847—that it is given a place at this point among the records of 1846.

Holt is said to have been born in Lancaster, England. There is some discrepancy in relation to his birth-date. In the 1850 Oregon census he stated his age to be 33, but an

189

obituary in the Oregon Historical Society collections fixes
the date as April 5, 1815. He came to America in 1832,
served in the Seminole War, and after living in Missouri
for a time, traveled overland to Oregon with the emigration of 1844. He took up one of the earliest land claims in
the Santiam Valley, about midway of the long Willamette
Valley, and this gave him an early interest in the project to
find a southern road into the fertile valley west of the Cascades. At a meeting in Salem on February 11, 1846, he
was appointed one of a committee to raise funds for a
roadmaking endeavor, as also to ascertain "who are willing
to go on the expedition, and are competent to go as
pilots." But he was not actually one of those who went
with Jesse Applegate in the eventually successful effort to
work out a road. He was secretary of a meeting to organ-
ize the Oregon Rangers at Salem on June 11, being elected
orderly sergeant; and on July 4 he led the march at
Salem which celebrated the anniversary of American Independence.

Clearly, Holt was much disturbed when reports began
to reach the settlements of the distressed condition of the
emigrants on the Applegate Cutoff. He was not the only
one who displayed enough energy and interest to ride to
the relief of the emigrants; but he must have been one of
the few who set out without having relatives or close
friends to succor.

Since his journal gives his first-hand account of his
experiences on the Applegate Road, no more will be said
of those experiences here. Sometime in 1847 Holt married
Leona, a stepdaughter of James Madison Bates, who had
settled near him on the site of Santiam City; and it is
recorded that in 1848 he was again elected orderly sergeant of the Oregon Rangers. Soon after he entered into
a partnership with Jacob Conser and N. B. Evans for
constructing a saw mill and grist mill on the Santiam
River. When Conser a little later located a ferry and
sawmill at another site, Holt again was his partner, and
thus he also became one of the founding fathers of the

town of Jefferson. His wife died at Jefferson in March, 1895, having borne him twelve children. Holt himself died of dropsy at the home of a daughter in Albany, Oregon, October 13, 1896, survived by ten of the children.

❀ ❀ ❀

The Holt Journal
For the *Oregon Spectator.*

Thomas Holt, in company with five half breeds and one Frenchman, started on the 3d of last December, to assist the immigration then coming in on the southern route. They had a band of 34 horses. The following is a memoranda of travel kept by Mr. Holt.

Dec. 4th. We crossed the Rickreal and traveled 15 miles and camped on the north fork of the Luckemute.[1] Some of the men started with the expectation that I had provisions for all hands, and did not bring any. I did not take any more than I wanted for my own use, as it was generally understood that Mr. Jones had started out with fifteen hundred weight of flour, and some beef cattle. I found out here that Mr. Jones had not started at all.[2] I had two hundred weight of flour, and Rev. J. B. Baldroach, 100 cwt. flour and one bacon ham, which he sent to be given to the needy. I found it necessary to get some more: I bought twenty-seven pounds of salt pork from Mr. J. Taylor.

Dec. 5th. Crossed the north and south fork of the Luckemute—swimming and bad crossing—traveled ten miles and camped on muddy creek.[3] We met the first wagons here: Mr. Goff is here—he is bringing Mrs. Newton in. Mr. Newton, her husband, was killed in the most barbarous manner. Three Indians came to Mr. Newton and gave him to understand that he had better camp where he was; if he went any further, he would not get as good a place, and accordingly he camped. The Indians begged something to eat, and some ammunition, with the promise to fetch in a deer: one of the Indians could speak a little English. He gave them three balls and some powder. The

Indian that could speak English, loaded his gun with the three balls, and remained about the camp. Mr. Newton suspected that all was not right, and wanted them to go away, but they would not go. He thought he would watch them, but he happened to drop asleep, and one of the Indians shot three balls into him: he was laying outside of the tent—he jumped inside of the tent to get his gun, and one of the Indians got an axe and cut his leg very nearly off. He died the next day of his wounds. The Indian robbed the tent of some articles and took an American mare and packed her off.[4]

Dec. 6th. Crossed Mary's river: there is a small canoe here that we cross our packs in, and swim our horses. Traveled nine miles and camped on the south bank; there are five families with their wagons here, and one family packing, camped here.[5]

Dec. 7. Traveled 18 miles and camped on the north bank of Lungtum river.[6]

Dec. 8th. Crossed our pack over the river in a canoe, and swam our horses. We overtook Capt. Campbell Mr. Goodman, Mr. Jenkins, and Mr. Harris, with 25 horses and some provisions. They all tell us that they are going to the kanyon.[7] We have more help than Capt. Campbell, and we travel faster—he started three days before us. We met three families packing, and one family with a wagon. They tell us they have had nothing to eat to-day— the children are crying for bread: we let them have fifty pounds of flour. Traveled 4 miles through a mirery prairie, and camped on a slough.

Dec. 9th. We met 8 wagons and as many families, all out of provisions: we gave 10 pounds of flour to each family. Traveled 5 miles and camped on the Willamette. We waited here for Capt. Campbell to go ahead with the provisions, as we have no more to spare.

Dec. 10. Traveled 14 miles and camped on Goose creek. There is a number of families encamped here, waiting for assistance: their teams have given out. Mr. Owens, Mr. Patten, Mr. Duskins, Mr. Hutchins, Mr.

Howell, and Mr. Burrows overtook us to day with 24 horses.[8]

Dec. 11th The Frenchman and three half breeds[9] turn back this morning: they are afraid if they go over the mountain, they will not get back this winter. I told Baptiste that Mr. Beers expected that he would go with me to the kanyon, and if he turned back, I could not go any further. He said that he did not think that the people back had any money to pay for being brought in. I told him that if he would go, that he should be paid— if the people was not able to pay him, that Mr. Beers would raise a subscription and pay him. He said that he owed Mr. Beers sixty dollars—that if I would see that paid, he would risk the rest; I told him I would see that paid.[10] We came across four or five families encamped, about noon, at a bute in the prairie. These families could not get any further without assistance. Mr. Goodman, Mr. Hutchins, and Mr. Howell stopped here to assist them in. We traveled 23 miles and camped at the foot of the mountain. There are three families here that are in a very bad situation; their teams have given out, and they have no provisions. Mr. Campbell let them have some flour. I feel for them; it is hard for me to pass them, but when I know there are other helpless families among hostile Indians; I am bound to go on and assist them.[11]

Crossed the Callapoia mountains; saw the carcasses of a good many dead animals today—met one family on the top of the mountains, packing—met two families on south side of the mountain, just ready to take the mountain; they were almost afraid to try to cross—their cattle were nearly given out, and their provisions all gone. Mr. Campbell let them have some flour. Traveled 12 miles and camped on a small creek in the Umpqua valley. Traveled 9 miles and camped on Deer creek. This is a very pretty valley, but it is small and scarce of timber. There is white and black oak, and some ash, but very little fir timber nearer than the mountain.[12]

Dec. 14th. Traveled 15 miles and camped on the north

fork of Elk river; there are five families here. Mr. Kennedy, Mr. Hall, Mr. Croizen, and Mr. Lovlen; they have neither flour, meat, nor salt, and game is very scarce. Baptiste killed two deer, and divided the meat among them. I gave them 50 pounds of flour.[13]

Dec. 15th. Crossed the north and south forks of Elk river, both swimming—we carried our packs across on logs. Mr. Campbell met his family here, and two others. Mr. Cornwall and Mr. Dunbar, Mr. Harris and Mr. Jenkins stopped here to help these families: there were not horses enough to take Mr. Cornwall's; he moved to the other family. Mr. Campbell left nearly all his property with him. We traveled 6 miles and camped on a spring branch.[14]

Dec. 16th. Traveled 9 miles and camped on the creek where Mr. Newton was killed by the Indians. We saw a camp of Indians on a small creek; when they saw us, they run. Baptiste told them to stop—he went up to them—they told him that the Indians that killed the Boston man[15] was on the south fork of the Umpqua river, and the mare that they stole was there also. We crossed the north fork of the Umpqua river in a canoe; the Indians made us give them a blanket for the use of the canoe; we swam our horses across.[16]

Dec. 17th. Traveled up the south fork of the Umpqua 10 miles and camped on a spring branch. We met the last company of immigrants here, consisting of five families. They rejoiced very much when they saw us.[17]

Dec. 18th. All hands busy making pack-saddles.

Dec. 19th. The Indians stole a horse belonging to Baptiste. To-day we took the back-track. Mr. Owens took Mr. Crump's family, Mr. Patten and Mr. Duskins took Mr. Butterfield's family and the widow Butterfield, Baptiste took Mr. James Townsend's family, Delore took Mr. David Townsend's family. Thomas Holt took Mr. Baker's family. These families had been out of bread for more than two months. Their teams have all about given out—they are taking their empty wagons along until they get to the river; there they will leave them. We traveled nine miles and camped on Rock creek.[18]

Dec. 20th. The Indians stole 3 horses and 1 mule belonging to Mr. Owens, Mr. Patten and Mr. Duskins. We pursued the Indians so close, that we got the mule. We traveled 6 miles and camped on a spring branch.[19]

Dec. 21st. Crossed the north fork of the Umpqua river. The Indians were very saucy: they told us that they would not let us have a canoe to cross—told us to go and hunt a ford; they knew the river was very high, and it could not be forded. We had to give a gun, valued at eight dollars, belonging to Delore,[20] before we could get a canoe. We traveled nine miles and camped on the north bank.

Dec. 22d. Traveled 5 miles and camped on a spring branch. Snowed all day.

Dec. 23d. Traveled 10 miles and camped on the south fork of Elk river. We leave the wagons here.[21]

Dec. 24th. It took us all day to cross the river. It is out of its banks. Drowned two oxen. Camped on the north bank.

Dec. 25th. Lay by to-day. It snowed all night. The snow is a foot deep.

Dec. 26th. Traveled a mile and a half and camped on the north fork of Elk river. We find these families in a very bad situation. Mr. Kennedy and Mr. Hall state to us, that their families have had nothing to eat for four days, but a little tallow boiled in water. Mr. Baker has three oxen that were driven from the settlement: he paid 75 dollars a yoke for them. I proposed to him to let these families have them. He said that he had lost nearly all his property in the kanyon, and these oxen were all he had to depend on. These people are not able to pay him for them—I thought it rather a hard case that he should lose them, and thought that under such circumstances, the people in the settlements would pay him by subscription. I told him that if he would leave them, I would insure his pay, whatever they cost him. He left them, and we divided them out, one to Mr. Kennedy's family, one to Mr. Hall's, and one to Mr. Croizen's family, and three quarters of one to Mr. Cornwall's family. I gave 50 pounds of beef to two men that are encamped here, for an axe, and sold them 10 pounds of tallow for one dollar. I gave the axe to Mr. Townsend, it being very cold weather, and he having no axe to cut fire wood with. Mr. Owens leaves us to day to go ahead. Mr. Duskins goes with him—as he has lost his horses, he can be of no more service to Mr. Butterfield. I let Mr. Townsend and Mr. Baker have 80 pounds each, of beef. I omitted to state, that Mr. Burrows returned on the 15th, and packed Mr. Lovlen's family in.[22]

Dec. 26th [27th]. We lay by to-day to dry our clothes. This is the first clear day we have had since we left the settlements.[23]

Dec. 28th. Traveled 6 miles and camped on a spring branch.[24] This is very slow getting along in consequence of having to pack oxen. I let the widow Butterfield have a horse to ride, the Indians having stolen her horse.

Jan. 1st. Crossed the mountain—the snow three feet deep in places. I *cached* some flour in the mountain, going out. I opened the *cache* to-day—our mouths water for some bread, as we have been out some time. Traveled 10 miles and camped at the foot of the mountain.[25]

Jan. 5th. To-day and the last three days traveled 25 miles and camped at the Skinner house. We met Mr. Powers here, with three horses to assist Mr. Butterfield.[26]

Jan. 6th. Mr. Butterfield gave a dollar and a half towards paying for Delore's gun: he lies by to-day. We traveled 6 miles and camped on the Willamette.

Jan. 8th. Very cold and frosty: swam two creeks— the women and children got wet and came very near freezing. We had to camp—traveled 14 miles yesterday and to-day.

Jan. 9th. Crossed Lungtum river, swimming—traveled 10 miles and camped at Scott's bute. Mr. Butterfield overtook us again to-day.[27]

Jan. 10th. Crossed Mary's river, swimming. Traveled 10 miles and camped on the north bank of the river.

Jan. 11th. Traveled 12 miles and camped on muddy creek. Mr. Butterfield was taken sick and stopped here.

Jan. 12th. Traveled 5 miles and remained with Mr. Williams on the Luckemute.[28] Very stormy and cold.

Jan. 17th. After lying by four days in consequence of storms and severe weather, traveled 7 miles and stopped with Mr. Harris.[29] Crossed the Luckemute below the forks, swimming. Very stormy. Baptiste traveled on the 14th and crossed the Luckemute, and drowned one of his horses. He left the two Townsend families at the forks of the Luckemute.[30]

Jan. 18th. Traveled 8 miles and stayed at Judge Nesmith's. Very cold and stormy—two horses gave out to-day.[31]

Jan. 19th. The horses are so stiff to-day that they cannot travel. I leave Mr. Baker's family here, I took the best horse that I have, to ride to Mr. Beers' house. I got as far as the Rickreall, and he gave out.

Jan. 20th. I took it a foot this morning, as far as Mr. Keyser's. I got a horse from Mr. Keyser, and stayed all night.[32]

Jan. 21st. Went to Mr. Beers' to-day. One horse died this day. On this day, Jan. 21st, 1847, I arrived at home, after having been gone fifty days, undergoing many privations and hardships, but I feel that I have done no more than my duty.[33] The public doubtless is aware of the humane object of our trip. It was to relieve our *fellow beings* who were suffering almost beyond description. As the painful news of their sufferings was not to be heard without prompting some of us to endeavor to relieve them as far as we could. We succeeded in relieving many who must have perished. Our party agreed to charge nothing for the use of our horses: and as yet we have not received any thing. And I feel it will be too great a loss on us as individuals, to be at the whole of the expense of the trip. Therefore, I appeal to the public to know if they will not bear a hand in defraying the expenses of the trip. It will not be felt by the many, but to be wholly defrayed by persons in as indigent circumstances as we are in, will be felt considerably.[34]

I therefore subjoin a bill of expenses:—

To provisions taken from home,	$12	00
For ferriage,	19	25
To pork bought on the trip,	3	12
” Horse stolen,	40	00
” Three beeves bought and distrib-uted, (Cash,)	112	00
” Horse drowned,	40	00
” Horse died,	50	00
” Baptiste Gardapie's services,	80	00
” Q. Delore's services,	60	00
” Sundry expenses,	10	00
Total	$426	37

THOMAS HOLT.

"Storm on the Prairie"

Diary of George McKinstry

With a Letter to P. B. Reading

With the diary he gave to H. H. Bancroft in 1871, George McKinstry returns us to Independence and the California emigration. He was the son of George and Susan (Hamilton) McKinstry, born at Hudson, New York. According to William Willis, *Genealogy of the McKinstry Family* (Boston, 1858), the date of his birth was September 15, 1810. This date seems incontestable, yet McKinstry himself, in registering as a voter in San Diego County, August 11, 1866, gave his age as 49; and on re-registering at Santa Ana, Los Angeles County, July 24, 1879, stated his age to be 63.

Educated in New York, there or later McKinstry acquired some knowledge of medicine, but when he found his way South, he entered upon a merchant's life; written on the cover of his diary is the firm name McKinstry,

Puckett & Co., Vicksburg, Mississippi. At Vicksburg, McKinstry became well acquainted with Pierson B. Reading, who went overland to the Sacramento Valley with the emigration of 1843, and this acquaintance may have directed McKinstry's attention to California when he wearied of a five-year struggle with chills and fever and in the spring of 1846 rode west in search of a more congenial environment.

Along the way, McKinstry purchased two guidebooks. One of these, presented to H. H. Bancroft with other records, has high associational interest, for it is a badly waterstained copy of Lansford Hastings' *Emigrants' Guide,* signed "Geo. McKinstry, jr. St Louis, Mo. 1846," and bearing a later note: "This pamphlet was among my baggage that I hired hauled to here of the Donner, party detained by Snow in the Serria Nevada Mountain the winter of ,46-,47. G. McKinstry, Jr." Still more important is John Bidwell's printed account of his own overland journey to California in 1841, sent back to Missouri and printed there at some undetermined date, probably 1843 or 1844. The copy McKinstry carried to California, and which he gave to H. H. Bancroft, after more than a century is still the only one known. McKinstry signed his name in this pamphlet on various pages, and pasted into it various clippings of historical interest, including Charles T. Stanton's letter of July 12, 1846, reprinted from the New York *Herald* in Volume II of the present work. McKinstry also made marginal notes, particularly valuable because they come from the period after his diary lapses. Where Bidwell mentions a "spring of cool, though unpleasantly tasted water" 22 miles northeast of Willow Spring, McKinstry signs the remark, "we camped at this Spring Monday July 6th." And where Bidwell tells of the abandonment of the Bartleson wagons at the foot of the Pequop Mountains in present Nevada, McKinstry comments: "We cooked our supper & breakfast with fires made from the remains of these Wagons." No date is supplied for this second note, but we may infer from

James Mathers' diary that McKinstry warmed his hands at these fires on the evening and morning of August 23-24.

As will be seen from his diary, McKinstry traveled most of the first stretch of the road to California as a member of the company led by William H. Russell. Quite early in the journey he began to think about leaving the wagons to go on with a pack party, and after reaching the North Platte he rode ahead to Fort Laramie with this end in view. Unfortunately his diary—one of the best we have for 1846—breaks off June 30, the second day after leaving the fort. If McKinstry kept a diary the rest of the way to California (the extant MS. is identified on the cover as "No. 1"), all trace of it has been lost. But his subsequent experiences can be pieced together after a fashion from records of his fellow-travelers and from two of his own letters, which here supplement the diary. Charles T. Stanton's letter of July 5 mentions McKinstry's overtaking the wagon train on June 30. He was then in company with Hiram Ames, James McCleary (or McClary), and the mountain man, Captain Wells, but these four packers went their separate ways. In his letter of November 2, 1846, to P. B. Reading, McKinstry says that he became so weak he "found it advisable to give up packing on the Great Salt Lake and take to the wagons," but it would not be surprising if we learned some day that he had fallen ill several weeks earlier, traveling much of the way from the Black Hills in some hospitable wagon.

McKinstry was one of those who traveled the Hastings Cutoff, as is apparent from the above and from his letter in the *California Star* of February 13, 1847. Thus his diary is curiously complemented by that of James Mathers, which begins at the crossing of the North Platte immediately after McKinstry's ends, and describes the journey on to California by the same route McKinstry traveled. McKinstry himself says that he reached Sutter's Fort October 19. His health too poor to permit him to have a part in the conquest of California, he remained at Sutter's. As he wrote Reading, he "accepted the appointment of Sheriff and Inspector of this district"—the appointment coming under the prevailing U. S. Navy jurisdiction—and thus he appears as Sheriff McKinstry in many happenings of the next year. It was this appointment which officially involved him in the Donner relief and its aftermath, and resulted in his acquiring a number of related papers, including Patrick Breen's diary, as seen on a later page.

The *California Star* contains a great many interesting letters written by McKinstry in 1847-1848, some signed, others identified only as having been written by "our Sacramento correspondent." It would be apparent that McKinstry was this correspondent, even had he not identified himself as the author in various personal letters. Within the compass of the present work, it is not possible to print all of these letters; a volume containing them would be a most interesting contribution to the history of California, and a lively personal chronicle as well.

A collection of McKinstry's papers in the California State Library shows that in the spring of 1848 he tried his hand at mining gold, but had to give it up—"the work of mining is too severe for my constitution and I do not think I can stand it long." He entered into a brief business association with John Bidwell, E. C. Kemble, and T. H. Rolfe, involving both mining and an Oregon supply speculation; he also began buying land up and down the Sacramento Valley, and for a time had a trading post on the Cosumnes River. The explosive change in progress was not much to his taste; as he wrote Edward M. Kern from San Diego in December, 1851, a letter now in the Huntington Library's "Fort Sutter Papers," the Country became "crowded with hungrey gold hunters and speculating Yankees. Times are not as they 'useter was.' " Accordingly, late in 1851, he traveled to southern California, "to look at the country," and possibly to "purchase a ranch and settle for life. From what I have seen of this part of the state I dont think the damned Yankees will crowd me much. . . ."

He located at Santa Ysabel in San Diego County and began to practice medicine. A strong Unionist, on June 2, 1862, McKinstry was appointed Inspector of Customs at San Diego, and he was still serving in this post three years later. A biographical note by Caroline Wenzel, printed in a *Keepsake* of the Book Club of California for January, 1948, relates that in after times McKinstry lived with John S. Minter (a fellow emigrant on the Hastings Cutoff in 1846) and Serafina (Wrightington) Minter, conducting his medical practice in the front rooms of their San Diego home. When the Minters moved to Santa Ana, McKinstry accompanied them, and there he died, about 1890.

McKinstry seems to have commenced his diary belatedly on May 21, while sitting beside the emigrant road on his baggage, waiting for the company behind to come along. Thus in the opening entries, the diary is a bit askew in its chronology. However, this is true even of the published journal of his fellow emigrant, J. Quinn Thornton. Once these discrepancies are straightened out, the diary plunges us absorbingly into life on the trail in the spring of 1846.

❀ ❀ ❀

THE McKINSTRY DIARY

Monday May 12th [11th] 1846. Camped on Indian creek 30 miles from Independence called a meeting to elect a captain and make laws the party numbered 120 wagons candidates put up Gov Bogges Col Wm H Russell and Geo Harlen Harlen & 40 wagons left before the election Col Russell was elected by a large majority committees appointed to draft laws Gov Bogges chairman meet at 2 O'clock today Acepted[1]

Tuesday 13th [12th] took up line of march went 35 [*i.e.*, 6?] miles to Camp creek[2]

Wednesday 14th [13th] travelled [16?] miles to camping place[3]

Thursday 15th [14th] to Sugar creek 12 miles[4]

16 Saturday [15th Friday] 10 miles to a large creek (Wakarusau). waited a day for Gov Bogges wagons[5]

17th Sunday [16th Saturday] camped on opposite side creek Gov Bogges came up traveled 8 miles camped.[6]

Monday 18th [Sunday 17th] travelled 10 miles and camped on Prairie Travelled 15 miles to a creek part of the company crossed the balance camped on opposite side Weather verry hot[7]

Tuesday 19th [Monday 18th] crossed the creek and proposed a division of the company as we found it too large and too long starting in the morn Col Russell and 35 wagons went ahead and crossed the Kansas River 3 miles distance and camped 3 miles beyond on a branch of the Kansas on the Kansas Valley [Remained at this encampment on Tuesday 19th][8]

Wednesday 20th traveled 7 miles and camped about 2 miles from the road to wait for Mr Boon[9] a brother in law of Gov Boogs Mr [Hiram] Ames[10] went ahead this morn and traveled some 5 miles crossing a large creek (Soldier creek) with bad banks camped with two wagons for oregon 200 yds from the Creek[11]

At this place the next morning Thursday 21 I took my baggage from his wagon and put it on side of the road to wait for Col Russells party the country we have traveled through five miles from Independence to this place is a beautiful rolling prairie on the creeks a small skirt of timber oak, elm, hickory &c the land on the Kansas is the most beautiful farming land I ever saw we crossed the Kansas 110 miles from Independence using the Missions (Methodist) with two flat boats owned by a half breed Frenchman charging one dollar for each wagon[12] the oxen & horses were swum over the river the river about 100 yds wide, we had a great deal of trouble and confusion in our party thus far cattle were young and wild great complaints about slow traveling Mr Lippingcott with his wagon & four mules and Mr Benton with his ox wagon left us some 18 miles from the Kaw and went ahead[13] they are now some 25 or 30 miles ahead

Harlans party (Judge Brown [Morin] capt.) are now some 25 or 30 miles ahead of us[14] I am now sitting on my bagage alone waiting for Col Russells party some 5 miles behind we are in the Kaw Nation said to be great theives[15] not a soul is in sight or hearing Mr Ames has joind 7 wagons for oregon that camped half a mile from us and gone ahead they number 10 wagons and expect to travel 10 or 12 miles to day I am in hopes that Mr Grayson Buchanan Putnam[16] and some 10 wagons will leave the party and go ahead as the party is so large that we are late in getting a start in the morning and travel very slow waiting for stray cattle every morning Mr Ames is travelling for his health and cares not whether he goes to California or oregon Says if he falls in with a clever set of men he will go to oregon but if Mr Grayson, Buchanan and some 10 wagons come up he will go with them I have found the journey thus far very labourious much more than I expected but think in a few days we will so divide our Company that we will travel with more ease and comfort had I have the experience I now have I could so arrange it that I could travel much more agreeably we find the women and children much in the way I should prefer going with a party of 20 to 30 men on muels one to ride and two to pack say start with 200 lbs on each mule as we used the provisions, the load would become much lighter the party ought to leave Independence on the first day of May I find that the best place to fit out is at Independence oxen can be had at 25$ pr yoke mules & Horses from 30 to 40$ pr head flour this year 4$ pr bbl Company should go out some 10 miles and remain a few days in camp they would then be able to organize and find out what things were necessary for the journey and could procure them at Independence and wait for those that are not ready or are to come on I do not think it necessary to organise untill reaching the Kaw as the company will then learn what is necessary to be done divide into messes and each man do his part of camp duty, 9 O'clock A. M. Messrs Kirkindall & Bryant came up to

look for camping ground and selected the spot occupied
by the 7 Oregon wagons last night[17] I rode back 2 miles
and meet the company to direct them as to the road around
a ditch and advise them to take of[f] part of team in
going down the bank of creek and double teams in going
up the carel [corral] is now being formed on a beautiful
rolling prairie numbering some 56 wagons a party haveing joined them yesterday[18] it is now $2\frac{1}{2}$ O'clock p.m.
having gone into Camp thus early to wait for Mr Boon
who is to be in this Evening Mr Boon with 11 wagons
came into camp this day at 6 o'clock the whole number
being 67 wagons[19] last night commenced driving cattle
into carel at night and turning them out mornings

Friday May 22^d 1846 This day has been somewhat
warm but have travelled 18 miles through the most beautiful farming land I ever saw and camped on east side
[blank] creek within $\frac{1}{2}$ mile of a Kansas village consisting of some 250 or 300 inhabitants[20] the most of them
were immediately in our Camp beging for provisions and
in every thing they could see put out an extra guard of
voulentiers 8 on each watch to assist the regular guard in
keeping off the Indians two of the guard brought in a
Kaw Indian who attempted to cross the lines with two
horses he was much alarmed but was set at liberty as he
had been hunting a stray horse to sell to one of our young
men report in Camp at 9 O'clock that the Pawnee
Indians had been at the Kaw village and had been fired
on by the Kaws[21] the two tribes being always at war
with each other we are camped on Hurricane Creek about
200 yds from the bank, the skirts of woods are beautiful,
medium size Oak clear of under growth the banks of the
creek not bad this evening company called together
under arms to make a show of strength before the Indians
and took a vote whether capt Dickenson & Mr Gordon
should be allowed to come back into our company the
meeting decided that they would take 2 or 3 days to think
of it and give them time to repent[22] Messrs Gordon &
Dickson with 14 wagons crossed the creek and camped

on the east side of a large creek (Sandy C.) with good banks but we found it necessary to throw in timber & brush to enable the teams to cross-

Saturday May 23d started at 7 ½ O'clock traveled 4 miles to a creek with bad banks and was some 4 hours crossing[23] we then travelled through a beautiful country some 8 or 10 miles makening the whole distance 12 to 14 miles and camped on side a small creek and found a beautiful Spring of water[24] went into camp at 6 o'clock p. m. this evening a man came in camp from Kansas River where he had left two wagons and wishes to join our party he was informed that he could join if he could catch up with us but could not wait for him he returns to the river to night he informs us that the Kaw Indians have stolen several horses and cattle from his party[25] the weather has been verry agreeable to day wind blowing fresh from South east we are now camped on a beautiful side hill the scenery is verry fine and the land of the finest quality.

Sunday May 24th, 46 travelled 12 miles and camped on the prairie near a beautiful spring the finest water that we found on the plains thus far.[26]

Monday May 25 travelled some 15 miles over quite a broken country in view of some beautiful buttes we crossed the "big Virmillion" a large creek with a steep bank on the east side and verry good road on the west we camped about 4 miles from the above creek on high prairie some water but no timber while the wagons were forming carel a most furious thunder storm arose with strong wind lasting for half an hour[27]

Tuesday May 26th started at 7 O'clock A. M. and travelled 10 miles to the "Blue earth" river and camped we found that the rains had raised the Stream some 20 feet and are now waiting for it to fall the part of our Company under Messrs Dickenson & Gordon that seperated from us some few days since last night and crossed the creek and were seen some three miles ahead on the opposite side of the creek under way when we came up this evening[28]

Wednesdy May 27th still in camp creek has fallen some few inches this morning at 8 O'clock a meeting was called to enact laws for the better regulation of the Company a committee haveing been sent out last night to report this morning this morning before the hour of meeting various reports were in circulation in camp the young men mustered their strength to vote down any obnoxious laws that might be offered by the Committee first law offered was as to Guard duty inflicting punishment for neglect of duty which was passed. Second was to give the Capt power to punish the members for all crimes I moved to strike out the whole of the article Mr E. Bryant moved to appoint a committee of 3 to whom the officers were to report and before whom the accused should have a trial I seconed the motion and the meeting passed it. Mr Ewing moved a committee of 5 be appointed to punish officers which was passed by a respectable majority the Capt Russell then resigned and the greatest confusion arose flameing speeches were made which became quite personal Mr Ewing nominated Gov Bogges for Capt Gov declined Mr Brenham nominated Russell which was carried and accepted the meeting adjourned as soon as possible with a determination not to hold any more meetings as the Young Men were determined to do their own voting and their own fighting[29]

Thursday May 28 The creek is now riseing the weather still unsettled have had showers the last three days the men are now out makeing Canoes to form a raft to cross the river this has been a general washing day all of us being obliged to do our own washing I find I have done my work badly and am much fatigued.[30]

Friday May 29 The creek fell some 3 1/2 feet last night and the company have concluded to wait for the creek to fall before crossing last night I mounted guard from 11 to 1 O'clock about day light this morning Mrs Keyse the mother of the wife of Mr Reed of Illinois died of consumption aged [*deleted*: about 67] 70 had been sick for a long time has been blind and deaf for some time past[31] her son in law Mr Reed is on his way to California she was to have accompanied him as far as Ft Hall to meet an only Son from Oregon[32] The funeral took place this evening at 2 O'clock which was attended by every member of the company Mr Cornwall[33] one of our party and a Presbyterian clergiman conducted the burriel and delivered a sensible sermon at the grave thakeing his text from Thessilonians "Trouble yourselves not about those that sleep" the grave is under an Oak tree beside the "Oregon road about ¼ mile west [east] of Blue earth river. Yesterday 8 wagons bound for California came into our Camp haveing made a forced march of but 7 days from Independence[34] yesterday a man came into our camp from Harlens company and reports that a son of Judge Morain died in camp a few days since and that an ox of the same gentleman was killed by lightning while in the yoke[35]

Saturday May 30th have been at work at the boats as the river falls slowly and th[e] banks muddy the boats are launched and are now being annexed and will try to cross the first division to day about a half mile from Camp up the spring branch on the right hand fork is a most beautiful spring and a fall of water of 12 feet Mr Bryant of our party has named it the "Alcove Spring" the water is of the most excellent kind the spring is surrounded with Ash Cotton wood & Cedar trees it is an excellent place to camp for a day or two to wash, recruit the cattle &c I this day cut the name of the spring in the rock on Table at the top of the falls[36] we have crossed 8 wagons this evening with the Canoes which are about 35 feet long and connected with cross pieces some 8 feet long we have found it necessary to put one log between the boats and one on the upper side—[37]

Sunday May 31st commenced crossing this morning immediately after breakfast in the canoes the river fell but 7 inches last night we crossed 5 wagons pr hour it commenced raining at 5 o'clock p. m. and continued the most of the night all the wagons were crossed by 10 O'clock p. m. the company were verry much fatigued no guard out this night[38] we formed Carell on the prarie about ½ mile from the river one of the most beautiful falling spring on the right of the camping ground wood in abundance I would advise emigrants to cross this creek before camping on account of the suden rise of the river after showers as we have been delayed 5 ½ days

Monday June 1st 1846 Started at 8 Oclock a.m. and travelled 12 Miles to a creek[39] plenty wood & water—

Tuesday June 2d last night courts were held to try a dutchman for insulting officers and to settle a disagreement between Col Thornton and his partner in the wagon great confusion prevailed and the meeting broke up in a row this morning a meeting was called and the oregon part of the party were requested to seperate and some 20 wagons lead off which reduced our number to about 40 wagons[40] we have travelled this day 12 or 14 miles to a small creek; we met two Shawnee Indians this evening and stoped them in our Camp until morn to enable the members of the company to write the settlements as they live near Westport Mo they are returning from the Platte river where the have been traping and Buffalo hunting.[41]

Wednesday June 3d started this morning ¼ before 7 Oclock a. m. and travelled through a broken country plenty of wood & water the ditches in the Praries verry bad several teams were stalled we traveled 20 Miles to a tributary of the little blue and camped about one mile from the little blue different members of the company saw some 8 or 10 Antelope & Elk on coming into Camp this evening some 2 or 3 men in the Company got into a quarrel a Knife was used on the fingers of one of them not much damage done.[42]

Thursday June 4th started at ¼ after 7 oclock and travelled about 25 miles over the finest road in the world to a branch of the "little blue" we saw several antelopes to day but have not been able to kill one yet Mr Grayson this day killed a deer the first blood drawn by the com-

pany[43] we had a fine chase after a wolf but on account of
the ditches we could not over take it the men run one
antelope within 200 yds of the Wagons the weather for
the past five days has been very cold thermometer from
44 to 50 at sun rise several attacks of bilious chills

Friday June 6th [5th] Thermometer at sun rise this
morning stood at 44 started ¼ before 8 O'clock some 25
miles over fine roads through several long bottoms and
camped on the little blue several antelopes seen this day
one man reports having seen some 40 or 50 and that he
shot one but was not able to get it[44]

Saturday June 7th [6th] Started at 8 O'clock detained
by loosing oxen traveled 20 miles over fine roads and
camped on the little blue near a fine creek running into
the blue the water clear & cold this day the weather has
changed and become very warm the muschetoes and knats
were very annoying to the Horses this day plenty of antelope and hares were seen but none killed excepting one
hare.[45]

Sunday June 8th [7th] Started at 7 OClock and traveled over fine roads up the little blue untill 12 O'clock
then left it in a north west direction and travelled untill
5 O'clock and went into Camp on a creek supposed to be
a tributary of the Platte we traveled some 17 Miles this
stoped early to wait for Mr Bryants wagon as the axle
was broken some 5 miles back we have found the soil
much poorer and the grass thin and short the last 3 or 4
days one duck was all the game killed this day great
numbers of the antelope were seen the Oregon party some
3 miles ahead of us saw a lot of Pawnees this morning on
the opposite side of the river the first we have seen since
we have been in the nation[46]

Monday June 9th [8th] Started at 7 Oclock and struck
the Platte river at the Grand Island about 5 O'clock and
traveling up three miles and camped we made some 20
miles over good roads this day Mr Grayson killed an
antelope to day the first one shot found the meat better
than the deer we found the wood for cooking our first

guard heard guns fired from the oregon camp some 3
miles ahead a scouting party of 7 men was detached and
sent on returned and reported that it was done by some
foolish young men our camp was formed on the river
bank a beautiful place the river stud[d]ed with small
islands the river high and muddy[47]

Tuesday June 10th [9th] Started at 8 Oclock traveled
along the bank of the Platte over good roads 18 miles the
weather pleasant and camped at 6 O'clock the oregon co
3 miles ahead saw a notice this day on a stick by the side
of the road that a company of 66 wagons for oregon &
California left that point on the Morning of the 8th [48] we
are traveling up the bottom of the Platte which is some 3
or 4 miles wide and perfectly level the soil sandy & mixed
with salt peter at the edge of the bottom is a continuous
range of sand hills verry broken

Wednesday June 11th [10th] started at 8 Oclock
traveled up the Platte 20 miles the soil and scenery the
same as yesterday[49]

Thursday June 12th [11th] started at 7 ½ O'clock
traveled 20 Miles

Friday June 13th [12th] Started at 8 O'clock traveled
18 miles and camped about one mile from the Platte on a
tributary a small quant[it]y wood

Saturday June 14th [13th] Stoped all day to wash and
repair wagons[50]

Sunday June 15th [14th] traveled 20 miles to day along
the Platte soil and scenery the same as before.

Monday June 16th [15th] started at 8 Oclock and
travelled 20 miles and camped at a fine spring one mile
from the river.[51]

Tuesday June 17th [16th] started at 8 O'clock traveled
some 20 miles and camped on the river at the forks[52] this
day met a party of some 15 men that left oregon the first
of March with pack horses & mules part of them Camped
with us until morning they report that a Company of
214 Wagons that went to oregon last year took a new
route from Ft Hall and 70 persons died from starvation

and fatigue Wrote and sent letters by Mr Wall to the States[53]

Wednesday June 18th [17th] Started 7 ½ O'clock travelled 17 miles crossed the Platte and camped on the opposite side the river about ¾ mile wide 2 ½ feet deep distance by way of the crossing one mile[54] the bottom of the river is coarse sand and gravel all the wagons crossed safe, the river was riseing some 6 or 8 inches pr day would not been able to cross next morning the roads all along the Platte are of the best quality no wood useing Buffalo Chips alltogether for cooking the men kill more buffalo than is wanted by the Company every day

Thursday June 19th [18th] Started at 8 ¼ O'clock weather clear and warm we have had no rain since we left the crossing of the blue a large Buffalo came into our Camp this Morning among the Cattle Mr B- gave chase & killed it. travelled up the south fork some 13 miles to the upper crossing and camped.[55]

Friday June 20th [19th] Started at 7 O'clock and travelled over to the North fork of the Platte distance 23 miles I this day rode ahead alone and arrived at the river at 12 O'clock found a Oregon company of 26 wagons in camp to burry a young man that died this morning [of] fever & disease of the heart[56] the road across from the South to the North fork is high barren prarillon five miles next the north fork is "ash hollow" the most wild barren pass that I ever saw a few scattering ash trees along the bottom the hills verry steep at the mouth of the hollow next the river we found a small log building put up by some Mackinaw boat men last winter as they were caught by the ice it is called "ash hollow Hotel" we found Memorandums of all the emigrating parties that have passed this spring I found a card from my self from Woodworth U. S. N. left on the 8th [57] we camped some two miles up the river

Saturday June 20th This day I left the Company with 10 men to go ahead to Ft Larimie we travelled some 30 or 35 Miles over sandy roads and over took Cap Dickenson

Co of 14 wagons and stopped with them over night this evening we had quite a thunder show the first rain since we left the blue[58]

Sunday June 21st Started at 7 O'clock passed McCutchens co 3 miles from our camp Campbells 6 miles & Coopers 15 miles[59] travelled 33 miles and camped on the bank of the river opposite the "Chimnies" 80 miles from Ft Larimie. went to the Upper base of the Chimnies the Chimnies about 100 feet composed of soft rock and hard white earth the hills in the vicinity resemble old forts the river stud[d]ed with small islands cov'd with grass the Scenery beautiful.[60]

Monday June 22[d] Started at 6 O'clock travelled 45 miles and camped on the banks of the Platte rain & cold at night[61]

Tuesday June 23[d] Started at 6 ½ Oclock raining nooned at Scotts bluff Scenery beautiful[62] stoped at Harlens & Youngs camp east of the bluff[63] arrived at Fort John or Bernard[64] about 3 O'clock went 7 or 8 miles to Ft Larimie stopped a few minutes passed Mr ames and some 20 Oregon [wagons?] 2 miles west of the Ft went on with Mr Lippincott five miles from the Ft. and camped with him and four wagons for Oregon[65] some 2500 Sius Iindians at the Ft making up a war party to fight the "Crows"[66] rained all night

Wednesday June 24th Morning clear and beautiful started fort Bernard via Larimie met Mr Ames got him to return with me arrived at the Ft Mr A sold his wagon fr two mules[67]

Thursday June 25th weather clear remain at the Ft to wait our company Coopers Dickenson, Craigs companies came up and camped.[68]

Friday June 26 Messrs Bryant and Jacobs sold their wagon for 7 pack mules— Col Russell also sold his.[69]

Saturday June 27 took out our baggage the company left at 12 Oclock A company of 5 men 1 woman & two children came up and camped two miles east of the fort stayed in camp with them gave a verry bad account of

California[70] report my friend Reading doing well

Sunday June 28th Col. Russell Messrs. Bryant Jacobs, Kirkendall Ewing, Holder, B[r]ookie, Nutall & Brown left on pack Mules[71]

Monday June 29 left the fort about 3 O'clock p. m. on pack mules with Messrs Ames, Wells & McCleary[72] travelled 20 miles & Camped at a large spring—

Tuesday June 30th Started before breakfast travelled 12 miles and camped on a creek for the day to repair packs &c passed Dunbars company two miles from the camp and also our old company under way at the crossing of the creek Capt Boggs just resigned[73]

GEORGE McKINSTRY, JR., TO PIERSON B. READING, NEW HELVETIA, NOVEMBER 2, 1846.[74]

Dear Reading,

I arrived at this place on the evening of Oct. 19th [75] and found your kind favor of 6th ult. Midshipman Byers of the Portsmouth was here at the time waiting to take down volunteers with the ships 1st cutter. I immediately wrote to you, to send by him, together with the letters of your Brother, but Capt. Sutter and others thought it doubtfull whether they could be forwarded to you with certainty. I concluded to wait for a more direct and safe conveyance which now offers by Mr. Burrows[76] who brought me yours of Oct. 22nd, dated off Monterey and I embrace the opportunity of writing to return my thanks for the kind attention you have shown me on my arrival in this country and to forward to you three letters from your Brother which you must be very anxious to peruse. I should have sent them ahead by Col. Russell but was fearful he might lose them and had my health been good I should have arrived a few days after him,[77] but I became so weak I found it advisable to give up packing on the Great Salt Lake and take to the wagons and after a long and tedious journey I have arrived in much better health than I could have expected on crossing the main California Mountain. The weather was extreamly disagreeable, snowing all the time. I had a severe attack of disease of the lungs and was obliged to be hauled in the wagons for a few days. On arriving at the Bear River Valley I took my mule and rode in for fear of being caught in more bad weather. The beautiful weather of this valley has strengthened me up and I am in better health than I have been for years. But I think I had better take your advice and remain here untill you return.

Capt. Sutter has received me with the utmost kindness and wishes me to assist him in his business as long as I wish. I shall do so untill I meet you, when I shall be ready to engage in any thing you may propose, that I am capable of doing. I am anxious once more to be most busily engaged in business and if my good health is only continnued it will afford me great pleasure.

I have taken much pains to make the acquaintance of all the immigrants from the U. S. this season and think I have done so favorably. Should you want to use them I would take great pleasure in assisting you. While packing I travelled and camped with all of them. The emigration is of a good character, entirely different from the Texas Emigrants that we knew in our Mississippi days. Good farmers and mechanics, with a small sprinkle of "Yankee peddlers."

The Russian American Co., have attached all the Real Estate of your friend Capt. Sutter to secure their debt of $27,000.[78] At the request of Capt. Sutter and Mr. Sinclair the alcalde, I have accepted the appointment of Sheriff and Inspector of this district and serve the attachment in this part of the country. It is only known by us three. I have written to Mr. Hastings and enclosed him copy and asked his opinion. Mr. Lei[des]dorf writes that the Co. only want to prevent the sale of the lands until their debt has been paid. I presume it was brought about by Lei[des]dorff although in his letter he denies it. At the request of Capt. Sutter I have written to Commodore Stockton at Monterey by T. O. Larkin offering him the

Fort and a sufficient quantity of land and referred him to you for discription of place and price. Capt. Sutter will write you on the subject by Mr. Burrows. He appears to be anxious to sell it and retire to his farm on Feather River. It is of course unnessary to ask you to lend your assistance in effecting the sale.[79] The Capt. thinks some of joining a volunteer emigrant corps now being raised by Messrs. Bryant, Brown, Jacobs and other gentlemen. They have requested him to take the command. Capt. S. has raised 100 Indians "horsethieves" that will accompany them if he accepts.[80] I shall be kept in charge of his business. I was extremely sorry at not getting in in time to see you but am happy to learn that you have been called to fill so honorable a station. Now [Had?] I have got here in time I should have joined you in some capacity but think with you that it would be imprudent for me to travell and camp out during the rainy season until my health is firmly established. While writing our friend Capt. Kerne[81] is in bed by my side (in the office) shaking finely with the chills, my old enemy that I have been fighting the past five years. I dimand a truce for a short time at any rate.

I have not time to give you history of my life since we parted and my long laborious trip over the American desert. When we meet which I hope will be soon we can talk over all old affairs.

Your Brother will give you the news of the East in his letters. I will give you yours of the Sunny South and the West. A small war party of Walla Walla Indians have just rode up in front of the fort in full costume, music and yells.[82] They will go down with Mr. Burrows party tomorrow. It will be some 8 or 10 days before the last emigrant party of volunteers will go down as some of them are back on the Mountains. I will do all I can to push their movements and forward them to your assistance at the earliest date. I hope the God of war will protect your little army and bring you out victorious. Let me hear from you at all times. I shall look for your return with great impatience. I have obtained a small set of books of one of the emigrants and will put the old Captains accounts ship shape as soon as possible. I hope he may be successful in selling this property to the U. S. Government. He will then be able to settle up his debts and retire to his farm with a very pretty fortune. The business of this place appears to be too much for him and it will be necessary for the U. S. Government to have a garrison at this point to protect the citizens and emigrants from the U. States.

Until we meet, farewell my dear Reading,

Yours truly,

GEO. MCKINSTRY.

Nov. 6th. Mr. Burrows has been detained untill this date mounting cannon but will start this morning with 25 or 30 men. I am sorry to learn by Mr. Foster that you have been quite unwell but am happy to be informed that you have recovered. Nothing of importance has occured since writing as above. No arrival from Sonoma. All things remain quiet here. The weather is bad. I am fearful the snow is too deep for the last Company of emigrants to cross the Mountains.[83] Mr. Burrows will find it difficult traveling with the cannon. It is thought the stream is swimming. Capt. Sutter has secured an excellent gardner from the emigration to make him a Nursery and garden on the Hock farm. If you could send him a lot of seed, fruit trees &c from below I presume he would be very grateful.

Yours,   McK.

"Indians Horse-Racing"

Diary of James Mathers

James Mathers' diary begins in mid-course, explained by a notation on the cover: "Journal of travels from Missouri to California 1846 Continued from another book.—" That first book has been lost; what is preserved to us is a volume commencing at the crossing of the North Platte on July 4 and continuing until his arrival at Mission San Jose on November 7. This abrupt beginning makes the record a fitting complement to George Mc-Kinstry's diary, which leaves off just before Mathers' begins. But if Mathers' own chronicle is incomplete, his interesting history before he embarked upon the overland trails may be developed from other sources; few who went west in 1846 did so with a comparable biography.

According to Thompson & West's *History of San Luis*

Obispo County (Oakland, 1883), p. 382, James Mathers was born March 15, 1790, emigrated in 1819 from New York State to Elkhart County, Indiana, and in 1832 removed to Will County, Illinois. Information obtained by Miss Frances Campbell from Mr. Sterling J. Patterson, Plainfield, Illinois, indicates that James and Sara Mathers came to Plainfield in 1833 and with four other couples were instrumental in organizing the Congregational Church there the following year. On the north edge of the village Mathers built a grist mill which he is stated to have operated until about 1844, when he sold it to a Mr. McCallister.

The date 1844 should doubtless be 1842, for in the fall of that year James Mathers, his wife, and their two nearly grown sons, Carolan and Marcellus, traveled to the Pawnee villages on the Loup Fork of the Platte in present Nebraska to become government farmers. A Presbyterian mission among the Pawnees had been opened by John Dunbar and Samuel Allis in 1834, but they had made slow headway, and young George B. Gaston, who had joined the Pawnee mission in May, 1840, had begun to agitate for stronger measures. When the Mathers family came out to the Loup Fork in the fall of 1842, he found in them willing allies. James Mathers had been appointed farmer to the Skidi or Loup Pawnees, and his eldest son, Carolan, who had been born in 1823, was made farmer to the nearby Pitahauerat or Republican Pawnees.

George E. Hyde has written in *Pawnee Indians* (Denver, 1951), pp. 151-164, that the elder Mathers immediately joined young Gaston in opposing Dunbar and Allis in their policy of coaxing the Pawnees along, Gaston and Mathers being for driving the Indians. "Mathers, setting to work as government farmer to teach the Skidis the first steps in civilization, was soon knocking the Indians down with his fists. He then took a whip to them, and in this his sons and young Gaston enthusiastically aided him." The protests of Dunbar and Allis fell on deaf ears; the new Indian Agent at Council Bluffs, Daniel Miller, came from a slave state and held the view that colored people, Negroes or Indians, "must be handled firmly and forced to do what was for their own good." Indeed, he made James Mathers superintendent of the government establishment among the Pawnees, placing Allis and the rest under Mathers' orders.

In the summer of 1844 the Mathers party whipped out of their fields hungry Pawnees who were gathering corn, whereupon a party forcibly looted Mathers' potato field. Failing to profit from this lesson, Carolan Mathers caught a Pawnee taking roasting ears from a field, and shot him in the back, inflicting an apparently mortal wound. He had previously whipped a Pawnee girl so severely that she almost died. The resulting crisis brought the Indian Agent out from Bellevue in October. As George Hyde says: "The agent began to storm up and down and roar. He shouted that the whites were right to whip or even to shoot Indians they caught stealing, and that the chiefs should then have the men whipped a second time. White men were whipped for stealing, and the Pawnees should also be whipped. At this most of the chiefs got up and started to leave the council. Miller yelled at them to come back, and a few returned. The agent then called the names of the few government employees the chiefs had spoken well of and dismissed these men on the spot . . . . "

Every man friendly with the missionaries was removed from the government payroll and ordered to depart. "Mathers was left in charge, to continue his policy of beating and driving the Indians. In the spring of 1845 Thomas Harvey, the Indian superintendent from St. Louis, visited the Loup Fork and, after listening to the statements of the chiefs and the white men, he warned the government employees that they must cease their harsh treatment of the Indians. But he left in charge men who believed in harsh treatment, and there was little change in the conduct of Mathers and his friends."

That spring there was trouble between the Pawnees and the Otos. One consequence was that when Mathers came to the Bellevue Indian Agency with six wagons to haul supplies to the Loup Fork, armed Otos forced him to unload all ammunition. "When the Pawnees came home from their buffalo hunting they inquired anxiously for the ammunition the government agent had promised them, only to learn that the Oto warriors had forced James Mathers to unload all of the ammunition and leave it at Bellevue. Not knowing whether to believe Mathers' story, the Indians were suspicious and angry. Soldier Chief, the Skidi head-chief, went to Mathers' farmhouse and demanded ammunition; but Mathers stated that only a small quantity was on hand, and he refused to give any to the chief. There was a violent quarrel. Many horns of powder were hanging on the walls of the room in which the two men were arguing, and Soldier Chief rushed to the wall and began taking down the powderhorns. Mathers shouted at him to stop, then seized an axe and hewed at the chief's arm, cutting through the bone and leaving the hand dangling by a few shreds of flesh. The chief ran in on his assailant as he raised the axe again and grappled with him, holding him with his wounded arm while with his sound hand he tried to wrench the axe out of his hand. Mathers' son Marcellus now rushed in to aid his father, but the wounded Pawnee hurled Mathers across the room and turned to face the younger man. Marcellus turned to run, and Soldier Chief pursued him; but he was now weak from loss of blood and, finding that he could not overtake the white man, he threw the axe and the blade sank into the flesh of young Mathers' back between his shoulders. Soldier Chief staggered out into the Pawnee Village, shouting for the people to avenge him until he fell unconscious.

"The village was in an uproar. The fallen chief was surrounded by a throng of furious Skidis. Indians were running for weapons; but from the roofs of some of the big earth-lodges the chiefs were haranguing the people, urging them not to kill the whites. Mathers and the other white men had barricaded themselves and their families inside their log houses and were preparing to fight for their lives. Among the Indians there was no leadership. The chiefs were calling for peace while some of the warriors were shouting for vengeance. If they could not kill the white men, there was the property of these white men to be avenged on. A number of warriors rushed to the farm buildings and began to shoot the cattle and destroy wagons, harness, and other articles; but before they could begin an actual attack on the whites some friendly chiefs placed a picked body of warriors inside the log houses. Faced with this opposition, the mob of angry Skidis sullenly withdrew to their village.

"This affair occurred just as the Indians were ready to set out on their winter hunt, and the chiefs, who were strongly opposed to killing the whites, hastened the departure of the tribe, hoping that before the people came home in the spring their anger would subside. Soldier Chief had died of his wound; young Mathers was dying. James Mathers had had enough of trying to civilize the Pawnees by violent methods . . . . Young Mathers died at Dunbar's mission house [in mid-November]; Mathers was dismissed from the government service and took his family to Bellevue, the whites fearing a general massacre if the Pawnees found this man at the settlement when they returned in the spring. Mathers and his wife bitterly accused the missionaries of causing all the trouble by supporting the chiefs in their opposition to what the Mathers family regarded as progress . . . . "

The foregoing account Hyde based largely upon letters by the Pawnee missionaries published in *Kansas Historical Collections,* 1915-1918, vol. XIV, pp. 570-784. One of these letters, begun by Timothy E. Ranney on January 12, 1846, contains a postscript dated January 15, "Since writing what I have I have heard that Mr. James Mathers was called from the country and is expected to leave today." This comment puts a period to Mathers' service among the Pawnees, but poses a question as to his movements during the next few months.

In all likelihood the Mathers family made their way into northwestern Missouri, and as the spring of 1846 came on decided to head for the Pacific. They may have visited their old home in Illinois, or they may merely have written home, but sometime during the spring they were joined by Otis Ashley, who clearly was a son-in-law.

A biographical sketch of Ashley in E. S. Harrison, *History of Santa Cruz County* (San Francisco, 1892), p. 232, says that he was born July 20, 1820, in Martinsburg, Lewis County, New York, and was the son of a farmer, obtaining a limited education at the district schools. He had married Sallie M. Mathers on December 29, 1841, and they had one daughter, Sarah E., born October 4, 1845. (Another account of Ashley printed in *Riptide,* October 19, 1950, relates that he was living in Plainfield, Illinois, "when the spirit of overland adventure struck." With their infant daughter "the couple proceeded to Peru on the Ill. river, thence by water to Weston, Mo., crossing to Calif. by ox team.")

In view of the troubles James and Carolan Mathers had experienced with the Pawnees, it is likely they took a more southerly route to reach the Platte, leaving the Missouri at Independence or St. Joseph rather than at Iowa Point. Presumably they passed through the Pawnee country uneventfully; had the first volume of Mathers' diary survived, it might have hinted at none of the violent disorders of the past few years, or the climactic tragedy in which his second son was mortally wounded. Nothing was said of this chapter of the past after the Mathers family arrived in California.

The Thompson & West county history says simply that Mathers came to California from Illinois in 1846, settled in Santa Clara County, and removed to San Luis Obispo County in 1858. "Mr. Mathers was an honest man, a good neighbor, and an excellent citizen . . . [who] died of old age on the 6th of April, 1870, at his rancho near Cambria." His wife Sarah (Clarke) Mathers, had died August 6, 1869, aged 68.

According to his granddaughter, Mrs. Mattie Bartol of Talent, Oregon, Carolan Mathers married Margaret Burrel in 1846, probably after reaching California. Five children in all were born to them. Like his father, Carolan settled eventually at Cambria, in San Luis Obispo County. He was a farmer, at various times also a real estate agent, surveyor, newspaper correspondent, and active Republican.

By E. S. Harrison's account, Otis Ashley reached Johnson's Ranch October 13, 1846 (a date the Mathers diary corrects as October 20). "After arriving he stopped at the Santa Clara Mission for a while, served three months under General Fremont [*i.e.,* in the California Battalion], and arrived in the Zyante Valley, in Santa Cruz County, March 13, 1847. He helped to build three sawmills on the San Lorenzo River. In 1848 he moved to San Jose where he remained until June, 1856, when he returned to Zyante Valley, settled on a piece of government land on the west side of the Zyante Rancho, and built a sawmill." Eight children were born to him and his wife Sallie, seven after reaching California. Otis Ashley died at Felton, Santa Cruz County, March 13, 1906.

After this long prologue we take up the James Mathers diary. Uncertain with whom or just when he reached the upper North Platte, we follow him southwestward as he sets out for Independence Rock on the Sweetwater River.

❁   ❁   ❁

THE MATHERS DIARY

July 4th 1846 Left our encampment—near the middle crossing[1] of the North Fork of the Platt 100 miles above Fort Larame and traveled a distance of about 15 m. over a high range of hills and encamped in a narrow valley by a large spring.[2] No timber near. A few buffalo were seen to-day and two killed by our party. The country rough and barren.

5th Sunday — Considerable consertion [*i.e.,* concern?] was felt this morning in consequence of the absence of Mr.

Dickinson a young man attached to our company.[3] He with others went out on yesterday to shoot some buffalo, and being on foot fell several miles behind the waggons, when a man in company with Mr. Dickinson becoming much fatigued stoped and requested him to go on and overtake the company and return with a horse. Dickinson thinking to cut off a bend in the road passed us without observing us after we had encamped and coming into the road about three miles ahead of us traveled on until some time in the night supposing we were still ahead— and did not come into camp until 2 O'Clock P. M. Did not remove camp today. A large black bear was seen to pass about a mile from camp. They appear to be plenty in this region.

6th Traveled 18 m and encamped near excellent springs of water, and had good grass but no wood[4] The country destitute of timber. Saw a black bear & buffaloe

7th Traviled 12 m. over a sandy road and encamped on the bank of Sweetwater about a mile below Independence Rock.[5] Saw many buffalo by the way & places once containing water but now covered with a white substance that bears some resemblance to saleratus. There is a large pond of this a little to the east of the Rock on the north side of the road. On the 6th we passed salt Springs, improperly called Soap mines.[6]

8th Stopped a short time at Independence Rock as we passed and then went about 3 m. and encamped above the pass of the river between the high rocks.[7] This is the most interesting sight we have met with on our journey.

9th Traveled 15 m. and encamped on the bend of the creek. The road sandy and hard traveling —

10th Met a man from California returning to the states and read us a letter from Mr. Hastings, giving information respecting the best road to that place.[8] Crossed the creek three times to-day, and passed thro' a narrow place between two high rocky hills.[9] Wile bateing at noon some of our party killed a black-tailed deer on the top of one of the hills. Encamped in the evening one or two miles below where the road leaves the creek Traveled 15 m.

11 Traviled 18 or 20 miles and encamped by the creek. The distance from where the road leaves the creek to where it touches it again is 16 m.[10] There is good Grass about 5 or 6 miles on the way but no water that is good.

12th Sunday — Traveled 9 or 10 miles to where the road leaves the creek again. Found good grass and the creek abounds with fish. The country is less rocky than we found it for two days past. Saw the sun go down behind the snow-capt mountains last evening. The days are hot and the nights, as a general thing not uncomfortable cool. Straw-berrys, curants, and goosberrys are found in the valley of the Sweetwater, but no wood except willow, a little birch, and a few kinds of shrubery—

13th Traveled 16 miles over high hills and through intervening valleys crossing two small brooks three ponds, one small branch of the Sweetwater and encamped on another branch of the same stream to the southeast of the Windriver.[11] The road to day was generally good, except two or three places where it is rocky—Saw large masses of white quarts & a rock dappled with red & white

14th Traveled 3 m. and crossed the Sweetwater to the west and leaving that stream we struck off over the hills dividing the waters of the Platte from those running into the gulf of California, and after traveling 12 m. we came to a marshy prairy made by springs from which issues a brook running to the S. W. where we encamped in the vicinity of 4 companies of emigrants.[12] The Wind river Mountains are a few miles to the N. E. of this place, and its peaks are spoted with Snow. The road sandy & gravelly.

15. Came to Little Sandy a distance of 14 m. Had a heavy fall of rain in the evening; also a light shower the day previous.

16th Our company separated to-day, eight waggons takeing the common rout and the others with Major Cooper took what is called the cutoff.[13] Encamped at 2 P. M. by the Big Sandy. Distance 10 m. The road good and land level. Had a light shower in the evening.

17th Traveled 16 m. and encamped again on the Big Sandy. The day cloudy & cool & the road good

18th Came to Green River—a distance of 7 m. and crossed at 11 A. M. and encamped 6 m. below the ford. The grass poor. Day cloudy & cool. —

19th Sunday — Went over to Blacksfork and encamped 2 m. up the same. Distance 16 miles, and road good. The course from Sweetwater to Little Sandy W. S. W. from Little Sandy to Green River S. W. and fromn Green River a little east of south and from thence to Blacks Fork S. S. W.

20th Traveled 20 m. and encamped again by Blacks Fork Saw [?] flax [?] a kind of thorn not seen before— Course to day nearly South. [*Written in margin*:] frost

21st Came to Fort Bridger a distance of 12 m.[14] cours S W [?]

22nd Remained in camp.

23rd Otis Ashley, Carolan and myself separated from the company and started on the new rout by the way of the Salt Lake the others prefiring the rout by the way of Fort Hall.[15] Traveled to Mud [?] Spring 5 m. road sandy and bad — a little grass—encamped by Mud [?] Creek 6 m. road mostly bad—[16] water & grass. Course to-day S.S.W. (11 [*Written in margin*:] frost

24th To a valley of excellent gras and springs of water 7 m. from thence 8 m. to a Spring and grass 9 m.[17] (16 Road hilly except some 4 or 5 m. Course S. S. W.

25th Traveled to Bear River a distance of 7 m. road hilly— Course S. W. Some pine timber along the river of a good height. Found Harlin's company encamped by the river, and learned that Mr. Hastings with 30 waggons had just left—All the waggons that has come to Bear River 57 — Distance from Fort Bridger to the river 34 m.[18] 34

26th Remained in camp.

27th Traveled 12 m. over a hilly road, but not bad in other respects, and encamped in a valley where there is abundance of grass and good water. Cours S. S. W.[19] 12

28th Traveled down the valley about 19 m.——

29th Came to Weaver's River 4 m. and turned down the same 3 m. and encamped. The whole length of the valley is about 23 m. Cours S. S. W. and there is generally plenty of grass and springs of good water in several places. Towards the lower end of the valley there is a brook [?] that runs into the river. This valley is walled up by mountains on either side, some of them are very high and precipitous, present a grand and imposing appearance. There is no wood except willow brush, a little popple and shrub cedar Scattered here and there on the sides of the mountains[20] 23 [?]

30th Traveled about 5 m. down the river, and then came to a narrow pass between the mountains where the vally was covird with a thick growth of willow brush and other timber, which rendered traveling exceedingly difficult for 5 m when we came into an open valley and encamped[21] Course S. W. —— — 10

31 Travelled a mile through brush, and then entered an open valley and went down the same 9 m. and encamped near a spring brook.[22] Course W.   10

August 1st Went about 3 m. and encamped near to the upper end of the narrows on the river——[23]

2nd Went down and examined the pass and found it to be impracticable for waggons to go thro' although a number of men were at work removing all rocks that were not immovable and digging down the hills to make a way over—an exhibition of most consumate folly.[24] In the evening went up and encamped with Fowler's company.[25]

3rd Early in the morning two parties were sent out to examine different parts of the mountains to find a way to get over into the plain which is but a few miles distant. In the evening two of the men returned without finding a pass where they went[26]

4th In the morning the other men that went out to look for a pass returned without finding one—It was resolved to make the attempt of passing thro' by the way of the river rather than go back 20 m. and take the rout over the mountain and we succeeded in geting about half way thro' and encamped among the rocks.[27]

5th Came out into the plain about the middle of the day much fatigued by the great exertions in geting our waggons over the rocks 5 m.[28]

6th Traveled South about 4 m. and came in sight of the Salt Lake and continuing our course over the plain a little to the left of the lake encamped in the evening near the foot of the mountain.[29] Distance 15 m   15

7th Traveled South crossing two or three brooks and the outlet of Yuta Lake and passing over a dry plain, and then [?] a salt marsh encamped by a mountain & had brackish water[30] 23 [? 20?]

8th Passed round the point of the mountain on the shore of the lake and steering west over the plain encamped abot 9 P.M. on the western side of the same Distance 20 m. We experienced great inconvenience in the former part of the day for the want of fresh water   20 There are a great many beautiful Springs but the water is, in many of them, strongly impregnated with salt. After leaving the mountain we found two very large spring coming out in a deep ravine but a few feet apart one was salt & the other fresh and very good but has a little alkaline taste.[31]

9th Sabbath — Remained in camp — had good grass in abundance and numerous springs, or rather pits, of good water but were much troubled on account of our cattle falling into them and were unable to extricate themselves without assistance[32] — The weather, since we came into this valley, has been hot

August 10th Traveled 15 m and encamped by a point of the mountain at a very large spring of brackish water and but little grass, and that so salt that the cattle would not eat it. Pased a great many salt springs, but none of fresh water.[33] Had a shower in the evening. Course nearly west   15

11th Started early and after traveling 6 [*written over*

5] m. came to grass and found several springs, one of which was fresh but a little impregnated with alcalie. 6 In the evening moved on to a Spring on the Side of the mountain — Distance 6 m. — 6 course S.[34]

12th Remained in camp.

13th Went up the valley 5 m and encamped by fresh water and grass —[35]

14 Remained in camp

15th Went to springs in the mountain[36] 12 m.

16th Started on the long drive and after traveling until near the middle of the next day without resting but a little we were obliged to leave two waggons and go on with the third so as to get the cattle to water the sooner, the distance still being more than 20 m. I remained with the waggons on the salt plain until the evening of the 20th when Carolan came back with the oxen and the next day about 11 o'clock we reached the camp at the foot of the mountains, the whole distance without water about 65 m. On the 18th there was a violent wind and the salt drifted over the plain like snow.[37] 65

22nd Removed our camp about 4 m[38] — Course on the long drive W. N. W. 4

23rd Drove 30 m. and reached water and grass about 2 o'clock A. M. on the 24th The road for 18 m. was bad except 3 m. from the top of the mountain it was better course south & west[39] 30

August 25th Traveled south parallel with the mountain 14 m.[40] — hard travelling — plenty of grass & water — days hot & nights cold — froze ice in a basin more than ¼ of an inch thick.

26th Started early and crossing the mountain (5 m) and the valley (10 m) encamped near the eastern side of another range of mountains.[41] Plenty of water & grass — road bad Course W. 15

27th Remained in camp

28th Passed over a mountain to the west and across a valley and encamped a mile from the foot of another mountain. Distance 14 m.[42] 14

29th Traveled 17 m. S. S. W. over a high ridge of land and diagonal across a valley to the foot of a very high range of mountains lying to the east of Marys river—[43] 17

30th Sabbath — Traveled 9 m. and encamped by excellent grass & water — 9 m. Course S — road good — abundance of grass in this valley[44]

Mo. 31st Traveled 17 m. S. and encamped by a number of large Springs — road mostly good[45] 17 m

Tuesday Sept. 1st 1846 Traveled 12 miles and encamped near to the pass thro' the mountain. Abundance of water & grass along the base of the mountain[46] 12

W. 2nd Passed over the mountain and encamped in the valley by a Small Creek — cours S. W. & N. W. — distance — 15 — heavy traveling.[47]

T. 3rd Went down the creek 10 m — road good cours north[48]

F 4th Remained in camp — morning extremely cold —

S. 5th Traveled down the valley 20 m — road mostly good — course a little west of north — 2 or 3 Small Springs about 10 m. on the left of the road[49]— 20 m.

Sabbath — 6th Went down the valley through a pass in a mountain and encamped above another pass — course N. W. — distance 4 Running water by our camp but the water Sunk a little below —[50]

M. 7th Went thro' the pass — distance 12 m. — road bad — crossed the channel of the creek a great many times — no water until within 2 m. of the plain where are large Springs — general course west but traveled in every direction[51] 12

T. 8th Traveled 5 m. and came to Mary's River & also the old road — course S. W.— Continued down the river 1 ½ m. and encamped in a pass[52] Distance to-day — 6 ½ m. Total distance from Fort Bridger to old road 459

W. 9th Went through the pass across the valley and 8 miles onto a high mountain and encamped by Springs of very good water & grass—Distance 16½ [*sic*] m[53] 18 m.

T 10th Went down the mountain 7 m. and down the

river 8 m. — 15

F. 11th Traveled 16 m. 16

S. 12th Traveled 14 m. 10 miles extremely dusty. 14 m.

Sabbath 13th Traveled 17 m road good cours to-day N. W. general course since we came to the Road S. W. 17

M. 14th Traveled 17 miles 12 m. road good 5 m sandy and one bad hill course N.W. 12 S.W. 5[54] 17

15th Traveled 16 m. course S. W. — road tolerably good. In the evening saw some Indians but none came to our camp — They lighted several fires within one mile of us and we felt alarmed for the safety of our cattle and kept watch through the night—[55] 16

16 Traveled 15 m — course S. & W. Road tolerably good except a few miles of sand There has been but little running water in the channel of the river for two or three days travel but a little below our last encampment a creek comes in from the north and there is now plenty of water[56] 15

Thu- 17th Traveled 16 m Course 8 m S. W. & 8 m. S 16

F 18th Traveled 8 m road bad — 4 m. deep sand Course nearly South 8 m

Sat. 19th Traveled 17 m — road good — Course S & S. W — The road to Oregon turned off at about noon — Since then water & grass Scarce[57] 17 m

Sabbath 20th Traveled 12 m. over a barren tract of table land — road exceedingly dusty and the days hot — the country extremely barren and grass Scarce — course a little east of South — 12 m

M 21st Traveled 14 m road Still dusty and the river at a distance—turned off from the road and found good grass Course S. 14

22nd Remained in Camp

23rd Traveled 12 m Course S. S. W. — — 12

24th Traveled 20 m to the Sink of the river — road good — water Scarce & brackish — Course S. S. W.[58] 20

25th Commenced the long drive to Truckey's River at 3 P. M. crossed over the valley a distance of 6 m. and

assend the low parts of the mountain and came to the hot
Spring a distance of 20 m. — thence to a place of brackish
water 5 m thence to the foot of the sand hill 10 m. thence
to Trucky's river 6 ½ m The road over the hills to the
spring is bad & from the sand hill to river very good the
whole distance 41 course S. W. There is no grass on
this rout — We left 2 waggons at the sand hill and returned for them on the 27th the sand is deep and loose to
the river — left one ox by the way —[59]

28th Moved on up Trucky's River - 6 m. Course S. W.

29th Traveled 9 m Course W. S. W.

30th Continued up the river 10 m — Course W. S. W.
10

Thursday October 1st Traveled 3 m to a wide valley
covered with grass and thence across the same 4 m - thence
over a sandy and stony ridge 4 m and encamped by the
river Grass scarce & poor — The road extremely bad
except on the valley — There is pine timber on the river
and on the mountains to the westward — Some of the
trees quite large General course to day West[60] 11 m.

F 2nd Continued up the river 6 m — found a patch
[?] of good grass — road bad Course W. 6 m

Sat 3rd Traveled 2 m. to where the road leaves the
river and passed over a very high mountain covered with
lofty pine & cedar and encamped in a small valley by a
spring — Course W. N. W. There is less stone on the
mountain than along the river and the road is not very
bad—over the mountains. 5 m.[61] 7 m.

Sabbath 4th Traveled 7 m to a creek and from thence
to a small valley of grass and Springs 5 m. road good
general course S. S. W.[62] 12

M. 5th Traveled 12 m and encamped in a forest of
small pine trees in the mountain near the head of a branch
of Trucky's River—road generally good—passed several
patches of grass and creeks or Springs of water General
course S. W.[63] 12

Tus. 6th West 3 m to the foot of a bold mountain that
looked to be almost impassable. The road was rocky and

some places steep others flat [?] We were now obliged to take most of the loading out of our waggs and pack it up the mountains 100 rods and 6 or seven yoke of oxen then drew up the waggons, and about noon on the 7th we were ready to move down the mountain and e[n]camped in a valley about 4 m from the summit. The weather was cold and on the 7th we had frequent squalls of snow and the braws [?] flew to the southwest — course W.64 7 m.

8th Continued down the mountain 10 miles and encamped at the last good grass for two or three days travel ahead the day clear but cold The road hilly & rocky Course W65 10 m

F 9th Traveled down the mountain 7 m. & the road rocky and extremely bad—almost impassable—the weather continues to grow warmer as we descend the mountain—grass scarce—Course W. 7 m.

10th Traveled 6 m. over a horrible road and encamped in the valley and drove our cattle onto the mountain—66 6

Sunday 11th Traveled from [?] a lake on the mountain to a valley of water & grass The road bad & the descent into the valley was steep & long—67 6 m.

M 12th Traveled 7 m the road mostly hilly but less rock than heretofore — encamped on the mountain, and went ½ a mile down a difficult place to water68— 7 m.

T 13th — Passed a spring and after traveling 4 m. passed other Springs and encamped on a high ridge 8 or 900 ft above the creek The road to day tolerably good but uneven69 7 m.

W. 14th Traveled 6 m and encamped by a creek—The mountains on both sides are high and steep — no grass — weather warm

Th. 15th Rested our oxen and took three waggons to the top of the mountain in the evening—

F. 16th Traveled 4 m and drove our cattle down to a creek where was a little grass — 4 m.

S. 17th Traveled 5 m. and found grass and water ½ m to the left of the road — The road to-day hilly but good in other respects 2 bad hills 4 [sic] m.

Sabbath 18th Traveled 7 m found a little grass and poor water — the road good but hilly — 7 m.

M. 19th Traveled 9 m. the road still hilly but the ground firm [?] The hills are covered with oak & but little pine is to be seen

T. 20th Traveled 11 m. and encamped 2 m above [?] Johnsons — The road to-day was good — the general course for 50 or 60 m is West[70]

W. 21st Went down to Johnsons and remained till friday morning—the weather cloudy & cool— 2

F. 23rd Traveled 6 m and encamped by a pond of water in the bed of a creek—weather cloudy & cool —

24th Traveled 16 m and encamped in a grove

Sunday 25th Went to the American Fork and encamped near to Mr. St. Clair's — 2 m from Sutter's fort — course from Johnson's nearly S — distance — 14 m.[71]

M & Tuesday 26 & 27th remained in camp

W 28th Started for the S. Joseph's Mission and encamped by a pond ¾ of a mile from wood — 10 m

T 29th Went to Murphy's 6 m.—It commenced raining the night previous and continued to rain through the greater part of the day 6 m

Fr. 30th Remained in camp — the weather fine

S. 31st Traveled 10 m. to a creek that was nearly dry—

Sunday Nov. 1st Traveled 8 m. to Mackasamah [Mokelumne] Creek — the road bad it having rained in the night 8 m

M. Nov. 2nd Traveled 18 m to a Spring — latter part of the road bad—land generally good

T. 3rd Went to and crossed the San Joiquin — 12 m.

W. 4th The morning was rainy but we traveled 10 m in the course of the day

Th 5th Traveled 14 m and encamped by a large rock in the mountain on the top of which we found good water — rainy part of the day 14

F 6th Traveled 14 m the day cloudy & wet — 14 m

S. 7th The day clear & pleasant — reached the St. Joseph Mission 7 m[72]

The 1849 map of T. H. Jefferson, showing the emigrant road from Independence, Mo., to San Francisco, Calif., is reproduced in sections on the following pages. In the original edition of Volume I published by the Talisman Press, Georgetown, Calif., in 1963, the map folded out and was inserted in a back pocket.

Part I. A: (reading from right to left, or east to west): Independence, Mo., to camp on Pawnee River, early June 1849

Part I. B: (right to left): from Pawnee River, early June, to Arapaho River, mid-June

Part II. A: (right to left): to Fort Laramie, late June

Part II. B: (right to left): from Fort Laramie to beyond Independence Rock, mid-July

Part III. A: (right to left): from near South Pass to Great Salt Lake, early August

Part III. B: (right to left): from Salt Lake to Valley of Fountains, early September

Part IV. A: (right to left): from Mary River, early September, to Truckey Pass, early October

Part IV. B: (right to left): from Truckey Pass to San Francisco

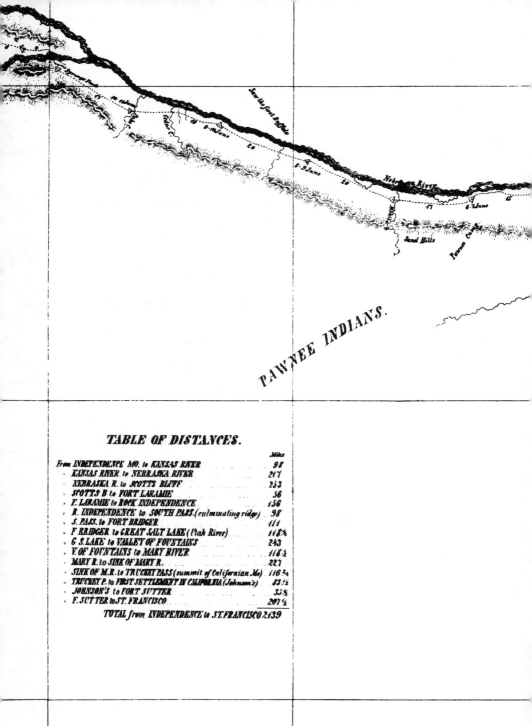

PAWNEE INDIANS.

TABLE OF DISTANCES.

	Miles
From INDEPENDENCE MO. to KANSAS RIVER	98
KANSAS RIVER to NEBRASKA RIVER	217
NEBRASKA R. to SCOTTS BLUFF	253
SCOTTS B to FORT LARAMIE	56
F. LARAMIE to ROCK INDEPENDENCE	156
R. INDEPENDENCE to SOUTH PASS (culminating ridge)	98
S. PASS. to FORT BRIDGER	111
F BRIDGER to GREAT SALT LAKE (Utah River)	118½
G S. LAKE to VALLEY OF FOUNTAINS	243
V. OF FOUNTAINS to MARY RIVER	118½
MARY R. to SINK OF MARY R.	227
SINK OF M.R. to TRUCKEY PASS (summit of Californian Mo)	116¾
TRUCKEY P. to FIRST SETTLEMENT IN CALIFORNIA (Johnson's)	83½
JOHNSON'S to FORT SUTTER	35½
F. SUTTER to ST. FRANCISCO	207½

TOTAL from INDEPENDENCE to ST. FRANCISCO 2139

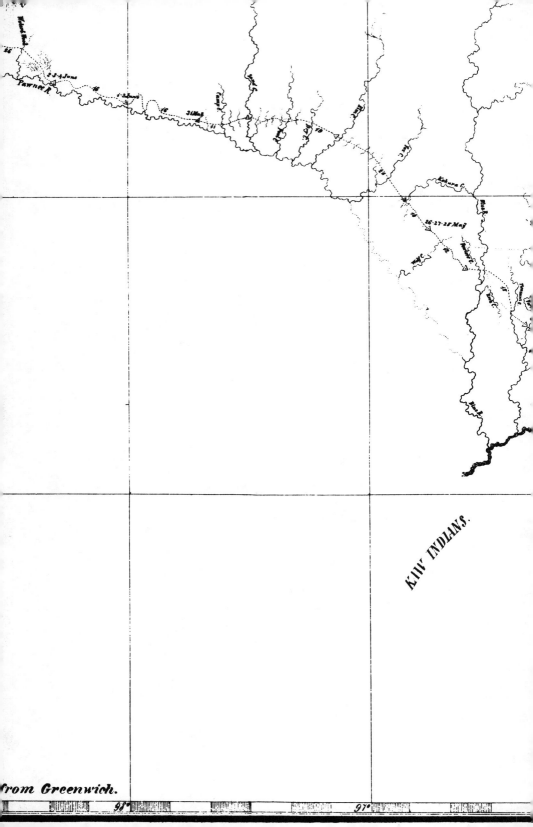

KIIV INDIANS.

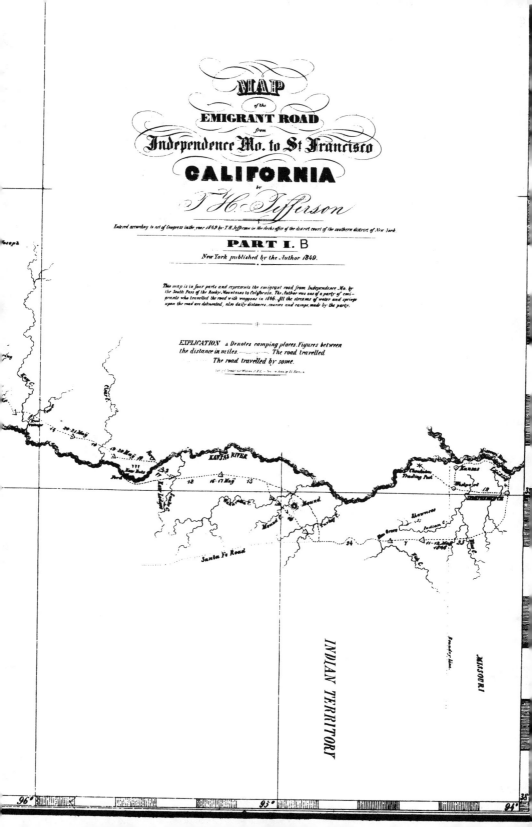

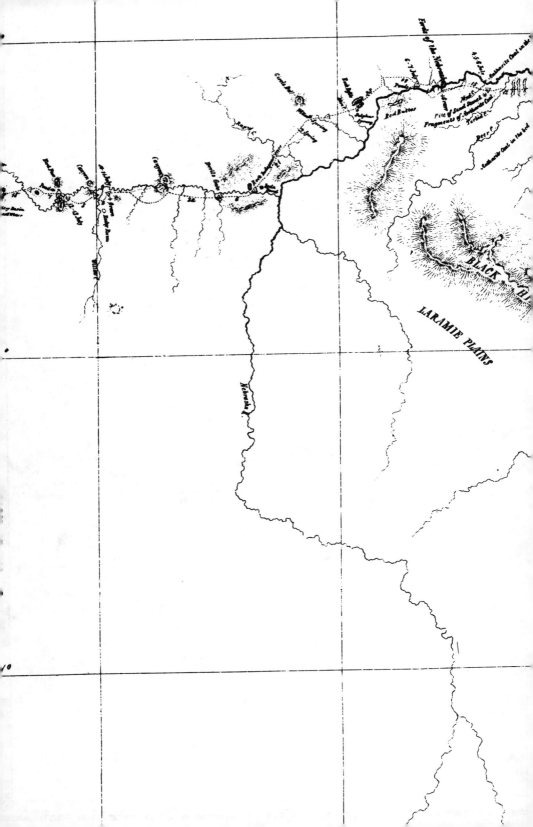

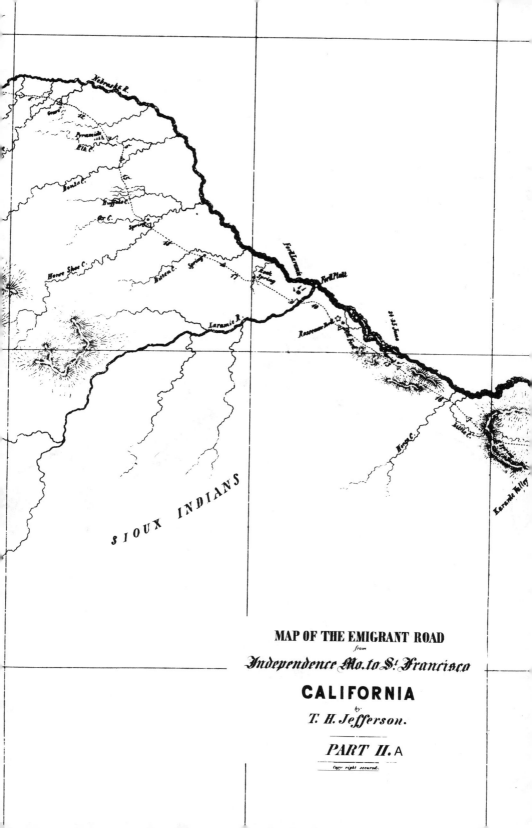

MAP OF THE EMIGRANT ROAD
from
Independence Mo. to St. Francisco

CALIFORNIA
by
T. H. Jefferson.

PART II. A

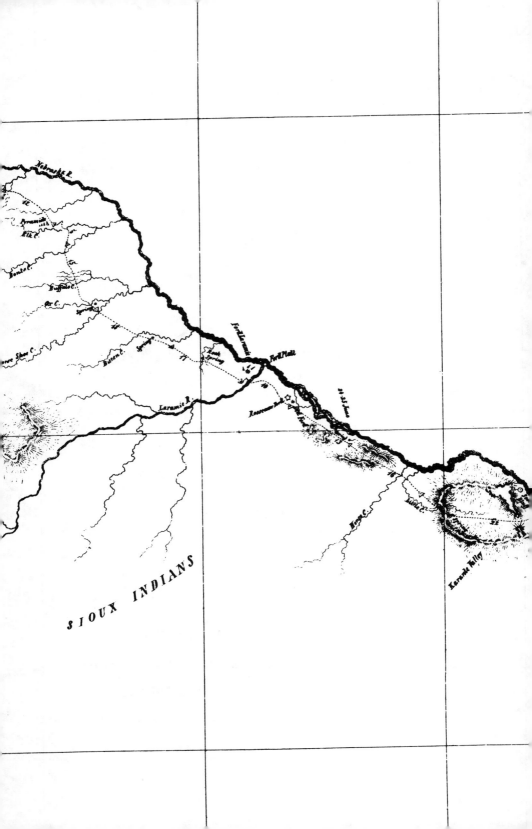

MAP OF THE EMIGRANT ROAD

from

Independence Mo. to S! Francisco

CALIFORNIA

by

T. H. Jefferson.

PART II. B

Copy right secured.

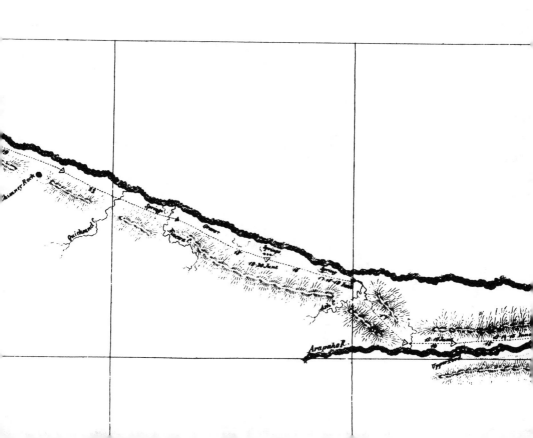

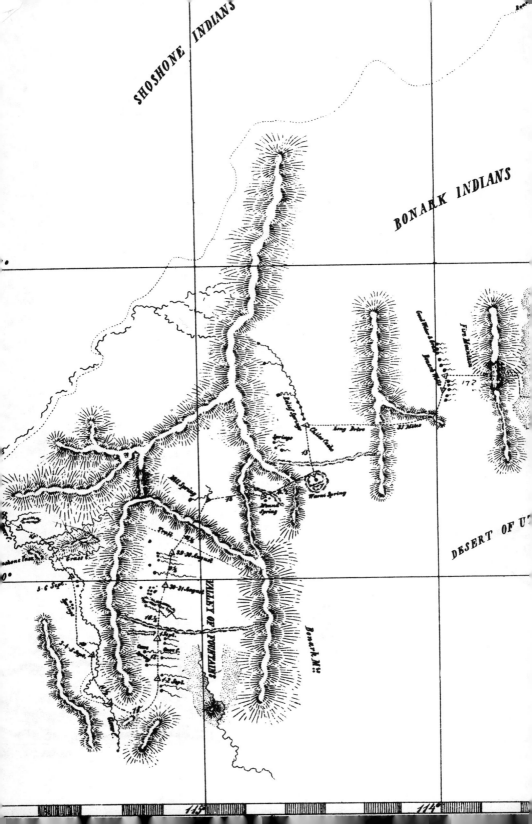

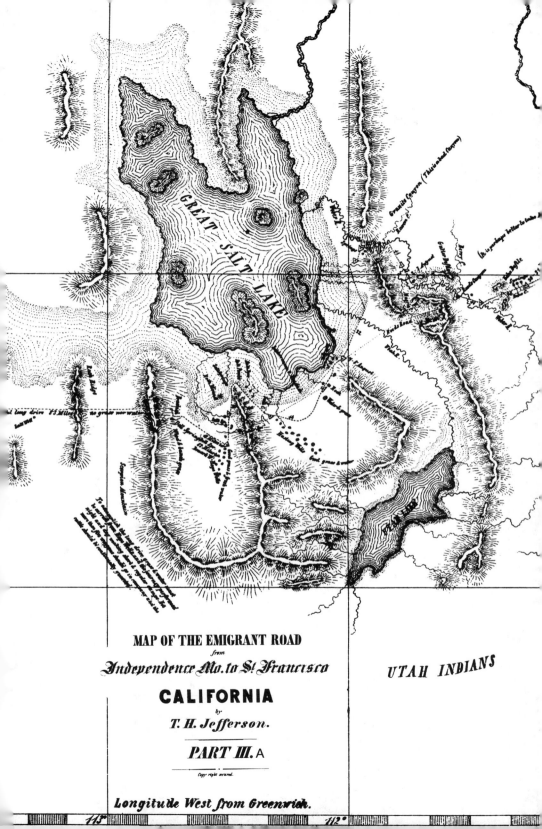

GREAT SALT LAKE

UTAH INDIANS

MAP OF THE EMIGRANT ROAD
from
Independence Mo. to St. Francisco
CALIFORNIA
by
T. H. Jefferson.

PART III. A

Copy right secured.

Longitude West from Greenwich.

115° 112°

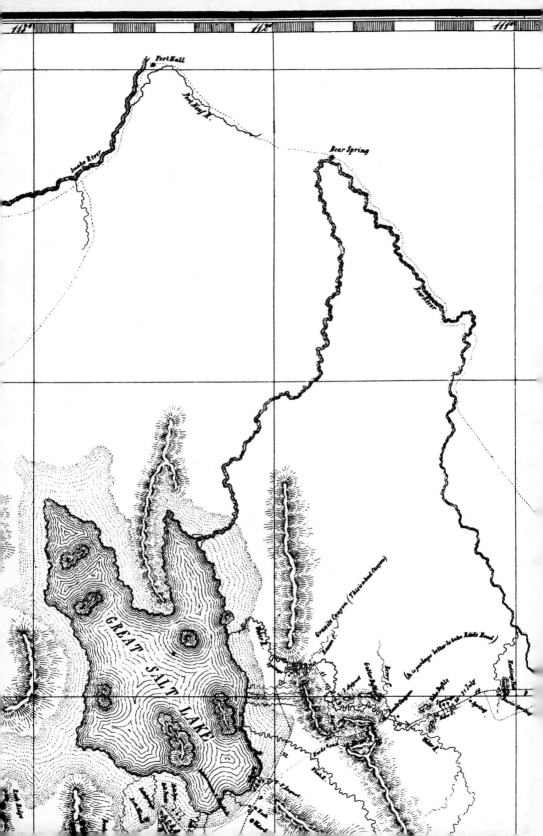

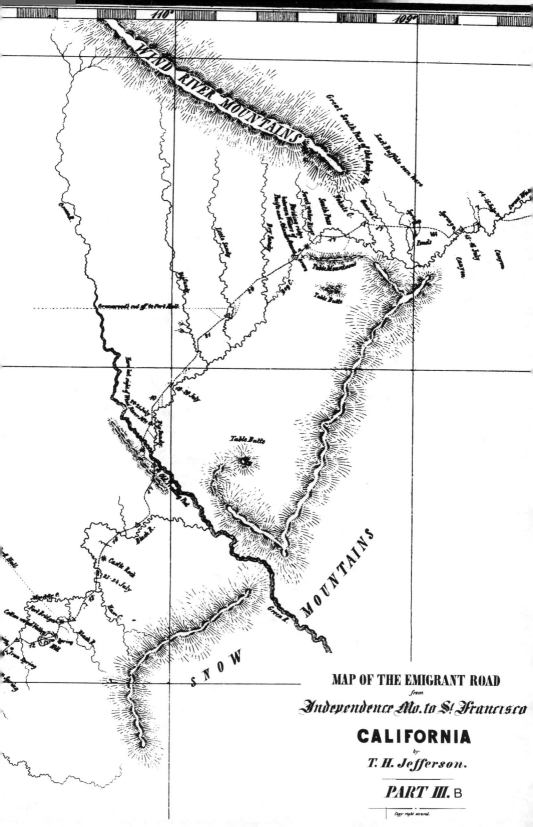

MAP OF THE EMIGRANT ROAD
from
Independence Mo. to St. Francisco

CALIFORNIA
by
T. H. Jefferson.

PART III. B

Copy right secured.

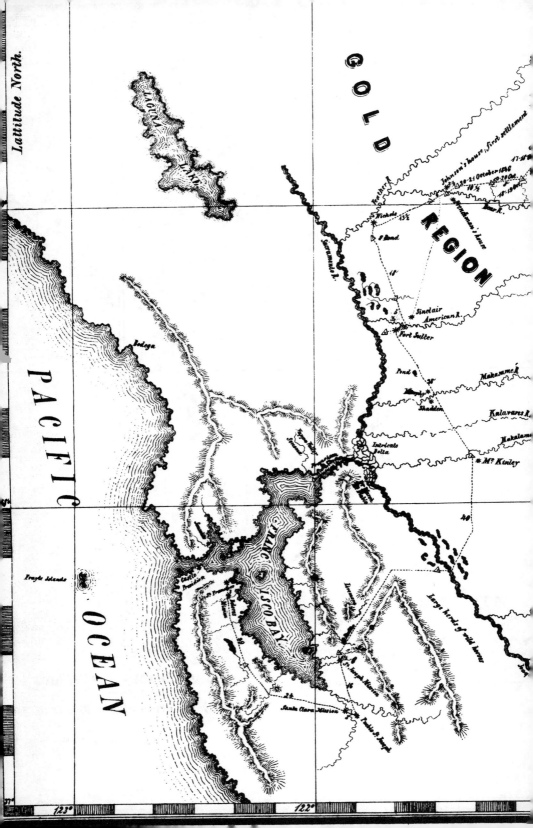

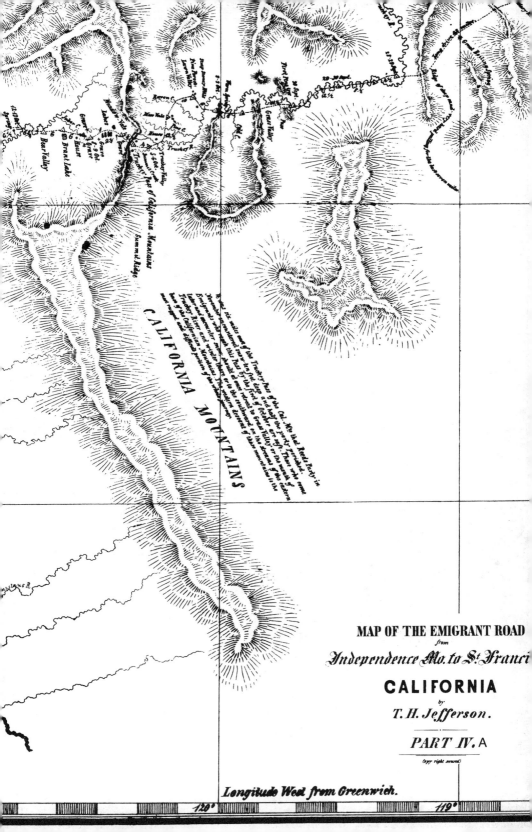

CALIFORNIA MOUNTAINS

MAP OF THE EMIGRANT ROAD
from
Independence Mo. to St. Franci

CALIFORNIA
by
T. H. Jefferson.

PART IV. A

Copy right secured.

Longitude West from Greenwich.

120°   119°

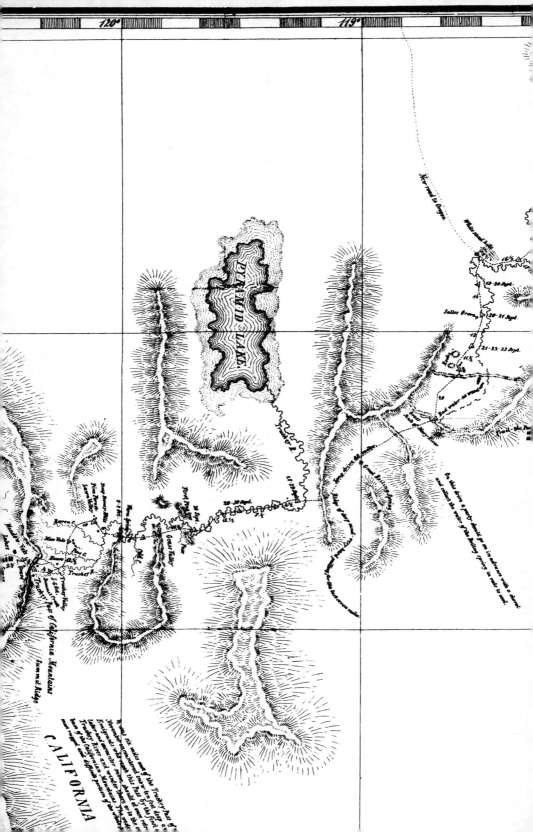

MAP OF THE EMIGRANT ROAD

from

Independence Mo. to St. Francisco

CALIFORNIA

by

T. H. Jefferson.

PART IV. B

"Going up the Truckey River"

The Map of T. H. Jefferson

The sections to be found between pages 236 and 237 are adapted from one of the great American maps, an extraordinarily original production which will always have a special place in the cartography of the West, and which add up to a trail document of high importance. This *Map of the Emigrant Road from Independence, Mo., to St. Francisco, California,* was published by T. H. Jefferson at New York in 1849, having been entered for copyright by the author in the clerk's office of the district court of the southern district of New York; it was "Eng^d in stone by Ed. Herrlein," and issued from the "Lith of G. Snyder 138 William St. N. Y." With its printed *Accompaniment* of 11 pages, it was sold by Berford & Co., 2 Astor House, New York City, at the stiff price of $3 a copy. At least one Forty-niner, J. Goldsborough Bruff, carried a copy overland in 1849, so the work ap-

237

peared early in the year. But no publication notice has
been found, nor have biographical details about the author
emerged except that he was, as might have been expected,
a New Yorker.

As will be seen by the selections from 1846 newspapers
printed in Vol. II of the present work, Jefferson was
glancingly mentioned after reaching Independence, without any intimation that he had the interest and the tech-
nical skills to produce a great map. He is not referred to
in any of the narratives that have thus far come to light.
One reason is that at the Kansas River Jefferson joined
one of the parties which has had no chronicler.

Specifically, Jefferson was one of the emigrants who
under the leadership of the Methodist minister, James
Dunleavy, split off from the William H. Russell Company on May 19, just before reaching the Kansas River.
The Dunleavy party, we observe from Jefferson's campsites (he unites date of arrival with date of departure)
got ahead when the Russell Company paused to allow
Alphonso Boone and others, including the Donners, to
catch up. Thus they reached the crossing of the Big
Blue ahead of the torrential rain which made that river
temporarily impassable. While the Russell Company delayed at the Big Blue from the evening of May 26 to
the morning of June 1, Jefferson and his companions
moved on west, reaching the Platte on June 5, three days
ahead of the Russell Company, though two days behind
the party with which Virgil Pringle traveled.

We observe by Jefferson's map that he reached the
Laramie River probably on June 26; it seems likely that
he paused in this vicinity for two days, and resumed his
journey on June 29. In view of the way most companies
on the trail broke up and recombined, it may be unsafe
to conclude that he was still traveling with Dunleavy.
The only check we have is that Charles T. Stanton, in
his letter of July 19, notes that "Dunlavy's" company
made camp on July 16 within a mile or two of where the
Donners and J. Quinn Thornton were encamped on the

Sweetwater. Jefferson's map shows that he was somewhat farther west this day. He crossed South Pass July 17, and it was not until the following afternoon that Thornton and the Donners reached Pacific Spring.

West of South Pass, Jefferson chose the route via Fort Bridger in preference to the Greenwood Cutoff, reaching the fort July 24. He was then three days behind James Mathers, who in fact set out on the new Hastings Cutoff July 23. It appears that Jefferson left Fort Bridger July 27 (four days ahead of the Donner Party), though we must infer this from a dated campsite of July 30-31 in Echo Canyon. He was evidently a day behind the little group with which Heinrich Lienhard departed Fort Bridger, but must have overtaken Lienhard and his fellows at the Bear River on the afternoon of July 28.

Details of Jefferson's further travels on the Hastings Cutoff, and on to the Sierra Nevada after regaining the established emigrant trail on the Humboldt River, are brought out in the Notes to the Mathers diary and will not be repeated here. It is enough to say that Jefferson reached "Johnson's house—first settlement" on October 20. Although he maps the rest of the emigrant road, south to Sutter's and then on to "Pueblo St Joseph" and "St Francisco," with campsites and mileages between camps, he provides no more dates, and the map ceases to be the personal document it had been, all across the West.

Some of the small legends may, perhaps, not be easily read. One of these occurs on Part III of the map, southwest of Great Salt Lake, in reference to the crossing of what later became known as the Salt Lake Desert: "To accomplish the long drive grass & water must be carried from Hope Wells and the journey performed night and day making short & regular camps. No more than five waggons should go in company and the cattle should be continually guarded." As we shall see, he repeated these views in the body of his Guide.

On Part IV of the map, near the Sink, one legend identifies a "Trail the Pautas escaped with the stolen

cattle from the sink of Mary's River." A little farther
west, with reference to what eventually became known as
the Forty Mile Desert, Jefferson notes, "On this drive
a party should go on in advance with a shovel and collect
the water of the Boiling spring in vats to cool." Beyond
the "Great Boiling Spring" he locates the "Ridge of deep
sand—very hard pulling for the last seven miles" before
reaching "Truckey R." And an extensive legend at the
"California Mountains" says: "It was six miles east of
the Truckey Pass of the Cal. M^{tn} that Reeds Party in
November encountered snow ten feet deep and half the
party perished. Emigrants who reach this Pass by the
first of October are safe. Those who come later and encounter snow, should at once retreat to Grass Valley [the
Reno area of today] or the mouth of Truckey River and
winter there or to the southward on the streams of the
eastern base of the Californian Mountains. The western
descent of these mountains is the most rugged and difficult portion of the whole journey."

No trace of Jefferson's visit to California has been
found, other than his map. It is assumed that he returned
east by sea, sometime in 1847 or 1848; had he gone home
via Fort Hall, his depiction of that branch of the California Trail would reflect the fact by improved detail.

The printed *Accompaniment to the Map of the Emigrant Road* contains some observations interesting enough
to be quoted. Jefferson begins by saying, "The journey is
not entirely a pleasure trip. It is attended with some
hardships and privation—nothing, however, but that can
be overcome by those of stout heart and good constitution.
A small party (10 or 20) of the *proper* persons *properly*
outfitted might make a pleasure trip of the journey.
Large parties are to be deprecated." He discusses the
pros and cons of packing, necessary equipment (with
commendation for the good wagons manufactured by Mr.
Murphy, of St. Louis), "Articles that may be taken,"
and other practical matters, incidentally mentioning that
the merchants at Independence "are polite and obliging,

and sell goods at reasonable rates. Messrs. Wilson & Clark, and J. S. Stone, dealt very honorably with me." He concludes:

"*Remarks.*—In the Buffalo region Indians are not apt to trouble oxen. Upon Mary river and the lower portion of Truckey river, the Indians steal oxen for food, and sometimes to secure them, shoot them with poisoned arrows.

"At Fort Laramie mules can be had for $60 per head. At Fort Bridger (recruited) work oxen can be bought for $40 per yoke—mules $40—horses $25. Mr. Jas. Bridger, the proprietor, is very obliging to emigrants.

"The elevated portion of the Black Hills are about 8000 ft. above the sea. Elevation of the South Pass of the Rocky Mountains, the culminating ridge, 7300 ft. above the sea. Peaks of the Wind River mountains, 13000 ft. Snow Mountains south of Fort Bridger, 13100 ft. Truckey Pass of the Californian Mountains, 9000 ft. Elevated peaks of Californian Mountains, 14000 ft.

"Look for a good camp on the east side of Green River, and stop one or two days that your cattle may feed and rest.

"The last good water that we found upon Mary River, was at the camp 20 miles north of the sink, in a slough. The water at the sink is strongly impregnated with soda; the cattle drink it; take care they don't get mired; the south side of the ridges is the best place to water; guard the cattle at night. The water of the boiling spring westward is clear, and but slightly impregnated with alkali; when cooled it will do very well for cattle; it overflows and forms a rill easily collected in vats. No grass from the sink to Truckey River.

"*Long drive, Desert of Utariah.*—Distance.—From Hope-Wells [Iosepa] to the East side Scorpion Mt. [Cedar Mountains], 12 miles. Road good, a level plain. East to west side Scorpion Mt., 9 miles. Road, steep hills, some sideling, rather bad. West side Scorpion Mt., to Rock Ridge [Grayback Mountain] 14 miles. Road good, hard marly plain.

"Rock Ridge to east side Fire Mt. [Silver Island], 32 miles. Road a vast desert plain, good hard marl in places, deep sand ridges in places, latter part damp or wet marl incrusted with salt, into which the wheels cut and make hard pulling. From east to west side Fire Mt., 8 miles. Road hilly, deep dust, bunch grass in places, rather hard. From west side Fire Mt. to Bonark Wells [Pilot Peak springs], 8 miles. Road a level plain of marl, damp, incrusted with fine table salt, rather hard pulling. Total distance 83 miles. Dell [Redlum] spring affords a small supply of brackish water, cedar trees, and some bunch grass; a good well could be made here. This would reduce the drive to 70 miles.

"Take in a supply of water and green grass at Hope-Wells. Three or four gallons of water per ox is enough. Water is more important than grass. Not more than five wagons should start upon the drive in company. Travel night and day; don't hurry the oxen; make a regular camp about every 20 miles. Remain at each camp two hours or more, and measure out the water to each ox in a basin. Unyoke at each camp and leave the cattle loose. Keep strict guard over them, and never for one moment allow them to leave your sight. Adhere to these rules and you will go through safe. Scorpion mountain affords cedar trees and some good bunch grass.

"North-east of Hope-Wells, upon the mountain, about two miles from the road, is situated Cedar spring. It affords an abundant supply of delightful water, has cedar trees and some bunch grass near it; a horse trail leads to it from Hastings-Wells [Grantsville], over the mountain. If the Indians catch an unarmed man alone, they will rob him.

"*Valley of Fountains.*—A large and fertile valley [Ruby Valley], abounding in springs of pure water; soil black and rich, and covered with excellent grasses; a variety of timber in the vales of the mountains, also currants and service berries; game abundant, such as antelope, geese, brant, cranes, plover, grouse, blue bird, robin, &c. The Digger Indians' 'bread root' is also found among the grass; it resembles a carrot. The north part of the valley is best. Grain of all kind could easily be cultivated. This valley affords a good site for a settlement or military provision post.

"The passage of the Rocky Mountains by the South Pass is quite easy, the road being remarkably good. The most difficult portion of the whole journey is the passage of the Californian Mountains, and particularly the descent of the western side. The only serious difficulty, however, is when you arrive late in the season, with a short supply of bread stuff, and encounter snow ten or fifteen feet deep. Those who expect to cross in safety must reach the Truckey Pass by the 1st of October. The snow does not usually begin falling till November, and remains upon the ground more or less till May. If you arrive late, however, and encounter snow, do not attempt to cross the mountain (as Reed's party did), but scatter at once into small parties, and retreat to the eastern base of the mountains, where you will find fertile valleys free from snow, which afford game, salmon, and roots, enough for small parties. You can winter there, and cross at the Truckey Pass when the snow is gone.

"I have no doubt but that you can go into California immediately, if you take the proper course. Travel leisurely south, feeling your way from river to river, and valley to valley. You will make some discoveries, and in time arrive at the south pass of the Californian mountain, which is practicable at all seasons. Here is a regular road or travelled trail leading to the Pueblo [de los] Angelos. There is also a nearer pass, leading into the head of the valley of the Joaquin river. To reach these passes you would not probably have to travel more than 250 or 300 miles from Truckey river.

"This vast country is open to exploration. Small parties of horsemen can go anywhere. Government should at once ·dispatch a dozen exploring parties in different directions.

The best road should be found speedily. Trappers, and emigrants with women and babies, have done more towards this object than government.

"We want a good wagon trail across this continent, and we must have one. It will not cost much to improve a few bad places, and thus create a good trail or road. At convenient distances upon this road military provision posts should be established. This journey then would become a pleasure trip.

"Why don't the government do something immediately that will be of practical utility to the emigrant or traveller across our own territory?"

With this peremptory question Jefferson concludes his Guide. Only two copies of the work, complete with *Accompaniment*, are known—one in the Philip Ashton Rollins Collection, Princeton University Library, the other in the Estelle Doheny Collection, Edward Laurence Doheny Memorial Library, St. John's Seminary, Camarillo, California. The Library of Congress has the maps, without the *Accompaniment*. The California Historical Society republished the Doheny copy, with introduction and notes by George R. Stewart, as its Special Publication No. 20 in 1945, and the maps herein are reproduced from that source. All four maps have been reproduced by Carl I. Wheat in the third volume of his *Mapping the Trans-mississippi West, 1540-1861* (San Francisco, 1959).

"Indian Skin Lodges"

The Miller-Reed Diary

With Letters by J. F. Reed and Virginia Reed

The diary kept by Hiram O. Miller on the California Trail from Independence, Missouri, to the Black Hills, continued by James Frazier Reed until his expulsion from the Donner Party far down the Humboldt Valley, is uniquely interesting and important as the only known daily record kept within the Donner Party until Patrick Breen began his laconic diary at the snow-covered cabin below Donner Lake.

The man who commenced this trail record, Hiram Owens Miller, gave his birthplace as Kentucky and his age as 48 on registering as a voter in Santa Clara County in August, 1866. It would appear that Miller was born about 1818; and there is some reason to think that he migrated from Kentucky to Illinois with his family. In 1866 he described himself as a blacksmith, and it may be that he followed such a trade at Springfield. Miller set out for California possibly as a hand for George Donner, but he had been intimately acquainted with the Reeds for some time before that, and he lived and died among the Reeds after reaching the Pacific shore.

At first glance Hiram Miller's diary is little more than an itinerary, thoroughly depersonalized, though it has points of interest about it. He abandoned his diary when Edwin Bryant, on July 2, prevailed upon him to join William H. Russell's pack party. Thus Miller went on ahead of the wagons, arriving at Sutter's Fort on August 31, 1846. But before he mounted his mule, he handed over to Reed the daily record he had commenced.

With Reed's first entry, July 3, an immediate change is seen in the character of the diary; it begins to reflect the fact that these were human beings on the trail to California. But whether because the diary had been commenced by another or because Reed's way of expressing himself was influenced by the severe impersonality of Miller's style, Reed continued the diary in a detached manner, keeping entries brief and referring even to himself in the third person. Only a professional analysis of the handwriting made it clear initially that it was Reed who had carried on Miller's trail record, though more ample study has made it abundantly evident that no one else could have written it.

The two diaries together give us a continuous daily chronicle of the Donner Party from May 12 to October 4. Miller provides a day-to-day record from the time the Donners left Independence until they caught up with the original William H. Russell company at the crossing of the Kansas River on May 19. After that, for a time, such other chroniclers as Edwin Bryant, J. Quinn Thornton, and George McKinstry furnish occasional data on the Donners. But Bryant went on ahead; Thornton turned off toward Oregon; and McKinstry seemingly gave up the effort to keep a diary. From the junction of the Greenwood Cutoff and the Fort Bridger road west of South Pass, the diary is again the only daily record of the Donner Party. Reed's contribution is far more important than Miller's, but clearly there would have been no Reed diary had there been no Miller diary, and for that we forgive Hiram Miller much.

Some account of Reed's earlier life is provided by John Carroll Power, *History of the Early Settlers of Sangamon County, Illinois* (Springfield, 1876), pp. 258-260, and by Frederic Hall, *History of San José and Surroundings* (San Francisco, 1871), pp. 369-370. According to Power, Reed "was born November 14, 1800, in County Armagh, Ireland. His ancestors were of noble Polish birth, who chose exile rather than submission to the Russian power, and settled in the north of Ireland. The family name was originally Reednoski, but in process of time the Polish termination of the name was dropped, and the family was called Reed. James F. Reed's mother's name was Frazier, whose ancestors belonged to the Clan Frazier, of Scottish history." Hall adds that Reed "came to the United States with his widowed mother when a very small child. After he arrived at a sufficient age to be of some service to himself, his mother sent him to the State of Virginia, to live with a relative of hers, when he was placed as a clerk in the store of that relative, and there remained until about the age of twenty-five. He then removed to the lead mine district of Illinois [Galena], where he engaged in the business of mining until the year 1831, when he changed his abode to Springfield, in the same State. He served in the Black Hawk war, and, after its termination, returned to Springfield. Abraham Lincoln . . . and Mr. Reed were privates in the same company in that war [and so was James Clyman]. That company was commanded by Jacob M. Early, uncle of Gen. Early, who served under Gen. Lee, in the late rebellion." Power says that

Reed afterward profitably manufactured cabinet furniture; Hall relates that Reed entered "the mercantile
business, made money, and purchased a farm . . . He
subsequently engaged in the railroad business, receiving
about the second contract given out in that State, and
subsequently numerous others, which would have yielded
him large profits, and made him a wealthy man, had not
the State repudiated the payment of railroad contracts;
that is, she passed laws, compelling contractors to compro-
mise on her own terms, whereby Mr. Reed became a
loser of many thousand dollars."

The Reed papers in the Sutter's Fort collection show
that he became a Freemason in 1844, and in December
of the same year was named U. S. Pension Agent for the
State of Illinois, serving in that capacity until the hour
of his departure from Springfield. By the spring of 1845
he had already made up his mind to go West, for letters
he wrote to various members of the Illinois delegation in
Congress in June of that year show him seeking an appointment as "Sub Indian agent west of the Rocky mountains"; he wanted such an appointment to commence by
the first of March, 1846, for "at that time I intend to
start for Oregon with my family office or no office." He
may have been the prime mover in organizing the Springfield contingent that has come down in history as the
Donner Party. That he sought conscientiously for information respecting the Western trails is shown by two
letters to him, printed in Volume II of the present work;
and other documents of the kind are preserved among the
Reed papers. These reveal that when he did leave Springfield he had the intention of establishing his family in the
San Francisco area and then visiting the Sandwich
Islands. On departing Springfield, he took with him
cordial testimonials from the governor and other prominent citizens.

According to a letter Virginia Reed Murphy wrote C.
F. McGlashan, May 24, 1879, Reed was originally affi-
anced to Lizzy (Elizabeth) Keyes, but she died during

their engagement. The only sister of his fiancee, Margret Willson Keyes, who was born at Union, Monroe County, (West) Virginia March 31, 1814, married Lloyd C. Backenstoe about the same time. To the Backenstoes was born an only daughter, Virginia Elizabeth. Her birthdate has usually been given as June 28, 1834, but in 1879 Virginia in a letter to McGlashan corrected this to 1833. Backenstoe died of cholera, and on October 13, 1834 (as usually stated; but to McGlashan Virginia formally corrected the year as 1835), James Frazier Reed married the young widow. According to Virginia, Margret was sick in bed at the time of their marriage, and Reed "stood by the bed side holding her hand during the cerimony. She had been sick ever since my own fathe died and papa persuaded her to not wait until she was *well,* but give him the right to nurse her as a husband." For many years afterward Mrs. Reed was afflicted with "sick headaches," and the hope that she might feel better in a different climate was a major consideration in Reed's taking his family to California. (These "sick headaches" disappeared under the stresses of the terrible winter of 1846-1847, but surely the cure was a radical one.)

As will be clear from the above, James Frazier Reed was the stepfather rather than the natural father of Virginia E. B. Reed, but throughout life they enjoyed a relationship as trusting and affectionate as Reed had with any of his own children, respectively Martha Jane (Patty), born February 26, 1837; James Jr., born March 26, 1840, Thomas Keyes, born April 2, 1842, and Dallas, born in July, 1844, only to die in February, 1846. Another son, Charles Cadden, was born after the Reeds settled in California.

One of Margret Reed's four brothers, Robert Cadden Keyes, had set out for Oregon in 1845 (though as the Reeds would learn, he had ended up in California). To see this son again was one reason Margret's mother, Sarah (Humphrey) Keyes, demanded to be taken along, notwithstanding she was in feeble health, suffering from consumption. She is usually stated to have been 70 years old, but Virginia Reed Murphy, in her "Across the Plains in the Donner Party (1846)," *Century Magazine,* July, 1891, says her grandmother was then 75. Her sons in Springfield, Gersham and James W. Keyes (the name was also spelled Keys) tried to dissuade Grandma "from the long and fatiguing journey, but in vain; she would not be parted from my mother, who was her only daughter. So the [wagon] in which she was to ride was planned to give comfort. The entrance was on the side, like that of an old-fashioned stage coach, and one stepped into a small room, as it were, in the centre of the wagon. At the right and left were spring seats with comfortable high backs, where one could sit and ride with as much ease as on the seats of a Concord coach. In this little room was placed a tiny sheet-iron stove, whose pipe, running through the top of the wagon, was prevented by a circle of tin from setting fire to the canvas cover. A board about a foot wide extended over the wheels on either side the full length of the wagon, thus forming the foundation for a large and roomy second story in which were placed our beds. Under the spring seats were compartments in which were stored many articles useful for the journey, such as a well filled work basket and a full assortment of medicines, with lint and bandages for dressing wounds. Our clothing was packed—not in Saratoga trunks—but in strong canvas bags plainly marked."

Virginia affirms that Reed "was the originator of the Springfield party, and the Donner brothers, George and Jacob, who lived just a little way out of Springfield decided to join him." (Further light is shed on the inception of the party by documents printed in Volume II.) On setting out, Reed had three wagons, two of which were laden with provisions. With his family went their domestic of many years, the nearly deaf Eliza Williams, Virginia-born and evidently destined to be an old maid, since she was already 31 years old. Eliza's half-brother, Baylis, who suffered from an impairment of his sight (he had good night vision but could scarcely see by daylight) was taken along, and other hired men were Milford (Milt) Elliott, James Smith, and Walter Herron. That Reed could hire his work done, and owned the only blooded horse in the company, contributed to the resentment of him felt by others in the Donner Party as the journey wore on.

The Reeds, the Donners, and Hiram Miller, accompanied to the west line of Missouri by Gersham Keyes, made their way to Independence by the second week of May, and launched out upon their journey May 12. Nine wagons comprised the original company from Springfield, Reed and the two Donner brothers having three wagons each. How the travelers fared after leaving the frontier is related in the documents which follow, and in letters printed in Volume II. Reed's diary breaks off in mid-entry on October 4. He was then probably a day behind with the record. Apparently it was on October 5, when Reed's family had reached the toilsome sand ridge west of present Redhouse, Nevada, that he had a fatal altercation with John Snyder, a hired man traveling with the late-joining Graves family. Snyder was killed, and Reed was forced to leave the company. He went on ahead to Sutter's, was prevented by the snow from returning, and in the end became one of the prime movers in the Donner Relief.

This story emerges in fuller detail on later pages; here let us remark that the Snyder tragedy interrupted diary-keeping, and led to Reed's preparing the sketch map reproduced herein which takes the place of a diary in reflecting his further travels on to Sutter's. Reed would have liked to expunge from memory all recollection of the unfortunate death of Snyder: in none of the letters written by him and Virginia in 1847 is there any mention of this tragedy, the reason for Reed's leaving the company. Many years later, provoked by some loose published reminiscences, Reed wrote a long statement respecting the Donner Party which was printed in two issues of the

Pacific Rural Press, March 25-April 1, 1871. He said then that he had "never appeared voluntarily, and never wished to, before the public" in reference to the history of the Donner Party, "having gained the ill-will of parties who wished to write books with reference to it by refusing. Myself and family have always refused giving particulars, but were always willing to give general items." Yet even in breaking his long silence, Reed had nothing to say of the Snyder tragedy; the Reed side of that affair came out only in the letters Virginia and Patty wrote C. F. McGlashan in 1879—letters now in the McGlashan collection at the Bancroft Library, the ultimate source of the account in McGlashan's *History of the Donner Party* —and in Virginia's *Century Magazine* article of 1891.

The Reed letters here reprinted consist initially of Reed's letter to his brother-in-law, James W. Keyes, written from the South Fork of the Platte on June 16, 1846, and printed in the Sangamo Journal, July 30, 1846; Virginia E. B. Reed's letter to a young cousin written from Independence Rock, July 12, 1846; and Reed's letter written from Fort Bridger, July 31, 1846, printed in the *Sangamo Journal,* November 5, 1846. These first three letters reflect the light-hearted early weeks of the journey. The fourth letter was written by Virginia to her cousin, Mary C. Keyes, from California's Napa Valley, under date of May 16, 1847; as the production of a 13-year-old girl it is one of the most moving documents of American history. Since James Frazier Reed made many emendations, this letter also is personal for Reed. Supplementary are the report of the Donner tragedy Reed sent home, which survives in the form it was published in the two Springfield newspapers late in 1847, and an accompanying letter he wrote from the Napa Valley on July 2, 1847, printed in the *Illinois Journal,* December 23, 1847. The sketch map was preserved among Reed's papers and is now in the Sutter's Fort Historical Monument collection. (Reed's diary of the Donner Relief is printed later in the present volume.)

Concerning the life of Miller and Reed after they reached California, little need be said. Both served briefly in the California Battalion; both had a large part in the Donner Relief. In the spring of 1847, when Reed was named guardian of the orphaned children of George Donner, Miller was made guardian of their cousins, the children of Jacob Donner. Reed was one of the more successful miners after the discovery of gold in 1848, and brought to San Jose a mule load of gold which he invested in land. Next year he was one of those most active in promoting the temporary designation of San Jose as the California State Capital. "In 1850, he had large offers made him for his real estate; but, believing in the growth of this city, refused to part with it. He afterward became involved, but prior thereto had secured to his family an estate which, by its enhancement, has provided them bountifully with the comforts of life." Reed was, Hall commented in 1871, "a most generous man, possessing much public spirit; social and entertaining at his own house. He is strong in his convictions, warm in his friendships, bitter in his hate; but honorable in apologising if satisfied that he has been in the wrong." Reed died in San Jose July 24, 1874. His wife had passed on November 25, 1861.

Hiram Miller lived with the Reeds much of the time after they settled in San Jose. Patty wrote McGlashan in 1879 to that effect, and added that Miller was exposed to smallpox when on a boat en route to Sacramento, contracted the disease, was taken to the pest house, and afterward came to the Reed home, an invalid for nearly five years until he died. Miller's death on October 19, 1867, "aged about 50 years," is noted in the San Jose *Mercury,* October 24, 1867, with the comment that he "never recovered from an attack of the small pox, a few years ago, which greatly disfigured his features. He was a quiet, truthful, inoffensive man, noted for his kindness of heart . . . "

Virginia E. Backenstoe Reed married John M. Murphy

on January 26, 1850. Nine children were born to them, two of whom were still living when she passed away at Los Angeles on March 14, 1921. She had made her home in San Jose until the fall of 1918, when she went south to live with a son. To her death Virginia retained the warm sense of life and the capacity for fun revealed in her letters of 1846-1847.

Perhaps this is the fitting place to bring out something of the later history of Virginia's classic letter of 1847. Her sister Patty, by then the widowed Martha Jane (Reed) Lewis, wrote C. F. McGlashan on April 11, 1879: "when I was looking over Papa^s old papers . . . I found the original letter written by my Sister Virginia, May 16th 1847 to our cousin, in Springfield Ill. I wish you to publish it, as it is, in full, I think it worthey of a share in your collums [the Truckee *Republican,* in which McGlashan was then printing Donner materials], if you can not study it out, please send it back to me, & I will copy it off . . . Sister was 12 [13] years old, it showes for its self. I need not tell you, Sister does not know I have it, & I do not intend to let her hear, of it, untill I get it back home again, I do not think she would send it, or allow me too if she knew of it, yet I think I am doing right, if I wound Sisters feelings, you will assist me in soothing it over, will you not?"

Virginia in turn wrote McGlashan on April 17-18, 1879: "I am so excited I hardly know what I am doing. My sister has Just been in and told me that she found the letter I wrote to my cousin thirty three years ago, in the bottom of my fathes old trunk and has sent it to you. I would not have you or any one else out of the family see that letter for all California, it was my first effort, the very first letter [actually, the second] I ever tried to write in my life, and sent it to my litle Cousin never dreaming for a moment that other eyes would ever rest on it. I had promised to write to her before I left home and I was trying to keep my promise I told you I would try and get the letter and intended picking out what ever was worth publishing to send you but never dreamed of your seeing the whole affair. I had no idea that my father had it hid away. Please don't publish it for it must be silly & foolish. What could a child wright at that age, not accustomed to writing either. I can onely say I must have had a good deal of curage to undertake it. The first time it went the rounds I did not care. I was too full of happyness then to care much for any thing as long as my fathe said 'never mind daughter it is all right' poore old letter the hands that hid you away, and the lips that spoke to me then are mouldering now in the dust. . . "

The editor of the *Illinois Journal,* on printing the text December 16, 1847, as a "Deeply Interesting Letter," dissented from Virginia's later view, and we agree with him: "The following letter is from a little girl, aged about twelve years, step-daughter of Mr. James F. Reed, and was one of the unfortunate company of emigrants, of whose sufferings last winter, we gave an account in our last week's paper. The artless manner in which the child details the sufferings of the party, and especially of her own family—the joyful meeting of her father after his absence of five months—can scarcely be read without a tear,—while her notice of the country, which she had reached with untold tribulations, will cause a smile. 'It is a great country to marry. Eliza is to be married; and this is no joke!' "

Toward the end of Virginia's life, George Wharton James was permitted to make a photostatic copy of the original letter, and from that copy, preserved in the Southwest Museum at Los Angeles, an exact text is now printed. By judicious use of brackets, an effort is made to present the letter as Virginia wrote it, and the emendations made by Reed.

✹　　✹　　✹

THE MILLER-REED DIARY

1846 Left Home th[e] 26 of April[1]

May Left Independence on the 12th went about 4 miles and camped[2]

13 next day travelled about 16 miles in the rain, bad roads and rainy night

14 15 Camped at "Heart Grove" Jackson County near the Indian line twenty two miles from Independence on the Big blue[3]

16 and from thir we Camped on the head of Rull [*i.e.,* Bull?] Creek twenty miles from Big Blue

17 the '5 night wee Camp on the wapulusa [Wakarusa] 18 mills from the head of Bull Creek and we Camped on the plains near the a Spring 18 miles from Wapulusa

18 and from thire wee Camped near the Creek 20 miles from plain Spring,

19 and from their wee Crossed the Cau [Kaw or Kansas] river and went about five miles and Camped[4]

20 and from their we Camp on prairie Creek 8 miles from the Same Creek

21 and from their we traveled a Bout 5 miles and Camped on prairie Creek

22 and from ther wee traveled a Bowt 15 miles and Campe on the wapalore[5]

23 and from their wee traveled 12 miles and Camped on prairie Creek

24 and from their wee traveled a Bout 14 miles and Camped near a Creek on the plains

25 and from their wee traveled a Bout 10 miles and came to the Big Vermilion and Crossed and traveled a Bout 5 miles and Camped on the plaines

26 and from their traveled a Bowt 10 miles and Camped on the Big Blue and Remained their the 27 and the twenty Eighth and twenty-ninth and thirtyeth

thirty first day wee Crossed over the Big Blue and Camped

June 1 1846 and from their we traveled a Bout 15

mills and Camped on prairie Creek

2 And from their wee traveled a Bout 15 mills and Camped on prairie Creek

3 And from their wee traveled a Bout 16 miles and Camped on the Bear Creek[6]

4 and from their wee traveled a Bout 20 miles and Camped on the Blue

5 And from their wee traveled a Bowt 20 miles and Camped on the litle Blue

6 and from their wee traveled up the little Blue a Bout 18 miles and Camped on the Blue

7 and from their wee traveled a Bowt 16 miles and Camped on the tributary of the Plat

8 and from their wee traveled a Bowt 18 miles and Camped on the plat

9 And from their wee traveled a Bowt 18 miles and Camped on the Plat near the 20 Ileands[7]

10 and from their wee Traveled a Bowt 18 miles and Camped near the Plat on a Small Creek

11 and from their wee traveled up the Plat a Bowt 18 miles and Camped near the Plat

12 and from their we traveled up the Plat a Bowt 18 miles and Camped near the Plat

13 wee Remained their one day and Repared their waggons

14 and from their wee traveled up the Plat a Bout 17 miles and Camped near a grove on the Plat

15 and from their wee traveled up the Plat a Bowt 18 miles and Camped near the Plat By a fine Spring near the Road no timber A Bout a half a mile from the forkes of the River

16 and from their wee traveled up the Sowth fork 14 miles and Camped on the Plat their is no timber [*See* Reed's letter of this date, *post.*]

17 and from their wee traveled a Bowt 14 miles and Came to the plat and Crossed over on the west Bank and Camped no timber

18 and from their wee traveled a Bout 10 miles and

Camped on the plat where the Road leaves the plat no timber

19 and from their wee traveled a Bout 18 miles and Came to a fine Spring and timber plenty and from their wee traveled a Bout 2 miles and Camped on the north plat

20 and from their wee traveled up the plat a Bout 18 mills and Camped near the plat

21 and from their wee traveled up the plat a Bowt 12 miles and Camped near the plat By a fine Spring no timber off to the left of the Spring on the Bluffs is a Beautiful pine ridge the first that i have Seen on the Rout[8]

22 and from their wee traveled up the plat a Bowt 20 miles and Camped near the Court-house on the Plat

23 and from their wee traveled up the plat a Bowt 10 miles and Came to the Chimney Rock and from their wee traveled a Bowt 8 miles and Camped near the plat

24 and from their wee traveled a Bowt 10 miles and Came to Scotts Bluffs and from their wee traveled a Bout 7 miles and Camped near Fremonts spring Betuen the divideing Ridge[9]

25 and from their we traveled a Bowt 10 miles and Came to horse Creek, and from their we traveled a Bowt 6 miles and Camped near the Plat

26 and from their wee traveled a Bowt 16 miles and Camped near fort Benard on the plat[10]

27 and from their we traveled up the plat a Bout 8 miles and came to lairome River near where it Emties in to the north plat and traveled up it a Bout a mile and Crossed Over to fort lairome and Camped[11]

28 and from their we traveled up the Lariome fork a Bowt 2 miles and Camped

29 and from their we traveled a Bowt 16 miles and Camped on willow Creek timber[12]

30 and from their we traveled a Bowt 14 miles and Camped near a Spring on the Rood and a Bout Eight miles from Lariomes peak[13]

July 1 1846

1 and from their we traveled a Bout 15 miles and Camped near a Creek their is a fine Spring and timber plenty we are now in the red mouns [*in margin*: devils Brick kilns][14]

2 and from their we traveled a Bowt 15 miles and Camped on a Creek their is plenty of water and timber[15]

3 we made this day 18 Miles and Camped on Beaver Creek here is a natural Bridge 1 ½ miles above camp[16]

4 we Celebrated the glorious 4th on the Camp and remained here to the morning of the 6th

6 we left Camp much rested and our Oxen mouved off in fine Style, and went 16 miles and encamped on the Bank of [   ] Creek about ½ a Mile from the North fork of the Platt which Stream we struck about 6 miles from Camp, where there is a fine Coal Bank[17]

7 left Camp in good order and mouved up Platt 16 and encamped on the Bank in a Beautiful grove of Cotton wood here we killed Buffalo

Wed 8 went up Platt this day Crossed over and encamped opposit the upper Crossing 12 be Certain to Come up on the South Sid & Cross- the road & ford is desidedly the best.[18]

Thur 9 left the Platt and encamped at the Spring in the bottom land of a dry Branch fine water and Plenty of it 5 Buffalos Killed 12 [Miles]

Fri 10 made this day 14 and encamped at the Willow Springs good water but little grass 3 Buffaloes Killed the Main Spring 1 ½ Miles above

Sat 11 Made this day 20 Miles to Independence Rock Camped below the Rock good water ½ way

Sun 12 Lay by this day [*See* Virginia Reed's letter of this date, *post.*]

Mo 13. left the Rock after Reading many Names and Made 20 Encaped at the Sand Ridge

Tus 14 left our encampmt and Crossed the Sand Ridge to the Narrows of sweet water a sandy Road 20 Bad Bad Road[19]

Wed 15 this day [*deleted*: went up Sweet Water and] Crossed a Ridges to Sweetwater and made 16 Encamped at the foot of the Mountain [*in margin*: and encamped on the last crossing]

Thur 16 Crossed the Mountain 14 [*The rest of this day's entry is crossed out*: here Some of our Cattle got poisoned from drinking bad water there are about 1 Mile from Our encampmt 3 or 4 hot Springs, the water Sinks near the road where the encampmt is usually made go if possible 3 miles further to the Crossing]

Frid 17 Came from the Mountain 16 [miles] to last Crossing of Sweet water

Sater 18 this day nooned on the Sumit of the pass. 6 miles from our encampmt and 2 miles below on the west Side is the green Spring which You Can See from the Sumit [*deleted*: 2 miles] and about 6 miles from this Spring is dry Sandy which You will avoid as Several Cattle got poisoned by drink[ing] the watter in the pools. [*In margin, with pointing hand*: Avoid this place, poison in the water that stands in pools at the Crossing][20]

Son 19 Made this day 10 Miles to little Sandy here Geo. Donner & J. Donner lost 2 oxen & J F Reed lost old Balley 5 miles west of this place from being poisond at dry Sandy Gurge also got poison there.

Mo 20 this day made 5 and encamped on little Sandy within 6 miles of Big Sandy

Tues 21 we encamped on little Sandy all day Geo Donner lost one Steer in this encampmt J. F Reed lost old George & one Ball faced Steer, by being poisoned at dry Sandy—on Saturday night last.[21]

Wed 22 left our encampmt and went to Big Sandy 6 Mr Dallin [Dolan] lost 1 steer from Poison on Dry sandy [*Deleted*: Tomorrow we have 28 miles to grass Big Sandy River enters a gorge below the Crossing and Consequently there is No grass.]

Thus 23 encamped on big Sandy grass Plenty 13

Frid 24 this day made green River in the morning and went down about 3 miles and made in all 8

Sat 25 Started this morning Early and went down green River about 4 miles to Bridgers New fort where we turned to the Right to Blacks fork making in all 16 the fort is now vacant, Bridger having remouved to his old Fort on Blacks fork[22]

Sond 26 left Blacks fork and Crossed Hams fork about 9 miles from our encampment and encamped on Black fork making this day 18

Mo. 27 left this day and encamped in a beautiful Grass bottom about ½ mile below Bridgers Old Fort now occupied by Bridger and Vascus—making 18

Tus 28 this day lay in Camp our Cattle much fatigued from the hard drive we made during the 2 last weeks

Wed. 29 still in Camp recruiting this day. J F Reed lost one of his best oxen Supposed to be murr[a]in

Thur 30 Still on Camp at Bridgers Fort on Blacks fork Our Cattl looks fine

Frid. 31 [*See* Reed's letter of this date, *post.*] We Started this morning on the Cut off rout by the south of the Salt Lake- & 4 ½ miles from the fort there is a beautiful Spring Called the Blue Spring as Cold as ice passed Several Springs and Encamped at the foot of the first Steep hill going west making this day 12[23]

Sat 1 Augt 1846—left Camp this morning early and passed through Sevral Valleys well watered with plenty of grass, and encamped at the head of Iron Spring Vally making 15[24]

Sond 2 this morning left Camp late on acct of an ox being missing Crossed over a high ridge or mountain with tolerable rough road an encamped on Bear river making 16 on a little Creek ab[o]ut 4 miles from Bear River we ought to have turned to the righ[t] and reached Bear River in one mile Much better road Said to be[25]

Mon 3 left our encampmt and traveled a tolerable rough Road Crossing Several Very high hills and encamped at the head of a larger [?] Vally with a fine little runing Stream passing by the edge of our Camp Cattle plenty of grass County appear more hale west Made this day 16[26]

Tus 4 this day left our encampmt about 2 oclock made this day about 8 our encamp was this day in red Run Valley [*interlined*: fork of weaver][27]

Weds 5 Started early and traveled the whole day in Red Run Valley and encampe below its enterens into Weavers Creek 15[28]

Thus 6 left our encamp. about ten oclock and encamp above the Cannon here we turn to the left hand & Cross the Mounten instead of the Cannon which is impassible although 60 Waggons passed through this day made 10[29]

Frid 7 in Camp on weaver at the mouth of Canon[30]

Sat 8 Still in Camp

Sond 9 Still in Camp

Mo 10 Still in Campe James F. Reed this evening returned he and two others having been Sent by the Caravan to examine the Canon and proceed after Mr Hastings, who left a Note on the road that if we Came after him he would return and Pilot us through his new and direct Rout to the South end of the Salt Lake Reed having examined the new rout entirely an reported in favour, which induced the Compay to proceed[31]

Tues 11 left Camp and took the New rout with Reed as Pilot he having examined the mountains and vallies from the south end of the Lake this day made 5[32]

Weds 12 left Camp late and encampe on Bosman Creek on new rout made 2[33]

Thurs 13 Made a New Rout by Cutting willow Trees &[c] on Basman Creek 2[34]

Frid 14 Still on Basman Creek and proceeded up the Creek about one mile and Turned to the right hand up a Narrow valley to Reeds Gap and encamped about one mile from the mouth making this day 2[35] [*In margin*: Spring of water]

Sat. 15 in Camp all hands Cutting and opning a road through the Gap.

Son 16 Still Clearing and making Road in *Reed* *Gap*.[36]

Mon 17 Still in Camp and all hands working on the road which we finished and returned to Campe

Tus 18 this morning all started to Cross the Mountane which is a Natural easey pass with a little more work and encamped making this day— 5 J F Reed Brok an axle tree[37]

Weds 19 this day we lay in Camp in a neat little valley fine water and good grass the hands ware this [day] on the other on West Side of Small mountain in a Small Valley Clearing a road to the Valley of the Lake we have to Cross the outlett of the Utah Lake on this Rout near the Salt Lake[38]

Thurs 20 Still in Camp and hands Clearing road

Frid 21 this day we left Camp Crossed the Small Mountain and encap^d in the vally runig into the Utah outlett making this day 4[39]

Sat 22 this day we passed through the Mountains and encamp^d in the Utah Valley making this day 2[40]

Son 23 left Camp late this day on acct. of having to find a good road or pass through the Swamps of the utah outlet finally Succeeded in and encamp^d on the East Bank of Utah outlett making 5[41]

Mo 24 left our Camp and Crossed the plain to a spring at a point of the Lake mountain and 1 ½ miles from the road traveled by the people who passed the Cannon[42] 12 [*In margin*: Brackish water] [*In margin still later*: it took 18 days to gett 30 miles][43]

Tues 25 [*corrected from* 24] left Camp early this morning intending if possibl to make the *Lower wells* being fair water 20 which we made and in the evening a Gentleman by the name of *Luke Halloran,* died of Consumption having been brough from Bridgers Fort by George Donner a distance 151 Miles we made him a Coffin and Burried him at the uper wells at the forks of the road in a beautiful place [*in margin*: fair water][44]

Wed 26 [*corrected from* 25] left Camp late and proceed to the upper wells One of them delightful water being entirely fresh the rest in N^o about 10 all Brackish

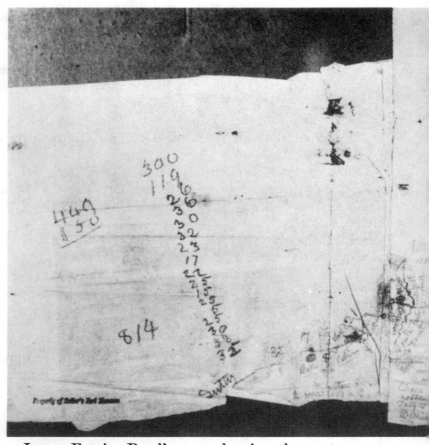

James Frazier Reed's map showing the route over the Sierra Nevada. See discussion on page 269.

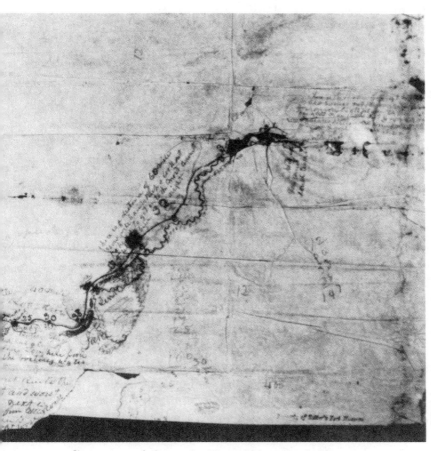

—*Courtesy of Sutter's Fort Historical Monument.*

this day Buried Mr Luke Halloran hauling him in his Coffin this distan[ce] 2 which we only mad and Buried him as above stated at the forks of the One Turning directly South to Camp the other West or on ward.[45]

Thur 27 [*corrected from* 26] left early this day and went west for half the day at the foot of the Lake Mountains the latter ½ of the day our Course S. W. to a N° of Brackish Wells making 16 *miserable water*[46]

Frid 28 [*corrected from* 27] left Camp and glad to do so, in hopes of finding fresh water on our way but without Success untill evening when it was time to Camp Came to a N° of delightful fresh water wells this Camp is at the Most Suthern point of the Salt Lake 20 miles Northwest we commence the long drive we are taking in water, Grass, and wood for the various requirements. 12[47]

Sat. 29 [*corrected from* 28] in Camp wooding watering and laying in a Supply of grass for our oxen and horses, to pass the long drive which Commen[c]e about [   ] Miles We have one encampm[t] between but neither grass wood or water of sufficentt quallity or quantity to be procured water Brackish [*in margin*: *Sulphur*], grass Short and No wood—[48]

Son 30 [*corrected from* 29] Made this day 12 to a Silphur Spring in the Mountain which ought to be avoided water not good for Cattle, emigrants Should keep on the edge of the lake and avoid the Mountain entirely here Commence[d] the long drive through the Salt desert.[49]

Mon 31 in dessert drive of Sixty 60 miles

Tusdy Sept 1 in dessert

Wed 2 in do Cattle got in Reeds Cattle lost this night

Thusdy 3 in [*deleted*: do some teams got in]

Fridy 4 [*deleted*: in do] lost Reeds Cattle 9 Yok by not driving them Carefule to water as directed by Reed— [*in margin*: Hunting Cattle 3 or 4 days the rest of teams getting in and resting Cattle all nearly given out]

Sat 5 Still in Camp in the west Side of Salt Dessert

Sond 6 Started for Reeds waggons lying in the Salt Plains 28 miles from Camp Cached 2 waggs and other effects[50]

Mon[d] 7 Cam in to Camp on the Night and the waggon Came in on Tuesdy morng

Tudy 8 Still fixing and resting Cattle

Weds 9 M[r] Graves Mr Pike & Mr Brin loaned 2 Yoke of Cattle to J F Reed with one Yoke he tried [hired?] to bring his family waggon along[51]

Thu 10 left Camp and proceeded up the lake bed 7[52]

Frid 11 left the Onfortunate lake and mad in the night and day about 23 Encamped in a Vally wher the is fine grass & water[53]

Sat 12 [*corrected as being the entry for the following day*][54]

Sund 13 South in the Vally to fine Sp[r]ing or Bason of water and grass—sufficient for Teams made this day 13[55]

Mond 14 [*corrected from* Sunday] left the Bason Camp or Mad Woman Camp as all the women in Camp ware mad with anger and mad this d[a]y to the Two mound springs 14[56]

Tus 15 left the 2 mound Sp[r]ings and Crossed the Mountain as usual and Camped in the West Side of a Valley and Made this day about 14[57]

Wed 16 left Camp Early this mornig Crossed flat Mounten or Hills and encamped on the east side of a Ruged Mountain plenty of grass & water 18[58] here Geo Donner lost little gray & his Cream Co[l] mare Margret

Thu 17 made this day South in the Mineral Vally about 16[59]

Frid 18 this day lay in camp

Sat 19 this day mad in Min[e]ral Vally 16 and encamped at a large Spring Breaking out of from the and part of large Rock Stream lage enough to turn one pr Stone passed in the evening about 10 Spring Branches Springs Rising about 300 Yds above where we Crossed[60]

Son 20 this day made 10 up the Mineral Vally passed last evening and this day 42 Beautiful Springs of fresh water [*in bottom margin*: 384 miles from Bridger][61]

Mon[d] 21 Made 4 miles in Mineral Vally due south turned to the west 4 Miles through a flatt in the mounton thence W N W. 7 miles in another vally and encamped on a Smal but handsome littl Branch or Creek making in all 15 miles[62]

Tus 22 Made this day nearly due North in Sinking Creek Valy about ten miles owing to water.[63] 10

Wed 23 Made this day owing to water about Twelve 12 miles Still in Sinking Creek Valley—

Thu 24 this day North west we mad down Sinking Creek valley about 16 [*corrected from* 17] and encamped at the foot of a Red earth hill good grass and water wood plenty in the Vallies Such as sage greace wood & ceder &C—[64]

Frid 25 September This day we made about Sixteen miles 16 for Six miles a very rough Cannon a perfect Snake trail encamped in the Cannon about 2 miles from its mout[65]

Sat 26 this day made 2 miles in the Cannon and traveled to the Junction of Marys River in all about 8[66]

Marys River, Son 27 Came through a Short Cannon and encamped above the first Creek (after the Cannon) on Marys River[67]

Mond 28 this day after leaving Camp about 4 miles J F Reed found Hot Springs one as hot as boiling water left the River Crossed over the Mounta[in] to the west Side of a Can[n], and encamp in Vally[68] 12

Tus 29 This day 11 O.Clock left Camp and went about 8 mils to the river again 2 grave had 2 oxen taken by 2 Indians that Cam with us all day[69]

Wed 30 left Camp about 10 oclock and made this day 12 Miles down the River[70]

Oct Thur 1 left Camp and made 15 Miles down the River encampe on a Rich bottom this night M Graves lost a fine mare by the Indians[71]

Frid 2 Still down the River Made to day 12 miles
Sat 3 left Camp early mad a this day 10 miles
Son 4 Still[72]

THE REED MAP

Reed's diary having been interrupted by the fatal altercation with John Snyder, which occurred October 5 where the road crossed a sandy ridge east of present Winnemucca, the map he sketched on a scrap of paper following his expulsion from the company takes the place of his diary in recording the rest of his journey to California. The map is reproduced herewith, from the original in the Reed Papers in the Sutter's Fort Historical Monument collection, but the legends are difficult to read, and it may be as well to transcribe them.

In his contemporary account of the Donner tragedy, printed in the *Illinois Journal* in December, 1847, and in Virginia Reed's narrative of May 16, 1847, edited by Reed himself, the travels displayed by the map are briefly described. But it is desirable also to quote the relevant passages from Reed's reminiscent account printed in the *Pacific Rural Press,* March 25 - April 1, 1871. Reed passes over the painful episode of Snyder's death, saying only that it was suggested he go in advance to California, see what had become of McCutchen and Stanton, and hurry up the supplies. The Company would take care of his family.

" . . . That being agreed upon I started, taking with me about three days provisions, expecting to be able to kill game on the way. The Messrs. Donner were two days drive in advance of the main party when I overtook them. With George Donner there was a young man named Walter Herren, who joined me; with all the economy I could use, our provisions gave out in a few days; I supplied our wants by shooting wild geese and other game when we could find any. The next day after I was joined by Herren, I proposed to him—I having a horse and he none—that we would ride half the day about; it was thankfully accepted; no game to be seen; hunger began to be felt, and for days we traveled without hope or help. We reached the Sierra Nevada mountains; I could have stopped here, and, hunting, found game. Then again I might not be successful. This would have delayed our progress and increased our hunger. The second day before we found relief, Herren wanted to kill the horse; I persuaded him from it by stating that we might find relief soon, but before we would perish, I would kill the horse. Soon after this he became delirious; this afternoon, while walking, I found a *bean,* and gave it to him, and then never was a road examined more closely for several miles than was this. We found in all *five beans.* Herren's share was three of them. We camped that night in a patch of grass a short distance off the road. Next morning, after traveling a few miles, we saw some wagons.

"We soon reached and ransacked the wagons, hoping to find something to eat, but found nothing. Taking the tar bucket that was hanging under one of the wagons, I scraped the tar off and found a streak of rancid tallow at the bottom. I remember well that when I announced what I had found, Herren, who was sitting on a rack near by, got up, hollooing with all the strength he had, and came to me. I handed the tar paddle to him having some of the tallow about the size of a walnut on it. This he swallowed without giving it a smell. I then took a piece myself but it was very repulsive. He, craving more, I gave him another piece. Still wanting more, I positively refused stating that it would kill him. After leaving the wagons probably fifty yards, I became deathly sick and blind. I rested myself against a rock, leaning my head on the muzzle of my gun. Herren, seeing my condit[i]on, came to me and said: 'My God, Mr. Reed, are you dying!' After resting a few minutes, I recovered, much to his joy.

"The wagons were within a short distance of the steep descent going down into Bear river Valley. After descending the first steep pitch, I discovered wagons in the valley below us. Herren, said I, there are wagons in the valley, pointing to them. When he saw them, he gave vent to his joy, hallooing at the top of his voice, but could not be heard ten rods off, he being so weak. The sight of the wagons revived him and he descended the mountain with all his ability.

"On reaching the wagons we found several families of emigrants who supplied us with bread. I here met Mr. Stanton with two Indians, on his return to the company with provisions sent by Capt. Sutter, on receiving my letter. Next morning Mr. Stanton started for the company and myself for Capt. Sutter's.

"When I arrived, making known my situation to him, asking if he would furnish me horses and saddles to bring the women and children out of the mountains, [I expected to meet them at the head of Bear Valley by the time I could return there], he at once complied with the request; also saying that he would do every thing possible for me and the company. On the evening of my arrival at the Captain's, I found Messrs. Bryant, Lippencott, Grayson, and Jacobs, some of the early voyagers in the Russel company, they having left that company at Fort Laramie, most of them coming on horseback. . . ."

Edwin Bryant, in *What I Saw in California,* dates this arrival at Sutter's in late October: "On the 28th, Mr. Reed, whom I have before mentioned as belonging to the rear emigrating party, arrived here. He left his party on Mary's river, and in company with one man crossed the desert and the mountains. He was several days without provisions, and when he arrived at Johnson's, was so much emaciated and exhausted by fatigue and famine, that he could scarcely walk. His object was to procure provisions immediately, and to transport them with pack-mules over the mountains for the relief of the suffering emigrants behind. He had lost all of his cattle, and had been compelled to *cache* two of his wagons and most of his property. . . ."

Reed turned back on the trail but the night he reached Sutter's it began raining in the valley, which meant snow in the mountains. He was unable to rejoin his family and eventually had to return to Sutter's. Our present concern, however, is his map.

This unique document portrays the course of Mary's River (soon to be renamed the Humboldt) from above its great bend east of present Winnemucca down to its Sink. The course of the emigrant road is shown, down the river, across the desert to the Truckee, up the canyon of the Truckee to the Sierra, and thence to Sutter's, though only a most perfunctory indication is given of the road and the country west of the divide.

Insofar as it can be made out, the first legend, beginning at the right hand side of the map, reads: "here is the Battle between [?] the Shosonies and the Emigrants [?] for oregon took place in which [?] one white man killed and 3 wounded The Indians killed and wounded several cattle & horses [*two or three words illegible*]." (Presumably Reed is referring to the incident which led Jefferson to show on Sheet IV of his map, at the great bend of the Humboldt, "Battle with the Paute Indians" and "Retreating trail of the Paute Indians.")

The next legend on the map, set edgewise, reads, "hard pass You must double teams." Presumably Reed is referring to the locality where the Snyder tragedy occurred, called by Jefferson "Pauta Pass," and located by him 16 miles east of the great bend of the Humboldt.

Just beyond, Reed has a slight legend apparently reading "Blue Clay," with what appears to be a representation of the unnamed Applegate Road going off to the west toward Oregon. His next legend reads, "here is a distance of 60 miles You will have to keep a look out a head to get the most convnet places before night." He is referring to the descent of the Humboldt from the later Lassens Meadows to the Sink.

After depicting the "Sink" and its accompanying "Lake", Reed shows the desert crossing, "40 miles Long Drive," with the notes "Sandy" and "Boiling Springs," and the remark, "We had a cup of fine Tea here from the boiling water." (He alludes to the present Bradys Hot Springs, half way across the desert to the Truckee.) Another legend, set edgewise, comments, "dry sandy for the last 10 miles and very dis hartning Neither grass or water— Son at 80° 13 octo 1846." Thereby he furnishes a valuable date for the record. Below, a legend written somewhat later says: "from the Salmon trout [Frémont's name for the Truckee River] to the little Vally 4 first and worst Chain of mountan the next is nothing and the distance from little vally to the American River is 6 miles fair Road Except loose Rock."

On reaching the present Reno area, the "Grass Valley" of the Jefferson map, Reed comments, "fine valley sufficet for 20000 head Cattle." Farther along, he notes the forks of the Truckee, "South fork S Trout" and "north fork." Beyond a ridge to the west is "little Vally with grass plenty and good watter." Reed locates the "Cabins" and (Donner) "Lake" above, as well as a more prominent "Lake" beyond the divide. It would seem that he took the Coldstream route south of Donner Lake, previously traveled by Carriger, and that he is referring to this stretch of the trail in saying at the bottom of the map, "Mountain 8 mi the worst road in creaton." "Sutters" is the only legend for the rest of the journey.

Reed kept an account of mileages, which on the face of the map may be read from right to left: 36 [?], 36 [?], 32, 35, 38, 30, 25, 5, 25, 15, 25, 21, 8, 17, 25. These mileages for the most part may be made out in the column of figures at the left of the map, evidently one of Reed's totals. Three other penciled columns of figures may be noted at right, with 12, 50, 12, 35, and 38 totaled as 147; again with 30, 25, 5, 25, 15, 25, 21, 17, and 28 erroneously totaled as 188 (and with a few other figures noted below); and at bottom, with 25, 5, 25, 15, 25, 21, and 17 in column. These calculations painfully reflect distances Reed had covered and which his family would have to cover in coming along behind.

*   *   *

James Frazier Reed to James W. Keyes South Fork of Platte, June 16, 1846[73]

To-day, at nooning, there passed, going to the States, seven men from Oregon, who went out last year. One of them was well acquainted with Messrs. [William B.] Ide, and [Robert] Cad[d]en Key[e]s,—the later of whom he says went to California.[74] They met the advance Oregon caravan about 150 miles west of Fort Larimere, and counted in all for California and Oregon (excepting ours), four hundred and seventy-eight waggons. There is in ours forty waggons, which make 518 in all; and there is said to be twenty yet behind.

To-morrow we cross the river, and by our reckoning will be 200 miles from Fort Larimere, where we intend to stop and repair our waggon wheels; they are nearly all loose, and I am afraid we will have to stop sooner if there can be found wood suitable to heat the tire. There is no wood here, and our women and children are now out gathering "Buffalo chips" to burn in order to do the cooking. These "chips" burn well.

So far as I am concerned, my family affairs go on smoothly, but I have nothing to do but hunt, which I have done with great success. My first appearance on the wilds of the Nebraska as a hunter, was on the 12th inst., when I returned to camp with a splended two year old Elk, the first and only one killed by the caravan as yet. I picked the Elk I killed, out of eight of the largest I ever beheld, and I do really believe there was one in the gang as large as the horse I rode. We have had two Buffalo killed. The men that killed them are considered the best buffalo hunters on the road—perfect *"stars."* Knowing that Glaucus could beat any horse on the Nebraska, I came to the conclusion that as far as buffalo killing was concerned, I could beat them. Accordingly, yesterday I thought to try my luck. The old buffalo hunters and as many others as they would permit to be in their company, having left the camp for a hunt, Hiram Miller, my self and two others, after due preparation, took up the line of march. Before we left, every thing in camp was talking that Mr so and so, had gone hunting, and we would have some choice buffalo meat. No one thought or spoke of the two Sucker hunters, and none but the two asked to go with us.

Going one or two miles west of the old hunters on the bluffs, and after riding about four miles, we saw a large herd of buffalo bulls, great [?] for choice young meat, which is the hardest to get, being fleeter and better wind— On we went towards them as coolly and calmly as the nature of the case would permit. And now, as *perfectly green* as I was I had to compete with old experienced hunters, and remove the *stars* from their brows; which was my greatest ambition, and in order too, that they might see that a Sucker had the best horse in the company, and the best and most daring horseman in the caravan. Closing upon a gang of ten or twelve bulls, the word was given, and I was soon in their midst, but among them there was none young enough for my taste to shoot, and upon seeing a drove on my right I dashed among them, with Craddock's pistol in hand—(a fine instrument for Buffalo hunters on the plains)—selected my victim and brought him tumbling to the ground, leaving my companions far behind. Advancing a little further, the plains appeared to be one living, moving mass of bulls, cows and calves. The latter took my eye, and I again put spur to Glaucus and soon found myself among them, and for the time being defied by the bulls, who protected the cows and calves. Now I thought the time had arrived to make one desperate effort, which I did by reining short up and dashing into them at right angles. With me it was an exciting time, being in the midst of a herd of upwards of a hundred head of buffalo alone, entirely out of sight of my companions. At last I succeeded in separating a calf from the cows, but soon there accompanied him three large bulls, and in a few minutes I separated two of them. Now having a bull that would weigh about 1200 lbs., and a fine large calf at full speed, I endeavored to part the calf from the bull without giving him Paddy's hint, but could not accomplish it. When I would rein to the right where the calf was, the bull would immediately put himself between us. Finding I could not separate on decent terms, I gave him one of Craddock's, which sent him reeling. And now for the calf without one pistol being loaded. Time now was important—and I had to run up and down hill at full speed loading one of my pistols. At last I loaded, and soon the chase ended.—and I had two dead and a third mortally wounded and dying.

After I had disposed of my calf I rode to a small mound a short distance off to see if Hiram and the others were in sight. I sat down, and while sitting I counted 597 buffalo within sight. After a while Miller and one of the others came up. We then got some water from a pond near by, which was thick with mud from the buffaloes tramping in it. Resting awhile the boys then wanted to kill a buffalo themselves. I pointed out to them a few old bulls about a mile distant. It was understood that I was not to join in the chase, and after accompanying the boys to the heights where I could witness the sport, they put out at full speed. They soon singled out a large bull, and I do not recollect of ever having laughed more than I did at the hunt the boys made. Their horses would chase well at a proper distance from the bull. As they approached he would come to a stand and turn for battle. The horses would then come to a halt, at a distance between the boys and the buffalo of about 40 yards. They would thus fire away at him, but to no effect. Seeing that they were getting tired of the sport and the bull again going away, I rode up and got permission to stop him if I could. I put spurs to Glaucus and after him I went at full speed. As I approached the bull turned around to the charge. Falling back and dashing towards him with a continued yell at the top of my lungs I got near enough to let drive one of my pistols. The ball took effect, having entered behind the shoulders and lodged in his lungs. I turned in my saddle as soon as I could to see if he had pursued me, as is often the case after being wounded. He was standing nearly in the place where he received the shot, bleeding at the nostrils, and in a few seconds dropped dead. I alighted and looped my bridle over one of his horns. This Glaucus objected to a little, but a few gentle words with a pat of my hand she stood quiet and smelled him until the boys came up. Their horses could not be got near him. Having rested, we commenced returning to the place where I killed the last calf. A short distance off we saw another drove of calves. Again the chace was renewed, and soon I laid out another fine calf upon the plains. Securing as much of the meat of the calves as we could carry, we took up the line of march for the camp, leaving the balance to the wolves, which are very numerous. An hour or two's ride found us safely among our friends, the acknowledged hero of the day, and the most successful buffalo hunter on the route. Glaucus was closely examined by many to-day, and pronounced the finest nag in the caravan. Mrs. R. will accompany me in my next buffalo hunt, which is to come off in a few days.[75]

The face of the country here is very hilly, although it has the name of "plains." The weather rather warm— thermometer ranging in the middle of the day at about 90, and at night 41.

The Oregon people tell me that they have made their claims at the head of Puget Sound, and say that the late exploration has made the northeast, or British side of the Columbia, far superior to the Willamette Valley, in quality and extent of territory.

Our teams are getting on fine so far. Most of the emigrants ahead have reduced their teams. The grass is much better this year throughout the whole route than the last.

Respectfully your brother,
JAMES F. REED.

VIRGINIA E. B. REED TO MARY C. KEYES, INDEPENDENCE
ROCK, JULY 12, 1846[76]

My Dear Couzin

I take this oppertuny to Write to you to let you know
that I am well at present and hope that you are well. We
have all had good helth——we came to the blue—the
water was so hye we had to stay thare 4 days—in the
mean time gramma died, she became spechless the day
before she died. We buried her verry decent We made
a nete coffin and buried her under a tree we had a head
stone and had her name cutonit and the date and yere
verry nice, and at the head of the grave was a tree we cut
some letters on it the young men soded it all ofer and put
Flores on it We miss her verry much every time we
come into the Wagon we look at the bed for her.[77] We
have come throw several tribes of indians the Caw Indians
the soux the shawnies, at the caw viliage paw counted
20050 Indians[78] We diden see no Indians from the time
we lefe the cow viliage till we come to fort Laramy the
Caw [Sioux] Indians are going to War with the crows
we have to pass throw ther Fiting grond, the Soux Indians
are the pretest drest Indians thare is, paw goes bufalo
hunting most every day and kills 2 or 3 buffalo every
day paw shot an elk some of our compians saw a grisly
bear We hve the thermometer 102°—average for the last
6 days We celebrated the 4 of July on plat [Platte
River] at Bever crick, severel of the gentemen in Springfield gave paw a botel of licker and said it shouden be
opend till the 4 day of July and paw was to look to the
east and drink it and they was to look to the West an
drink it at 12 o clock paw treted the compiany and we all
had some lemminade, maw and paw is Well and sends
there best love to you all. I send my best love to you all
We have hard from uncle Cad severl times he went to
california and now is gone to oregon he is well. I am a
going to send this letter by a man [Wales B. Bonney]
coming from oregon by hisself. He is a going to take his

family to oregon[79] We are all doing well and in hye sperits so I must close your leter, you are for ever my affectionate couzen

VIRGINIA E. B. REED

JAMES FRAZIER REED TO [JAMES OR GERSHAM KEYES?][80]

Fort Bridger, one hundred miles from the Eutaw or Great Salt Lake, July 31, 1846.

We have arrived here safe with the loss of two yoke of my best oxen. They were poisoned by drinking water in a little creek called Dry Sandy, situated between the Green Spring in the Pass of the Mountains, and Little Sandy. The water was standing in puddles.—Jacob Donner also lost two yoke, and George Donner a yoke and a half, all supposed from the same cause.[81] I have replenished my stock by purchasing from Messrs. Vasques & Bridger, two very excellent and accommodating gentlemen, who are the proprietors of this trading post.[82]—The new road, or Hastings' Cut-off[83], leaves the Fort Hall road here, and is said to be a saving of 350 or 400 miles in going to California, and a better route. There is, however, or thought to be, one stretch of 40 miles without water; but Hastings and his party, are out a-head examining for water, or for a route to avoid this stretch.[84] I think that they cannot avoid it, for it crosses an arm of the Eutaw Lake, now dry. Mr. Bridger, and other gentlemen here, who have trapped that country, say that the Lake has receded from the tract of country in question.[85] There is plenty of grass which we can cut and put into the waggons, for our cattle while crossing it.

We are now only 100 miles from the Great Salt Lake by the new route,—In all 250 [!] miles from California; while by way of Fort Hall it is 650 or 700 miles—making a great saving in favor of jaded oxen and dust. On the new route we will not have dust, as there are about 60 waggons ahead of us.[86] The rest of the Californians went the long route—feeling afraid of Hasting's Cut-off. Mr. Bridger informs me that the route we design to take, is a fine level road, with plenty of water and grass, with the exception before stated. It is estimated that 700 miles will take us to Capt. Suter's Fort, which we hope to make in seven weeks from this day.

I want you to inform the emigration that they can be supplied with fresh cattle by Messrs. Vasques & Bridger. They have now about 200 head of oxen, cows and young cattle, with a great many horses and mules; and they can be relied on for doing business honorably and fairly. Mr. Bridger will go to St. Louis this fall and return with the emigration in the spring, and will be very useful as a pilot. He will be found during winter in St. Louis, at Mr. Robert Campbell's (merchant.)[87] I must put you on your guard against two or three persons who have left California and Oregon for horse stealing and other crimes. Of course they dislike those countries. They are perfect vagabonds.[88]

I have fine times in hunting grouse, antelope or mountain goat, which are plenty. Milford Elliott, James Smith and W[alter]. Herron, the young men who drive for me, are careful, first rate drivers,—which gives me time for hunting. We are beyond the range of buffalo.

The independent trappers, who swarm here during the passing of the emigrants, are as great a set of sharks as ever disgraced humanity, with few exceptions. Let the emigrants avoid trading with them. Vasques & Bridger are the only fair traders in these parts.

There are two gentlemen here—one of them an Englishman of the name of Wills, and the other a yankee named Miles—who will leave here in a few days to settle at some favorable point on the Salt Lake, which in a short time will be a fine place for emigrants to recruit their teams, by exchanging broken down oxen for good teams.[89]

VIRGINIA E. B. REED TO MARY C. KEYES "NAPA VALLIE CALIFORNIA" MAY 16th 1847[90]

My Dear Cousin

I take this opportunity to write to you to let you [k]now that we are all Well at presant and hope this letter may find you all well [*deleted*: to] My dear [Dear] Cousin I am [*deleted*: a] going to Write to you about our trubels [in] geting to Callifornia; We had good luck til we come to big Sandy thare we lost our best yoak of oxen [Balley & George & cathin] we come to Bri[d]gers Fort & we lost [Two] another one we sold some of our provision & bau[gh]t a yoak of Cows & oxen[91] [*deleted*: &] they [the people at Bridges Fort] pursuaded us to take Haistings cut off over the salt plain thay said it saved 3 Hondred miles, we went that road & we had to go through a long drive [as they said] of 40 miles With out water or grass Hastings said it was 40 [miles] but i think it was 80 miles We traveld a day and night [*deleted*: & a nother day] and at noon [next day papa] pa went on to see if he Coud find Water, he had not [*deleted*: been] gone long till some of the oxen give out and we had to leve the Wagons and take the oxen [*deleted*: on] to water [*deleted*: one of the men] [Walter Herron & Bailos,] staid with us and the others [boys Milt Elliot & J Smith] went on with the cattel to water pa [papa] was [*deleted*: a] coming back to us with Water and met the men thay was about 10 miles from water pa [papa] said thay [would] get to water that night, and the next day to bring the cattel back for the Wagons any [and] bring some Water pa [papa] got to us about [*deleted*: noon] [daylight next morning] the man that was with us took the horse and went on to water We wa[i]ted thare [*deleted*: throug] [thinking thay would] come we wa[i]ted till night and We thought we [would] start and walk to Mr doners [Donners] wagons that night [distant 10 miles] we took what little water we had and some bread and started pa [papa] caried Thomos and all

the rest of us walk we got to Donner and thay were all
a sleep so we laid down on the ground we spread one shawl
down we laid down on it and spred another over us and
then put the dogs on top [Tyler, Barney, Trailor Tracker
& little Cash] it was the couldes night you [*deleted*: most]
ever saw [for the season] the wind blew [very hard] and
if it haden [not] bin for the dogs we would have Frosen[92]
as soon as it was day we went to Miz [Mrs] Donners she
said we could not walk to the Water and if we staid we
could ride in thare wagons to the spring so pa [papa] went
on to the water to see why thay did not bring the cattel
when he got thare thare was but one ox and cow thare
[*deleted*: &] none of the rest had got to Water Mr Donner come out that night with his cattel and braught his
Wagons and all of us in we staid thare a week and Hunted
for our cattel and could not find them [the Indians had
taken them] so some of the companie took thare oxen and
went out and brought in one wagon and cashed the other
tow and a grate man a [many] things all but what we
could put in our Wagon we head [had] to devied our
provisions [*deleted*: out to them] [with the Company]
to get them to carie them [carry it][93] We got three yoak
with our oxe & cow so we [went] on that way a while and
we got out of provisions and pa [papa] had to go on to
callifornia [california] for provisions[94] we could not get
along that way, in 2 or 3 days after pa left we had to cash
our wagon and take Mr. graves [Graves] wagon and
cash some more of our things well we went on that way
a while and then we had to get Mr Eddies [Eddys]
wagon we went on that way a while and then we had to
cash all of our close except a change or 2 and put them in
Mr Brins Wagon and Thomos & James rode the [*deleted*:
other] 2 horses and the rest of us had to walk, we went on
that way a Whild and we come to a nother long drive of
40 miles [between Marys and Truckeys Rivers] we went
with Mr Donner We had to Walk all the time we [*deleted*: was a] [ware] traveling up the truckee [truckey]
river we met [*deleted*: a man] [a Mr T C Stanton who]

and [*deleted*: a] [2] Indians that we had sent on for provisions to [Captn] Suter Fort [before papa Started][95] thay had met pa, not fur from Suters Fort he looked very bad he had not [*deleted*: had] ate but 3 times in 7 days and the [three last] days without any thing his horse was not abel to carrie him thay give him a horse and he went on[96] so we cashed some more of our things all but what we could pack on one mule and we started Martha and James road behind the two Indians it was a raing then in the Vallies and snowing on the montains so we went on that way 3 or 4 days tell we come to the big mountain or the Callifornia Mountain the snow then was about 3 feet deep thare was some wagons thare thay said thay had atempted to cross and could not,[97] well we thought we would try it so we started and thay started again with thare wagons the snow was then up to the mules side the farther we went up the deeper the snow got so the wagons could not go so thay packed thare oxens and started with us carring a child a piece and driving the oxens in snow up to thare wast the mule Martha and the Indian was on was the best one so thay went and broak the road and that indian was the Pilot so we went on that way 2 miles and the mules kept faling down on the snow head formost and the Indian said [*deleted*: thay] he could not find the road [we] stoped and let the Indian and [*deleted*: man] [Mr. Stanton] go on to hunt the road thay went on and found the road to the top of the mountain and come back and said they thought we could git over if it did not snow any more well the Weman were all so tirder caring there Children that thay could not go over that night so we made a fire and got something to eat & ma spred down a bufalo robe & we all laid down on it & spred somthing over us & ma set up by the fire & it snowed one foot on top of the bed so we got up in the morning & the snow was so deep we could not go over & we had to go back to the cabin [built by emigrants 2 Years ago] & build [*deleted*: built] more cabins & stay thare all Winter [to 20 Feby] without Pa[98] we had not the first thing to eat Ma maid

arangements for some cattel giving 2 for 1 in callifornia
we seldom thot of bread for we had not had any since
[*word or two obscured*] & the cattel was so poor thay
could note hadley git up when thay laid down we stoped
thare the 4th of November & staid till [*deleted*: March]
and what we had to eat i cant hardley tell you & we had
[*deleted*: that man] [Mr Stanton] & Indians to feed
[*deleted*: to] well thay started over a foot and had to
come back so thay made snow shoes and started again &
it come on a storme & thay had to come back[99] it would
snow 10 days before it would stop thay wated tell it stoped
& started again I was a goeing with them & I took sick
& could not go—thare was [*number corrected to* 15]
started & thare was 7 got throw 5 Weman & 2 men it
come a storme and thay lost the road & got out of provisions & [*deleted*: the ones] that got throwe had to eat
the them that Died[100] not long after thay started we got
out of provisions & had to [put] Martha at one caben
James at another Thomas at another & Ma & Elizea &
Milt Eliot & I dried up what littel meat we had and
started to see if we could get across & had to leve the
childrin[101] o Mary you may think that hard to leve them
with strangers & did not now wether we would see them
again or not we could [*deleted*: not] hardle get a way
from them but we [*word deleted*] told them we [*deleted*:
to] [would] bring them Bread & then thay was willing
to stay we went & was out 5 days in the mountains Elieza
giv out & had to go back we went on a day longer we had
to lay by a day & make snow shows & we went on a while
and coud not find the road & we had to turn back I could
go on verry well while i thout we wer geting along but
as soone as we had to turn back i coud hadley git along but
we got to the cabins that night[102] [I froze one of my feet
verry bad] & that same night thare was the worst storme
we had [*deleted*: that] winter & if we had not come back
that night we would never got back we had nothing to
eat [then] but ox hides o Mary I would cry and wish I
had what you all wasted Eliza had go to Mr Graves

cabin & we staid at Mr Breen thay had meat all the time
[*deleted at a later time*: we had to kill littel cash the dog
& eat him we ate his head and feet & hide & evry thing
about him] o my Dear Cousin you dont [k]now what
trubel is yet a many a time we had on the last thing a
cooking and did not [k]now wher the next would come
from but there was awl wais some way provided there
was 15 in the cabon we was in and half of us had to lay a
bed all the time thare was 10 starved to death [while we
ware] there we was hadley abel to walk we lived on litle
cash a week and after Mr Breen would [cook] his meat
[and boil the bones Two or three times] we would take
the bones and boil them 3 or 4 days at a time ma [Mama]
went down to the other caben and got half a hide carried
it in snow up to her wast it snowed [*word deleted*] and
would cover the cabin all over so we could not get out for
2 or 3 days [at a time] we would have to cut pieces of
the loges in sied to make fire with I coud hardly eat the
hides [*deleted*: and had not eat anything 3 days] Pa
stated out to us with provisions [*deleted*: and then came
a storme and he could not go] [on the first of November
and Came into the Great California Mountain, about 80
miles and in one of the Severest Storms Known for Years
past, A raining in the Valley and a Hurrican of snow in
the mountains it Came so deep that the horses & mules
Swamped So they could not go on any more] he cash his
provision and went back [*deleted*: &] on the other side of
the bay to get compana of men and the San Wakien got
so hye he could not crose well thay Made up a Compana
at Suters Fort and sent out we had not ate any thing for
3 days & we had onely a half a hide and we was out on
top of the cabin and we seen them [the party] a coming

O my Dear Cousin you dont [k]now how glad i was,
we run and met them one of them we knew we had
traveled with them on the road[103] thay staid thare 3 days
to recruet a little so we could go thare was 20 started all
of us started and went a piece and Martha and Thomas
giv out & so the men had to take them back ma and Eliza

James & I come on and o Mary that was the hades thing
yet to come on and leiv them thar [One of the party Said
he was a Mason and pledged his life that if we did not
meet Pa in time he would come and help his children]
did not now but what thay would starve to Death Martha
said well ma if you never see me again do the best you
can the men said thay could hadly stand it it maid them
all cry but they said it was better for all of us to go on for
if we was to go back we would eat that much more from
them thay give them a littel meat and flore and took
them back and we come on [Ma agreed to leave Thomas
& Martha from the promise of Mr Glover, if we should
not meet Pa which we did in few days.] we went over
great hye mountain as steap as stair steps in snow up to
our knees litle James walk the hole [whole] way over all
the mountain in snow up to his waist, he said every step
he took he was a gitting nigher Pa and somthing to eat
the [*deleted*: Bears] [Cacadues, or Fishers][104] took the
provision the men had cashed and we had but very little
to eat when we had traveld 5 days travel we met Pa with
13 men going to the cabins o Mary you do not nou how
glad we was to see him we had not seen him for [*deleted*:
6] [5] months we thought we woul never see him again
he heard we was coming and he made some seet cakes
[the night before at his Camp] to give us [and the other
Children withe us] he said he would see Martha and
Thomas the next day he went in tow days what took us
5 days [when pa went to the Cabins] some of the compana
was eating [*deleted*: from them] [those] that Died but
Thomas & Martha had not [to] ate any Pa and the men
started with 12 people Hiram O Miller Carried Thomas
and Pa caried Martha and thay were caught in [*deleted*:
storms?] [a Snow Storm which lasted two days & nights]
and thay had to stop [Two] days it stormed so thay
could not go and the [*deleted*: Bears] [Fishers] took
their provision and thay weer 4 days without anything
Pa and Hiram and and all the men started one of Donner
boys Pa a carring Martha Hiram caring Thomas and

the snow was up to thare wast and it a snowing so thay
could hadley see the way thay raped the children up and
never took them out for 4 days & thay had nothing to eat
in all that time Thomas asked for somthing to eat once
[*deleted*: those] [Those] that thay brought from the cabins some of them was not able to come [from the Starved
Camp as it is called,] and som would not come Thare was
3 died and the rest eat them thay was 10 days without
any thing to eat but the Dead Pa braught Thom and
pady on to where we was none of the men [*deleted*: was
abel to go] [Pa had with him ware able to go back
for Some people Still at the Cabins,] there feet was
froze very bad so they [thare] was a nother Compana
went and braught them all in thay are all in from the
Mountains now but [*deleted*: five?] [four] [*deleted*:
they was] men went out after them and was caught
in a storm and had to come back thare [*deleted*: is?]
[was] another compana [*deleted*: gone thare was half
got through that was stoped thare] [sent to their relief]
thare was but [2] families [*deleted*: got] that all of them
got [*through*] we was [ware] one[105] O Mary I have
not wrote you half of the truble [we have had] but I hav
Wrote you anuf to let you [k]now what truble is but
thank [*deleted*: the Good] god and the onely family that
did not eat human flesh we have left everything but i dont
cair for that we have got [through with our lives but]
Dont let this letter dishaten anybody never take no cutofs
and hury along as fast as you can

My Dear Cousin
We are all very well pleased with Callifornia particularly with the climate let it be ever so hot a day thare is
all wais cool nights it is a beautiful Country it is mostley
in vallies it aut to be a beautiful Country to pay us for
our trubel geting there it is the greatest place for catle
and horses you ever saw it would Just suit Charley for
he could ride down 3 or 4 horses a day and he could lern
to be Bocarro that [is] one who lases cattel the spanards

and Indians are the best riders i ever saw thay have a
spanish sadel and woden sturups and great big spurs
[*deleted*: the wheel of them is] 5 inches in diameter and
they could not manage the Callifornia horses witout the
spurs, thay wont go atol if thay cant hear the spurs rattle
they have littel bells to them to make them rattle thay
blindfold the [wild] horses [*deleted*: and then] [so the]
sadel them and git on them and then take the blindfole
of and let run and if thay cant sit on thay tie themselves
on and let them run as fast as they can and go out to a
band of bullluck and throw the reatter on a wild bullluck
and but it around the horn of his sadel and he can hold
it as long as he wants a nother Indian throws them and
when thay [*deleted*: git] take the reatter of of them thay
are very dangerous they will run after any person thay
see thay ride from 80 to 100 miles a day [*deleted*: & have]
some of the spanard have from 6 to 7000 head of horses
and from 15 to 16000 head Cattel we are all verry fleshey
Ma waies 10040 pon and still a gaing I weigh 80 tel
Henriet if she wants to get Married to come to Callifornia
she can get a spanyard any time that Eliza is a going to
marrie a a spanyard by the name of Armeho and Eliza
weighs 10070[106] We have not saw uncle Cadon yet but
we have had 2 letters from him he is well and is a coming
here as soon as he can Mary take this letter to uncle
Gurshon and to all that i know to all of our neighbors
[*interlined*: and tell Dochter Mcniel][107] and every girl i
know and let them read it Mary kiss little Sue and
Maryann for me and give my best love to all i know to
uncle Gurshon aunt Percilla and all the Children and to all
of our neighbors and to all the girls i know Ma sends
her very best love to uncle James aunt Leida and all the
rest of the famla and to uncle Gursham aunt Persilla
and all the Children and to all of our neighbors and to
all she knows so no more at presant [*interlined*: pa is yer-
bayan][108]

My Dear casons
VIRGINIA ELIZABETH B REED

Illinois Journal, Springfield, December 9, 1847

Narrative of Sufferings
Of a Company of Emigrants in the Mountains of
California, in the Winter of '46 and '7 by
J. F. Reed, late of Sangamon County, Illinois

[The following narrative was prepared for the press by Mr. J. H. Merryman, from notes written by Mr. J. F. Reed. We copy from the *State Registe*[r],—omitting the list of those who survived and those who perished,— having published the same several week's since.][109]

Through the kindness of Mr. James W. Keys, Esq., we are enabled to lay before our readers an abstract of the journal of Mr. James F. Reed, who emigrated from this place, some two years since, to California.

He says that his misfortunes commenced on leaving Fort Bridger, which place he left on the 31st of August [July], 1846, in company with eighty-one others. Nothing of note occurred until the 6th of September [August], when they had reached within a few miles of Weaver [Weber] Canon, where they found a note from a Mr. Hastings, who was twenty miles in advance of them, with sixty wagons, saying that if they would send for him he would put them upon a new route, which would avoid the *Canon* and lessen the distance to the great Salt Lake several miles. Here the company halted, and appointed three persons, who should overtake Mr. Hastings and engage him to guide them through the new route, which was promptly done. Mr. Hastings gave them directions concerning this road, and they immediately recommenced their journey.[110] After traveling eighteen days they accomplished the distance of thirty miles, with great labor and exertion, being obliged to cut the whole road through a forest of pine and aspen.[111] They halted upon the south end of the great Salt Lake, where they remained several days. Mr. Reed describes the water of this lake, to use his own expression, as "strong enough to brine beef." Leaving this place on the 20th of September [August], they proceeded on their way, crossing a large desert, devoid of water, on account of which they lost several of their finest cattle.—When within nine hundred miles of the California settlements they discovered that their stock of provisions was insufficient to last them until they had traveled that distance; therefore, they appointed two persons, Messrs. C. F. Stanton, of Chicago, and William McClutchem [McCutchen], of Clay county, Mo., who should proceed with all possible haste to Fort Sacramento, owned by Capt. Sutter, procure supplies, and return as soon as possible. They accordingly started on their errand, and although having near a thousand miles to go, they calculated that they would return in a short time.[112] The company then proceeded, and after traveling three hundred miles, giving ample time, as they supposed, for the return of Messrs. Stanton and McClutchem, and fearing that some accident had befallen them, they determined to send another messenger. Mr. Reed was at once chosen as the most proper person for this service, and providing himself with seven days provision, he commenced his lonesome march. Before him lay a journey of six hundred miles, which he must accomplish on foot, for although he had a horse, it was so weak that it could not carry his saddle-bags and blanket. He left the company at Mary's river.[113] On the second day's march he overtook the Donners, who were in advance, on account of the superior condition of their cattle.—Here he was joined by Walter Herron. He found the Donners subsisting on the carcases of some of their cattle, which had been killed by the Indians in a night attack two days previous. In company with Herron he pursued his way; the scanty supply of provisions soon gave out; along the banks of Mary's and Tucker's [Truckee] rivers they found a little game; after leaving the latter they saw none at all. For seven days they journeyed through that wilderness, during which time they ate but two meals, and they were made of wild onions. Fortunately, at the end of the time they reached Bear river valley, where they found a small party

S. W. for the 3 last days M^rs [Phillipine] Key burg
started & left Keysburg here unable to go I Burried
pikes Child this Moring in the snow it died 2 days ago,
Paddy [Patty] Reid & Thos. Came back [brought by]
Messrs Grover [Aquilla Glover] & Mutry [R. S. Mou-
try]

Tues^d. 23 froze hard last night today fine & thawey
has the appearance of Spring all but the deep Snow wind
S. S. E. shot Towser today & dressed his flesh M^rs
Graves Come here this morning, to borrow meat dog or
ox they think I have meat to spare but I know to the
Contrary they have plenty hides I live principally on
the same

Wen^d. 24th froze hard last night to day Cloudy looks
like a storm wind blows hard from the W. Commenced
thawing there has not any more returned from those who
started to cross the M.^ts

Thurs^d. 25th froze hard last night fine & sun shiney
to day wind W. Mrs Murphy says the wolves are about
to dig up the dead bodies at her shanty, the nights are
too cold to watch them, we hear them howling

Frid 26th froze hard last night to day clear & warm
Wind S:E. blowing briskly Marthas jaw swelled with
the tooth ache; hungry times in camp, plenty hides but
the folks will not eat them we eat them with a tolerable
good apetite, Thanks be to Almighty God, *Amen* M^rs
Murphy said here yesterday that thought she would Commence on Mil^t. & eat him, I dont [think] that she has done
so yet, it is distressing[11] The Donnos told the California
folks that they [would] Commence to eat the dead people
4 days ago, if they did not succeed that day or next in
finding their cattle then under ten or twelve feet of snow
& did not know the spot or near it I suppose They have
done so ere this time

Sat. 27th beautiful morning sun shineing brilliantly,
wind about S. W. the snow has fell in debth about 5 feet
but no thaw but the sun in day time it freezeing hard
every night, heard some geese fly over last night saw none

Sun^d. 28th froze har^d. last night to day fair & sun
shiney wind S. E. 1 Solitary Indian passed by yesterday
come from the lake[12] had aheavy pack on his back gave me
5 or 6 roots resembleing Onions in shape taste some like
a sweet potatoe, all full of little tough fibres
Mon^d. March the 1st to [day] fine & pleasant froze hard
last night there has 10 men arrived this morning from
bear valley with provisions[13] we are to start in two or
three days & Cash our goods here there is amongst them
some old [mountaineers] they say the snow will be here
untill June

"Arrival of the Second Relief"

Diaries of the Donner Relief

Misgivings were felt in respect of the emigrants who had failed to cross the Sierra Nevada before snow blanketed the mountain heights, and the fathers James F. Reed and William McCutchen, separated from their families, were prey to the deepest anxiety, but the desperate situation of the Donner Party became known only with the arrival of William H. Eddy and his companions at Johnson's Ranch on January 18, 1847. Of fifteen who had hazarded the journey from Truckee Lake, only seven had come through alive.

News of their arrival was printed in the *California Star* of February 13, 1847, as may be seen in Volume II; the relief efforts already in progress were given added impetus and formal status, as inhabitants of the Bay Area and U. S. Navy authorities gathered means and men. But before anything could be done out of Yerba Buena, emigrants wintering at the frontier settlements set on foot a relief effort of their own, backed by John A. Sutter and John Sinclair.

George Tucker, who was 16 years old in 1847, recalled for the benefit of C. F. McGlashan in 1879, a long narrative now preserved among the McGlashan Papers in the Bancroft Library:

"as Soon as we got these Seven [Snowshoers] in and got them made as Comfortable as Circumstances would admit and learned the Condition of the rest of the Company they had left behind we then Commenced to devise Some plan to releave them but at Johnson's Ranch there was onely 3 or 4 families of poor Emigrants beside Johnsons and nothing Could be done without help from other Setlements Sutters fort was the nearest point and it had been raining nearly all winter and the Country was all Covered with water Bear River was banks full so it could not be forded and if it could the Sacramento plains was one vast quag mire from there to Sutters fort 40 miles

"John Rhodes one of our neighbors an Emigrant that had crost the plains that Season Said if there was no other way he would go on foot we had no means of crossing the river So we made a boat by lashing 2 pine loggs to gather with Strips of rawhide the next morning we set John Rhodes a crost the river on our raft he took his Shoes in his hand Roled his pants up above his knees and Started for Sutters fort through water from one foot to 4 foot deep a good part of the way. he reached Sutter's Sometime that nite, and informed Captan Sutter and the Setlers of what had hapened and what was wanted—, Captan Sutter and Alcalda St Clair whoo lived on what is now Called Norrises Ranch 2 ½ miles from Sutter's fort on the American River—and one of the welthiest men in the Country, furnished Some provisions Such as flour Sugar Coffe &c and five or Six men that was liveing in the Settlement Volenterrd to go with the Suplies in the corse of Six or Eight days Six men Came up with the Suplies mean while we had butchered five or six fat beaves, furnished by Johnson and was drying and Jirking the meat we Scowered the country far and near to get horses and mules to ride and pack— & Sadles and pack Sadles It was ten or 12 days before we could get every thing ready—the day before we Started Alcalda St. Clair Came up to assist us in getting Started— in the morning we got all the animals Sadled and packed when St Clair took out his pencil and paper and took down all the names of those that were to go.—then he got up and made us a Speech he said we wer about Start- ing on a very hazardous Journey—that nothing would Justify us in undertaking what we wer about to do onley the obligation we owed to our fellow man—urged us to do all that was in our power without Sacrificing our own lives to Save our Suffering Brothers from Starvation and death. he then appointed my Father R. P. Tucker Captan of the Company.''

A parallel account dictated by Daniel Rhoads for H. H. Bancroft in 1873 anticipates the first of our diaries, but should be quoted at length:

"The day after the arrival of Eddy at Johnsons a party started from the latter place to bring in [William] Foster and the four women, which they accomplished in two or three days.

"On the receipt of the news at the Fort letters were at once sent . . . to Yerba Bueana and the Settlements around the Bay of San Francisco.

"Captain Sutter made a call for volunteers, to proceed to the assistance of the emigrants. A party of fourteen, of which I was one, was made up and at once started for Johnsons Ranch. Here we prepared for our expedition. We killed some beef cattle and dried the meat over fires. We pounded some wheat in Indian stone mortars and ground some in coffee-mills (no grist mills nor flour nor meal of any kind in those days). We cut the hides of the animals we killed into strips for the future construction of the snow-shoes.

"Although we worked night & day without intermission except short intervals for sleep these preparations occupied us three days. The provisions were then packed on mules and we started on our journey, without a guide, and trusting to the judgment of our leaders, John P. Rhoads (my brother) and — Tucker to find our way. Until we 'struck' the snow we took the emigrant trail . . . .

"Our road was in very bad condition and at frequent intervals we had to unpack the mules and drag them out of the mire. In about five or six miles a day we reached the snow which we found three feet deep. Through this we worried along some five miles when it became too deep for the mules to go any further it being eight feet deep and falling all the time; a regular storm having set in. Our encountering the snow so deep and so much sooner than we had been led to anticipate utterly disheartened some of the party and six men turned back.

"We made a camp and left the mules in charge of one of Sutter's men a German who went by the *soubriquet* of 'Greasy Jim' [*i.e.,* James Weinberg, otherwise known as Adolph Bruheim?] Jim was to take care of the animals and to pasture them on hill sides with a Southern exposure and such other bare spots as he could find, until our return.

"Our party now consisted of seven. John P. Rhoads,— Tucker (now in Napa valley) Sept. Mootry (now in Santa Clara), — Glover (dead), a sailor named George [Joseph] Foster [otherwise known as Joseph Sels], a sailor named Mike [*i.e.,* Edward Coffeemeyer], and myself. Each man made a pair of snowshoes. These were constructed by cutting pine boughs, stripping off the bark, heating them over the fire and bending them in the shape of an ox-bow about two feet long and 1 wide with a lattice work of raw hide, for soles We attached them to our feet by means of the rawhide strips with which we were provided. On these we had to travel continuously except at brief intervals on hill-sides & bare spots where we took them off.

"Each man also took a single blanket a tin cup, a hatchet and as near as the captains could estimate 75 pounds of dried meat. Thus equipped we started. [William] Foster had told us that we should find the emigrants at or near Truckee lake, (Since called Donner lake) and in the direction of this we journeyed. Of course we had no guide and most of our journey was through a dense pine forest but the lofty peak which overlooks the lake was in sight at intervals and this and the judgment of our two leaders were our sole means of direction . . . When we first started from the fort Capt Sutter assured us that we should be followed by other parties as soon as the necessary preparations could be made. For the guidance of those who might follow us and as a signal to any of the emigrants who might be straggling about in the mountains as well as for our own direction on our return trip; we set fire to every dead pine tree on and near our trail At the end of every three days journey (15 or 20 miles) we made up a small bundle of dried meat and hung it to the bough of a tree to lighten the burden we carried and for subsistence on our return.

"The first day we made 7 or 8 miles. At Sunset we 'made Camp' by felling pine saplings 6 inches in diameter and cutting them off about 12 feet long, & placing them on the snow making a platform 6 or 8 feet wide. On this platform we kindled our fire, roasted some meat for supper and then throwing our blankets over our shoulders sat, close together, around the fire and dozed through the night the best way we could. If we had made the fire on top of the snow without the intervention of any protecting substance we should have found our fire, in the morning 8 or 10 feet below the surface on which we encamped. In this manner we passed every night of our journey both to and from the lake on the part of the road Covered by snow

"We went on making from four to six miles per day leaving a very sinuous trail by reason of the impossibility

of pursuing a straight course through the dense forest
and of our having to wind around the sides of hills and
mountains instead of going over them. The snow increased
as we proceeded until it amounted to a depth of eighteen
feet as was afterwards discovered by the stumps of the
pine trees we burned.

"We travelled in Indian file. At each step taken by
the man in front he would sink in the snow to his knees
and of course had to lift his foot correspondingly high
for his next step. Each succeeding man would follow in
the tracks of the leader.—The latter soon became tired
fell to the rear and the second man took the head of the
file. When he became fatigued by breaking the track he
would fall back & so on each one in his turn.

"At sunset of the 16th day we crossed Truckee lake on
the ice and came to the spot where we had been told we
should find the emigrants. We looked all around but no
living thing except ourselves was in sight and we thought
that all must have perished. We raised a loud halloo and
then we saw a woman emerge from a hole in the snow.
As we approached her several others made their appearance in like manner coming out of the snow. They were
gaunt with famine and I never can forget the horrible,
ghastly sight they presented. The first woman spoke in
a hollow voice very much agitated & said 'are you men
from California or do you come from heaven.'

"They had been without food except a few work oxen
since the first fall of snow, about 3 weeks [*sic*] They had
gathered up the bones of the slaughtered cattle and boiled
them to extract the grease and had roasted some of the
hides which formed the roofs of their cabins. We gave
them food very sparingly and retired for the night having
some one on guard until morning to keep close watch on
our provision to prevent the starving emigrants from
eating them which they would have done until they died
of repletion.

"When these emigrants had first been stopped by snow
they had built small cabins using the skins of the slaught-

ered oxen for roofs Storms nearly continuous had caused
the snow to fall to the depth of 18 feet so that the tops of
their cabins were far beneath the surface When we
arrived they were eating portions of the hides forming
their roofs, which hides being under the snow were in a
putrid condition. The bodies of those who had perished
were lying on top of the snow, covered with quilts. When
a person died an inclined plane was dug to the floor of
the cabin and the body slid up to the surface; the inmates
being too weak to lift the corpse out. So far the survivors
had not been compelled to partake of human flesh. I
remember seeing but 3 living men Louis Keeseberg was
lying on his back unable to rise. Patrick Breen and one
other were the only ones left. Very few women or
children had died up to this time.

"The morning after our arrival John P. Rhoads and
Tucker started for another camp distant 8 miles East,
where were the Donner family, to distribute what provisions could be spared and to bring along such of the
party as had sufficient strength to walk. They returned
bringing four girls and two boys of the Donner family
and some others

"The next morning we started on our return trip accompanied by 21 emigrants mostly women & children.
John Rhoads carried a child in his arms which died the
second night. On the third day an emigrant named John
Denton, exhausted by starvation and totally snow-blind,
gave out. He tried to keep up a hopeful & cheerful appearance, but we knew he could not live much longer.
We made a platform of saplings, built a fire on it, cut
some boughs for him to sit upon and left him. This was
imperatively necessary. The party who followed in our
trail from California found his dead body a few days after
we had left him, partially eaten by wolves.

"As we were now guided by the stumps of the pine
trees we had burned on our way out as we never had to
stop to determine the road and as the ground we travelled
over was mostly descending we made much more rapid

progress than on our journey East being only five days from the lake to the camp where we had left our mules. Had we not made the journey thus quickly I do not know how we ever could have got through as will be seen. The first night after leaving the lake we consumed the last of our dried meat expecting that our next days journey would bring us to one of our 'caches' of provisions which we had left hanging to the boughs of trees. When we reached this point (2nd night) we found that some 'varmint' (predatory animals) had climbed up and eaten our 'cache' so that we had to make a supper of some strips of raw hide which we still carried, & which we cut from our snow-shoes roasted. We passed the night on our usual platform—there had to be several to accommodate the entire party—This rawhide was our sole subsistence for 3 days until just before we reached our 'mule camp' when we met a party going East under the guidance of a half-breed named Brit Greenwood who acted as pilot. Greenwood told us that when his father, an old Rocky Mountain hunter and trapper, heard that our party of seven had started over the mountains without a guide, he offered to wager the money he was to receive for piloting a party, that not one of us would ever come back alive: and the bet was not taken

"When we reached the camp where we had left our mules we remained until next day During the night, the food in Camp not being guarded sufficiently, the eldest boy of the Donner family managed to eat so much dried meat that he died the next day We here found a party of sailors from the U. S. Squadron commanded by Lieutenant Selim E. Woodworth U. S. N. and piloted by old man Greenwood before referred to. This was a novel business for the Sailors and I heard that they suffered terribly when they reached the deep snow

"Glover & myself were the weakest of the party suffering greatly from exhaustion caused by deprivation of food and want of sleep We mounted mules and returned to the Fort It was a long time before I recovered from the effects of the expedition. My brother John Rhoads made a second and third trip with relief parties none of which however met with the difficulties experienced by our party. . . ."

This retrospective account by Daniel Rhoads may be read in comparison with the contemporary notes made by M. D. Ritchie and Reasin P. Tucker. The diary here printed is a copy in the handwriting of John Sinclair, with some additions made by Sinclair, preserved in the James Frazier Reed Papers in the Sutter's Fort Historical Monument collection. A copy supplied to C. F. Mc-Glashan in 1879 by Patty (Reed) Lewis was used to some extent in the second edition of McGlashan's *History of the Donner Party,* and it was printed from the manuscript in the Reed Papers in Carroll D. Hall's *Donner Miscellany,* 1947. The only known diary of the First Donner Relief, it is incorporated into our text before we take up James Frazier Reed's diary of the Second Donner Relief.

1
NOTES KEPT BY M. D. RITCHIE
ON THE JOURNEY TO ASSIST THE EMIGRANTS—1

Names of the Party[2]—
Capts. R. P. Tucker
    —A. Glover
Men Joseph Sell
    "   R. S. Moutrie   "   Edward Coffymier
    "   John Rhodes   "   M. D. Ritchie
    "   Daniel Rhodes   "   Adolph Brueheim
    "   George Tucker   "   W. H. Eddy
    "   Wm. Coon   [*Deleted*: Curtis]

Feby 5th 1847—First day travelled [from Johnson's Ranch] 10 miles bad roades often miring down horses & mules. The 6-7th days travelled 15 miles road continued bad commenced raing before we got to camp continued to rain all of that day and night very severe here we laid by on the 8th to dry our provisions and clothing

9th Travelled 15 miles swam the animals one creek and carried the provisions over on a log—

10th day travelled 4 miles came to the snow continued about 4 miles further animals belly deep in snow and camped at the Mule springs³

11th Mr Eddy started back with the animals left Wm Coon and George Tucker to guard what provisions were left in camp,⁴ the other ten men each taking with the exception of one man (Mr Curtis who took about 25 pounds) about 50 lbs and travelled on through the snow having a very severe days travel over mountains making about 6 miles Camped on Bear River under a cluster of large Pines—

On the 12th moved camp about two miles and stopped to make Snow Shoes tried them on and found them of no benefit cast them away and on the 13th made Bear Valley upon digging for Curtis's waggon found the snow ten feet deep and the provisions destroyed by the Bear.⁵ Rain and snow fell upon us that night—Morning of the 14—fine weather.

From this on the journal was kept by Mr R. P. Tucker

15th Fine day three of our men declined going any farther W[M?]. D. Ritchie A. Bruheim—Curtis only 7 men being left the party was somewhat discouraged we consulted together and under existing circumstances I took it upon myself to insure every man who persevered to the end five dollars per day from the time they entered the snow⁶ we determined to go ahead and that night camped on Juba after travelling 15 miles—

16 Travelling very bad and snowing, made but 3 miles and camped in snow 15 feet deep—

17 Travelled 5 miles—

18th Travelled 8 miles and camped on the head of Juba on the Pass we suppose the snow to be 30 foot deep—

19th at sundown [*deleted*: we] reached the Cabins and found the people in great distress such as I never before witnessed there having been twelve deaths and more expected every hour the sight of us appeared to put life into their emaciated frames

20th My self and two others went to Donnors camp 8 miles and found them in a starving condition the most of the men had died one of them leaving a wife and 8 children, the two families had but one beef head amongst them, there was two cows buried in the snow but it was doubtful if they would be able to find them we left them telling them that they would soon have assistance if possible on the road back I gave out but struggled on until sundown when I reached the other cabins—

22[d] Left camp with twenty three of the sufferers 2 of the children soon gave out and two of our men carried them back and left them with Mr. Brin they were childreen of Mrs. Reed[7]

23 Got to the first cash and found half of the contents taken by the Bear being on short allowance death stared us in the face, I made an equal divide and charged them to be careful—

24th started 3 men on ahead of the Company—We had travelled about two miles when one man gave out (John Denton) I waited for him some time but in vain he could go no further I made him a fire and chopped some wood for him when I very unwillingly left him telling him he should soon have assistance but I am afraid he would not live to see it[8] travelled 7 miles and camp

25th This day a child died and was buried in the snow[9] travelled 5 miles and there met with some provisions half of a cash small allowance—

26—at noon had a small divide of shoe strings roasted and eat them and then proceeded about half a mile when we met two of our men with provisions we struck fire and feasted on our dry beef when we travelled about one mile farther and camped—

27th Travelled 4 miles and met with a another Company[10] hear Mr. Reed met with his wife and two children the meeting was very affecting; travelled about 3 miles farther and camped in our old camp head of Bear Valley here we found plenty of provisions and was waited on by Mr. Thompson a man of good feeling and judgement—[11]

28th remained in camp but after all our precaution three of the party eat to excess and had to be left in the care of an attendant

March 1st Travelled 10 miles and camped on the mountain side in the morning Mrs. Reed was very sick and we had to stop that day

on the 2d met Lieut. Woodworth and three men well loaded with provisions and blankets 10 miles from Bear Valley[12] Travelled on 3 miles and reached the Mule Springs at our old encampment where we met with nourishment Tea and Sugar which revived us a good deal—

3d Mrs. Reed reached Mule Springs and was waited on by Mr Thompson about 4 o'clock John Gordon arrived with two of the three that were left behind sick the other a boy about 15 (Wm. Donnor) had died and was buried in the ground by the side of a tree—[13]

March 4th Lay still waiting for Mr. Kern I am sorry to say but fear he dont do his duty the time is wasting and not much doing on his part.[14] Mr Kern arrived at 9 o'clock with horses and packs—

5 left Mule Springs and came to Rocky Run to Kerns Camp their he had 8 Baqueros to tend camp he shared very close with us keeping the best for himself and his Indians

7 at 3 in the evening reached Johnsons—[15]

Mr. Sinclair arrived at Mr. Johnson's on Sunday the thirty first of January having left his residence the day previous on foot. immeidiately after his arrival he requested Mr. Johnson to have all the horses [*deleted*: called] that were scattered about in that neighbourhood brought in in order to select a sufficient number for [*deleted*: car] packing the provisions and taking the men as far as practable on their journey he succeeded with considerable trouble in getting and with the aid of a few Bullock Hides *rigging* them out so that the whole party had saddles to ride with the exception of one (two of the Ladies there having kindly loaned their side saddles for the trip), as many cattle as was necessary for the expedition Mr Johnson cheerfully furnished and every man of the Party exerted himself to the utmost in cutting and drying the beef for the journey all hands were actively engaged until twelve o'clock on Thursday the fifth of February in completing the arrangements at that time the horses were brought up and part of them saddled when unfortunately a few of them got away and recrossed the river Mr. Sinclair having done all that could be done then called the party together and addressed a few words [*deleted*: to] of encouragement to them requesting them never to turn their backs upon the Mountains until they had brought away as many of their suffering fellowbeings as possible, he then left us to return home while several of the men crossed the river at the same time to bring back the horses which got away from us when the horses were brought over there was every appearance of a storm coming on the day being nearly spent the party considered it best to remain until morning rather than risk the destruction of their provisions by the rain which in a short time after fell in torrents accompanied by one of the heaviest hurricanes ever experienced on the Sacramento

On the 4th day after Mr Sinclair arrived Mr Kerns came and encamped on the opposite side of the river where we [*deleted*: was] dried our meat and had our horses saddled and prepared for starting. Mr Kerns never for the first time attempt to cross, the creek the *balsey* or raft that Mr Sinclair and others crossed in was still there and as for a boat I do not think there ever was such a craft on Bear Creek and as for Mr Kerns having any thing to do directly or indirectly he had not, nor did he ever give any directions or instructions, he arrived the day before we left, and I returned home [*deleted*: next],

when he had his frolick out, since my return I understood
Mr Kerns Crossed bear Creek and went to Mr Kysers &c
on the day after we had started for the mountains[16]
to be attached to Mr Tuckers Journal of the 7 March

[evening] of the 7—I went [to] Mr Kerns and asked
him to give the onfortunate emigrants that I had under
my Charge some pork that [I] understood the good people
of Yerba buna had bought for their benefit his answer
was there was none for them, he had no mor than would
do himself and Indians [*deleted*: but] and at last handed
me about two pounds which I Cut in small pieces and
divide [*deleted*: it] between [*deleted*: the people] the
women and Children when on the next mornig I saw
him Kerns and his Indians faring sumtiously on Pork and
superfine flour and when I asked him for Some of the
flour that was Sent for the use of the emigrants [*deleted*:
I] he told me he would give them none they might eat
hard Tack old dry sea bread which was broke to Crumbs
in a bag he also stated that he must and would take care
of his boys meaning the Indians (about 8 in number) and
did not care a *dam* for any one *Else*

when I met Mr Woodworth he informed me he had left
liqure at the camp where Kerns was and instructed me to
get some for [*deleted*: them] people and when I Came to
the Camp I made application for it and was told by Kerns
that there was none there for them when the same night he
and one or two others of his party ware drinking it [*deleted*: during the night follow]

2

For James Frazier Reed's own preface to his diary of
the Second Donner Relief, as written a few weeks after
the events, the reader should turn back to p.289. Reed's
reminiscent account, as printed in the *Pacific Rural Press,*
April 1, 1871, should also be quoted before we take up
the diary.

After relating his unsuccessful effort to recross the
mountains in the fall of 1846, Reed says that he returned

to Sutter's, where the Captain "was no way surprised at our defeat . . . He made an estimate and stated that if the emigrants would kill the cattle, and place the meat in the snow for preservation, there was no fear of starvation until relief could reach them. He further stated that there was no able bodied men in that vicinity, all having gone down the country with and after Fremont, to fight the Mexicans. He advised me to proceed to Yerba Bueno, now San Francisco, and make my case known to the naval officer in command.

"I left Capt. Sutter's by way of San Jose, for San Francisco, being unable to come by water. When I arrived at San Jose, I found the San Francisco side of the bay was occupied by the Mexicans. Here I remained and was attached to a company of volunteers, commanded by Capt. Webber [Charles M. Weber], until after the fight at Santa Clara.

"The road now being clear I proceeded to San Francisco, with a petition from some of the prominent citizens of San Jose, asking the commander of the navy to grant aid to enable me to return to the mountains. Arriving at San Francisco, I presented my petition to Commodore Hull, also making a statement of the condition of the people in the mountains as far as I knew; the number of them, and what would be needed in provisions and help to get them out. He made an estimate of the expense that would attend the expedition, and said that he would do anything within reason to further the object, but was afraid that the department at Washington would not sustain him, if he made the general out-fit. His sympathy was that of a man and gentleman.

"I also confered with several of the citizens of Yerba Bueno, their advice was not to trouble the commodore further. That they would call a meeting of the citizens and see what could be done. At the meeting the situation of the people was made known, and committees were appointed to collect money. Over a thousand dollars was raised in the town, and the sailors of the fleet gave over three hundred dollars. At the meeting, [passed] midshipman Woodworth volunteered to go into the mountains. Commodore Hull gave me authority to raise as many men, with horses, as would be required. The citizens purchased all the supplies necessary for the out-fit and placed them on board the schooner——, for Hardy's Ranch, mouth of Feather river. Midshipman Woodworth took charge of the schooner, and was the financial agent of the government.

"I left in a boat for Napa by way of Sonoma, to procure men and horses, and when I arrived at Mr. Gorden's, on Cache creek, I had all the men and horses needed. From here I proceeded to the mouth of Feather river for the purpose of meeting Mr. Woodworth with the provisions. When we reached the river the boat had not arrived. The water was very high in the river, the tule lands being overflowed. From here I sent a man to a point on the Sacramento river opposite Sutters Fort, to obtain information of the boat with our provisions, he returned and reported the arrival of the boat at the fort.

"Before leaving Yerba Bueno, news came of a party of 15 persons having started from the emigrant encampment and only 7 getting in to Johnson's. I was here placed in a quandary—no boat to take us across the river, and no provisions for our party to take into the mountains. We camped a short distance back from the river, where we killed a number of elk, for the purpose of using the skins in covering a skeleton boat. Early next morning we started for the river and to our delight saw a small schooner, belonging to Perry McCan [McCoon], which had arrived during the night. We immediately crossed, McCutchen and myself, to the opposite bank of the river. I directed the men to cross and follow us to Johnson's ranch. We arrived there early that day. Making known our situation, he drove his cattle up to the house, saying 'there are the cattle, take as many as you need.' We shot down five head, staid up all night and with the help of Mr. Johnson and his Indians, by the time the men arrived the next morning, we had the meat fire dried, and ready to be placed in bags. Mr. Johnson had a party of Indians making flour by hand mills, they making during the night nearly 200 lbs.

"We packed up immediately and started. After reaching the snow, the meat and flour was divided in suitable packs for us to carry, we leaving the horses here. At Johnson's, I learned that a relief party had passed in a few days previous, being sent by Capt Sutter and Mr. Sinclair.

"Leaving a man at this camp with all the extra provisions we could not pack, with instructions to prepare a camp for the parties coming out, we passed on and at the head of Bear Valley met the party returning with a party of women and children. Among them was my wife and two of my children. We delayed no time, only a few minutes, and pushed on until the snow became too soft for us to travel on. Then stopping until it froze sufficient to bear us, we traveled all this night, and about the middle of the next day we arrived at the first camp of emigrants, being Mr. Breen's. If he left any provisions here it was a small amount. He and his family not being in want. We then proceeded to the camp of Mrs. Murphy, where Keysburg and some children were. Here we left provisions and one of our party to cook and attend them. From here we visited the camp of Mrs. Graves some distance further east. A number of the relief party remaining here, while Messrs. Miller, McCutchen and one of the men and myself proceeded to the camp of the Messrs. Donner's. This was a number of miles further east.

"We found Mrs. Jacob Donner in a very feeble condition. Her husband had died early in the winter. We removed the tent and placed it in a more comfortable situation. I then visited the tent of Geo. Donner, close by, and found him and his wife. He was helpless. Their children and two of Jacob's having come out with the party we met at the head of Bear Valley.

"I requested Mrs. Geo. Donner to come out with us as I would leave a man to take care of both Mr. George Donner and Mrs. Jacob Donner. Mrs. Geo. Donner positively refused saying that as her children were all out she would not leave her husband in the situation he was in. After repeatedly urging her to come out, and she as positively refusing, I was satisfied in my own mind that Mrs. Geo. Donner remained with her husband from pure love and affection, and not for money, as stated by Mrs. Curtis.[17]

"When I found that Mrs. Geo. Donner would not leave her husband, we took the three remaining children of Jacob Donner's, leaving a man to take care of the two camps. Leaving all the provisions we could spare, and expecting the party from Sutter's Fort would be in in a few days, we returned to the camp of Mrs. Graves, where all remained during the night, except McCutchen, Miller and myself, we going to the cabin of Mr. Breen where two of my children were. Notice was given in all the camps that we would start on our return to Sutter's early the next day. About the middle of the day we started, taking with us all who were able to travel. In a short time we reached Donner Lake. Traveling on ice a short distance, we made camp on the eastern side. Here were several springs; in the water were many small fish. The next day we traveled up to the head of the Lake on the ice, making camp here for the night. From this camp I sent in advance of us two of our men, Jondrieux and Dofar, good mountaineers, for the purpose of getting the provisions in our last cache and returning with them, they to meet us on the road the next day.

"When coming in we made three caches, or deposits of beef. Two of them were made by taking a bag of dried beef to the top of a pine sapling, then securing it, cutting all the limbs off the tree to prevent animals from getting up and destroying the meat.

"The next morning we proceeded up the mountain and in the evening came to one of the camping places of the party we had met in Bear Valley. With a little repairs everything necessary for building a fire on the snow, which was twenty feet at least in depth, was here. We camped for the night. During all this day the sky had been overcast, threatening a storm. This night a heavy snow storm burst upon us, continuing all this night and the following day and night, and up to the middle of the next day. Our provisions gave out, and one of the children died. I expected the two men, Jondrieux and Dofar, at the latest to be back the morning after we made camp here. But the storm had overtaken them. They found the cache had been destroyed by animals and had proceeded on to the next one, finding that partly destroyed, there they were snow-bound, and were nearly perishing.

"As soon as the storm abated we made preparations for leaving. All that were able started, with the exception of Mr. Breen and family. He stated that if he had to die, he would rather die in camp than on the way. A strange proceeding of Mr. Breen, when he and his family were all strong enough to travel. We remonstrated with him, advising him to come with us; that if we perished, let us all die together in the effort to get out. Finding that we could not prevail upon him, I asked some of the men standing by to witness, that I then told Mr. Breen 'that if his family died, their blood be upon his head, and not on ours.'

"We had not proceeded far before the weather became intensely cold and when we stopped for the night many of the party had their feet frozen. The next day our travel was slow, many in pain. When night came on those in advance camped, the next coming straggling in making considerable noise. This gave the camp of Mr. Woodworth the first intimation of our proximity to them. He sent some of his party to us requesting that we come down to his encampment; but the most of us having laid down for the night, declined going, but would be glad if he would send something to eat, which he did, and some of the party who had not camped went down. Next morning Mr. Woodworth proceeded on with all haste, and my impression is that two or three of our party went back with them.

"We proceeded slowly and the second night, we reached the encampment at Bear valley, in company with Mr. Woodworth, he returning to Sutter's Fort. From here a majority of the party rode to Sutter's, I stopping at Mr. Sinclair's."

So ends Reed's statement of 1871. The original draft of this statement is still preserved among his papers, together with the diary that now follows. A copy of this diary was furnished to McGlashan in 1879, along with the Ritchie-Tucker memoranda, by Reed's daughter Patty, but was first printed from the original manuscript in Carroll D. Hall's *Donner Miscellany*. A portion of it was again printed in the 1960 edition of Stewart's *Ordeal by Hunger*.

THE REED DIARY OF THE SECOND DONNER RELIEF[18]

Feby 7 1847 Sund Mo 8 left Francisco half past one oclock on Sundaye in a Launch for Sonoma and arrived on Tuesday morning

Tus 9 Remained at Sonoma today· got from Lieut. [William L.] Maurey every assistance required and Ten government *horses* 4 Saddles & Bridles.

10 Weds. left this morning for Nappa with 5 men for the Mountains. 18 [miles]

11 Thus Remained at Mr. George Yo[u]nts on acct of [Caleb] *Greenwood* here I engaged three men more and bought *Two horses.*

12 Frd left Nappa and arrved at Mr. Childs [Joseph Chiles] where I bought 1 horse & 1 mule also 2 waggon Covers for Tents. 12 [miles]

13 Sat this day very Rough road we encamped near Berrissas [Berreyesa's] 9 [miles]

14 Sun left and had as usual a bad road encamped

about 15 miles west of Mr [William] Gordons up Cach River. 15 [miles]

15 Mo   had a good Road and encamped about 1 o'clock opposit Mr. Gordons on account of high water [*smudged*: in Cach River?] 15 [miles]

16 Tues   Crossed Cach river water up to the backs of our horses I went to Wm Gordons and bought 5 horses, returnd to the men and traveled about 4 miles. 4 [miles]

17 Wed left Camp early I left the *Caravan* and went a head to Mr. Nights [William Knight's] where I found the water was high in the Sacramento and the Sliews swimming left here and proceeded to Mr. [Thomas M.] Hardys at the mouth of Feather river where we encamped for the night the boys Shot Two *elk* out of a band of about 100—here I hoped to meet our spplies with Comdr Woodworth in a Launch sent from Yerba buena, but unfortunately the head winds prevented his arrival F[ea-ther] Riv was our [place?] of rendezvous. [*word or two illegible*] 24 [miles]

18 Thur   We broke Camp this morning intending to Cross the Sacramento at the mouth of Feather River in Skin Boats, for which purpose I intended to use the elk hides, we ware relieved the trouble [*deleted*: in the morning] by Mr. [Perry] McCoon who had his Launch at Mr. Hardy's [*interlined*: and kindly offered her to cross our Bagage when I found our supplies had not arrived] I Crossed my horse and proceeded to Mr. [William] Johnsons, 25 miles distant for the purpose of having prepared flour and Beef. 25 [miles]

19 Frd   I was at Mr Johnsons to day the boys had not arrived being detained in Crossing on acc^t of the high winds which arose when I landed on the East side

20 Sater   Still at Mr Johnson preparing Beef by drying and Keeping his Indians at work Night & Day [Grinding?] in a small hand mill

Sundy 21   this morning the men arrved with out any accident excepting one horse that run back I got him from Mr [Abram?] Combs at Mr Gordons. I kept fire under the Beef all night which I had on the Scafold and next morning by Sun rise I had about 200 lbs dryed and baged we packed our horses and started with the [*deleted*: addition of 5 men and one Indian,] our supplies 700 lbs flour [*interlined*: including what Greenwood had dried Sunday] 4 ½ Beeves [*deleted*: 25 horses in all 17 men in my party] and Mr Greenwood had [*deleted*: 2 men] 3 Men including himself- [*deleted*: & 2 boys][19] traveled this day about 10 miles

23 Tues left camp early this morning and packed today and encamped early on acct grass tommorrow we will reach the snow 20 [miles]

24 Weds encamped at the Mule Spring this evening mad[e] preparations to take the snow in the morning there is left at camp our saddles Bridles etc 15 [miles]

25 Thus Started with 11 horses & mules lightly packed about 80 lbs traveled about 2 miles and left one Mule, and pack, made this day with hard labour for the horses, in the snow [*deleted*: made only] about 6 miles Our start was late.

26 Frid [and 27 Sat] left our encampment early thinking the snow would bare the horses. proceeded 200 yard with dificulty when we ware Compelled to unpack the horses and take the provision on our backs here for a few minutes there was silence with the men when the packs ware ready to sling on the back [*deleted*: when] the hilarity Commenced as usual Made the head of Bear Valley a distance of 15 miles we met in the vally about 3 miles below the Camp Messrs Glover & Road belonging to the party that went to the lake for the people who Informed me they had Started with 21 persons 2 of whome had died John Denton of Springfield Ils & a Child of Keesberger [*deleted*: left] Mr Glover Sent 2 men back to the party with fresh provisions they men ware in a Starving Condition and all nearly give out I here lightened our packs with a suficiency of provisions to do [*deleted*: 28] the people when they should arrive, and [*deleted*: started a man back on evening of 27 to bring more by

tomorrow]

& 27 Sat I Sent back to our camp of the 26 2 men to bring provision [*deleted*: for the people] [they would] they will return tomorrow and left one man to prepare for the people which ware expected today and I left Camp early on a fine hard snow and proceeded about 4 miles when we met the poor unfortunate Starved people, as I met them Scattered allong the snow trail I distributed Sweetbread that I had backed the 2 nights previous I give in small quantities, here I met [*deleted*: my own wife] Mrs. Reed and two [*deleted*: of my little] children two still in the mountains, I cannot describe the [*deleted*: unfortunate] death like look [*deleted*: of them] they all had Bread Bread Bread Bread was the beging of evry Child and grown person [*deleted*: except my wife] I give to all what I dared and left for the sene of desolation and now I am Camped within 25 miles which I hope to mak this night and tommorrow we had to camp soon on account of the softness of the snow, the men falling in to their middles. [*Deleted*: Two of the party one man and one Child died since the party left] One of the party that passed us to day a little boy Mrs Murphy's son was nearly blind, when we met them. they ware overjoyed when we told them there was plenty of Provision at Camp I made a Cach 12 miles and encamped 3 m eastward on Juba, snow about 15 feet. 15 miles

28 Sund [*and* 29 Mond] left Camp about 12 o'clock at night and was Compl to Camp about 2 o'cl, the Snow Still being soft. left again a bout 4 all hands and made this day 14 miles in camp early Snow soft. Snow her 30 feet 3 of my men [C. L.] Cady, [Nicholas] Clark & [Charles] Stone [*interlined*: I told if they wished the might] kept on during the night [*interlined*: which they intended but halted] [*deleted*: to] within 2 miles of the Cabins [*deleted*: halted] and remained without fire during the night on acc^t of 10 Indians which they saw [*interlined*: the boys not having arms] and supposed they had taken the cabins and destroyed the people in the morning

they started [*deleted*: all ware] and arrived all alive in
the houses give provision to [*deleted*: two] Keesberger,
Brinn, Graves and [*deleted*: then two] two then left for
Donners a distance of ten miles which they made by the
middle of the day I came up with the Main body of my
party Informed [?] the people that all who ware able
Should have to Start day after tomorrow made soup for
the infirm washed and clothed afresh Mrs Eddy & Fosters
children and rendered evry assistance in our power I left
with Keesbergs people Mr Stone to cook and watch the
eating of Mrs Murphy Keesberge & 3 children

Tus March 1st left early this morning with 3 of the
men and went to Donners where Cady & Clark had arrivd
on Yesty found all alive cheered [?] them [?] and sent
Cady back for more provisions say 7 day found here
but 3 child of J Donner that Could Com with us at
George Doner tent there was 3 Stout harty children his
wife was able to travel but preferred [proposed?] to stay
with her husband until provisions should arrive, which
was confidently expected by Comd Woodworth, who was
at Cap Suters the day [*deleted*: I] before I left Mr
Johnsons, here I left two of my men Cady & Clark one
with each tent to cook and as fast as possible resusitate
the enfeebled so that they might in a few days Start, took
3 children of J Donner and the men I took in and returned
the same day making this 20 miles carrying 2 of the child
got back to the other cabins about 8 o'ck, much worn
down, as I passed Mrs Graves told them I would be of[f]
in the morning, the men that remained with her[?] today
Cached the principal of her effects and got for her out of
one of the waggons about 800 in gold & silver which was
[*deleted*: fastened] concealed in a slat or bracket that
was nailed in the middle of the bed the money being
placed in grooves close made for the purpose.

March 2 Weds after leaving with Keesberger Camp 7
day prov[isions] and Mr Stone to get wood cook and
take care of the helpless I left with the following persons
P Brin Mrs Brin, John Brin, youg man and 4 other

Smaller Children 2 of which had to be Carried in all of Brins. 7—Mrs Graves— & 4 children 2 of which had to be Caried in all of her family 5 Solomon Hook youg man and Ma[r]y & Isaac Donner in all 3—with two Children of my own one a girl of 9 Years the other a little boy 4 in all 2—making in all 17 souls—proceeded About 2 miles and incamped on the edge of the lak[e] on a bare spot of ground

3 Thurs left Camp early traveled on the lake 2 miles an[d] encamped under the mountain made this day about 4 miles, nothing of interest occ[urre]d.

4 Fri this morning [*interlined*: after Breakfast I had 2 Scanty meals left for all hands, which would do to the night following] I sent ahead 3 men J Jandrou M Dofar & [John] Turner whoe ware of my best men for the ocasion, to push to our first Cach and if not disturbed to bring it up while the other Two proceed on to bring up our Second and if they should meet our Supplies which we all [*deleted*: had aright] expected clace at hand to hurrey them on, (but to our misfortune there was none nigher than 65 miles and at this Juncture no prospect of Starting which I learned afterwards) to be the fact from Comd Woodworth himself[20]

I mouved camp and after a [*deleted*: great] fatiguing day arriv^d at the praire now Starved Camp at the head of Juba it was made by the other Compy who had passed in but a few days previous. here the men began to fail being for several days on half allowance, or 1 ½ pints of gruel or sizing per day. the Sky look like snow and everything indicates a storm god for bid wood being got for the night & *Bows* for the beds of all, and night closing fast, the Clouds still thicking terror terror [*deleted*: to many, my hartte] I feel a terrible foreboding but dare not Communicate my mind to any, death to all if our provisions do not Come, in a day or two and a storm should fall on us. Very cold, a great lamentation about the Cold.

5 Saturday Still in Camp the last of our provisions

gone lookig anxiously for our supplies none. My dreaded
Storm is now on us comme[nce]d snowing in the first
part of the night and with the Snow Commed a perfect
Hurricane [*deleted*: of] in the night. A great crying
with the Children and with the parents praying Crying
and lamentations on acc^t of the Cold and the dread of
death from the Howling Storm the men up nearly all
night making fires, some of the men began to pray [*deleted*: a part] several became blind I could not see even
the light of the fire when it was blazing before me I
Continued so to the next day then my sight returned[21]
Young Brine fell of[f] his feet into the pit the heat of the
fire had made in the snow to the depth of [*deleted*: 20]
15 feet. it has snowed already 12 inches, still the storm
Continues the light of Heaven, is as it ware shut in from
us the snow blows so thick that we cannot see 20 feet
looking against the wind I dread the Coming night 3
of my men only able to get wood the rest give out, for
the present. After some time wood being secured we had
a great dificulty in fixing a foundation for our fire the snow
having melted to a great depth I think now [*deleted*: 20]
15 feet—and no earth in sight it must be from 6 to 10
feet Snow before the earth is seen in the fire pit. the
manner of making our fires on the snow are as follows,
we lay 2 ps of timber or saplin about 10 feet apart—then
[*deleted*: com] Roll [*interlined*: close together] large
green logs on the Two pcs in a transverse position these
form a bed for the dry logs to lie on [*deleted*: and] so as to
prevent the coals of the dry wood which we lay on from
falling through into this deep pit which was melted below.
Still Storming verry cold so much so that the few men employed in Cutting the dry trees down have to Come and
warm about very 10 minutes, hunger hunger is the Cry
with the Children and nothing to give them freesing was
the [*deleted*: almost] Cry of the mothers with reference to
their little starving freesing Children Night Closing fast
and with it the Hurricane Increases—not quite so much
snow falling as before night.

6th *Sunday* thank god day has once more appeared although darkened by the Storm Snowing as fast as ever and the Hurricane has never Ceased for ten minuts at atime during one of the most dismal nights I ever witnessed and I hope I never shall witness Such in a similar situate of all the praying and Crying I ever heard nothing ever equaled it Several times I expected to see the people perish by the extreme Cold at one time our fire was nearly gone and had it not been for Mr McCutchen's exertions it would have entirely [*deleted*: out and] disapeared had [*deleted*: it] the fire been lost Two thirds of the Camp would have been out of their misery before morning but as god would have it we soon [*deleted*: got it] blazing in Comfortable order and the sufferings of the people became less—At this time [*deleted*: their] hope began to animate the bosoms of many Young and old when the Cheering blaze Rose through the dry Pine logs we had piled together, one would say thank god for this fire another how good it is the little half starved half frozen poor Children would say I'm glad I'm Glad we have got some fire Oh how good it feels, it is good our fire didn't go out At daylight I discovered the Storm to Slack by hushing as it ware entirely [*deleted*: up] for a few minutes and then it would burst forth with such fury that I felt often alarmed for the safety of the people on acct of the tall timber that surrounded us—the Storm Contines to lull Snow now nearly Ceased, the location of our camp [*deleted*: is] [*interlined*: a bleek point] under the summit of the great California Range about 1000 feet Consequently our altitude about 8300 above the *Sea* with a small Prarie on our south and west about 3 miles in length & one in breadth here the snow & wind had full sweep this Camp was used by the other party that had passed out of the mountain [*deleted*: and See] the under or bed logs for the fire having remained it saved the men from [*deleted*: a gr] considerable labor in cutting and rolling green logs together I estimate the snow in this valley about [*deleted*: 25] 20 feet deep and at the cabins on the east side of the

Mountain, about 10 feet on the average. the Storm did
not rage with such fury on the east side of the great Chain
as with us as I learned by two of my party that left the
Cabins the day after the Storm was over.

3

Reed's diary does not tell of the further travels of the
Second Relief, from this "Starved Camp" on to Bear
Valley and the settlements, though he supplied details in
his account of 1847 and his reminiscence of 1871, as we
have seen. When Reed's party started on, they left in
the camp on the Yuba the seven Breens, Mrs. Graves and
her four children, and Mary Donner, whose foot, burned
in the fire, would not bear travel. There was no food to
be distributed, but a three-day supply of wood was piled
up.

The two men referred to by Reed in the concluding
passage of his diary were Charles Cady and Charles Stone,
who with seven days' provisions had remained behind with
Nicholas Clark, instructed to get the enfeebled survivors
at the lake and on Alder Creek in condition to travel.
The suggestion has been made that three men were rather
more than enough to care for the few still alive, and that
an interest in the property of the Donner Party may have
motivated them beyond humanitarian impulses.

On Reed's departure, Cady and Clark were at the Donner tents on Alder Creek, Stone at the cabins just below
the lake. Reed was scarcely out of sight when Stone
made for the Donner encampment, where he found Clark
off on a bear hunt. As Eliza P. Donner Houghton tells
the story in her *The Expedition of the Donner Party and
Its Tragic Fate* (Chicago, 1911), pp. 107-108, Stone
arrived to tell Cady "that the other members of the Relief
had become alarmed at gathering storm clouds, and had
resolved to select at once the ablest among the emigrants
and hasten with them across the summit, and to leave
Clark, Cady, and himself to cut the necessary fuel for the
camps, and otherwise assist the sufferers until the Third

Relief should reach them.

"Cady and Stone, without waiting to inform Clark, promptly decided upon their course of action. They knew the scarcity of provisions in camp, the condition of the trail over the mountains, the probability of long, fierce March storms, and other obstacles which might delay future promised relief, and, terror-stricken, determined to rejoin their party, regardless of opposition, and return to the settlement.

"Mother, fearing that we children might not survive another storm in camp, begged Messrs. Cady and Stone to take us with them, offering them five hundred dollars in coin, to deliver us to Elitha and Leanna [George Donner's children by an earlier marriage] at Sutter's Fort. The agreement was made, and we collected a few keepsakes and other light articles, which she wished us to have, and which the men seemed more than willing to carry out of the mountains. Then, lovingly, she combed our hair and helped us to dress quickly for the journey. When we were ready, except cloak and hood, she led us to the bedside, and we took leave of father. The men helped us up the steps and stood us up on the snow. She came, put on our cloaks and hoods, saying, as if talking to herself, 'I may never see you again, but God will take care of you.'

"Frances was six years and eight months old and could trudge along quite bravely, but Georgia, who was little more than five, and I, lacking a week of four years, could not do well on the heavy trail, and we were soon taken up and carried. After travelling some distance, the men left us sitting on a blanket upon the snow, and went ahead a short distance where they stopped and talked earnestly with many gesticulations. We watched them, trembling lest they leave us there to freeze. Then Frances said,

" 'Don't feel afraid. If they go off and leave us, I can lead you back to mother by our foot tracks on the snow.'

"After a seemingly long time, they returned, picked us up and took us on to one of the lake cabins, where without a parting word, they left us."[22]

Cady admitted to McGlashan many years later that the children had been left on the snow, but explained that the party had seen a coyote and were attempting to get a shot at it. McGlashan says that probably the two men "became aware of the impossibility of escaping the storm, and knew that it would be sure death, for both themselves and the children, should they take them any farther. In view of the terrible calamity which befell Reed's party on account of this storm, and the fact that Cady and Stone had a terrible struggle for life, every one must justify these men in leaving the children at the cabins."[23]

At all events, the three small Donner children were left at the Murphy cabin, Cady and Stone crossed the divide to rejoin their fellows, and were with Reed when he reached Woodworth's camp in Bear Valley.

Something must now be said of Selim Woodworth's conduct of the Donner Relief. It was praised in the *California Star,* as will be seen in Volume II, but Reed and others roundly damned his behavior at the time, and few voices since have been raised in his defense. His own diary, should it appear, may give us another viewpoint, but the extant records show Woodworth lacking in energy, liking to command but indisposed to lead, and perhaps afraid of the snow, which had brought on so many disasters. He did not push the early preparations and did not follow up Reed's Second Relief as he should have, content to establish a base camp just above the snow line in Bear Valley and never stir far from there.

The Third Donner Relief, for which no diary is known, therefore owes most to the initiative of the two fathers, William H. Eddy and William Foster, the lone male survivors of the Snowshoers who had come out of the mountains in January. Eddy had set out from Johnson's Ranch with the First Donner Relief on February 5, but not fully recovered from his earlier ordeal, had turned back with the animals after reaching Mule Springs.

J. Quinn Thornton, whose contemporary account of the Donner tragedy was based to a large extent upon interviews with Eddy late in 1847, relates that four days after Woodworth's party left Johnson's Ranch, Foster and Eddy obtained horses purchased under the order of Captain J. B. Hull, and set out to meet Reed and his party.

"Mr. Eddy had heard that his wife and one of his children had perished, but he cherished a feeble hope that he was not left to mourn the loss of all; and that he would find one of his children with Mr. Reed; and in any event he felt it to be a duty which he owed to suffering humanity, to do all in his power to rescue others, although his wife and children might be no more. Mr. Foster believed that his child yet survived. He hoped also to find his mother-in-law, Mrs. Murphy, and his brother-in-law, Simon Murphy, alive.

"On the second day after they left, they arrived at Bear River valley, where they found Passed-midshipman Woodworth remaining in camp with one man to bring water, make fires, and cook for him. There were also other men in other ways to assist him. Messrs. Eddy and Foster believed that at that time he was over the mountain, and upon inquiring of him why he was not, he replied that he could not go without a guide. Mr. Eddy replied that he had the best guide in the snow trail of those who had preceded him. Mr. Woodworth promised that he would set forward on the following morning, but he advised Messrs. Foster and Eddy not to attempt the passage of the mountain. They informed him that they had passed over under vastly more difficult circumstances, and that they would certainly attempt it again.

"They accordingly set out, eight in number, on the following morning. Having crossed a ridge, they arrived at Yuva [Yuba] river, where Passed-midshipman Woodworth, who had become tired from carrying his blanket, proposed, at about 3 o'clock, P. M., to encamp. That night two of Mr. Reed's men came to Mr. Woodworth's camp, and informed him that Mr. Reed's party were encamped about one mile in advance (in the direction of the mountains). Mr. Woodworth then went to Mr. Reed's camp, and after conversing with him, returned. Mr. Reed had informed him that some miles from that place he had left fourteen of the sufferers. Mr. Woodworth asked the men with him, if they would go to the relief of these emigrants, and received a reply in the negative. Messrs. Foster and Eddy proposed to make themselves responsible for almost any sum to persons who would go with them. To this it was replied that they, having lost all their property and money, were irresponsible. J. F. Reed and Hiram Miller said that they would be responsible for any amount, for which Messrs. Eddy and Foster would engage. But these it was said were in the condition of the first. Mr. John Starks [Stark] offered to go out without any reward beyond that derived from the consciousness of doing a good act. But the snow made it prudent to have only light men for the service. It was necessary for each man to carry fifty pounds of provisions; and this, added to Mr. Starks' own weight, of two hundred and twenty-four pounds, made it imprudent for him to go.[24]

"Being unable to induce any of them to consent to go, Messrs. Eddy and Foster were about to set out alone. Mr. Reed, however, remonstrated against this, and at length induced them to consent to return to Bear River valley, where he said he would use his utmost efforts to prevail upon Mr. Woodworth and his party to enter upon the enterprise. Upon returning to Bear River valley, Mr. Woodworth finally said that he would engage, under the authority he had received from Capt. Hull to pay three dollars per day to every man who would go, and fifty dollars in addition to every man who would bring out a child not his own. Mr. Eddy hired Hiram Miller, formerly of Springfield, Illinois, engaging to pay him fifty dollars. [Thornton personally saw this debt paid, late in 1847.] Mr. Foster hired a Mr. [William] Thompson for the same sum. Howard Oakley, John Starks, and Mr. Stone looked to Capt. Hull for their wages."

The company thus organized, the Third Donner Relief,

consisted of seven men, of whom Miller and Stone had been members of the Second Relief. They set out the following morning, encamping that night about half way up the Yuba, in fifteen feet of snow. Late the next afternoon they reached the "Starved Camp" where Reed had had to leave the Breens and others. There the fire had melted the snow down to the ground, making a hole some twenty-four feet deep and from twelve to fifteen feet in diameter. "The picture of distress which was here presented," says Thornton, "was shocking indeed. And yet Patrick Brinn and his wife seemed not in any degree to realize the extent of their peril, or that they were in peril at all. They were found lying down sunning themselves, and evincing no concern for the future. They had consumed the two children of Jacob Donner [who had died before Reed's departure]. Mrs. Graves' body was lying there with almost all the flesh cut away from her arms and limbs. Her breasts were cut off, and her heart and liver taken out, and were all being boiled in a pot then on the fire. Her little child, about thirteen months old, sat at her side, with one arm upon the body of its mangled mother, and sobbing bitterly, cried, Ma! ma! ma! . . ."

The men had not been prepared for such a situation. Still alive were seven Breens, three Graves children, and Mary Donner, but only Mrs. Breen and her son John were able to walk. "A storm appeared to be gathering upon the mountains," writes McGlashan, "and the supply of provisions were very limited. The lonely situation, the weird, desolate surroundings, the appalling scenes at the camp, and above all, the danger of being overtaken by a snow-storm, filled the minds of Oakley and Stone with terror. When it was found that nine of the eleven people must be carried over the snow, it is hardly to be wondered at that a proposition was made to leave a portion of the sufferers. It was proposed to take the three Graves children and Mary Donner. These four children would be quite a sufficient burden for the three men, considering the snow over which they must travel. The Breens, or at least such of them as could not walk, were to be abandoned. [Obviously there was not much sympathy for the Breens, who could have saved themselves by going on with Reed.] This was equivalent to leaving the father, mother, and five children, because the mother would not abandon any member of her family, and John, who alone could travel, was in a semi-lifeless condition."

The men are said to have voted upon a course of action, all but Stark agreeing to leave the Breens for a hypothetical future relief. McGlashan says that Stark had stood apart. Now he replied, "No, gentlemen, I will not abandon these people. I am here on a mission of mercy, and I will not half do the work. You can all go if you want to, but I shall stay by these people while they and I live."

Stark was a son-in-law of M. D. Ritchie, one of the First Relief, and as previously remarked, a man of giant frame. John Breen wrote McGlashan: "Stark was finally left alone. To his great bodily strength, and unexcelled courage, myself and others owe our lives. There was probably no other man in California at that time, who had the intelligence, determination, and what was absolutely necessary in that emergency, the immense physical powers of John Stark. He was as strong as two ordinary men. On his broad shoulders, he carried the provisions, most of the blankets, and most of the time some of the weaker children. In regard to this, he would laughingly say that he could carry them all, if there was room on his back, because they were so light from starvation."

The financial records of the Donner Relief[25] show that Stark was eventually paid $117 for thirty-nine days service from March 2 to April 9, and was also paid $50 "For bringing out John Graves," a reference to 7-year-old Jonathan. Oakley headed back for the settlements with Mary Donner; Stone carried the Graves baby. But Stark shepherded down to Bear Valley Jonathan and Nancy Graves and the seven Breens: no man in the history of the Donner Relief took a more honorable part.

The four others of the Third Relief, Foster, Eddy,

Miller, and Thompson, pushed on across the divide to the emigrant cabins, arriving before noon next day, evidently on March 13. En route, they encountered Nicholas Clark of the Second Relief, in company with Jean Baptiste Trubode. After the departure of Cady and Stone, Clark had been importuned by Tamsen Donner to hike over to the lake cabins and inquire after her children. He found them at Keseberg's cabin, says McGlashan, "and witnessed such scenes of horror and suffering that he determined at once to attempt to reach California. Returning to Alder Creek, he told Mrs. Donner of the situation of her children, and says he informed her that he believed their lives were in danger of a death more violent than starvation. He informed her of his resolution to leave the mountains, and taking a portion of the little [bear] meat that was left, he at once started upon his journey. John Baptiste accompanied him." To Clark's discredit, it is remembered on Thornton's authority that he carried a pack of goods upon his back, weighing about forty pounds, and also two guns . . . which weighed more than did a child he left behind to perish."[26]

There had been more deaths since the departure of Reed's Second Relief, including Elizabeth Donner and her two young sons Lewis and Samuel, at the encampment on Alder Creek. George Donner was still alive but in a dying condition; and injury which had incapacitated him during the autumn had become gangrenous, and there was no hope he could survive. But what mattered most to Foster and Eddy was the fate of those in the cabins at the lake. The Murphy cabin had housed Lavina Murphy, her son Simon, her grandchild George Foster, little James Eddy, and the three small Donner girls, as well as Lewis Keseberg. All were alive save George and James. The story was that Keseberg had taken George Foster to bed with him and next morning the child was dead: from this circumstance sprang the tale that Keseberg took a child to bed and ate him up before morning. Although the tale was not true, for a fact the dead body had soon been

devoured. James Eddy's fate had been similar. William
Eddy came close to killing Keseberg there at the lake, and
came near doing as much later, after all the survivors
had reached California.

The same morning that the four men of the Third
Relief reached the cabins, Tamsen Donner came over
from Alder Creek to ascertain whether her children were
safe. She could not be persuaded to leave her dying
husband, and in the face of a threatening storm, the
others were not willing to delay an hour. Keseberg and
Tamsen Donner would not come along, and George Donner and Lavina Murphy were in no condition to travel.
When at noon the third Relief set out for the settlements,
Foster carried his young brother-in-law, Simon Murphy,
and the other three each carried a Donner child; Mrs.
Murphy had to be left to die. They reached Bear Valley
on March 17, and soon after were safely in the settlements.

The last week of March another effort was made to
cross the mountains. Though the party included such
proved men as John Rhoads, Reasin P. Tucker, Joseph
Sels, and Edward Coffeemeyer of the First Relief, John
Stark and William Foster of the Third Relief, and
young Billy Graves, they got no farther than Bear Valley,
turning back to report that the snow had become too
soft for travel.[27] So the stage was set for the final Donner
Relief. That expedition was frankly a salvage operation.
Its origins are shown by a document preserved in the
Reed Papers, dated Magistrates Office, Sacramento District, Territory of California:

"Know all men by these presents that it is mutually
agreed by John Sinclair on the one part acting in behalf
of the Heirs of Jacob Donner deceased and by the undersigned on the other part that they shall proceed to the
Cabins in the California mountains where the property
of said Jacob Donner deceased now is and if the property
still remains there that they shall bring away all or as
much of said property as they possibly can the property
so brought away to be delivered into the hands of said

John Sinclair when an equal division of said property shall be made the undersigned receiving one half of said property for their services. It is likewise understood and agreed that should George Donner and Wife be dead they shall likewise bring all of their property for the benefit of their Heirs on the same terms as is agreed upon relative to the property of the late Jacob Donner. And should their be any property which they cannot bring away belonging to the Estates of the above named persons that they shall *Cash* it as secretly and securely as circumstances will admit of. It is likewise understood that should there be any money either in Gold or Silver that the undersigned shall receive one half the same as any other description of Property which they may find belonging to the Estates of the Persons within mentioned.

"On their arrival at the Cabins should they find George Donner or Wife alive they the undersigned can then and there make any arrangements with both or either of them that will be satisfactory to all concerned taking care that whatever arrangement is entered into that it be drawn up in writing and a copy of said agreement brought in and delivered to John Sinclair in case of any accident happening to either of the parties after the date of the agreement.

WILLIAM FALLON

HIS

JOHN x RHOADES

MARK

JOSEPH SEL

"Signed in my presence this tenth day of April A. D. 1847.

JOHN SINCLAIR

Justice of the Peace"[28]

The head of this Fourth Relief was a mountain man of note, William Fallon, Herculean of frame yet strong and active as a cat, known generally as "Big" or "Le Gros." Originally from St. Louis, he had come to California by way of New Mexico early in 1845, soon afterward participated in the Micheltorena War, and in the fall of 1846 had served with Frémont's California Battalion.[29] His journal of the Fourth Relief was printed in the *California Star,* June 5, 1847, and is now reprinted with the *Star's* introductory remarks. His party consisted of Reasin P. Tucker, John Rhoades, Joseph Sels, Sebastian Keyser, William Foster, and Edward Coffeemeyer.[30]

EXTRACTS FROM A JOURNAL
WRITTEN BY A MEMBER OF THE PARTY
LATEST FROM THE CALIFORNIA MOUNTAINS.

The extracts which we give below are full of thrilling interest. Mr. Fellun, the writer, better known as "Capt. Fellun," set out from the settlements in April last with six others, to extend relief to the remaining sufferers of the emigration, still within the mountains, and also to collect and secure the scattered property of both living and dead. He succeeded in reaching the cabins, and with the exception of Kiesburg not a soul survived. They returned, bringing with them this man, and large packs of valuable property. Kiesburg was found in truly a lamentable situation; a long subsistance upon the bodies of his deceased comrades had rendered him haggard and ferocious-looking, and the unsatiable appetite of the cannibal displayed itself on frequent occasions, even after animal meat had been placed before him. This fondness for human flesh he had suffered himself to acquire in preference to the beef or horse meat of which he had an abundance. And it is to be feared that his conduct in the mountains was far from justifiable, and a hidden transaction of guilt remains yet to be brought to light.[31]

We commend the diary as being a plain though well written document, and we have published it in the writer's own language, abating nothing from it in point of interest. Mr. Fellun certainly deserves credit for his management of the affair, as it will be seen that he effected the desirable end.

"Left Johnson's on the evening of April 13th, and arrived at the lower end of the Bear Valley on the 15th. Hung our saddles upon the trees, and sent the horses back, to be returned again in ten days, to bring us in again. Started on foot, with provisions for ten days, and traveled to the head of the valley and camped for the night snow from 2 to 3 feet deep.

15th. Started early in the morning and traveled 23 miles, snow 10 feet deep.

April, 17th. Reached the Cabins between 12 and 1 o'clock. Expected to find some of the sufferers alive, Mrs. Donner and Kiesburg in particular. Entered the cabins and a horrible scene presented itself,—human bodies terribly mutilated, legs, arms, and sculls scattered in every direction. One body, supposed to be that of Mrs. Eddy, lay near the entrance, the limbs severed off and a frightful gash in the scull.[32] The flesh from the bones was nearly consumed and a painful stillness pervaded the place. The supposition was that all were dead, when a sudden shout revived our hopes, and we flew in the direction of the sound, three Indians [who] were hitherto concealed, started from the ground and fled at our approach, leaving behind their bows and arrows. We delayed two hours in searching the cabins, during which we were obliged to witness sights from which we would have fain turned away, and which are too dreadful to put on record.—We next started for "Donner's camp" 8 miles distant over the mountains. After traveling about half way, we came upon a track in the snow, which excited our suspicion, and we determined to pursue it. It brought us to the camp of Jacob Donner, where it had evidently left that morning. There we found property of every discription, books, calicoes, tea, coffee, shoes, purcussion caps, household and kitchen furniture scattered in every direction, and mostly in the water. At the mouth of the tent stood a large iron kettle, filled with human flesh cut up, it was the body of Geo. Donner, the head had been split open, and the brains extracted therefrom, and to the appearance, he had not been long dead, not over three or four days at the most. Near by the kettle stood a chair, and thereupon three legs of a bullock that had been shot down in the early part of the winter, and snowed under before it could be dressed. The meat was found sound and good, and with the exception of a small piece out of the shoulder, wholly untouched. We gathered up some property and camped for the night.

April, 18. Commenced gathering the most valuable property, suitable for our packs, the greater portion requiring to be dried. We then made them up and camped for the night.

April 19. This morning, [William] Foster, [John] Rhodes, and J. Foster [Joseph Sels] started with small packs for the first cabins intending from thence to follow the trail of the person that had left the morning previous. The other three remained behind to cache and secure the goods necessarily left there. Knowing the Donners had a considerable sum of money, we searched diligently but were unsuccessful. The party for the cabins were unable to keep the trail of the mysterious personage owing to the rapid melting of the snow, they therefore went direct for the cabins, and upon entering discovered Kiesburg lying down amidst the human bones and beside him a large pan full of fresh liver and lights. They asked him what had become of his companions, whether they were alive, and what had become of Mrs. Donner. He answered them by stating they were all dead; Mrs. Donner, he said, had in attempting to cross from one cabin to another, missed the trail, and slept out one night; that she came to his camp the next night very much fatigued, he made her a cup of coffee, placed her in bed and rolled her well in the blankets, but the next morning found her dead; he eat her body and found her flesh the best he had ever tasted! He further stated that he obtained from her body at least four pounds of fat! No traces of her person could be found, nor the body of Mrs. Murphy either.—When the last company left the camp, three weeks previous, Mrs Donner was in perfect health though unwilling to come and leave her husband there, and offered $500, to any person or persons who could come out and bring them in, saying this in the presence of Kiesburg, and she had plenty of tea and coffee, we suspected that it was her who had taken the piece from the shoulder of beef in the chair before mentioned. In the cabin with Kiesburg was found two kettles of human blood, in all supposed to be over one gallon[33] Rhodes asked him where he had got the blood, he answered, "there is blood in dead bodies,"—they asked him numerous questions, but he appeared embarrassed and equivocated a great deal, and in reply to their asking him where Mrs. Donner's money was, he evinced confusion and answered, that he knew nothing about it,—that she must have cached it before she died—"I have'nt it" said he, "nor the money, nor the property of any person, living or dead!" They then examined his bundle and found silks and jewelry, which had been taken from the camp of the Donners, and amounting in value to about $200; on his person they discovered a brace of pistols, recognized to be those of Geo. Donner, and while taking them from him discovered something concealed in his waistcoat, which on being opened was found to be $225, in gold.

Before leaving the settlements, the wife of Keysburg had told us that we would find but little money about him; the men therefore said to him that they knew he was lying to them, and he was well aware of the place of concealment of the Donners' money; he declared before heaven, he knew nothing concerning it, and that he had not the property of any one in his possession; they told him that to lie to them would effect nothing, that there were others back at the cabins, who unless informed of the spot where the treasure was hidden, would not hesitate to hang him upon the first tree. Their threats were of no avail, he still affirmed his ignorance and innocence, and Rhodes took him aside and talked to him kindly, telling him that if he would give the information desired, he should receive from their hands the best of treatment, and be in every way assisted, otherwise, the party back at Donners' camp, would, upon his arrival and refusal to discover to them the place where he had deposited this money, immediately put him to death; it was all to no purpose, however, and they prepared to return to us, leaving him in charge of his packs, and assuring him of their determination to visit him in the morning, and he must make up his mind during the night. They then started back and joined us at Donner's Camp

April 20, We all started for Bear River Valley with packs of 100 cwt. each; our provisions being nearly consumed, we were obliged to make haste away. Came within a few hundred yards of the cabin which Kiesburg occupied and halted to prepare breakfast, after which we proceeded to the cabin. I now asked Kiesburg if he was willing to disclose to me where he had concealed that money; he turned somewhat pale and again protested his ignorance: I said to him, 'Kiesburg, you know well where Donner's money is, and d—n you, you shall tell me! I am not going to multiply words with you, nor say but little about it— bring me that rope!' he then arose from his pot of soup and human flesh and begged me not to harm him—he had not the money nor the goods; the silk clothing and money which were found upon him the previous day, and which he then declared belonging to his wife, he now said was the property of others in California. I then told him I did not wish to hear more from him, unless he at once informed us where he had concealed the money of those orphan children, then producing the rope I approached him; he became frightened, but I bent the rope about his neck, and threw him, after a struggle, upon the ground, and as I tightened the cord and choked him he cried out that he would confess all upon release; I then permitted him to arise. He still seemed inclined to be obstinate, and made much delay in talking, finally, but with evident reluctance, he led the way back to Donner's camp about 10 miles distant, accompanied by Rhodes and Tucker. While they were absent, we moved all our packs over to the lower end of the lake, and made all ready for a start when they should return. Mr. Foster went down to the cabin of Mrs. Murphy, his mother-in-law, to see if any property remained there worth collecting and securing; he found the body of young [Landrum] Murphy, who had been dead about three months, with the breast and scull cut open, and the brains, liver and lights taken out, and this accounted for the contents of the pan which stood beside Kiesburg when he was found. It appears that he had left at the other camp the dead bullock and horse, and on visiting this camp and finding the body thawed out, took therefrom the brains, liver and lights.

[Reasin P.] Tucker and Rhodes came back the next morning, bringing $273, that had been cached by Kiesburg, who after disclosing to them the spot, returned to the cabin. The money had been hidden directly underneath the projecting limb of a large tree, and the end of which seemed to point precisely to the treasure buried in the earth.[34]—On their return and passing the cabin, they saw the unfortunate man within, devouring the remaining brains and liver, left from his morning repast! They hurried him away, but before leaving, he gathered together the bones and heaped them all in a box he used for the purpose, blessed them and the cabin and said, 'I hope God will forgive me what I have done, I could'nt help it! and I hope I may get to heaven yet!' We asked Kiesburg why he did not use the meat of the bullock and horse instead of human flesh, he replied he had not seen them. We then told him we knew better, and asked him why the meat in the chair had not been consumed, he said 'oh! its too dry eating!' the liver and lights were a great deal better, and the brains made good soup! We then moved on, and camped on the lake for the night.

April, 21st. Started for Bear River valley this morning, found the snow from six to eight feet deep, camped on Juba River for the night—On the 22d., traveled down Juba about 18 miles, and camped at the head of Bear River valley.—On the 25th, moved down to the lower end of the valley, met our horses, and came in."[35]

*   *   *

When the Fourth Relief brought Keseberg down from the mountains, the history of the Donner Party in one sense was complete. In another sense it will never be complete, but for this volume the chronicle is closed by a roll-call. In the list below, organized by families, the names of all who perished are italicized. Those not otherwise accounted for died in the snow.

BREEN FAMILY: Patrick, Margaret, and their children John, Edward, Patrick, Jr., Simon P., Peter, James, and Isabella.

GEORGE DONNER FAMILY: *George, Tamsen,* their children Frances E., Georgiana, Eliza P., and George Donner's children by a deceased wife, Elitha Cumi and Leanna C.

JACOB DONNER FAMILY: *Jacob, Elizabeth,* their children George, Mary M., *Isaac, Samuel, Lewis,* and Elizabeth Donner's children by a deceased husband, Solomon E. Hook and *William Hook.*

EDDY FAMILY: William H., *Eleanor,* and their children *James* and *Margaret.*

GRAVES FAMILY: *Franklin Ward* and *Elizabeth,* their unmarried children Mary Ann, William C., Eleanor, Lavina, Nancy, Jonathan B., *Franklin Ward, Jr.,* and Elizabeth, Jr. Another daughter, Sarah, was married to *Jay Fosdick.*

KESEBERG FAMILY: Lewis, Phillipine, and their children *Ada* and *Lewis, Jr.*

McCUTCHEN FAMILY: William, Amanda, and their child *Harriet.*

MURPHY FAMILY: the widow *Lavina,* her unmarried children *John Landrum,* Mary M., *Lemuel B.,* William G., and Simon P. Her daughter Sarah was married to William M. Foster, and they had a child, *George.* Another daughter, Harriet, was married to *William M. Pike* (killed by Foster through an accidental gunshot wound after reaching the Truckee River), and they had two children, Naomi L. and *Catherine.*

REED FAMILY: James Frazier, Margret, their children Martha J. (Patty), James Frazier, Jr., Thomas K., and Mrs. Reed's daughter by her first marriage, Virginia E. Backenstoe (Reed).

WOLFINGER FAMILY: *Wolfinger,* first name unknown, said to have been murdered on the Truckee by Reinhardt and Spitzer; wife Doris.

UNMARRIED MEMBERS OF THE PARTY:

Antonio, New Mexican herder.

Karl Burger, believed to have been a teamster for Keseberg.

John Denton, Englishman traveling with the George Donner family.

Patrick Dolan, Irishman travelling with the Breen family.

Milford (Milt) Elliott, teamster for Reed.

Luke Halloran, invalid taken in by the George Donners at Fort Bridger, who died at the south end of Great Salt Lake.

Hardcoop, first name unknown, traveling with Keseberg and by him left to die on the Humboldt River.

Walter Herron, teamster for Reed who traveled with him to California and remained there.

Noah James, teamster for one of the Donner families.

Joseph Reinhardt, said to have been traveling with Spitzer.

Samuel Shoemaker, teamster for one of the Donner families.

James Smith, teamster for Reed.

John Snyder, teamster for Graves, killed by Reed in an altercation on the Humboldt.

Augustus Spitzer, said to have been Reinhardt's partner.

Charles T. Stanton, traveling unattached.

Jean Baptiste Trubode, New Mexican teamster for

George Donner.
Baylis Williams, with half-sister Eliza, hired man and
girl for the Reeds.

In addition, Sutter's two California Indians, *Luis* [or
Lewis] and *Salvador,* who had accompanied Stanton
across the mountains with provisions died with Stanton
as members of the Snowshoe Party. In all, thirty-nine
died among the eighty-seven who set out from Fort
Bridger on the Hastings Cutoff, with Luis and Salvador
swelling the death toll to forty-one; the name of the aged
Sarah Keyes, who died at the crossing of the Big Blue
River in Kansas, is not usually included in the accounting.

Notes

DIARY OF WILLIAM E. TAYLOR
AND LETTER OF JOHN CRAIG

1. Elk Horn, later renamed Crab Orchard, was a village 9 miles northwest of Richmond, Ray County, Missouri.

2. Apparently "Mr. Lad" was John W. Ladd, who went on to Oregon. As seen in Volume II, the *Oregon Spectator* of October 29, 1846, speaking of those entering the Willamette Valley by the Barlow Road, says, "Mr. J. W. Ladd's wagon was at the head of the line, and arrived in this city on the 13th of last month. . . ."

3. The St. Joseph *Gazette*, April 3, 1846, contains a "Ferry Notice" by Evan Parrott, dated St. Joseph, March 27, 1846: "The shortest road to Wolf River, the Iowa Sub-Agency &c, by crossing at PARROTT'S FERRY, four miles above St. Joseph. A good lot for the safe keeping of animals immediately at the landing. Rates of Ferrage established by law."

4. What Taylor calls the Iowa Agency was properly the Great Nemaha Subagency, created in April, 1837, for the Iowas, Sacs, and Foxes, who had just ceded their lands east of the Missouri. The Iowas technically had a reservation of their own, north of that jointly occupied by the Sacs and Foxes. These "twin preserves," lying north of Wolf River, were formally surveyed in the summer of 1838. The Presbyterians, who in 1835 had opened a work among the Iowas, moved in the fall of 1837 across the Missouri, thereafter embracing all three tribes. For details, see Louise Barry, "Kansas Before 1854: a Revised Annals," *Kansas Historical Quarterly*, Spring, Summer, Autumn, 1963, vol. 29, *passim*.

5. In view of what Taylor says here, evidently there were three wagons, including Ladd's, in the Craig & Stanley party at this time. Presumably we can think of the full company of 27 wagons as Captain Martin's company—thus far, at least.

6. Concerning the "discord" over the election of officers, see the comments by John R. McBride, quoted in the Introduction.

7. Apparently Taylor's company camped on the Big (Black) Vermilion, supposing it to be the Big Blue, then discovered their mistake.

8. Having crossed the Big Blue proper near Marysville, Kansas, Taylor soon struck the emigrant road from Independence.

9. Horse Creek would seem to be the present Walnut Creek, northwest of Fairbury, Nebraska. The next stream mentioned, the Sandy, is still so called.

10. The Nebraska or Platte River was reached near the head of

Grand Island. Here Fort Kearny was founded late the following year.

11. Taylor seems to say that he crossed the South Fork 28 miles above the Forks of the Platte. This would be the "upper ford" of the Jefferson map. Here Taylor records the violent storm John R. McBride recalled as having occurred at the crossing of the Big Blue.

12. The name Ash Hollow was only now coming into use. Although the fur traders had applied the name Ash Creek to two streams entering the Platte from either side, recognizing the novelty of the ash trees growing on their banks, they had known the area as "the Cedar Bluffs." For further details on Ash Hollow, consult the Index.

13. Taylor's "Sandy" was the present Pumpkin Creek, which enters the Platte east of what Taylor calls Castle Rock, a formation which through Fremont's influence was becoming known as Court House Rock. Together with Chimney Rock, a few miles to the west, Court House Rock had become one of the most famous landmarks along the Platte. For the origin and early evolution of the various placenames marking the road to the mountains, see a forthcoming work edited by Dale L. Morgan and Eleanor T. Harris, *The Rocky Mountain Journals of William Marshall Anderson.*

14. Scotts Bluff acquired its name apparently in 1827-1828, when Hiram Scott, abandoned by a fur caravan returning from the mountains, died in this vicinity. See Dale L. Morgan, ed., *The West of William H. Ashley* (Denver, 1963).

15. In saying that the company divided, Taylor perhaps supplies a date and more correct place for the incident John R. McBride places on the Little Blue. Taylor evidently continued with the Martin company when it separated from the main body of the St. Joseph emigration, and again when it parted from the Burnett train, as described by McBride.

16. As seen by Joel Palmer's narrative, the Martin company was at the head of the emigration on reaching Fort Laramie June 10.

17. The Bitter Cottonwood is now termed simply Cottonwood Creek. For this travel through the Black Hills (Laramie Mountains), refer to the Jefferson map.

18. Horseshoe Creek is still so called.

19. Taylor's "Butte Creek" is clearly a mistake for Labonte Creek.

20. "Black Creek" is La Prele Creek, so known even in 1846. What Taylor calls "Red Rock" appears on Jefferson's map as "Pyramids"; William Clayton observed in June, 1847, that the emigrant road here passed over "a kind of red earth or sand about the color of red precipitate. Most of the rocks and bluffs are of the same red color, only a deeper red. It affected my eyes much from its brightness and strange appearance."

21. The wagon road emerged from the Black Hills a few miles east of Deer Creek. In 1849 a ferry was established near this creek, but

earlier emigrants continued up the North Platte some distance before attempting to cross.

22. Usually the North Platte was not fordable until late July or August. The customary crossing place was about 4 miles west of present Casper. Difficult to identify are the "Return emigrants" Taylor encountered June 18; they were not the Clyman party from California (which he fails to mention on June 23); it seems unlikely they were stragglers from Palmer's company; and the only other sizable contingent from Oregon would be met on the Sweetwater June 26. Clyman, on June 20, while descending the Sweetwater, referred to an Oregon party "six or eight days ahead of us," and at Bear River on June 10 had noted that "a large party of horses and mules had passed appearantly some 5 or 10 days previous." Perhaps these were not mistaken references to Palmer's party, and there was a third company from Oregon this year. But no newspaper recorded their separate arrival on the frontier.

23. The Red Buttes at the west end of the Casper Range were and are a famous landmark, depicted on the Jefferson map. Taylor is one of the few who had kind words for any spring other than Willow Spring after leaving the North Platte.

24. The Willow Spring was appreciated both for its fine water and for its grass. This day Taylor passed Clyman's party.

25. "Rock Independence," the original form of the name now fixed as Independence Rock, was named from the circumstance that William L. Sublette, bound for Wind River with the first wagons ever taken to the northern Rockies, celebrated the national holiday here in 1830.

26. This "Kenion on Sweet water" was only now becoming generally known as Devils Gate. Mountain sheep frequented the cliffs from earliest times, and were usually first seen here by overland travelers.

27. The "party of men" encountered this day would seem to have been the Oregonians who left The Dalles May 1, as seen in the Introduction, and whom for convenient reference we shall hereafter call the Genois company. See Index.

28. The "eternal snow" (a much-favored phrase in these years, employed by emigrants not accustomed to snow in summer) might have been seen on the Bear River Divide, far to the west, but Taylor was perhaps applying the name "Bear River mountans" to the present Uintas, running east and west along the Utah-Wyoming border.

29. Taylor's firm placement of Lansford W. Hastings on the Big Sandy on July 2 is a service to history. It is to be noted that he did not in the course of the next few days mention encountering Wales Bonney, the lone traveler from Oregon.

30. The Green River, called by Taylor the "colorado of the west," was usually crossed on the Fort Bridger road a little above the mouth

of the Big Sandy.

31. As shown by the Jefferson map, Part III, after crossing the Green River, the wagon road descended the west bank about 8 miles, then at a point marked by the ruins of the original (?) Fort Bridger (called by Jefferson Old Trading Post, and further discussed in connection with the Miller-Reed diary), angled southwest to Blacks Fork.

32. It was very common for emigrants to be prostrated by sickness in this region, an affliction called mountain fever. The illness was too general to be attributed to the tick-borne disease now called Rocky Mountain Spotted Fever, and probably reflected oxygen starvation in men not accustomed to physical exertion at high altitudes.

33. Solomon Sublette's three companions were Charles Taplin, Walter Reddick, and one whose name is not known. They had reached Fort Bridger by a southern route in company with Joe Walker, and had resumed their journey probably on July 6. It will be seen in Volume II that when Sublette reached St. Louis in September he related having "met the first company of emigrants to California, under the command of Mr. Davis, eighteen miles on the other side of Green River, on the 8th of July last; they had eighteen wagons." This "Mr. Davis" has not been identified. It is noteworthy that Sublette met the first emigrants on the 7th (Taylor's date) and the last on the 16th; but he was going against the current—the interval between the first and the last along this stretch of the trail was more than three weeks.

34. Since Taylor was in the first company to reach Fort Bridger, we regret again the extreme brevity of his diary; what he failed to write is our lost history. He is the first to record the presence of Joe Walker at Fort Bridger; the last such note was made two weeks later by Heinrich Lienhard. Edwin Bryant on July 17 was introduced at Fort Bridger to "Captain Walker, of Jackson county, Missouri, who is much celebrated for his explorations and knowledge of the North American continent, between the frontier settlements of the United States and the Pacific. Captain W. is now on his return from the settlements of California, having been out with Captain Fremont in the capacity of guide or pilot. He is driving some four or five hundred Californian horses, which he intends to dispose of in the United States. They appear to be high-spirited animals, of medium size, handsome figures, and in good condition. It is possible that the trade in horses, and even cattle, between California and the United States may, at no distant day, become of considerable importance. Captain W. communicated to me some facts in reference to recent occurrences in California, of considerable interest. He spoke discouragingly of the new route via the south end of the Salt Lake."

Walker had left Fremont's service near Monterey the previous March 4. According to his nephew, D. F. McClellan, who accom-

panied him east (together with the "Monro" who crops up in Francis
Parkman's trail record), Walker and "some of his men" drove a herd
of horses south to the Chino ranch, beyond Los Angeles, then in late
May set out for the east, going via the Cajon Pass and the Spanish
Trail to Utah Lake. "Passing by the southern extremity of this, they
traveled up the Provo, one of the tributaries of the lake, and thence
over a range of the Bear Mountains, ultimately arrived in safety at
Fort Bridger, on Black's fork of Green river. Every one here was
well acquainted with Capt. Jo, and here the party remained for
some time." The quotations are from John C. McPherson's interview
with McClellan in the Oakland *Daily Transcript,* January 26 and 29,
1873, and should be compared with the account given by Solomon
Sublette to the *Missouri Republican* in September, 1846. Sublette
said that ten men in all comprised the party originally, so it may be
that the Walker company as such consisted of six men. Since Sublette
traveled with Walker, it is demonstrated that Edwin Bryant was
mistaken in saying that Sublette came via Fort Hall, and historians
who have inferred rather unreasonably that Walker drove his herd
east across Walker Pass, then ascending the Humboldt, must revise
their ideas. Walker had reached Bent's Fort by August 26, when Lieutenant Abert encountered him.

35. The Little Muddy, on which camp was made, had water with
a perceptible saline or mineral taste.

36. The road from Fort Bridger reached the Bear River by way
of what is now called Bridger Creek, 6 miles south of present Sage,
Wyoming. The Greenwood Cutoff, not mentioned by Taylor, joined
the older trail a little south of Smiths Fork, near present Cokeville,
some 18 miles farther down the valley of the Bear.

37. Soda Springs, just east of the great bend of Bear River, was
one of the most famous stopping places along the overland trail.
Emigrants usually had much to say about quaffing the waters, but
Taylor was more preoccupied with the summer thunder showers.

38. It would seem that on July 19 the Craig & Stanley party,
having decided for California, and undeterred by their small size,
parted from the Oregon-bound company of William J. Martin. (The
two companies nevertheless traveled the same road as far as Raft
River.) At Soda Springs in 1849, the Hudspeth Cutoff took off to
the west, past the "old Crater" Taylor mentions, in the hope of
eliminating the elbow bend north by way of Fort Hall and shortening
the distance to the head of the Humboldt. That effort at a cutoff
(named for Benoni Hudspeth, not for Hastings' trail companion of
1846, James Hudspeth) was a logical consequence of Lansford W.
Hastings' arguments and trail labors in 1845-1846, but Jesse Applegate and others argued in 1847-1848 that a more convenient route
from the Bear to the Humboldt must exist.

39. The Portneuf River where Taylor reached it was flowing south. The trail ascended the river, then crossed a divide to Ross's Fork, a tributary which joins the Portneuf in the Snake plain.

40. Unusual is Taylor's reference to "the Blue Spring 5 miles from fort Hall," though Joel Palmer, traveling to Oregon in 1845, mentioned camping 5 miles short of the fort "at a large spring of cold water."

41. The American Falls on the "Snake or Saptin River" ("Saptin" was a corruption of Shahaptin, a name applied to the Nez Perces) had been so known since the overland journey of the Astorians in 1811.

42. "Casua" is one of many variations of the French-Canadian term Cajeux, applied to small rafts, and therefore a French version of the name Raft River. The following day, after reaching this stream, Taylor mentions parting from "the Oregon Road." His diary is one of the earliest describing this section of the California Trail, preceded only by Jacob R. Snyder's diary of 1845 (printed in Society of California Pioneers, *Quarterly,* December, 1931, vol. 8, pp. 224-260), though as noted in the Introduction, William H. Winter briefly recounts an east-bound journey in the spring of 1845.

43. On this day, July 28, Taylor crossed the divide from Raft River to Goose Creek. The existence of the afterward-celebrated City of Rocks is barely intimated by his comment, "Road Bad," and that may have applied primarily to what is now known as Granite Pass.

44. The "verry hot spring" presumably was one of the springs in the southern arm of what became known as Thousand Springs Valley, the "Hot Pools" of William H. Winter's narrative. Beyond, in reaching "the head of Marys River," Taylor may have struck upon Bishops Creek, down which seems to have gone the original road of 1843-1844, or he may have taken the slightly longer but more open route to the south via the Humboldt Wells, which Jacob Snyder says was used by his own party under Caleb Greenwood's guidance in August, 1845, "a new route said to be 2 days nearer than the old road."

45. This meeting with Jesse Applegate and Black Harris on August 3 is important for date and place, as pointed out in the Introduction. In his letter written from Fort Hall on August 9 (see Volume II) Applegate tells of meeting Larkin Stanley a few days earlier.

46. The term "digger" has no ethnological meaning, since most mountain Indians dug for edible roots at the proper season. Indians encountered here probably were Western Shoshoni. Below the great bend of the Humboldt they would more likely be Northern Paiutes.

47. The "Remarkabley hot Springs" passed on August 6 were doubtless those at present Elko, Nevada.

48. These hot springs probably were those at present Carlin, 25 miles west of Elko. Here, as the Jefferson map shows but as Taylor

neglects to say, the emigrant road left the Humboldt for some distance, Palisade Canyon being impassable for any but railroad builders. Jefferson's road, the Hastings Cutoff, rejoined Taylor's just east of the Carlin area, after having been separate since leaving Fort Bridger; the Jefferson map pictures the rest of Taylor's journey to California.

49. The "Natural Soap" Taylor remarked was precipitated alkali on the Humboldt plain west of present Battle Mountain. The "Salaeratus" noted on August 13, similar to that observed by emigrants on the Sweetwater, would have been seen near present Winnemucca, at the great bend of the Humboldt.

50. The new "oregon road," the Applegate Cutoff, separated from the California road at a bend in the Humboldt near present Mill City, at the south end of the Eugene Mountains.

51. Jefferson's map shows how the road cut across the bend of the Humboldt mentioned in the preceding Note.

52. Taylor's terse account of being overtaken by William H. Russell's pack party must be supplemented by Edwin Bryant's narrative. Having left Fort Bridger on July 20, nine days after Taylor, and done their share of exploring on and adjacent to the Hastings Cutoff, the Russell party had come back to the established trail in the Humboldt Valley near the present Halleck on August 8.

"The proprietors of the two wagons," Bryant says, "were Messrs. Craig and Stanley, from Ray county, Missouri, accompanied by six or eight young men. I learned from them that they left Fort Hall on the 23d day of July, and are some twelve or fifteen days in advance of all the other emigrant trains bound for California. The intentions of Messrs. Craig and Stanley, are to visit California first; and after travelling over it, to explore the fertile districts of Oregon; and if upon examination they are pleased with either of these countries, they design to dispose of their property in the United States, and settle on the Pacific. Messrs. C. and S. are highly intelligent and respectable gentlemen, and I derived from them much interesting and useful information in regard to the emigrant route, via Fort Hall. . . .

"Messrs. Craig and Stanley, in the course of the afternoon, although their supply of provisions was not more than equal to their probable consumption, before they would reach the settlements of California, generously furnished us with a quantity of flour and bacon, which I believed would be nearly or quite sufficient for our wants. They would accept of no compensation for this very great favor; and I consider myself, as well as every member of our party, under the highest obligations to them, for their most liberal manifestation of kindness and hospitality."

Bryant also says, doing the reporting Taylor shirked, that toward sunset two Digger Indians came into camp, one mounted on a "miserably lean and broken down horse," with whom the ceremony of smoking was performed. "A member of Messrs. Craig and Stanley's party, who for a number of years had been a trapper in the mountains, and was considerably skilled in the significance of Indian signs, afterwards held a conversation with the principal Indian [the one who rode the horse], and learned from him, that a short day's journey would bring us to some pools of standing water, and that after this, we would find no water or grass for a long distance. The time was indicated by pointing to the course of the sun and its positions when the incidents respecting which we inquired would take place. Other matters were explained by a similar reference to objects connected with and illustrative of those inquired about. The information derived from this conversation was not sufficiently clear to solve the doubt, as to whether this was or was not the 'Sink' of Mary's river. . . ."

53. Although Bryant does not specifically say so, the Russell party rode ahead, reaching the Sink (described as marked by pools of standing water, covered with a yellowish slime, and emitting a most disagreeable fetor), about 2 P.M. Some wanted to encamp, forbidding as the locality looked, since it was reported to be another 45 miles to the Truckee, but finally the Russell party rode on as far as Bradys Hot Springs, where Clyman's spaniel had died in May. Bryant estimated the day's travel as 45 miles.

54. Russell's pack party reached the Truckee a little after noon on August 20, the course of the river "indicated by a line of willows, grass, and other green herbage, and a number of *tall* trees,—the last a sight that has not saluted us for five hundred miles. Our animals, as if reinvigorated by the prospect of grass and the scent of water, rushed forward with great speed, and we were soon in the middle of the stream, from the clear current of which all drank copious daughts. We immediately crossed to the bottom on the opposite side and encamped. . . . Distance 20 miles." Bryant says that when he rose next morning "Messrs. Craig and Stanley were riding towards our camp, and they informed us that their wagons had just reached the opposite bank of the river just before daylight, having travelled all night, and that they were now crossing the stream for the purpose of encamping for the day. I was much gratified that these, our good friends, had crossed the desert in safety, and had reached a point where they could recruit their animals. . . ."

The Russell party started up the Truckee on the 22nd, and though Taylor tells us that the wagon party also resumed the journey that day, Bryant saw no more of these fellow travelers until after they arrived at Sutter's.

55. As we now conceive the geography, Taylor had not yet reached the Sierra Nevada when he started up the canyon of the Truckee, but there is much to be said for his point of view.

56. The "spur of the mts" crossed on August 25 lies immediately

west of present Verdi, where almost on the California-Nevada line the Truckee makes a right-angle bend. On the west side of this ridge flows the Little Truckee River, called by Clyman in the spring Wind River. The road continued on by way of what was then called John Greenwood's Creek, now Prosser Creek, to Donner Lake.

57. Bryant had passed "Truckee Lake" about mid-afternoon on August 25, consequently gained two days on the wagons in ascending the Truckee. He mentions, as Taylor does not, the cabin at the foot of the lake which had sheltered Moses Schallenberger during the winter of 1844-1845, and which would similarly provide a home for the Breen family in the winter of 1846-1847.

58. The "worst mountain that waggons ever crossed" is Taylor's obeisance to Donner Pass. In fact, the wagons in 1844-1845 had been got up to the summit only with the aid of a windlass. What this climb to the summit involved is more clearly conveyed in a letter of April 17, 1846, written by one of the emigrants of 1845, William L. Todd, and reprinted from the Springfield *Illinois Journal* in the New York *Tribune* of August 20, 1846: "We left Fort Hall on the 9th of August, in company with ten wagons, and on St. Mary's river we were joined by fifteen more. We went on smoothly until we reached the California mountains, which were about 300 miles from our destination. There we met with tribulations in the extreme. You can form no idea, nor can I give you any just description of the evils which beset us. From the time we left the lake on the North [East] side of the mountains [Donner Lake] until we arrived at the lake on the top [Marys Lake], it was one continued jumping from one rocky cliff to another. We would have to roll over this big rock, then over that; then there was bridging a branch; then we had to lift our wagons by main force up to the top of a ledge of rocks that it was impossible for us to reduce, bridge or roll our wagons over, and in several places we had to run our wagons broadside off a ledge, take off our cattle, and throw our wagons round with handspikes and heave them up to the top where where our cattle had been previously taken. Three days were passed in this vexatious way and at the end of that time we found ourselves six miles from the lake on the North side of the mountain, and you never saw a set of fellows more happy than when we reached the summit. . . ."

59. For Taylor's travels since reaching the crest of Donner Pass, compare the Jefferson map, though Jefferson reached the summit south of Donner Lake, by way of Coldstream Creek. The road passed through Summit Valley, then dropped down the canyon of the upper Yuba, suitably characterized by Taylor between August 31 and September 3. On September 5, near present Cisco Butte, the Craig & Stanley party left the Yuba to climb a ridge to the southwest, passing what Jefferson calls Brant Lake, the present Crystal Lake, and after

winding along a narrow hogback, descending a steep slope into upper Bear Valley, often mentioned the following winter in the Donner chronicle.

60. The rugged travel Taylor describes on September 7-8 covered the stretch of trail from what became known as Mule Springs, in the Bear Valley, over a high ridge and down into Steep Hollow. After that, the road to Johnson's Ranch presented no problems.

61. Johnson's Ranch was located along the north bank of the Bear River, at present Wheatland, Yuba County. The Irish-born William Johnson arrived in California in 1840 as an American sailor, and subsequently was naturalized. Don Pablo Gutierrez, the original grantee for the area, was killed in 1845, in consequence of which his grant was sold at auction on April 28 of the same year, the purchasers being Johnson and Sebastian Keyser. The two men separately sold out their half-interests in 1849. Johnson took several Indian squaws as wives, but in June, 1847, married Mary Murphy, one of the survivors of the Donner Party. That marriage gave up the ghost by November of the same year. The teen-age girl remarried, and her name survives in present Marysville.

62. Far West had been the original seat of Caldwell County, Missouri, when organized for the benefit of the Mormons in 1836-1837. After the expulsion of the Mormons from Missouri the town declined, and in 1843 a new seat, Kingston, was selected a few miles away. George Boosinger, to whom John Craig addressed this letter, had been a Mormon, but he fell away from the faith during the troubled times of 1838-1839.

63. Some long passages of Craig's letter relating to these business concerns are omitted.

64. The year 1844 was marked by epic floods which greatly delayed the Oregon emigrants who set out from Independence and St. Joseph. It is interesting that Craig says much malarial illness followed the inundation: the 1844 flood may have been a large factor in the 1845 emigration to Oregon and California, with a secondary effect upon the emigration of 1846.

65. It is not entirely clear when Craig and Stanley changed their destination from Oregon to California. The decision may have been made after encountering Solomon Sublette on July 7, but see note 38 above.

66. Craig has a rather freewheeling account of the enlistment of Fremont's California Battalion. A more satisfactory history is given by Edwin Bryant in relating events from October 27 to November 30.

67. Larkin Stanley's death on December 12, when the California Battalion was nearing Mission San Luis Obispo, is described by Bryant under date of December 13: "Mr. Stanley, one of the volunteers, and one of the gentlemen who so kindly supplied us with provi-

sions on Mary's river, died last night. He has been suffering from an attack of typhoid fever since the commencement of our march, and unable most of the time to sit upon his horse. He was buried this morning in a small circular opening in the timber near our camp. The battalion was formed in a hollow square surrounding the grave which had been excavated for the final resting-place of our deceased friend and comrade . . . . The cold earth was heaped upon his mortal remains in silent solemnity, and the ashes of a braver or a better man will never repose in the lonely hills of California."

68. We have seen in the introduction to the Taylor diary that by early March Craig had made up his mind to return home, and that he advertised his purpose in the *California Star* of April 10, the expectation then being that he would leave Sutter's about May 1. In his letter of April 29 from New Helvetia, printed in the *Star* on May 22, George McKinstry commented, "The water is so high that Messrs. Craig and company, who advertised to rendezvous here previous to their departure for the U. States, have not been able to get here from Sonoma. . . ." It was not until May 22 that the New Helvetia Diary recorded: "Mr Craig left here for his journey to the U. S." The same diary noted that "a good many volunteers [members of the California Battalion] arrived from below," including "Myers (who is going with a band of horses to the big salt lake, his new established trading post)." That was a reference to Miles Goodyear, who would accompany Craig on the journey. Seven men in all comprised the party, Goodyear and his two herders, and three others who like Craig himself were returning to the States. The name of only one of the three is known, one Truitt or Truete who was probably Samuel Truitt. The New Helvetia Diary has two entries concerning him: On May 31, "Truet arrived & left again." And on June 1, "Truet left this morning for the Mountains." According to Craig, the party set out the next day, no doubt from Johnson's Ranch.

69. Craig is here saying that he traveled the Hastings Cutoff, perhaps employing Clyman's route of the previous year.

70. Apparently Craig visited on July 4-5 Miles Goodyear's new Fort Buenaventura on the site of Ogden, founded after the emigration passed by in 1846, concerning which more is said in the notes appended to James Frazier Reed's diary and letters.

71. It was on July 10, not July 11, that Craig met the Mormon Pioneers at Bear River. Albert Carrington mentioned meeting "Miles Goodyear & 2 men & a Mr. Craig of Ray County Mo & a Mr Truete of Shelby County Ill. & 2 other men," adding that "on the lower or Hastings route a drive of 75 miles over a salt plain without water Craig & Company lost 5 horses." Orson Pratt noted in his journal on July 10 that at Bear River the Pioneers found "a small party from the Bay of St. Francisco, on their way home to the States. They

were accompanied by Mr. Miles Goodyear, a mountaineer, as far as this point, where Mr. Goodyear learning from us that the Oregon emigration was earlier than usual, and that they, instead of coming by way of Bridger's had taken a more northern route, concluded to go down Bear River, and intersect them for the purposes of trade." On July 11 Pratt remarked further, "Mr. Craig and three others proceeded on their journey for the States. Mr. Goodyear and two Indians went down Bear River. . . . ."

72. The family migration which followed upon the heels of the Pioneers is remembered in Mormon history as the "second company" of 1847. They reached the Valley of the Great Salt Lake in late September and early October. Interesting is the intimation that some of the Mormons expected to go on to "California proper."

DIARY OF NICHOLAS CARRIGER

1. The Nodaway River forms the boundary between Andrew and Holt counties.

2. Davis Creek, still so called, flows into Mill Creek about 3 miles south of present Oregon, Holt County.

3. I have not identified what Carriger calls in his diary "Thompsons; Hameys Ferry," and in his autobiography "Thompson and Hayman's ferry." It was located at Iowa Point, a short distance below the present Kansas-Nebraska boundary, where Cedar and Mill creeks reach the Missouri.

4. This camp of May 6-10 was evidently on present Cedar Creek, by Carriger called Honey Creek.

5. The route Carriger was taking, which he is the first emigrant to describe, made for the Platte essentially by the Burlington Railroad's Kansas City, Atchison and Columbus line as far as Lincoln, thence on to Bellwood near the mouth of the Loup Fork by the Union Pacific's branch line. Carriger would seem to have camped on May 13 near the future Nebraska line, then made successive camps on the Nemaha south and southwest of Falls City, and west of Salem; near Elk Creek and St. Mary on the North Fork of the Nemaha, near Adams, and on May 22 near Roca on Salt Creek. The 23rd brought him to Middle Creek at present Lincoln; which he rightly calls "a branch of the blue Earth [Big Blue River]"; and he then went on to the Platte past Valparaiso, Brainerd and David City (Oak Creek being the stream he mentions on May 26 and 27).

6. Curious is this allusion to a bridge. Constructed by these emigrants of 1846?

7. Major Stephen Cooper's announced intention of going to California may be found in Volume II, as reprinted from the St. Joseph

Gazette of March 13, 1846. He was born in 1797, moved to Missouri from Kentucky in 1807, and was active in the Santa Fe trade in the 1820's, an Indian subagent at Council Bluffs in the 1840's, and a member of Abert's detachment of Fremont's Third Expedition of 1845. In the 1870's and 1880's, after a varied life in California, he gave out sundry reminiscences of his Western experiences which are not uniformly accurate. One of these, printed in Oakland, 1888, at the behest of his grandchildren as *Sketches from the Life of Maj. Stephen Cooper,* says in part:

"In the spring of 1846 I started with my family for California; was at the head of seven wagons, three of these my own. We soon fell in with a large train of thirty-five wagons, bound for Oregon. We camped together two nights; the second morning at daylight there was a flag flying on one of our wagons with large, conspicuous letters, 'Bound for California.' This got up great excitement, and the Oregonians threatened to shoot the flag down. I said to them, 'Bring out your brave men and shoot down some old woman's flag if you want to.' This made them ashamed of themselves.

"We soon rolled out and twenty-one of the Oregon wagons fell in with us, making twenty-eight wagons in my train, which I brought to California. Through my influence at least sixty-five wagons came to California that had started for Oregon. . . ."

Cooper died at the age of 91 on May 16, 1890, at Winters, California. Apparently on July 4 Carriger saw Cooper for the last time on the 1846 journey.

8. The "Pawney Village" Carriger mentions on June 1 had been a well-known abiding place of the Chauis or Grand Pawnees for twenty years; it was situated opposite present Clarks, about 10 miles northeast of Central City.

9. Compare Carriger's account of this council with the Pawnees in his autobiography, quoted in the introductory sketch.

10. The junction with the Independence-St. Joseph road was a few miles east of the site of Fort Kearny, selected by Lieutenant D. P. Woodbury in the fall of 1847. Edwin Bryant seemingly adds to the history of the company in which Carriger had been traveling when he says on June 9, the day after arriving on the banks of the Platte by the Independence road: "A sort of post-office communication is frequently established by the emigrant companies. The information which they desire to communicate is sometimes written upon the skulls of buffaloes,—sometimes upon small strips of smooth plans,—and at others a stake or stick being driven into the ground, and split at the top, a manuscript note is inserted in it. These are conspicuously placed at the side of the trail, and are seen and read by succeeding companies. One of the last-described notices we saw this morning. It purported to be written by the captain of a company from Platte

county, Mo., a portion of which was bound for California, and a portion for Oregon. It consisted of sixty-six wagons. They had travelled up the Platte a considerable distance, passing through the Pawnee villages, with which Indians they had had some difficulties. They had also suffered much from the rains and high waters. They were now one day in advance of us."

11. The tragedy Carriger recounts on June 14 evolved out of the accident which had occurred eight days earlier. Both Edwin Bryant and J. Quinn Thornton have long accounts of the occurrence, Bryant having been summoned from the Russell company to amputate the boy's gangrenous leg. He saw that an operation would only heighten the boy's sufferings in the moments before his death, so he declined. A "Canadian Frenchman, who belonged to this emigrating party . . . stated that he had formerly been an assistant to a surgeon in some hospital, and had seen many operations of this nature performed, and that he would amputate the child's limb, if . . . the mother desired it. . . ." The boy died as the operation was concluded. Bryant adds that the father of the dead boy was lying prostrate in his tent, "incapable of moving a limb, with an inflammatory rheumatism. . . . He was suffering from violent pains in all of his bones . . . [and] told me that he had been unable to walk or sit upright for four weeks." After leaving some medicines with this man, Bryant examined the wife of one of the emigrants (evidently Redwood Easton), "who had been ill for several weeks of an intermittent fever. She had taken large quantities of medicine, and her strength and constitution appeared to be so much exhausted, that I had no hopes of her recovery, unless the company to which she belonged could suspend their march for a week or more, and give her rest." (That, of course, was not done; for the sequel see Carriger's diary entry for June 21.) Bryant also told another young man who applied for relief, and who seemed to be "laboring under a disease of the heart," that the journey might effect his cure, "but that no medicine which I possessed would have any other than an injurious effect." For the apparent sequel to *this* case, see Note 15.

12. J. Quinn Thornton was on hand to relate the story of the boy's gruesome death because he was then traveling in the "Oregon Company of 20 Waggons" to which Carriger refers, captained by Rice Dunbar. Afterward he conducted Bryant to his camp, where that night they attended the wedding of a Miss Lard to Sept Moutry (though Thornton drew a long face over a woman marrying upon the road: "It looks so much like making a sort of a hop, skip, and jump into matrimony.") In yet another company a child was born, so that both Thornton and Bryant reflected upon the fact that a death, a funeral, a wedding, and a birth should have occurred within two hours' time and within a space only two miles in diameter.

13. Evidently Carriger crossed the South Platte by Jefferson's "Upper Ford."

14. Carriger this day, June 18, reached Ash Hollow.

15. Presumably "Eli Griggery," buried on the 19th, was the young man with heart disease Bryant had examined a few days earlier, as set forth in Note 11 above. McKinstry's diary mentions this "Oregon company of 26 wagons in camp to burry a young man that died this morning [of] fever & disease of the heart." Carriger's "Cedar Creek" is the present Ash Creek.

16. "Col Russels & Boggses" company of 40 wagons was that in which McKinstry, Bryant, James Frazier Reed, and a good many others were traveling at this time. (In his diary for June 20-21 Carriger also refers to the death and burial of "Easton's Wife," and we may suppose that this was the woman whose future Bryant had so ominously forecast.)

17. Taylor had not mentioned Horse Creek, though on June 4 he "Saw wild horses" below Castle Rock. Wild horses frequented the country between the forks of the Platte at least as early as 1812, when Robert Stuart noted their presence.

18. The trading house briefly mentioned on June 25 was Fort Bernard, more fully discussed elsewhere; see Index.

19. By "fort" Carriger means Fort Laramie, or as it had been properly known since 1841, "Fort John." The "bitter Water" to which Carriger moved next day was (Bitter) Cottonwood Creek.

20. "Campbells & Crabtrees California Company" presumably ended up in Oregon. Thornton on July 5 tells of passing "two companies of Oregon emigrants, one led by a Mr. Campbell, the other by a Mr. Crabtree," and on July 19, preparing to separate from the Donners at the Little Sandy, he mentions Crabtree and Campbell as among those encamped nearby. In his 1878 address to the Oregon Pioneer Association, Thornton elaborated upon his journal entry of July 5 by saying that the second company was led by "Jimmy Campbell, a better man than whom never came to Oregon." Mrs. Campbell died on the Greenwood Cutoff on July 28, as Thornton relates in his journal and his 1878 address. Thornton last mentions him on August [14], beyond Fort Hall.

21. One of the three companies encamped at the crossing of the North Platte on July 4 was that in which Heinrich Lienhard and the Kellogg family were traveling; see B. F. Kellogg's letter written there, printed in Volume II. Not far off, James Mathers was commencing the second volume of his diary, as printed in these pages.

22. What Carriger terms the "muddy Spring," in the valley of present Poison Spider Creek, was more usually termed a mineral spring. William Clayton's *Latter-day Saints' Emigrants Guide* of 1848 said that it was "Considered poisonous. No bad taste to the water,

unless the cattle trample in it. In that case it becomes black, and is
doubtless poisonous." Passing earlier in the season, William E. Taylor
on June 22 had thought it a "good Spring."

23. The night encampment might have been on present Strawberry
Creek, preliminary to going on to the last crossing of the Sweetwater
next day. The Sweetwater runs through a canyon here, familiar to
the early trappers, but not often viewed after wagon travel began.

24. This day, July 16, Carriger crossed South Pass to the Dry
Sandy, unfavorably known for poison water.

25. Carriger's traverse of the Greenwood Cutoff is the earliest recorded in an emigrant's diary, but should be compared with the account
of J. Quinn Thornton, who embarked upon the cutoff next day, July
19, and reached Bear River July 29, five days after Carriger.

26. Carriger's "black Creek" would seem to have been present
LaBarge Creek, but possibly was Fontenelle Creek.

27. The encampment of the 21st would seem to have been on Crow
Creek.

28. Carriger had now reached Hams Fork. Some improvements
were made on this stretch of the Greenwood Cutoff by Joe Walker,
in giving a hand to an emigrant company of 1848, which makes Carriger's earlier account, however sparse in detail, that much more
valuable. It is apparent that Carriger crossed the divide separating
Crow Creek from Hams Fork, instead of descending Crow Creek to
Hams Fork and ascending the latter stream as an easier way of reaching the same objective.

29. On July 23 Carriger probably encamped on Rock Creek after
a characteristically hard climb up to the Hams Fork Plateau.

30. Interesting is this allusion to "a trading house on bear river"
near what was clearly Thomas Fork; see John R. McBride's account
of Pegleg Smith as quoted in the Introduction. It was not until 1848
that Pegleg established, a little farther down the Bear at present
Dingle, Idaho—a locality then better known as the Big Timbers—
the trading post that received so much attention by emigrants of
1849. In May, 1845, the British botanist Joseph Burke had encountered Pegleg higher up the Bear; next month Overton Johnson, eastbound from Oregon, set out from Fort Hall in search of "the camp
of Messrs. Vasques and Smith, (Peg Leg,),'' eventually finding their
camp not on the Bear but on Green River, and noting that Vasquez
had left his trading house (Fort Bridger) "for fear of the Sioux and
Shians." On August 2, 1845, the west-bound Joel Palmer encountered
at Big Timbers "a company of trappers and traders attached to
Bridger's party," but whether Pegleg was with them is not stated;
Pegleg at this time reportedly was making his returns at the British
establishment, Fort Hall.

31. Carriger moved down the Bear another 17 miles, apparently to

present Montpelier Creek, and passed a second "Trading house." Two such houses at this date are provocative. Perhaps one was conducted by Pegleg, the other in the interest of Bridger & Vasquez. Or some independent, like Miles Goodyear, might have been bidding for the emigrant trade; Goodyear had set out from Independence the previous autumn with a small outfit and the avowed intention of opening a "half-way house," as will be seen in connection with James Frazier Reed's letter of July 31, 1846.

32. On the 27th Carriger traveled down (not up) the Bear River Valley to encamp near the present Bannock-Bear Lake county line. The "spur of the mountain" over which he passed lies north of present Georgetown, Idaho, where the Preuss and Aspen ranges adjoin.

33. A small piece has eroded from the manuscript, and it is impossible to be sure just how many miles of travel Carriger recorded this day. Probably he crossed Gem Valley to camp on the Portneuf River west of present Hatch, having made a long drive of 23 miles or so.

34. On July 30 Carriger ascended the upper Portneuf and crossed the divide to Ross's Fork drainage.

35. This camp of July 31 was on Ross's Fork, which flows into the lower Portneuf a few miles below the site of Fort Hall.

36. Carriger reached Fort Hall nine days behind Taylor, who had passed by on July 23, and six days ahead of Pringle. The interesting question arises whether Carriger's company hired Caleb Greenwood and his sons as their guides. His diary nowhere mentions the Greenwoods, but as seen in the introductory comments, his autobiography tells of having "Mr Greenwood" as pilot after arriving at the Sierra Nevada. No really definite information has come forth relating to the movements of the Greenwoods after Clyman and Hastings separated from them in the Humboldt Valley on May 16. It is my conviction that they went on only as far as Fort Hall, and there awaited the arrival of emigrants, as in 1845.

In some recollections of the 1846 overland journey, "Across the Continent in a Caravan," *Journal of American History,* Fourth Quarter, 1907, vol. I, pp. 617-632, Joseph Aram declared that a company under Charles Imus, in which Adna A. Hecox and himself traveled, had an "old pilot, Greenwood," from some point east of the Green River as far as the Truckee; however, the Aram account is full of misinformation, and no credence can be given particular statements. Hecox, whose reminiscences were printed in the *San Jose Pioneer* in 1878, and again in *The Grizzly Bear,* December, 1911, vol. 9, pp. 7-9, mentions Greenwood, but only as one said to have guided the emigrants of 1844.

37. Carriger's description of his travel from Fort Hall to Raft River (by him called Cassia Creek) is serenely vague. The river he crossed on August 5 cannot have been the Snake and was therefore

the Portneuf; and what he calls a lake was probably a slough at or near the mouth of the Bannock River. He went 14 miles on the 6th to "a small Creek" which was probably Rock Creek, not mentioning that outstanding landmark, American Falls. On the 7th he possibly camped a little short of Raft River. On the 8th he may have written his diary entry originally, before amending it as printed, "thence up the Creek Crossing the same 15 [16? 10?] miles to the Creek a very good road."

38. The two days, August 8-9, evidently brought Carriger up the Raft River and its western affluent, Cassia Creek. Probably on the 8th he met Jesse Applegate, making for Fort Hall; but Carriger mentions none of the east-bound travelers encountered on the trail this year.

39. The camp of August 11 was in the City of Rocks area, much better described by Virgil Pringle three days later.

40. On August 12 camp was evidently made on Birch Creek, a tributary of Goose Creek, after passing from City of Rocks to the upper Raft, then crossing the Goose Creek Mountains by Granite Pass.

41. It would seem that the divide crossed this day was simply the ridge between Birch and Goose creeks.

42. As seen in the introductory remarks, John Lewis was Carriger's brother-in-law.

43. This day Carriger turned south from Goose Creek to camp in the northern arm of what became known as Thousand Springs Valley.

44. I have not elsewhere encountered the name "horse spring"; we are entitled to wonder if Carriger had it from Old Greenwood.

45. These hot springs in the southern arm of Thousand Springs Valley gave that valley its primary celebrity.

46. Again we may wonder if Old Greenwood was performing guide service, for Carriger clearly has taken the original wagon road down Bishops Creek rather than the route to the south via the Humboldt Wells which Greenwood opened in 1845. See the Taylor diary, Note 44.

47. The hot spring in Bishops Creek Canyon identifies this route in many overland narratives.

48. On the 20th Carriger came approximately to where the present Marys River joins Bishops Creek from the north.

49. This day Carriger camped in the vicinity of present Elko after having reached the site of Halleck on the 21st. His "sal a ratus fork" is presumably the North Fork of the Humboldt.

50. The child's death which Carriger recorded, the second in nine days, exemplifies the new character the California Trail acquired this year. Few such incidents can have occurred in prior years; Jacob R. Snyder mentioned none in 1845. The Chisman baby was buried in the

vicinity of present Osino.

51. Camp was made about 10 miles east of present Carlin, the site of which was reached the following day. The Jefferson map, which now begins to reflect the Carriger route, shows the wagon road from Fort Hall descending the south bank of the river here.

52. After passing down the Humboldt 10 miles through Moleen Canyon (Jefferson's "Wall Defile"), on the 24th, on the 25th Carriger left the river at present Carlin. Here Jefferson shows a "Robin Creek" which would be either Maggie Creek or Susie Creek. It would seem that Carriger's company passed what became known as "Emigrant Springs" and went on to reach the Humboldt again near present Beowawe, the area later well known as Gravelly Ford.

53. Carriger's mention this day of Meadows Vanderpool's company is very interesting, for it was one of the two at the front of the emigration on the Applegate Cutoff. Vanderpool is described by Tolbert Carter as an old mountaineer.

54. When Gregg's company separated from Carriger's and became a "pack Co." remains to be seen. Apparently Gregg was bound for Oregon. A. E. Garrison, in his recollections written in 1887, published in 1943 as *Life and Labour of Rev. A. E. Garrison* . . ., set out from the Missouri in the same company with Carriger. He says they organized on May 10 by electing as captain "Riley Gragg of Platte County Missouri" (compare Bryant's comment quoted in Note 10). This is the only source I have seen which supplies Gregg's first name, and aside from Carriger's, the only first-hand account of the portion of the 1846 emigration which crossed the Missouri at Iowa Point.

55. The 62 miles traveled between the 27th and the 31st brought Carriger to the "bad ridge" where James Frazier Reed later killed John Snyder, in the vicinity of present Iron Point.

56. The hot springs were at present Golconda.

57. Scott and Dearborn remain unidentified among the 1846 emigrants, whether to Oregon or to California; but for the battleground itself, near present Winnemucca, see the Jefferson and Reed maps.

58. For the junction with the Applegate Cutoff, see the Taylor diary, Notes 50 and 51.

59. The area below present Lovelock in early times boasted a considerable marsh or "lake," the last stage of the Humboldt above its ultimate "Sink."

60. Jefferson's map shows the "Trail the Pautes escaped with the stolen cattle from the sink of Mary River," east toward the Humboldt Mountains. Jefferson was more than two weeks behind Carriger, so it is evident that later-comers were preyed upon in their turn.

61. Carriger's is the fifth earliest diary recounting a crossing of the Forty Mile Desert, antedated only by Snyder in 1845 and by Clyman, Bryant, and Taylor in 1846.

62. As seen in the introductory sketch, Mrs. Wardlaw was Carriger's sister-in-law. Her baby was buried probably in the vicinity of present Sparks; Carriger overestimates the distances traveled in ascending the Truckee. For the crossings of the Truckee, compare the Jefferson map.

63. Carriger had now reached the Little Truckee. See the Taylor diary, Note 56.

64. Prosser Creek, as it is now called, had been named John Greenwood's Creek the previous year; Clyman on May 2, 1846, referred to it as Johns Creek. Jefferson uses the name Pine Creek.

65. The next few entries of the Carriger diary have prime importance, for it would appear that he is describing the pioneering of the route up Coldstream Valley. On the 21st he left Prosser Creek and its tributary Alder Creek, and crossed a "small hill" to reach Donner Creek above where it enters the Truckee River near present Truckee, California. Instead of going up the north side of Donner Lake as Taylor seems to have done, Carriger's company took a route south of the lake, ascending Coldstream Valley, up which the Southern Pacific grade today makes its deep hairpin bend in gaining elevation to reach the summit. The "foot of the mountain" was at present Horseshoe Bend, where Emigrant Canyon reaches Coldstream Valley from the heights above.

66. Compare Carriger's diary entries for September 21-22 with what he says in his autobiography, as quoted in the introductory sketch. It may be that the Greenwoods are primarily to be credited with this effort to improve upon the fearful difficulties at Donner Pass as described in the Taylor diary, Note 58. By this alternate route, Carriger reached the crest of the Sierra between Mount Judah and Mount Lincoln, about 1½ miles south of Donner Pass, and at an elevation some 200 feet higher than the 7,088 feet of Donner Pass. See Irene D. Paden, "Facts About the Blazing of the Gold Trail, Including a Few Never Before Published," *Pacific Historical Review,* February, 1949, vol. 18, pp. 3-13.

67. Obviously the lake Carriger reached on September 24 was Mary Lake in Summit Valley. The 8 miles would refer to the final ascent described the two previous days, for Mary Lake was only a mile north of where he gained the summit.

68. Jefferson locates several graves in Summit Valley, but not necessarily those of Carriger's father and sister-in-law. Refer again to Carriger's autobiography for these deaths, the burials, and his journey on to Johnson's Ranch.

DIARY OF VIRGIL K. PRINGLE

1. Near present St. Peters, on Dardenne Creek.

2. Pringle was traveling a ridge road between the watersheds of the Mississippi and the Missouri; from St. Charles to Camden, he followed essentially what is now the route of the Wabash Railroad. His "Auvaux" River is more easily recognized as the Loutre, Harrison's Branch as Clear Fork.

3. Evidently near Martinsburg, just beyond the Montgomery County line.

4. Pringle repeats his entry for this day in nearly the same words.

5. The Grand Prairie was a distinguishing feature of the divide along which Pringle was traveling.

6. Properly Cottleville in St. Charles County.

7. The route to Brunswick was past Foristelle, Pendleton, Montgomery City, Martinsburg, and Mexico. At Brunswick, beyond which Pringle crossed the Grand River, the Missouri reaches its northernmost point inside Missouri.

8. Moss Creek is the most southerly fork of Wakenda Creek. Here Pringle refers to the 1844 flood on which John Craig had commented.

9. Mathano (or Manthano) Brown's home appears to have been a couple of miles west of Camden. Mrs. Tabitha Brown, in her letter of August, 1854, says: "I expected all three of my children to accompany me, but Mathano was detained by sickness, and his wife was unwilling to leave her parents." This letter, originally printed in *Congressional Work,* June, 1903, is reprinted in Oregon Historical Society *Quarterly,* June, 1904, vol. 5, pp. 199-205.

10. Pringle may have crossed the Missouri at Waterloo, but possibly at Napoleon, a few miles to the west.

11. Blue Mills was situated on Little Blue Creek, east of Independence.

12. The Big Blue River of Missouri, sometimes confused with the Big Blue River of Kansas, much farther west.

13. Usually known as the Lone Elm, once called Elm or Round Grove, on present Cedar Creek.

14. The Oregon road separated from the Santa Fe Trail a little west of present Gardner, Kansas.

15. Compare the Jefferson map, which in the vicinity of the present Blue Mound shows variant routes used in 1846.

16. John Robinson; see Note 22 and Index.

17. This Shawnee was evidently Charles, one of three sons of the Shawnee chief Fish (otherwise known as William Jackson), who died in 1834. Charles Fish had been a government blacksmith or assistant smith among the Kansas (Kaw) Indians since 1839. The ferry was at present Topeka. See the McKinstry diary, Note 12.

18. Probably Soldier Creek. Compare McKinstry's diary.

19. This was Fool Chief's village, noted by Bryant (in the plural) at the Little Vermilion ("Black Paint Creek") on May 22. Beyond the Little Vermilion the trail turned northwesterly toward the crossing of the Big Blue.

20. Apparently an incident from the 1843 emigration to Oregon.

21. See Introduction for Parkman's account of this defection.

22. Parkman's diary tells of being delayed on the 25th by a broken axle, in consequence of which Keithly's four wagons camped farther on. Six days later he mentions overtaking Robinson's party of about 40 wagons and adds, "Keathley, with the 4 waggons that had joined us, was ahead about a mile. Disorder in both these parties." His book adds in connection with Keithly, "thenceforward for a week or two we were fellow travelers," which lightened the guard duty for both.

23. This company of 13 wagons was the Gordon-Dickenson party; see the McKinstry diary, Note 22.

24. Properly, this "Republican Fork" was the Little Blue. To Jefferson it was Pawnee Fork.

25. The Platte was reached just east of the site of Fort Kearny. Pringle was two days ahead of Carriger at the junction.

26. P. D. Papin's party. See Index references.

27. The prairie-dog towns along this stretch of the Platte were a novelty described by Edwin Bryant, Heinrich Lienhard, and many others.

28. The misfortunes of Elam Brown's company are a recurring theme in this book. John R. McBride, as quoted in the Introduction, tells of Brown's early prominence in that part of the migration which made an early departure from St. Joseph. Two biographical sketches, one published in *San Jose Pioneer,* January 26, 1878, the other separately as *Biography of Elam Brown, of Lafayette, Contra Costa County, California* (Martinez, 1879), concur in saying he was born in New York in 1797, moved to Ohio in 1804, to Illinois in 1818, and to the Platte Purchase of Missouri in 1837. With his wife, a daughter of Thomas Allen, he set out for California in 1846, as captain of a company of sixteen wagons. Assertedly, this train crossed the Missouri at St. Joseph on May 1, and by the time they reached the Forks of the Platte had increased in number to "about thirty wagons." The 1879 sketch says, "Soon after dark the cattle took a stampede, supposed to have been caused by buffaloes. After considerable trouble and a delay of one week in searching for them, they succeeded in finding all except 120 head, of which 62 were oxen. That was a serious loss. It left their teams very much broken up, but they managed to buy some cows from other trains, and by working those and what cows and oxen they had, they were enabled to proceed on their journey." The 1878 sketch says Brown was compelled to leave one of

his wagons and work four cows in his teams the rest of the way to California, "and they stood the trip equally as well as oxen." For the further fortunes of the Brown company, see Index.

29. Again, compare the Jefferson map.

30. Pringle's is one of the best accounts of Ash Hollow in 1846. Bryant came along six days later to find "near the mouth of 'Ash Hollow,' a small log-cabin, which had been erected last winter by some trappers, returning to the 'settlements,' who, on account of the snows, had been compelled to remain here until spring. This rude structure has, by the emigrants, been turned into a sort of general post-office. Numerous advertisements in manuscript are posted on its walls outside; descriptive of lost cattle, horses, etc. etc.; and inside, in a recess, there was a large number of letters deposited, addressed to persons in almost every quarter of the globe, with requests, that those who passed would convey them to the nearest post-office in the states. The place had something of the air of a cross-roads settlement; and we lingered around it some time, reading the advertisements and overlooking the letters." Compare McKinstry's diary for this day.

31. Pringle derives his name for Courthouse Rock from Samuel Parker's *Journal of an Exploring Tour Beyond the Rocky Mountains* . . . (Ithaca, 1838), pp. 62-63. Parker viewed the "old castle" from the other side of the Platte on July 21, 1835.

32. Compare Merrill J. Mattes, "Chimney Rock on the Oregon Trail," *Nebraska History,* March, 1955, vol. 36, pp. 1-26, with reproductions of many sketches of the Rock made between 1841 and 1874.

33. Afterward called Roubidoux Spring, for a younger Antoine Roubidoux who had traded in this area for the past ten years. Parkman encountered him on June 12.

34. This feasting of the Sioux was one of the notable events attendant on the 1846 emigration. Elam Brown took a prominent part in this affair, related at length in the biographical sketches cited in Note 28 above.

35. Still called the Warm Spring. It is instructive that Pringle calls the cutoff route over the hills the "old road" and the usual one.

36. Cottonwood Creek.

37. The two detachments of Clyman's party, which had separated at Independence Rock five days earlier, on June 21.

38. It is hard to believe that any part of this country had not been trapped since 1831.

39. Pringle crossed the North Platte a little above the site of Casper, fording without any trouble. The preceding winter had been an open one, so the river did not remain high, as in other years. Different was Taylor's experience, less than two weeks earlier.

40. The mineral spring on Poison Spider Creek.

41. Willow Spring.

42. Having made excellent progress, Pringle was one able to celebrate the Fourth of July at Independence Rock.

43. See the Taylor diary, Note 26. This camp was about 8 miles above Devils Gate, which Pringle does not mention.

44. Later well known as the Three Crossings.

45. Presumably "mountain fever."

46. Table Rock, a flat-topped eminence in South Pass, is now known as Pacific Butte.

47. Pringle this day crossed South Pass to camp on the Little Sandy. He does not mention the junction with the Greenwood Cutoff in continuing on by the Fort Bridger road.

48. Similarly Pringle does not mention the ruins of Bridger's trading post, to be seen near where he camped.

49. Pringle arrived at Fort Bridger two days after Hastings left there with the first wagons to attempt his cutoff. He had ascended Blacks Fork, not Hams Fork, to reach Bridger's post.

50. The Big Muddy, near present Carter, Wyoming. Next day Pringle reached and began to ascend the Little Muddy.

51. Pringle had again intersected the Greenwood Cutoff, which came down to the Bear River just south of Smiths Fork. By this route J. Quinn Thornton reached the Bear late the following afternoon.

52. Although he had been making good time, Pringle had lost ground relative to Taylor, who had arrived at the Soda Springs July 17, fifteen days before.

53. To Ross's Fork, actually a branch of the lower Portneuf.

54. As seen by his letter of August 9, Jesse Applegate kept on to Fort Hall, arriving on the 8th, not on the 9th, as we might infer from Pringle's diary. For further details, see Volume II. Had Pringle been three days farther along, he would have gone on to the Willamette by the old road, knowing nothing of the new Applegate Cutoff. According to David Goff's statement of April 3, 1847, reprinted in Volume II, the first Oregon company to take the new road, captained by Harrison Linville, encamped at the forks on the evening of August 7 and entered upon the cutoff the following morning.

55. City of Rocks.

56. The northern arm of Thousand Springs Valley.

57. Pringle's diary so contrasts with Carriger's as to suggest that he took the route via Humboldt Wells in preference to that down Bishops Creek Canyon.

58. Emigrant Wells. Pringle had left the Humboldt at present Carlin, and next day returned to it a few miles east of Beowawe.

59. Pringle wasted few words while descending the Humboldt, but his diary becomes more descriptive as he reaches the Applegate Cut-

off; it is our only daily record for this route in 1846. J. Quinn Thornton's diary containing his entries after August 22, when he left Thousand Springs Valley en route to the Humboldt, was afterward lost, and his book relates subsequent events from memory.

60. Antelope Springs, 12 miles into the desert. Pringle's estimates of mileage must be used with caution.

61. Rabbit Hole Springs. See Lindsay Applegate's narrative, quoted in the Introduction.

62. Black Rock Springs.

63. In his Waybill, more fully discussed in Volume II, and printed in *Oregon Spectator,* April 6, 1848, Jesse Applegate gives the distance to this "Last Hot Spring" as 5 miles from Black Rock Spring. Thornton agrees with Pringle in locating the "Great Hot Springs" 8 miles on.

64. Called by Applegate in 1848 "Salt Valley," now Mud Meadows.

65. High Rock Canyon, one of the most noteworthy stretches of the Applegate and Lassen cutoffs. See Irene D. Paden's modern description in *Prairie Schooner Detours* (New York, 1949), pp. 175-181.

66. Between High Rock Canyon and what is now known as Little High Rock Canyon, up which Pringle traveled next day.

67. Most teams traveling this route were worn down by the deserts just crossed.

68. Compare Pringle's entry for September 29; perhaps 21 wagons were in his train.

69. Travel on the 16th and 17th took Pringle across what is now known as Forty-nine Hill via Forty-nine Canyon, called by Jesse Applegate "Little Mountain Pass." According to Applegate, "Four miles from the last water of high rock creek to a good camp at a running brook, two miles further there are springs left of the road, fine grass and water at the pass on both sides of the ridge."

70. Pringle had now entered Surprise Valley, on the eastern side of which this warm spring rises. Applegate gave the distance as 12 miles from Little Mountain Pass.

71. Applegate's note says: "The road in 1846 run directly across the dry lake [Middle Alkali Lake] to plum creek about 12 miles from the warm springs.—*The front company last year, having nooned at the warm springs*—left the road, and struck off to the left for the foot of the mountain in order sooner to make a camp, the rest of the emigrants followed—the old road is 3 or 4 miles shortest. . . ." (The words I have italicized were inadvertently omitted by the Misses Read and Gaines when they reprinted the Applegate waybill in their *Gold Rush.*) The incident Pringle relates, of livestock shot with arrows, may be that recalled by A. E. Garrison (*op. cit.,* p. 32), though by Garrison placed at Goose Lake: "here the Indians made a break

on us, killing several head of our cattle and driving off quite a number, leaving many wagons almost without a team, here my old friend Mr. Lancefield lost several of his oxen but supplied the place with cows. . . ."

72. The Warner Range was crossed by what became known as Lassen or Fandango Pass.

73. Near the mouth of Willow Creek, from which the road followed the south shore of Goose Lake. The later Lassen trail to the California mines separated from the Applegate road along the stretch Pringle traversed this day, turning more to the southwest and making for Pit River.

74. An affluent of Fletchers Creek, down which Pringle moved next day. He traveled north of the "Timbered Mountain" mentioned by Lindsay Applegate, as quoted in the Introduction. The mountain, still so called, rises about 12 miles west of Goose Lake.

75. Having camped on the 25th near the present Steele Swamp Ranch and on the 26th near the point Lost River flows from Clear Lake, Pringle camped this day at the north shore of that "pretty lake," now a reservoir.

76. The Modoc Mountains, hills separating Clear Lake and Tule Lake. The night encampment was near present Malin, Oregon.

77. Compare the entry for September 14. Pringle had now reached the forefront of the emigration. The Modoc Indian incursion he describes is recounted at much greater length by Tolbert Carter in his recollections printed in Oregon Pioneer Association, *Transactions,* 1906, pp. 67-72. See also the sketch of Albert L. Alderman in Elwood Evans, ed. *History of the Pacific Northwest. . . .* (Portland, 1889, 2 vols.), vol 2, pp. 190-191.

78. Like the Applegates and many others at the time, Pringle supposed Lost River to be the upper Sacramento. It flows out of Clear Lake and into Tule Lake. The "stone bridge" by which Pringle crossed is about 2 miles east of present Merrill, Oregon.

79. South of present Keno, Oregon.

80. From Pringle's description, the Applegate Road in 1846 forded the Klamath River at the site of Keno, then crossed a ridge to camp on the river several miles below. Later, the road bypassed Keno to the west, going through Bear Valley, over the shoulder of Chase Mountain, and fording the Klamath near Pringle's place of encampment. Compare Buena Cobb Stone, "Southern Route into Oregon: Notes and a New Map," *Oregon Historical Quarterly,* June, 1946, vol. 47, pp 135-154, in which this other route is discussed.

81. Between Buck Mountain and Hayden Mountain. The road Pringle follows the next few days runs somewhat north of the present

Oregon State Highway 66, the "Green Springs Highway."

82. Having camped on the 6th in Long Prairie, Pringle this day crossed the northern shoulder of Parker Mountain to camp probably on Jenny Creek in Round Prairie. A. E. Garrison says, "We crossed the Klamath river just at the outlet of the Lake at a very rocky ford, next was the Siskiou mountains which was heavily timbered and a great job it was to cut a road across, but we had a long way back provisioned and sent young men ahead to open the road, so we got over the mountain quite well."

83. One of the sources of Emigrant Creek.

84. South of the Green Springs Grade used by the present highway in crossing from Keene Creek to Emigrant Creek drainage.

85. Pringle encamped on Bear Creek north of present Ashland, having intersected the California pack trail, which wound down from the Siskiyou Mountains to the south.

86. After camping near Medford on October 12, Pringle reached the Rogue on the 14th near the site of Fort Lane.

87. At the present town of Rogue River.

88. After camping near Grants Pass on the 17th and near Sexton Mountain on the 18th, Pringle moved on to what ever since has been known as Grave Creek. Tolbert Carter interestingly tells of the burial and the subsequent history of the Crowley grave.

89. Pringle provides only an eliptical account of the working of the road through the hereafter celebrated "Umpqua Canyon," the Canyon Creek Pass road by which U. S. 99 today makes its way to Canyonville on the South Umpqua River. He seems to say that the wet season began on October 26, but at Oregon City George Gary wrote in his diary on the 28th, "Meridian it commences raining as though winter is about to set in. We have had very fine weather up to this time." Far to the south, this same storm turned back the Donner Party, just short of Donner Pass. Edwin Bryant says that the rain began at Sutter's on the night of the 28th. Now emigrants on both the California and Oregon trails would begin to know real hardship and suffering.

90. Evidently the wagon was Tabitha Brown's. In her letter of 1854, speaking of "the Umpqua Mountains, 12 miles through," she says: "I rode through in three days at the risk of my life, on horseback, having lost my wagon and all that I had but the horse I was on. Our families were the first that started through the canyon, so that we got through the mud and rocks much better than those that followed. Out of hundreds of wagons, only one came through without breaking. The canyon was strewn with dead cattle, broken wagons, beds, clothing, and everything but provisions, of which latter we were nearly all destitute. Some people were in the canyon two or three

weeks before they could get through. . . ." Compare the accounts from the *Oregon Spectator* in Volume II.

91. Having got along to Myrtle Creek on the 2nd and Round Prairie on the 3rd, Pringle tells of the departure of his son to seek help in the Willamette Valley. Octavius, then 14 years old, amplifies the record of these weeks in the reminiscences noted in the introductory sketch.

92. Pringle crossed Roberts Mountain on November 4, camped near Roseburg on the 5th, and reached the North Umpqua River near present Winchester on the 6th.

93. Probably near Deady on Sutherlin Creek.

94. The Elk Creek of 1846 is the present Callapooya Creek.

95. Evidently on upper Yoncalla Creek in Pleasant Valley. Next day Pringle moved on to Scotts Valley.

96. The four miles on November 17 brought Pringle perhaps to Lees Creek, an affluent of present Elk Creek.

97. On the 18th Pringle probably camped southeast of Anlauf on Buck Creek; on the 19th reached and began ascending Pass Creek, perhaps encamping near Comstock; on the 20th encamped beyond Divide; on the 21st reached the site of Cottage Grove; and on the 22nd moved along to the vicinity of Creswell Butte. He now proudly notes that his wagons were among the first to reach the Willamette Valley on the Applegate Cutoff. Although in the next entry Pringle speaks of being about seventy miles "from settlement," Eugene Skinner already had begun erecting a cabin on the site of Eugene, which Pringle reached on the 25th.

98. Near Junction City.

99. A. E. Garrison has much to tell of Lancefield during the previous weeks, and also says that "he and Mr. Lebo as soon as they struck the Willamette dug out a large canoe and leaving their wagon and cattle descended the river with their families. . . ." Tabitha Brown relates the fortunes of Pringle's family during his absence.

100. The fortunate encounter with Orus Brown on the Long Tom River (with its variously spelled name) is thus described by Tabitha Brown: "Orus Brown's party was six days ahead of ours in starting; he had gone down the old emigrant route and reached the settlements in September. Soon after he heard of the suffering emigrants at the south and set off in haste with four pack horses and provisions for our relief. He met Mr. Pringle and turned about. In a few days they were at our camp. . . . Orus, by his persuasive insistence, encouraged us to more effort to reach the settlements. Five miles from where we had encamped we fell into the company of half-breed French and Indians with packhorses. We hired six of them and pushed ahead again. Our provisions were becoming short and we were once more

on an allowance until reaching the first settlers. There our hardest struggles were ended. On Christmas day, at 2 p.m. I entered the house of a Methodist minister, the first house I had set my feet in for nine months. . . ."

101. At the confluence of the Willamette and McKenzie rivers, where Pringle had decided to "locate." But he settled in Marion County.

JOURNAL OF THOMAS HOLT

1. Presumably Holt set out from the French settlement near Salem. What he calls the Rickreal (now Rickreal), as often appears in early documents as La Creole. (The origins of the name have been endlessly debated.) After crossing this stream, he went on to camp on what he calls the "north fork," the Little Luckiamute River in the vicinity of present Lewisville.

2. It would seem that Holt's Mr. Jones was John Jones, earlier a member of Jesse Applegate's exploring company. After getting back to the settlements with Applegate, he started out again to meet the incoming emigration, accompanied by Brown and Allen, sons of Elam Brown and David Allen, and several others. Jones, Thornton says, "brought two large fat cattle, for the relief of the almost starving emigrants. These he killed and sold to the emigrants, after driving them several hundred miles through the wilderness, at a price that did not exceed that which he had paid for them in the settlements." Thornton says he met this relief party October 18, on the Rogue River. Jones turned back to the settlements, and evidently was thought to be preparing a second relief when Holt came along.

3. Apparently the present Soap Creek.

4. The murder of John Newton, who with his wife had been mentioned by Edwin Bryant near Independence on May 8 ("recently from Virginia, and bound for California"), was a notable tragedy of 1846 and has given name to Newton Creek, remarked below. Peter H. Burnett relates the story by hearsay in Volume II; J. Quinn Thornton, traveling in close proximity to the Newtons at the time, gives it attention in his book; and it is referred to by Bryant and by Applegate in his 1848 Waybill.

5. South of present Corvallis, at which place Tolbert Carter recalls that a pole cabin already existed, raised by J. C. Avery. Carter (north-bound) says Marys River was crossed, "as near as I can recollect, near where the grist mill now stands."

6. North of present Monroe. The name of the present Long Tom River has been spelled so many ways as to defy accounting; the root seems to be an Indian word.

7. James Campbell had previously been mentioned in connection with Carriger's diary. A sketch of his life in Sarah Hunt Steeves, *op. cit.,* pp. 86-87, says that he went on to the Willamette Valley, for supplies, and that during his absence J. H. Bridges took charge of the party. "The eldest daughter, Mary Campbell, died during these trying weeks and almost every soul in the train was ill. . . . when Mr. Campbell returned to meet the train after having reached the settlement, there was much rejoicing. . . ." He afterward settled in the Waldo Hills, dying there in 1872. The Mr. Harris mentioned by Holt must be Moses (Black) Harris. The term "the kanyon" as used here always means the one in the Umpqua Mountains south of present Canyonville.

8. Goose Creek, where Holt mentions this new relief effort, would seem to have been at present Eugene.

9. Holt does not specifically identify the men who turned back on December 11. He gives the names of those who went on with him as Baptiste Gardapie and Q. Delore. (Jean Baptiste Gardepie had come out to Oregon in 1811 as an overland Astorian.)

10. Alanson Beers had been a prominent member of the Methodist community in Oregon since 1837, described by H. H. Bancroft as "a man of low stature, dark complexion, thin features, and rigid alike in his views of religion and social propensities, an honest, worthy character, entitled to respect."

11. Apparently Holt met the first families near Creswell Butte, the others near the site of Cottage Grove.

12. Holt seems to say that he traveled 12 miles and nooned (probably on Pass Creek near Aunlauf), then went on nine miles more to what is clearly Elk Creek in Scotts Valley.

13. Holt applies the name "north fork of Elk river" to the present Cabin Creek. He apparently met the families of Ezekiel Kennedy, R. B. Hall, Henry Croizen (or Croysnt), and one Lovlen or Lovelin.

14. On this day Holt crossed Cabin Creek and Calapooya Creek, by him called the north and south forks of Elk river, and camped south of Oakland. J. A. Cornwall is discussed in Volume II; see Index. Rice Dunbar had been the captain of the company in which J. Thornton traveled. Next day Holt went on to Newton Creek on the northern outskirts of present Roseburg.

15. "Boston man" was a common expression on the Northwest Coast for Americans, harking back to ship captains trading on the coast.

16. The North Umpqua was crossed at present Winchester.

17. The last company of emigrants, encountered at or near Roberts Creek, west of Canyonville, consisted of the families of James Townsend, John Baker, David Butterfield, and one Crump.

18. Perhaps Rock Creek is the present Parrott Creek, south of Roseburg.

19. The spring branch was south of Winchester, where the North Umpqua was recrossed the next day.

20. Q. Delore, one of the half-breeds with Holt.

21. At Calapooya Creek, north of Oakland, again.

22. See Holt's entry for December 10. Possibly this was William Burrows, then a resident of the Tualatine Plains. Holt was again on Cabin Creek.

23. As remarked in the Pringle diary, Note 89, the savage winter storms which assailed the Donner Party in the Sierra Nevada were part of a weather-pattern common to the whole Pacific area. George Garry's diary at Oregon City remarks the continuously bad weather after October 28, a characteristic entry for November 23 being: "Dark, Dark, Dark weather. Rain, Rain, Rain. The weather is truly rather gloomy." On December 17: "The sun smiles upon us again, an uncommon event these days." On December 24, "the sun shines today," but again on December 28: "Our weather is cloudy and rainy. It is sometimes hard to keep the blues away in this dark and gloomy weather."

24. Near the head of Pleasant Valley. Holt omits from this journal entries for December 29-31 while moving north to Pass Creek.

25. At Cottage Grove, having crossed the Calapooya Mountains.

26. At Eugene.

27. Holt camped north of present Junction City on January 8, and perhaps near Dawson on the 9th; I suppose "Scott's bute" to have been the present Green Peak.

28. I have not identified this Williams specifically, but a "Williams' Mill" is shown on the Little Luckiamute in a map of the "Wallamette Valley" made by George Gibbs and Edward A. Starling in April and May, 1851. This map, in the National Archives, provides much enlightening information as far south as the "Callapooya Range."

29. Presumably this is again a reference to Black Harris, and helps to establish where he lived before leaving Oregon in the spring of 1847.

30. See Holt's entry for December 19.

31. James Nesmith, an emigrant of 1843, was a a son-in-law of David Goff, as will be seen in Volume II.

32. Perhaps Thomas D. Keizer, who established himself north of Salem.

33. Clearly, all had been done out of Holt's humanitarian feelings.

34. In the next issue after printing Holt's journal, March 18, 1847, the *Oregon Spectator* said: "A subscription has been opened at this office for the relief of Thomas Holt and others, who went to the succor of the immigrants by the southern route, and thereby incurred indebtedness which they cannot sustain. Call and subscribe." Let us hope the response was liberal.

DIARY OF GEORGE McKINSTRY

1. See the accounts of the organization of the Russell company by George L. Curry and Nathan J. Putnam printed in Volume II. The company was then on Indian Creek, west of the Missouri line. Edwin Bryant, who acted as chairman, says that George Harlan and his party attended but "moved a postponement of the election of officers, until the emigrants had passed the Kansas river. This motion was rejected. Mr. H. then requested leave to withdraw from the meeting, and by a vote his request was granted. He then withdrew, stating, however, before he left, his belief that companies of moderate size would travel with much more convenience and celerity than large companies, and that his party added to those on the ground, he believed, would render the train too unwieldy for convenience and progress. This view was afterwards found to be entirely correct."

2. McKinstry's travel of 35 miles is plainly excessive. Bryant gives the distance as 6 miles, to "a small branch, (head of Blue Creek,)" so McKinstry's "Camp Creek" was doubtless upper Indian Creek, east of present Olathe.

3. Bryant went 16 miles this day to a camp on what would appear to have been present Bull Creek, west of Gardner, Kansas.

4. According to Bryant, the largest part of the company camped on the Wakarusa after going 15 miles, but a number of wagons remained behind. He tells of crossing "a diminutive tributary of the Wakarusa creek," possibly the Little Wakarusa, but McKinstry's "Sugar Creek" more likely was present Captain Creek.

5. Much more is said of Lilburn W. Boggs, Missouri's governor from 1836 to 1850, in Volume II. On May 11, before the departure from Indian Creek, Bryant mentions a visit from Boggs during the evening (a term which in these pages usually means afternoon). Boggs then returned to Independence, stating "that it was impossible for his wagons to come up with us until Thursday [May 14]."

6. Boggs arrived in company with J. Quinn Thornton, who had fallen in with him along the road from Independence on the afternoon of the 13th. They reached camp on May 15, not the 16th, as McKinstry's entry would indicate.

7. The company moved on this day to Shunganunga Creek, east of present Topeka. A member of one of the advance trains arrived from Independence with a *Missouri Republican* having news of "the first overt acts of hostility between Mexico and the United States. . . an account of the defeat and capture of a company of dragoons on the Rio Grande, under the command of Captain Thornton, by the Mexicans, and also of the supposed critical situation of the United States troops composing the command of General Z. Taylor." Notwithstanding, says Bryant, "none of the emigrants to California, so far as I

could learn, manifested a disposition to turn back. . . ."

8. Bryant relates that on the evening of the 17th, after encamping, "it appeared from a speech delivered by Mr. Dunleavy, that a portion of the company had determined to separate from the main party, being dissatisfied with its present organization." Next day, in a conference, "it was proposed that the company should divide, it being too numerous and cumbrous for convenient progress. Those who were in favor of remaining with the originally organized company were requested to move towards the ferry. Thirty-five of the wagons moved forward, and the remainder separated from them." Despite the fact that the Dunleavy company for the time being remained behind, they got ahead when the Russell company paused on the north bank of the Kansas; their movements for a time may be followed by the dated campsites on the Jefferson map. McKinstry himself crossed the Kansas and camped on Soldier Creek.

9. Alphonso W. Boone was one of three grandsons of Daniel Boone who went to Oregon this year. His sister Panthea was Bogg's wife.

10. The name of the St. Louisan, Hiram Ames, recurs in these two volumes. He was killed the following December on the Salinas plains in a skirmish known as the battle of Natividad. The McKinstry Papers in the California State Library contain an inventory of his estate showing that Ames became associated with the Harlan party. Among the papers are notes signed by George Harlan on August 24, 1846, concerning the purchase of a mule, another signed by Harlan four days later agreeing to pay one mule and $10 within three months; and a fourth, signed by Harlan and P. L. Wimmer September 10, 1846, agreeing to return within 15 days of arrival in California, a brown mule or one of equal value, plus the sum of $10. Ame's personal property included books valued at $4.13 (a copy of Fremont's report was valued at 25 cents). Wimmer was administrator, and one of his accounts, September 20, 1847, charges $50 for hauling Ame's effects from Salt Lake to Sutter's, boarding him twelve weeks at $5 per week, etc. These details reflect the history of the Hastings Cutoff.

11. McKinstry had got ahead of the Russell company, and while waiting for it to come along began to write up this diary, as the next few lines disclose.

12. The reference to the Methodist mission seems muddled. The mission, which terminated this same year, had been founded in 1836 on American Chief Creek, 12 miles above where the company crossed the Kansas. Russell had first contemplated saving money by fording the river there, but in fear of rain and rising water used the ferry at the Topeka site. Presumably the "half breed Frenchman" was the Shawnee, (Charles?) Fish, mentioned a few days earlier by Virgil Pringle, though for at least three years Joseph Papin had maintained

a ferry here.

13. When Bryant fell in with Benjamin S. Lippincott and his companion near Ash Hollow on June 19, he gave the man's name as Burgess, rather than Benton, "two gentlemen who left us at Kansas, and had joined some of the advance companies."

14. Harlan's party is mentioned in Note 1, as elsewhere in this work. An account of their experiences appears in the book by his nephew, Jacob Wright Harlan, *California '46 to '88* (San Francisco, 1888), and incidental information is found in W. W. Allen and R. B. Avery, *California Gold Book* (San Francisco & Chicago, 1893), a narrative primarily concerned with the Wimmer family. Heinrich Lienhard also set out from the frontier in the Harlan company. For a considerable distance Josiah Morin served as captain. Morin eventually went to Oregon, while the Harlans kept on to California.

15. The Kansas or Kaw Indians had been much corrupted by civilization but emigrants felt safer in their country than when exposed to Pawnee depredations, beyond the Little Vermilion.

16. For Andrew Jackson Grayson, John C. Buchanan, and the brothers Charles and Nathan Putnam, see the letters printed in Volume II.

17. Bryant does not mention this search for a campsite. Presumably his companion was William Kirkendall. (The name appears in these pages as Kirquendall, Kuquendall, Kuyhendall, etc. Which form, if any, is correct, I have not determined. An elder man of the same name, Isaac, was evidently his father.)

18. The Reeds and Donners joined the Russell company on May 19, bringing the total to 50 wagons, by Bryant's accounting. The six wagons which swelled the total on May 20 remain to be identified.

19. With the accession of Boone's 11 wagons on May 21, the Russell company was restored to approximately its original size.

20. Fool Chief's village, was usually found on Soldier Creek, but this summer the Soldier Creek site was deserted. Fool Chief was on the Little Vermilion, to a branch of which Bryant and McKinstry apply the name Hurricane Creek. Bryant met and described "Ki-he-ga-wa-chuck-ee, (words importing 'the rashly brave,' or 'fool-hardy.')" this same day at what he calls Black Paint Creek or the Sandy, alternate names for the Little (or Red) Vermilion.

21. Bryant says: "Several of the young men from our camp visited the nearest Kansas village after dark. They had not been in the village long, before the cry of 'Pawnee! Pawnee! was raised by the Indians, and several guns were discharged immediately. This alarm was probably raised by the Indians, to rid themselves of their white visitors, and the *ruse* was successful. The Pawnees, as I learned, had a short time previously made an attack upon the Kansas, and besides killing a number of the latter, had burnt one of their villages."

22. According to Bryant, that same morning, the 22nd, "thirteen wagons, about half of which belonged to Mr. Gordon, of Jackson county, Mo., separated from the main party, assigning as a reason therefor, that the company was too large, and that as a consequence of this, our progress was too slow for them. This is the second division in our party which has taken place since we started, and there is a strong possibility that soon there will be others. A restlessness of disposition, and dissatisfaction from trivial causes, lead to these frequent changes among the emigrating parties." Joseph Gordon and Gallant D. Dickenson were the prime movers in this party. Some account of the latter is given by his daughter-in-law, Luella Dickenson, *Reminiscences of a Trip across the Plains in 1846 and Early Days in California* (San Francisco, 1904). Beyond the Big Blue, some members of the Harlan train joined the company captained by Dickenson, including Lienhard and other German-speaking emigrants, but in the characteristic fashion of 1846, split off again beyond the crossing of the South Platte. If the Dickenson party applied for readmission to the Russell company this date, the reason was alarm over the stories told about the Pawnees.

23. This would be, presumably, the Little Vermilion, referred to by McKinstry the day before as the Sandy, and by Jefferson called Kaw C.

24. The Russell company had now left the banks of the Kansas to make for the Big Blue, as shown by the Jefferson map, which illuminates all these entries in McKinstry's diary.

25. Without mentioning this incident, Bryant tells of meeting during the afternoon four trappers returning to the settlements from the Rockies, accompanied by several Delawares, "all of whom spoke English so as to be understood."

26. Jefferson applies the name Spring C. to what is clearly Rock Creek, already beginning to be known by that name.

27. Jefferson shows the Big (Black) Vermilion to be a tributary of the Kansas, rather than of the Big Blue.

28. The storm that had raised the Big Blue so it could not be crossed occasioned the first of the delays which would finally bring the Donner Party to its fate. The Harlan train and the Dickenson party had crossed the river before the waters rose, therefore could keep going. So could the Dunleavy company in which Jefferson was traveling.

29. It would seem that McKinstry's sympathies lay with the "Young Men" in these proceedings. Long accounts of the occurrence are given by Bryant and by the writers of letters in Volume II. Thornton says: "A man named E—, made use of violent language against our leader, Col. Russell, and the sub-captain, Mr. Jacob, a modest and amiable young man. E— had been disappointed in not

being elected to the latter post. He finally moved the appointment of a committee to try the officers, when charged with neglect of duty, or improper treatment of any of the party. The motion prevailed, whereupon the officers resigned. A few moment's reflection showed the evil consequences of permitting E— to control in any degree the company. The resolution was rescinded by a large majority, and the former officers re-elected by acclamation." This incident may be one explanation of why Ewing turned back to the States after reaching Fort Laramie.

30. Bryant and Thornton have longer accounts of the decision to construct the "Blue River Rover."

31. The death and burial of Sarah Keyes was one notable event in 1846 trail history; see Index.

32. Robert Cadden Keyes had left Illinois for Oregon the previous year, only to end up in California. It was evidently a misunderstanding on McKinstry's (and Bryant's) part to think that he would come east to meet his mother; yet he may have thought of meeting the Reed family on the trail this summer. Instead he went up to Oregon by the pack trail, as will be seen hereafter.

33. J. A. Cornwall ended up in distressed condition on the Applegate Cutoff. See Index.

34. This arrival is mentioned neither by Bryant nor by Thornton.

35. Bryant says Judge "Bowlin's" child died on the 27th.

36. Not the least interesting entry in McKinstry's diary is this record that it was he who carved its enduring name on Alcove Spring. (For photographs, see Charles Kelly, *Salt Desert Trails,* Salt Lake City, 1930, pp. 52, 54, and for a modern account of the locality, on the McNew Ranch 6 miles north of present Blue Rapids, see Irene D. Paden, *The Wake of the Prairie Schooner,* New York, 1943, pp. 48-52.) Bryant describes the discovery of Alcove Spring on the afternoon of May 27. J. F. Reed carved his name and the date, "26 May 1846," at Alcove Spring. Thornton says it was "John Denton, an Englishman from Sheffield," later to die in the snows of the Sierra, who carved upon "a decent slab of stone" the inscription "Mrs. Sarah Keyes, died May 29, 1846: Aged 70," marking the grave near camp which James Clyman was to note a few weeks later, and many travelers after him.

37. Much difficulty, says Bryant, "was experienced in working the boat, on account of the rapidity of the stream and the great weight of many of the wagons. The current was so strong, that near the shore, where the water was not more than three or four feet in depth, the strength of a man could with difficulty breast it. One of the canoes was swamped on the western side in drawing the third wagon from it." By his account and Thornton's, nine wagons and their contents were ferried over this afternoon.

38. Bryant and Thornton vividly depict the labors of this exhausting day.

39. "Near our camp," remarks Bryant, "there is a dead ox [probably killed by lightning], and two graves of children, which have died and been buried within the last four days. A stone with the inscription, 'May 28, 1846,' stands at the head of one of the graves; at the head of the other, there is a small wooden cross. One of these graves would be that of the Morin child.

40. Here McKinstry performs a service to history by relating events that Thornton, so verbose usually, saw fit to omit from his narrative; described here is the inception of the Rice Dunbar company. On June 1 Bryant says: "There has been for several days, a very troublesome dispute between two Oregon emigrants, partners for the journey, one owning the wagon and the other the oxen. The claimant of the oxen insists upon his right to take them from the wagon. The proprietor of the wagon denies this right. The difference was brought to a crisis on the road to-day, by a personal encounter produced by an attempt of the ox claimant to take the oxen from the wagon, and thus to leave it to move along by the best mode that could be invented for such an exigency." On June 2 Bryant finishes off the tale:

"A scene of angry altercation, threatening to terminate in violence and blood, occurred last night about eleven o'clock, during the sitting of the committee of arbitration on the oxen and wagon controversy which I mentioned yesterday. Happily, through the interposition of those roused from their slumbers by the loud threats, epithets, and language of defiance, which passed between the parties at variance and their respective friends, the affair was quieted without more serious consequences. This morning the men composing the company were summoned, at an early hour, to meet at the guard-tent for the purpose of adopting measures for the prevention of similar outbreaks, disturbing the peace and threatening the lives to an indefinite extent, of the party.

"The two individuals at variance about their oxen and wagon, were emigrating to Oregon, and some eighteen or twenty wagons, now travelling with us, were bound to the same place. It was proposed, in order to relieve ourselves from the consequences of disputes in which we had no interest, that all the Oregon emigrants should, in a respectful manner and a friendly spirit, be requested to separate themselves from the California emigrants, and start on in advance of us. This proposition was unanimously carried, and the spirit in which it was made prevented any bad feeling, which otherwise might have resulted from it. The Oregon emigrants immediately withdrew their wagons from the *corral* and proceeded on their way."

Although Thornton borrowed liberally from Bryant's book in writ-

ing his own up to this point, he limited himself to the austere notation on June 2: "Twenty wagons, including mine—all for Oregon,
except Mr. [William Squire] Clark's—separated from the California
wagons, and proceeded on in advance." A. B. Rabbeson, another
member of the party, related the affair to H. H. Bancroft in 1878 as
follows: "Thornton had fitted out a wagon with a man by the name
of Good [John B. Goode]. Good had furnished the means and Thornton had furnished the brains, and the means & brains together did not
work very well. They cut the wagon in two and gave Thornton half
and the other half to Good; and divided the team. Thornton went on
with the Californians although he had started for Oregon. He had a
wife and Good had none. The Californians were stronger than the
Oregonians, and the consequence was in a meeting to settle the difficulty, they decided that the Wagon and team had to go with Thornton,
because he was a man of family, and Good was a single man. That
caused trouble; and the consequence was a bigger force of men was
with the Oregonians. The Oregonians by force took the wagon out
of the train, and divided the team and wagon & gave each half. The
whole party got mixed up in the dispute. The amount of it was,
that Good was to furnish the means, and Thornton having nothing
was to take a proportionate part of the labour on his shoulders.
Instead of that he did nothing. He took advantage of his position
and got Goods temper up. Both the Oregonian & Californian Company divided again. . . . " (Antonio B. Rabbeson, Growth of Towns,
MS., Bancroft Library.) Here compare Thornton's entry for July 8,
at Willow Spring, and his slightly more explicit account in his 1878
address to the Oregon Pioneer Association, there referring to his
antagonist as "G."

When in subsequent entries McKinstry speaks of the Oregon company, he is to be understood as referring to the train in which Thornton traveled henceforth. By the same token, the Thornton narrative
now becomes a separate trail chronicle.

41. These Shawnees duly reached the frontier, as seen in Volume II.

42. Bryant describes this same affray, which might have been more
serious except for the intervention of William Kirkendall. He also
mentions the upsetting of a wagon "belonging to a German emigrant
named Keyesburgh, whose wife carried in her arms a small child,
and was in a delicate situation," the woman and child escaping without
material injury. This is the first mention in the 1846 trail record of
the family so unhappily celebrated in the annals of the Donner Party.

43. A demonstration of why no dependence could be placed upon
hunting to subsist a party beyond the limits of the buffalo. Bryant
mentions the fine, fat doe shot by Grayson.

44. Bryant's wagon was injured in crossing one of the gravelly
streams this day, compelling him to stop and repair it, a typical trail

exigency: "A fire was lighted, irons heated, and the 'art and mystery' of blacksmithing, without anvil, and with axes and hatchets for hammers, in the course of two hours repaired the injury. The train in the mean time moved on, and we were left far in the rear."

45. "Our amateur hunters, several of whom have been out all day, brought in no game. They saw large numbers of antelope, but never were so successful as to approach within rifle-shot of them." (Bryant)

46. Bryant describes the second accident to his wagon, the breaking of an axletree. The job of repair was done by "Mr. Eddy, a carriage-maker by trade," afterward of Donner Party celebrity. Thornton tells of the meeting of the Oregonians with the Pawnees, and the fraternal embrace given the Pawnee chief by Rice Dunbar.

47. Bryant tells much the same story as McKinstry about Oregonians and Pawnees.

48. This company was the Craig-Cooper party in which Nicholas Carriger was traveling. For Bryant's comment, see the Carriger diary, Note 10. On June 13 Thornton "came up with thirty wagons and a great number of cattle from that portion of Missouri known as 'The Platte Country.' They were a part of a company consisting originally of sixty wagons that had been ahead of us, the proprietors of which, not being able to agree, had finally consented to disagree, and to separate in peace."

49. McKinstry does not mention the fur traders' boats encountered this day. Bryant writes on the 10th: "We saw from our encampment this morning eight small boats, loaded, as we ascertained by the aid of a glass, with bales of furs. The boats were constructed of light plank, and were what are called 'Mackinaw boats.' The water of the river is so shallow, that the men navigating this fleet were frequently obliged to jump into the stream, and with their strength force the boats over the bars or push them into deeper water." Bryant also tells of a similar encounter late on the morning of June 11. He came upon a man in a buckskin shirt, pantaloons, and moccasins leaning upon his rifle: "he informed me that his name was Bourdeau;—that he was from St. Charles, Mo., and was one of a party which left a small trading-post on the Platte, a few miles below Fort Laramie, early in May. They were navigating two 'Mackinaw boats' loaded with buffalo skins, and were bound for the nearest post on the Missouri. He stated that they had met with continual obstructions and difficulties on their voyage from its commencement, owing to the lowness of the water, although their boats, when loaded, drew but fifteen inches. They had at length found it impossible to proceed, and had drawn their boats to the shore of the river, and landed their furs. Their intention now was to procure wagons if they could, and wheel their cargo into the settlements. Bryant mentioned among the members of this party "Mr. Richard, Mr. Branham, formerly of Scott county, Ky., a half-breed

Mexican, an Indian, and several creole Frenchmen, of Missouri."
(Perhaps the Mexican was the "Hosea" or Jose who subsequently
served the Mississippi Saints, as noted in the Introduction.)

50. More informatively, Bryant says on June 13: "The wood-
work of many of the wagon-wheels have contracted so much from the
effects of the dry atmosphere on the Platte, that the tires have become
loose, and require resetting. There being sufficient wood to make the
fires necessary for this purpose at this encampment, it was determined
that we should remain for the day." Grayson and Boggs, who had
crossed the Platte on a buffalo hunt the day before, returned successful.

51. Bryant had gone forward on the 14th, summoned by Carriger's
party, as previously seen, for a medical exigency. He adds little to
McKinstry's now rather laconic entries until his train came up on
the morning of the 15th; he then says, "Colonel Russell, our captain,
had been seized during the night with a violent attack of chills and
fever, and I found him in his wagon quite ill." Both Bryant and
Hiram Miller mention the fine spring at which camp was made;
Bryant says it was about a mile from the junction of the north and
south forks of the Platte.

52. This sentence seems to be a repetition of the previous day's
entry. By Bryant's account camp was made on the South Platte after
traveling 17 miles from the spring (the cold waters of which were
blamed for "violent and painful sickness" experienced by some of the
party: by most overland emigrants the ruddy river water was regarded as somehow more healthful).

53. See the Index references to Wall; this was a portion of Palmer's
company from Oregon. Bryant also has a considerable account of
meeting Wall, by whom he sent home the letter printed in Volume II.

54. It appears that the Russell company used a crossing of the
South Platte intermediate between the two shown on Jefferson's map.

55. McKinstry omits to make an important notation on June 18.
Bryant writes: "This evening, after we encamped, Colonel Russell,
who has been suffering for several days from an attack of bilious
fever, tendered his resignation of the office of captain of our party.
His resignation having been accepted by a vote of the company
assembled, Ex-governor Boggs was called to the chair. A motion was
then made by E. Bryant, and unanimously adopted, that the thanks of
the company be expressed to Colonel Russell for the manner in which
he has discharged his duties since his election to the office of captain.
The other subordinate officers then resigned their places. These were
Messrs. Kirkendall, Donner, Jacob, and West. A similar vote of
thanks was adopted in regard to them. Mr. F. West was afterwards
appointed captain pro tem., and the meeting adjourned."

56. See Carriger's diary for June 19 and accompanying Notes 11

and 15.

57. See Virgil Pringle's diary for June 13, accompanying Note 30 quoting the remarks by Edwin Bryant on this day, June 19. McKinstry's entry usefully dates the passage of Selim E. Woodworth at Ash Hollow.

58. Since May 21 McKinstry had meditated the advantages of packing. Bryant's journal for the previous day commented: "A party of eight or ten persons, including myself, had determined, on our arrival at Fort Laramie, to change our mode of travel, provided we could make suitable arrangements. If mules could be obtained for packing, our design was to abandon our oxen and wagons, and all baggage not absolutely necessary to the journey. This would enable us to proceed with much greater expedition towards the point of our destination." After reaching Ash Hollow, he added on the 20th, "Having made my arrangements for the purpose, last night, with a view of carrying into effect the design of changing our method of travel I left the encampment early this morning, accompanied by Messrs. Kirkendall, Putnam, Holder, and Curry, for Fort Laramie, about one hundred and fifty miles distant. In the course of the day we were joined by Messrs. Lippincott, Burgess, Brown and Ewing." Nothing is said of McKinstry, but he did not ride on to Fort Laramie in a separate party. In the course of this journey, McKinstry usefully locates other companies, beginning with Dickenson's. Bryant also tells of remaining overnight with the Dickenson company, now consisting of 21 wagons.

59. McCutchen's company conceivably is that of William McCutchen, subsequently celebrated in the Donner party. (But see Note 63.) Campbell must be James, and Cooper is Stephen.

60. Bryant mentions none of the companies passed, but has an extended description of Chimney Rock, estimated to be about 3 miles from their camp.

61. According to Bryant, the pack party rode 45 miles, passing Scotts Bluff to encamp beyond Horse Creek.

62. Here a discrepancy must be resolved in Bryant's favor, for it is clear that the nooning at Scotts Bluff occurred on the 22nd. Evidently McKinstry brought his diary up to date later, in the process scrambling the sequence of events.

63. Although the date must be corrected, the Harlan party placed east of Scotts Bluff on the 22nd, rather than the 23rd, McKinstry's notation is valuable in pinpointing the Harlans at a time and a place. His usage "Harlan & Young" is in conformity with the modern terminology by which the first train to attempt the new Hastings Cutoff is called the Harlan-Young Company. Samuel C. Young would seem to have set out from Missouri with the Gordon-Dickenson party, for in "Samuel C. Young — a Pioneer of 1846," San Jose

Pioneer, November 9, 1878, it is declared that Young's group consisted, besides himself, of "Arthur Caldwell, Mrs. Margaret Caldwell, John McCutchen, Mr. Buchalass [Benjamin Bukelew?], Joseph Gordon, Jacob Gordon, [Gallant] Duncan Dickenson, W. Hooper and wife," besides four young bachelors, "Jacob Ross, Simpson, McMonagill [William McDonald?] and one other."

64. Fort John was the proper name of Fort Laramie, the opposition Fort Bernard was the post McKinstry had just reached. See George L. Curry's description in Volume II. Bryant says they arrived about 2 P. M. "I had a letter of introduction to Mr. [John] Richard, the principal of this trading-post, from his brother, one of the party which we met on the Platte. Mr. R. received us with mountain cordiality, inviting us to remain with him over night. We declined the invitation, having determined to proceed as far as Fort Laramie. . . . Several traders from Taos and the headwaters of the Arkansas in New Mexico were collected here, to whom the herd of mules we saw belonged. They had packed flour, some four hundred miles, for the purpose of trading with the Sioux Indians." Observe that Bryant says the traders had mules, not horses (compare note 69).

65. After a long and interesting description of Fort Laramie and the Sioux Indians there, Bryant says: "The numerous herds of horses belonging to the Indians having grazed off all the grass from the plain surrounding the fort, and it being unsafe to trust our animals with theirs, we determined to proceed and encamp for the night about five or six miles further, at a point where we were informed there was good grass. Distant from our last encampment to Fort Laramie, 40 miles—to this camp, 46 miles."

66. This project of the Sioux to war upon the Crows dominates the diaries and many of the letters of 1846 and was interesting to Francis Parkman. Nothing came of it.

67. Ames thus became McKinstry's trail companion as far as his diary takes us. How it happens that they traveled the Hastings Cutoff with the Harlan train remains to be learned.

68. Cooper and Dickenson we have met before; and whether the name is Gregg, Grieg, Gragg, or Craig, we find an echo from Carriger's diary in the other company mentioned on the 25th. Bryant says: "Several emigrant companies which we have passed in the last day or two, arrived this evening, and encamped near the fort. A party of Sioux Indians, headed by two chiefs, on their way to join the main body in their expedition against the Snakes [perhaps not a mistake; The Sioux had a baleful eye on the Snakes, too], halted here for the night. The two chiefs had recently returned from a victorious expedition against the Pawnees, bringing with them twenty-five scalps, and a number of horses. They held a 'talk,' and smoked a pipe of peace and friendship at the camp of Capt. Cooper. A contribution of flour

and meat was made by the emigrant for their benefit." In treating the Sioux, Cooper was following the example of Elam Brown two days earlier.

69. Whether driven by their original teamster, one Brownell, or by his present partner, R. T. Jacob, Bryant's wagon reached Fort Bernard on the afternoon of the 26th. He says: "We entertained at supper, this evening, all the trappers and traders at the fort. The banquet was not very sumptuous, either in viands or the manner in which it was served up; but it was enjoyed, I dare say, with a higher relish, than many a feast served in a thousand dishes of porcelain and silver. The mountaineer who has subsisted for months on nothing but fresh meat, would proclaim bread, sugar, and coffee to be high orders of luxury." According to Bryant, it was on the morning of the 27th that he concluded a trade with "Mr. [Bill] New, a trader from the head-waters of the Arkansas, by which Mr. Jacob and myself realized seven mules with pack-saddles and other trappings for packing, for our wagon and three yokes of oxen and their appendages." In his diary McKinstry does not have a great deal to say about the traders he saw at Fort Bernard. Some of these may have come from California in the spring with Jim Waters and Jim Beckwourth (driving stolen horses if we correctly size up Beckwourth's *Life and Adventures*). In a letter of September 3, 1847, written from "Fort Sacramento" to the *California Star* of September 18, 1847, McKinstry said: "A few very bad persons left this country last year of the Genus Horse Thief; they reported throughout the Western States, that California was a miserable country, that it had not rained here for two years, and all the Americans were moving to Oregon. [See as one example the Norris Colburn letter written from Santa Fe July 17, 1846, reprinted in Volume II]. I met one of them last year at Fort Laramie with a large drove of horses, (that I have since learned were stolen). Among other falsehoods, he told me that seven bushels of wheat per acre was a large crop in this country. [Such?] falsehoods turned a large number of farmers to Oregon last year."

70. McKinstry's remark quoted in Note 69 might apply to a member of this company, except for what is said about having "a large drove of horses." McKinstry is now speaking of the party which had left California with Clyman, further discussed by George L. Curry in Volume II. Bryant adds, as his own contribution: "A party of eight or ten persons, some of whom were returning from California, and some from Oregon, to the United States, encamped a small distance below on the Platte. One of these came up to the fort to purchase provisions. He gave a most discouraging description of California; representing it as scarcely habitable. He stated, that he had resided in that country four years, during which time not a drop of rain had fallen; that no crops had been raised; that vegetation had perished,

and that the population there must necessarily perish for want of food. His account of the people was not more flattering than that of the soil and climate . . . . This man made himself very busy among the emigrant parties for California, who had halted here, or who were passing; and many of them, I have reason to suppose, were credulous enough to believe him. It was easy to perceive, however, that he had a motive for his conduct, more powerful than his regard for the truth."

J. Quinn Thornton, who in Dunbar's company camped this afternoon "within ten miles of Fort Laramie," remarks: "A company of travelers, consisting of persons of both sexes, most of whom were from Oregon and California, returning to the States, were encamped upon a plain about a mile distant. They presented a very woebegone appearance; and brought us, moreover, an evil report of those lands. The Californians affirmed that the country was wholly destitute of timber, and that wheat could not be raised in sufficient quantities for bread; that they had spent all their substance, and were now returning to commence the world anew, somewhere in the vicinity of their former homes." Thornton adds an item of information on one of Clyman's trail companions on this final stage of his journey: "Among the Oregonians was a Mr. McKissick, an old gentleman, suffering from blindness caused by the dust of the way, when he first emigrated into Oregon. He was now being taken back to the States, with the hope that something might be done to restore his sight." Possibly McKissick had traveled south to California and then come east, but conceivably he had come from Oregon direct, as a member of the hypothetical party discussed in the Craig diary, Note 22. Such a party could have lost separate identity on reaching Fort Laramie.

71. McKinstry does not explain why he did not join the Russell pack party in going on from Fort Bernard. Bryant says: "The party which started consisted, including myself, of Messrs. Russell, Jacob, Kirkendall, Brown, Curry, Holder, Nuttall, and Brookey. Not one of us had ever seen a mule packed before this morning. Some New Mexicans who came in with the trading-party gave us our first lesson, and it was a very valuable one. . . . " He tells of camping for the night at "our old camp, six miles beyond Fort Laramie . . . We passed a company of Oregon emigrants, from one of whom I learned that Ewing had joined a party of traders, bound for Taos or the headwaters of the Arkansas. I did not hear from him after this." Obviously McKinstry is mistaking as listing Ewing among Russell's party. (For Ewing's further adventures, see Volume II.)

72. McKinstry's diary does not continue long enough to explain why he and Ames separated from the others, but on July 3 Bryant writes: "We were joined to-day by Capt. Welles and Mr. [James] McClary, the first a mountain-trapper, intending to accompany us as

far as Fort Bridger, and the last an emigrant bound for California. Capt. Welles, as he informed us and as I was informed by others, had once held a commission in the British army. He was in the battles of Waterloo and New Orleans. He was a man of about sixty, vigorous and athletic, and his manners, address, and general intelligence, although clothed in the rude buckskin costume of the wilderness, confirmed the statements in regard to him, made by himself and others. . . ." McKinstry encamped apparently at Warm Spring.

73. For McKinstry's arrival in camp, bringing all the latest news, see Charles T. Stanton's letter of July 5, printed in Volume II. Thornton, who had reached Fort Laramie in Rice Dunbar's company on June 28 and continued on again next day, noted on the 30th: "great confusion prevailed in camp, in consequence of some of the Californians whom we had overtaken in the morning, and some of our own party, desiring to remain in camp; while others of both parties wished to proceed. Finally the Californians all determined to go forward. Messrs. Crump, Vanbebber, and Luce, who had left us on the preceding Sabbath [June 28], continuing with them." McKinstry's diary ends on Cottonwood Creek.

74. McKinstry's letter to P. B. Reading is derived from a typed copy in the Reading Papers, California State Library. It would appear that the original was given by a Reading descendant to a member of the McKinstry family.

75. Perhaps McKinstry's arrival at Sutter's should be dated October 20. The McGlashan Papers in the Bancroft Library contain a transcript of a short note to Sutter dated "Monday Morning 20th Oct." which says in a postscript, obviously after leaving the fort en route back to the Sierra, "Saw Mr. McKinstry this morning who will be with you in a day or two."

76. Charles D. Burrass was killed at the same time as Hiram Ames, in the battle of Natividad the following month.

77. Russell (with Bryant) reached Sutter's Fort September 1.

78. This debt had been incurred by Sutter's purchase of Fort Ross.

79. Sutter's New Helvetia was then occupied by U. S. forces, with Captain Edward M. Kern in charge. Officially it was called Fort Sacramento.

80. Payrolls for these Indian troops are preserved in the McKinstry papers.

81. Had Reading and McKinstry met Kern before coming to California in 1843? Or was he a new acquaintance of both?

82. For several years these Walla Walla Indians from the Northwest had enlivened the California scene, especially the vicinity of Sutter's, by their comings and goings. Bryant has a full account of the recruiting of emigrant volunteers for service in Fremont's California Battalion. He himself had left the fort just two days earlier.

83. The rainy season had now begun, and McKinstry feared for the Donner Party, which he knew by Reed's arrival on October 28 was perilously far back on the trail.

DIARY OF JAMES MATHERS

1. Mathers is the only emigrant who mentions a "middle crossing" of the North Platte in 1846, though its existence could be inferred from the Jefferson map. All three fords were not far from present Casper.

2. To the Mineral Spring on Poison Spider Creek, Jefferson's "Mire C.," beyond Emigrant Gap.

3. If "Dickinson" was one of the sons of Gallant Duncan Dickenson, Mathers at this time was traveling with the Gordon-Dickenson company. Heinrich Lienhard for a time had been identified with that train, but had separated; his little group may be referred to as the Jacob D. Hoppe company. Lienhard reached the ford of the North Platte this day, July 4.

4. Willow Springs. Jefferson arrived here a day later.

5. Mathers reached the Independence Rock vicinity four days ahead of our tail-end diarist, James Frazier Reed. William E. Taylor had arrived June 24, thirteen days earlier.

6. In this entry Mathers refers both to the "Soda Pond" north of the Sweetwater (shown on the Jefferson map), a welcome source of saleratus, and to an alkali area probably on Poison Spring Creek passed on the 6th.

7. Devils Gate, a name Mathers seems not to have known; emigrants familiar with the name could not refrain from using it.

8. Wales B. Bonney, returning from Oregon, not from California. See Index.

9. The Three Crossings of the Sweetwater, Jefferson's "Bird Pass."

10. As Jefferson indicates, the Wind River Mountains were first seen on this stretch, across a northerly bend of the Sweetwater.

11. After encamping at the fifth crossing of the Sweetwater on the 12th, on the 13th Mathers left the canyoned river to the left, passing the Lewiston Lakes, Strawberry Creek and Rock Creek to camp on Willow Creek. The U. S. Geological Survey has now published topographical quadrangles covering the whole trail from Fort Laramie to South Pass, in the light of which the diaries here printed may be studied with more enjoyment.

12. From the last crossing of the Sweetwater Mathers moved on Pacific Creek, which rises in Pacific Springs.

13. Are we to infer from this entry that Mathers had been traveling in Stephen Cooper's company, or merely that some of his company joined Cooper's in taking the Greenwood Cutoff?

14. Mathers reached Fort Bridger the day after the Russell pack party (guided by James Hudspeth), and the Harlan-Young wagons (guided by Lansford Hastings) set out on the new cutoff.

15. The little Mathers party presumably consisted of Mathers and his wife, their son Carolan, and Otis Ashley, wife, and child, six in all. The entry for August 16 shows that they had three wagons, so five wagons continued on by the Fort Hall route.

16. For a detailed study of the route Mathers had now adopted, with ample quotation from the Mormon diaries of 1847 as well as from the California diaries of 1846, see J. Roderic Korns, *West from Fort Bridger* (Salt Lake City, 1951); published as *Utah Historical Quarterly*, vol. 19, and including an independent translation of Lienhard, the one quoted here respecting the Hastings cutoff. What Mathers calls Mud Spring Reed calls Blue Spring, on the east side of Bridger Butte; Lienhard and the 1847 Mormons refer to it without applying a name. He went on to camp on the Big Muddy, beyond Bridger Butte.

17. Mathers ascended Spring Valley, nooned in Pioneer Hollow, then crossed the Altamont Divide to camp in the valley of Sulphur Creek, now known as Hilliard Flat.

18. This important entry shows that the Harlan-Young train continued southwesterly across Hilliard Flat and over a low ridge to Bear River near the mouth of Mill Creek. As recorded by Reed's diary, the Donner party used this same road (shown by Jefferson) when they came along seven days later. Heinrich Lienhard, who had left Fort Bridger on July 26, reached Mathers' campsite of the 24th on July 27, just in time to meet Hastings returning from the advance or reconnaissance Mathers mentions. Lienhard says Hastings met the Hoppe train on the afternoon of the 26th; "he turned back again with us and remained overnight in our camp." On Hastings' recommendation, Lienhard and his fellows crossed the low ridge west of Sulphur Creek to arrive almost immediately on the banks of the Bear. (On August 2 Reed says in his diary that the Donners should have taken this road: "much better road said to be.") Jefferson as well as Lienhard traveled this cutoff, and it was adopted by the Mormons next year, becoming the standard road west of Bear River. The two trails appear to have come back together again on the divide west of Yellow Creek.

With all the rest, we are indebted to Mathers for an accounting of the number of wagons that had thus far taken the Hastings Cutoff, the total of 57 presumably including the three of his own little party. The Harlan-Young company is said to have numbered some 40 wagons when it left Fort Bridger. Lienhard speaks of 52 wagons ahead of his own, but this may merely have been the number Hastings knew about when he left the Harlan camp at Bear River on July 25. If we accept Mathers' total of 57 as including his own contingent, the total of 66 in advance of the Donner Party, as given by J. Quinn Thornton in his account of the Donner tragedy, would seem to be about right; the Lienhard (Hoppe) group may have had about 9 wagons. James Frazier Reed was convinced that 60 wagons preceded the Donners on the cutoff, but this seems too low a figure. Writing in the *California Star* of February 13, 1847, as seen in Volume II, McKinstry estimates "some seventy-five." Bryant says "about eighty." Bridger told the Mormons next year that "nearly a hundred wagons" had taken the Hastings Cutoff in 1846, which would have included the 23 wagons in the Donner party.

19. Presumably by the roundabout route to the south shown by Jefferson, this day's travel brought Mathers to Yellow Creek, or to Cache Cave beyond. The compass course he gives does not seem quite right; there should have been more northing. Perhaps we should reflect further on something Lienhard says. Hastings had camped on the night of the 27th with Lienhard's company. Next day they crossed the Bear about 7 miles southeast of present Evanston, and Lienhard says: "After we had gone about 7 miles, we camped near the channel of a nearly dry brook, where however we found a spring of excellent water, together with sufficient grass for our cattle. The 52 wagons traveling ahead of us here had taken two different routes, and Hastings had shown us still another which he considered the better way, and which we thought to put to the test. Hastings left us in the evening to overtake a company in advance of us." Jefferson shows the route Lienhard described, via "Hastings Pass," and on to what we now call The Needles, east of Yellow Creek. But from Lienhard's language, those ahead had reached this vicinity by two different routes. Perhaps Mathers traveled a route intermediate between that of the Harlan wagons and that of Lienhard and Jefferson, from Bear River across the ridge to Yellow Creek.

20. On the 28th Mathers descended Echo Canyon, coming on the 29th to the Weber River, which he descended to a campsite opposite present Henefer.

21. This day's travel brought Mathers (with a small detour through Croyden Valley) down the canyon of the Weber below Devils Slide to Round Valley above present Morgan. On Jefferson's map, this part of the canyon is given the name Gutter Defile in recognition of the twin limestone dikes which distinguish the south wall of the canyon below the mouth of Lost Creek (Berry C. on Jefferson's map.) Mathers was three days ahead of Lienhard and Jefferson at this point. His is the earliest diary recording travel through this canyon, no diary for the Harlan train having yet been found. James Hudspeth, guiding the Russell pack company in a search for a possibly better road, had taken a more northerly route from Bear River, eventually descend-

ing Lost Creek to the Weber. He was unable to work out a good route down Weber Canyon, so on July 24 conducted Russell (and Bryant, who tells the tale) south over the divide to East Canyon, the route he had used eastbound with Clyman in June, then by a perilous Indian trail high on the mountainside descended East Canyon to Morgan Valley. Leaving the Russell party to rest for a day, on the 25th he "rode down the valley to explore Weber's river to the Salt Lake. He returned in the afternoon, having passed through the next *canon*." On the 26th, while Russell and Bryant tackled the difficult lower canyon, Hudspeth and two emigrants with him left "to explore the *canon* above, and ascertain the practicability of wagons passing through it." Hudspeth got back to the Russell party early on the morning of July 29, at the mouth of the lower canyon. He and his men "had forced their way through the upper *canon,* and proceeded six miles further up Weber river, where they met a train of about forty emigrant wagons under the guidance of Mr. Hastings, which left Fort Bridger the same day that we did." This would indicate that the advance company of the Harlan train reached the mouth of Echo Canyon on the afternoon of the 27th, about a day ahead of Mathers. That night Hastings camped at Bear River with Lienhard, so he had no part in the decision to descend the Weber. Hudspeth's voice may have been decisive. Bryant says: "The difficulties to be encountered by these emigrants by the new route will commence at that point [Henefer]; and they will, I fear, be serious. Mr. Hudspeth thinks that the passage through the *canon* is practicable, by making a road in the bed of the stream at short distances, and cutting out the timber and brush in other places."

22. As Mathers says, a mile of difficult travel below Round Valley brought him on July 31 to the open Morgan Valley. He encamped near present Peterson.

23. Here the lower canyon of the Weber begins, above Devils Gate.

24. The Samuel C. Young sketch cited in the McKinstry diary, Note 63, says "the male portion of these four companies [the advance contingent on the Hastings Cutoff] spent four days clearing the boulders out of the way, and then they could make but one and a half miles per day." Jacob Wright Harlan recalled that the company "worked six days building a road, and got through on the seventh day."

25. For William Fowler, see Index.

26. Mathers' entry for August 3 is interestingly complemented by Lienhard's. With Jefferson, Lienhard had encamped in upper Morgan Valley on August 2. "On the 3rd of August as we were making our way down along the river in a northerly [northwesterly] direction, and after we had traveled about 5 miles, we encountered Captain Hastings, who had returned to meet us. By his advice we halted

here. He was of the opinion that we, like all the companies who had gone in advance of us, were taking the wrong road. He had advised the first companies that on arriving at the Weber River they should turn to the left which would bring them by a shorter route to the Salt Lake; this advice they had not followed, but by good luck they had been able to make their way down the river. We thereupon turned our wagons around and went back about 2 miles, where we encamped."

Thus we learn that it had never been Hastings' intention to descend the Weber through its canyons. Instead, he had proposed that the emigrants cut a road across the mountains, following essentially the same trail he had traveled with Clyman, eastbound in June. Hastings, when Lienhard met him, must have been going back up the Weber to leave near present Henefer the notice which would result in the Donner Party's opening the road over the Wasatch to the site of Salt Lake City.

27. We may judge that one of the two exploring parties sought a way across the last ridge of the Wasatch from Morgan Valley—a route that simply does not exist. The second party Mathers mentions might have crossed the divide north into Ogden Hole, only to find Ogden Canyon worse than Weber Canyon. Lienhard writes on the 4th, "A few of the company endeavored to seek out a better route but returned to camp without having effected their object."

28. Lienhard, who similarly made the passage of the lower canyon on August 6, graphically describes the difficulties involved in getting four of their wagons through, "directly down the foaming riverbed, full of great boulders." Allen and Avery, in *The California Gold Book,* pp. 62-63, picture the problems surmounted by the Harlans: "The canyon is scarcely wide enough to accommodate the narrow river which traverses it, and there was no room for roads between its water and the abrupt banks. In many places great boulders had been rolled by the mountain torrents and lodged together, forming an impassable way. . . . Three such obstacles were encountered, and only about a mile a day was average for more than a week. The sides of the mountains were covered by a dense growth of willows, never penetrated by white men. Three times spurs of the mountains had to be crossed by rigging the windlass on top, and lifting the wagons almost bodily. The banks were very steep, and covered with loose stones, so that a mountain sheep would have been troubled to keep its feet, much more an ox team drawing a heavily loaded wagon. On the 11th [1st?] of August, while hoisting a yoke of oxen and a wagon up Weber mountain, the rope broke near the windlass. As many men as could surround the wagon were helping all they could by lifting at the wheels and sides. The footing was untenable and before the rope could be tied to anything, the men found they must abandon the wagon & oxen to destruction, or be dragged to death themselves. The

faithful beasts seemed to comprehend their danger, and held their ground for a few seconds, and were then hurled over a precipice at least 75 feet high, and crushed in a tangled mass with the wagon on the rocks at the bottom of the canyon." This seems to describe specifically the Devils Gate blockage in the canyon, to which Mathers reacted in his entry for August 1, before the Harlans found it feasible to take their wagons down the riverbed itself. Jefferson's comment, "Granite Canyon (This is a bad Canyon)," and his reflection, "(It is perhaps better to take Reed's Route)," would seem fully warranted. Mathers apparently encamped on August 5 at the mouth of the canyon, present Uintah.

29. Mathers evidently passed over the Sand Ridge, from which he could view Great Salt Lake while continuing south to camp near present Farmington.

30. On the 7th Mathers made a long drive, but Jefferson made a longer one of 32 miles, so that both camped this night beyond the Jordan River, near the site of Garfield. Lienhard went only as far as the Jordan, then known as the "Utah Outlet." For a discussion of alternate trails along this stretch, see Korns, *op. cit.*, pp. 134-137.

31. On the 8th Mathers passed along the margin of the lake around the northern end of the Oquirrh Mountains, then in Tooele Valley rolled on more nearly west to the site of Grantsville, variously known in 1846 as Twenty Wells or Hastings Wells.

32. During this day of rest, Lienhard briefly caught up with Mathers. He describes similarly the tendency of the cattle to tumble into the "deep holes of spring water." Lienhard remained here until August 14, so Mathers again moved ahead on the 11th. One important fact Mathers does not mention; seeking more information about the mountain route Hastings had proposed, James Frazier Reed left the Donner party below the mouth of Echo Canyon on the afternoon of August 6 or the morning of August 7, and with McCutchen and Stanton set out to overtake Hastings with the emigrants ahead. After an exhausting ride, he probably rode into camp on August 8. According to Reed's recollection in 1871, he overtook Hastings "at a place we called Black Rock, south end of Salt Lake." This was probably what became known as Adobe Rock in Tooele Valley, not the Black Rock which later gave name to a Great Salt Lake beach; Mathers might have nooned thereabouts on the 8th. Perhaps Hastings for the time being was with a rear company of the Harlan train, Mathers toward the front. Having ridden as far back on the trail as Big Mountain, in the Wasatch east of Salt Lake City, to point out the road to Reed, Hastings turned west to overtake his emigrants. Lienhard remarks his return in an entry of August 12 (cast in the past tense): "Mr. Hastings had returned; he was of the opinion that we should give our cattle more opportunity to recruit." Very likely Hastings reached

the camp at Grantsville late on the 11th.

The picture of Hastings given us by Lienhard and Mathers goes far to rehabilitate his reputation. Historians in recent years on insufficient evidence have united in the opinion that Hastings' behavior on the trail in 1846 was reckless and irresponsible. On the contrary, we begin to find that he showed extraordinary activity in behalf of the emigration; but affairs got out of control. Had the Harlan train taken his recommended route across the Wasatch, many more hands would have been available for cutting out the road, and it would have been made much faster than the Donner party found possible.

33. It has been conjectured that the Harlan-Young party waited patiently at Twenty Wells for Hastings to return from the excursion with Reed, Lienhard's long period of recruiting giving authority to this view. But we now find from Mathers' diary that the emigrants began moving on at least as early as the 10th. The Russell party had camped at Twenty Wells on July 31. Instead of continuing on around the Stansbury Mountains, as Clyman had done earlier and as Mathers was now doing, they crossed the mountains into Skull Valley by way of North Willow Canyon. This was a pack trail (shown by Jefferson), not feasible for wagon travel. Mathers went on to camp close to the Big Spring near present Timpie.

34. On the 11th Mathers traveled south along the east side of Skull Valley, apparently nooning at Muskrat Spring after passing Burnt Spring, then continuing on to camp at the springs west of Salt Mountain.

35. Evidently Mathers on the 13th moved 5 miles farther south, perhaps to the present Deseret Ranch on Big Creek.

36. This day, August 15, Mathers crossed Skull Valley to what Jefferson calls Dell Spring, now Redlum Spring, on the east side of the Cedar Mountains. Lienhard's company, which had been recruiting at Twenty Wells, resumed its journey on the 14th and early on the 15th "arrived at the last fresh water springs, of which there were several, and fortunately we found also a great abundance of grass. Here again we overtook the last immigrant company in advance of us, including the Harlans and Weimer [Wimmer], with whom we had begun the journey from Indian Creek." It would seem that Mathers set out before Lienhard arrived, one of the first to tackle the "long drive."

37. Like a good many emigrants after him, including Reed, Mathers was so disorganized by the crossing of the Salt Desert to Pilot Peak that he preserved only a fragmentary record of the experience. Writing with his trail diary at hand, but with the advantage of retrospect, Lienhard gives a much fuller account of this hard passage across the salt waste. A particularly interesting feature of Lienhard's account is that it includes a clear reference to Mathers. Lienhard had reached Redlum Spring on the afternoon of the 17th, then gone ahead

in search of a well reportedly dug by the emigrants in advance, 15 or 20 miles farther on. Giving up this search, he waited near Grayback Mountain for his company to come along, then went on with them. Lienhard says that west of Grayback, on the afternoon of the 18th, they came to "a small Sahara desert. The wind blew strongly from the northeast and drove the whitish-yellow sand before it as our wagons wound their way among numerous sandhills from 10 to 12 feet high; the air was darkened so that we could scarcely perceive the sun; one might have supposed that already twilight had come, although it was yet too early; this flying sand perhaps most resembled a very heavy snowstorm. Fortunately, this Sahara . . . could not have been more than 4 or 5 miles wide here where we crossed it. When we had left it behind, the wind died away almost entirely."

Lienhard kept on after darkfall, and in the small hours of the 19th learned from some of the party who had gone ahead that "a short distance from here they had come upon a man [Mathers] who had remained behind to take care of several wagons; from this man they had learned that the distance to the nearest freshwater springs and grass was at least 24 miles. We soon came up to the wagon in which this man was staying, and from him we learned that those ahead of us had left many wagons behind and driven the cattle ahead to the springs, there to recover strength, after which they would come back for the wagons." At sunrise Lienhard could see Silver Island ahead; up to that time, he says, "we had passed 24 wagons which had been left behind." This would indicate that the Harlan-Young train abandoned temporarily in the desert a third of their wagons. Lienhard passed abandoned cattle, some already dead, others barely alive, and on the salt plain between Silver Island and Pilot Peak met "a considerable number of men with oxen, a few mules, and horses, who were going back into the barren desert to recover their abandoned wagons." About 4 p.m. on the 19th the company in which Lienhard traveled, "Hoppe's Company," reached the springs at the foot of Pilot Peak: "We were told that the companies which had gone in advance of us had been generally of the opinion that our party would suffer most in crossing this long desert, to the point, perhaps, of perishing altogether. Here we were, however, the only company which had had to leave behind neither a wagon nor an animal, at which they were not a little amazed." (Lienhard's comments here should be read in conjunction with Jefferson's remarks on the "Long drive, Desert of Utariah," quoted in the next section of this book.

38. The 4 miles were actually in a southerly direction along the base of Pilot Peak; see the Jefferson map. From this day, till perhaps October 8, Jefferson reflects Mathers' daily travels with his own. In quest of better grass, Lienhard had moved to these springs on the 21st, noting that "many others were there." He did not go on till

the 24th.

39. This second long drive was across the Toano Mountains by Silver Zone Pass to the springs at the present Johnson Ranch in Gosiute Valley. On this day's journey Mathers was following the track made in 1841 by the Bartleson party, which had reached Pilot Peak by a course north of Great Salt Lake and along the west edge of the Salt Desert. At the springs in Gosiute Valley, confronted by the Pequop Mountains, the emigrants of 1841 abandoned their wagons, which accounts for Jefferson's notation, "Chiles Cache," at "Relief Springs." (Joseph Chiles had been one of the Bartleson party.) McKinstry, who carried west John Bidwell's published diary, here made the marginal notation, not dated, "We cooked our supper & breakfast with fires made from the remains of three [*i.e.*, eight?] wagons." Lienhard, arriving at "Relief Springs" about 11 a.m. on August 25 to find "another company already encamped there," also mentions the relics of an earlier emigration: "they had abandoned their wagons there, burying in the ground what they could not carry with them. After they left, the Indians had burned the wagons; the travelers in advance who had recently arrived here had found what was left of the wagons." Evidently it was at "Relief Springs" that George Harlan began his transactions with Hiram Ames, referred to in the McKinstry diary, Note 10.

40. Travel on the 25th was to Flowery Lake, Jefferson's "Warm Spring."

41. Across the Pequop Mountains by Jasper Pass (under which the Western Pacific later tunneled) to camp in Independence Valley at Mound Springs near the foot of Spruce Mountain. At this spring, or at nearby Chase Springs, Fremont divided his party, westbound in 1845. Lienhard arrived here on the 28th.

42. Over the Spruce Mountain Ridge and across Clover Valley to the base of the East Humboldt Mountains, where rises what is now called the Warm Spring (Jefferson's "Mill Spring").

43. Over the shoulder of the East Humboldt range to the north end of Ruby Valley and a camp at the base of the Ruby Mountains. Talbot's detachment of Fremont's party in 1845 made for Secret Pass between the East Humboldt Mountains and the Rubies, veering to the right of Mathers' travel this day; and Hastings had come east with Clyman by that trail in May. This trail (indicated by Jefferson) was not practicable for wagons in 1846, and the emigrants had to make a long detour, south around the Ruby Mountains. As Mathers notes, the drainage basin of the Humboldt lay west of the Rubies.

44. Lienhard's account of this travel down the east side of Ruby Valley is not quoted here, but students will be interested to compare it with Mathers' diary, and both with Jefferson's map.

45. North of Cave Creek, so called today as in Jefferson's time.

46. Near the later Overland Ranch, near the foot of what was long called Hastings Pass, now Overland Pass.

47. To a campsite on Huntington Creek near the future Elko County line. Jefferson's "Glover Creek" may be an engraver's misreading of Clover Creek, but it is possible that Aquilla Glover, later prominent in the Donner Relief, had found this creek, scouting ahead.

48. To near the present Sadler Ranch. Observe that Jefferson as well as Mathers remained in camp on the 4th. Perhaps they were waiting upon the efforts of road-hunters, again out ahead.

49. Down Huntington Creek nearly to its confluence with Smith Creek. The three springs mentioned by Mathers and shown by Jefferson still rise west of Huntington Creek, about 11½ miles north of the Sadler Ranch.

50. On the 6th Mathers followed Huntington Creek past Smith Creek (which apparently is Jefferson's "Grass C."), on through its canyon ("Shoshone Pass") and on past its confluence with the South Fork of the Humboldt (which Jefferson shows without naming), camping finally near the mouth of Ten Mile Creek. Below that point the canyon of the South Fork begins.

51. This day Mathers passed through the canyon to camp near its mouth on the Humboldt plain.

52. On the 8th Mathers reached the Humboldt and the old road via Fort Hall, camping at the head of Carlin Canyon near Moleen. He would now follow Carriger's route the rest of the way to the summit of the Sierra Nevada.

53. To this point the diary had been written in ink; the rest is in pencil. Mathers passed through Carlin Canyon on the 9th, then left the river to camp near Emigrant Springs. He variantly states the distance traveled, first 16, then 18 miles.

54. Mathers moved along to Gravelly Ford, then down the Humboldt to camp near Beowawe, at the head of Whirlwind Valley, on the 10th. Next day he crossed the river at present Dunphy after going about 8 miles, and camped near present Kampos Station on the Western Pacific Railroad. On the 12th he camped on the Humboldt about 3 miles north of present Battle Mountain, paralleling present Rock Creek (Jefferson shows two variant routes here). On the 13th he crossed the Humboldt after about 6 miles and camped in Pumpernickel Valley, 6 miles northwest of Valmy. On the 14th he camped near Golconda after passing the bad hill to the east where Reed was to kill John Snyder the following month; the present highway cuts across this elevation by Golconda Summit; on the emigrant road, which kept more to the north, the locality became known as Iron Point. For Jefferson, this was "Pauta Pass."

55. On the 15th Mathers camped northeast of Winnemucca; his remarks about the Indians are given point by Jefferson's maps and

Carriger's previous comments.

56. The night encampment on the 16th was near present Rose Creek Station; the creek Mathers mentioned is the Little Humboldt, not shown by Jefferson.

57. Keeping steadily down the river, Mathers camped on the 17th west of Congrave, about 8 miles north of Mill City, on the 18th about 2 miles northwest of Mill City, and on the 19th, after passing the junction with the Applegate Cutoff, on the Humboldt west of Humboldt Station. He crossed the river this day, and remained on the right bank thereafter.

58. On the 20th Mathers camped near present Rye Patch, where Jefferson locates "Salles Grave," discussed in Volume II, on the 21st moved along to a camp southwest of Oreana, where he (and Jefferson) remained over the 22nd, and on the 23rd camped about 2 miles south of present Lovelock. Next day he reached the ultimate sink of the Humboldt above present Miriam, at which point the Trinity Range on the west and the West Humboldt Range on the east elevate the land somewhat to make the ridge shown by Jefferson and mentioned by Mathers on the 25th.

59. By way of explaining Mathers' trek to the Truckee: He reached Bradys Hot Springs at the end of a 20-mile desert stretch, west on to a desert playa "brackish water" between the Truckee Range and Hot Springs Mountain, and after paying the usual toll to the "sand hills" below the Truckee Range reached the haven of the Truckee after sunrise on the 26th.

60. Mathers' ascent of the Truckee may be described briefly. He does not trouble to mention the many river crossings Jefferson scrupulously shows on his map. He encamped on September 28 near Derby Siding, on the 29th near Clark Siding, and on the 30th near Hafed Siding (Jefferson noting the first pine trees here), and on October 1 emerged into what Jefferson calls Grass Valley, below present Sparks. He crossed the valley past the site of Reno, passing Steamboat Creek (which Jefferson shows without naming), and after traversing a stony slope of the Carson Range, camped near the upper limits of modern Reno.

61. On October 2 Mathers and Jefferson camped near the hot spring at present Lawton, after crossing Hunter Creek (Jefferson's "Cold C."). Next day they reached the bend of the Truckee at present Verdi and turned northwest with the road to camp in Dog Valley (Jefferson's "Lawn Valley") while circling Verdi Range ("Steep Stoney Hills"). Both travelers noted the pine forests here.

62. On the 4th our travelers went on to the Little Truckee ("Raven C."), then again south to a camp in "Moss Vale," north of Prosser Creek ("Pine C.").

63. Mathers does not mention Truckee or Donner Lake, though

he refers to Donner Creek. Jefferson, however, shows both the lake and the house Moses Schallenberger had occupied at its foot in 1844-1845. Camp was made this day in Coldstream Valley south of the lake; Jefferson applies the name "Summit Creek" to Cold Creek.

64. On October 6 Mathers and Jefferson ascended Cold Creek to the mouth of Emigrant Canyon, and after a hard struggle reached the summit on October 7 where Carriger had on September 24, a mile and a half south of Donner Pass. Jefferson's "Meadow Vale" is the present Summit Valley, at the time called the Yuba Valley. Although the rainy season had not yet begun, the snow squalls Mathers mentions had ominous implications and were remembered in later years by some of the emigrants, with the conviction that they had crossed the divide just a few hours before the abortive attempt by the Donner Party. Actually, it is clear that all others had crossed the summit before James Frazier Reed and Walter Herron came along in advance of the Donner train.

65. Mathers was now descending the rocky Yuba. He may have encamped near present Cold Springs; see the next Note.

66. There is a serious discrepancy in the estimated mileages of Jefferson and Mathers on the 9th, enough to suggest that they had parted company. Yet their travels on succeeding days seem approximately the same; and Jefferson's 2 miles on the 9th fits the geography better than Mathers' 7 miles. If they were traveling together, as I suspect was the case, they probably encamped on the 9th near present Rainbow after going about 3 miles. On the 10th they kept on down the Yuba to where the road left the river, about a mile north of Cisco Butte. The "House" located by Jefferson was another relic of the 1844 emigration.

67. On the 11th Jefferson and Mathers descended into upper Bear Valley by way of Emigrant Gap. Jefferson's "Brant Lake," mentioned by Mathers, was Crystal Springs, now dammed to form Crystal Lake.

68. On October 12 our travelers camped on the divide called Lowell Hill Ridge near Nigger Jack Hill. Mathers may have watered his animals down on Steephollow Creek.

69. The camp of the 13th was north of present Dutch Flat on the narrow ridge between Steephollow Creek and Bear River.

70. On the 14th Mathers and Jefferson descended into Steephollow, the latter giving the name Oak C. to the stream on which they encamped. After resting on the 15th, they moved along apparently to Greenhorn Creek on the 16th and on the 17th to a point northeast of Taylor Crossing. Camp was made on the 18th probably in Long Hollow, on the 19th near Bushy Mountain, and on the 20th near present Horstville, east of Wheatland. This is the last dated campsite we have for Jefferson.

71. Mathers' travels of October 21-25 need not be described at any length, since Jefferson well displays the road and most of the campsites.

72. Mathers started on to Mission San Jose none too soon, for the rain which began to fall on the night of the 28th as part of that widespread Pacific Coast storm would soon turn the valley roads into quagmires. Jefferson shows the road and the streams. For his Maka-same read Cosumnes; for his Kalaveras (Mathers' nearly dry creek of the 21st) read Calaveras; for his Mokalame and Mathers' Makal-ama read Mokelumne. On November 6 Mathers passed the Livermore Valley without wasting much space on it, and on the 7th he concludes his diary at the "St. Joseph Mission," 16 miles north of the modern city of San Jose.

DIARY OF HIRAM O. MILLER AND JAMES FRAZIER REED WITH LETTERS BY VIRGINIA E. B. REED AND JAMES FRAZIER REED

1. This opening entry repeats a remark inside the front cover, also in Miller's hand: "Left Home. Hiram O. Miller April 26 1846 and Milford Elliott." This might point to some particular relation-ship with Elliott, of which there is no other indication. "Home" is of course Springfield, Illinois.

2. Thus is dated precisely the departure of the Donner Party from Independence. See Tamsen Donner's letter of the previous day, printed in Volume II.

3. "Heart Grove" is a term I have not elsewhere seen, applied to the crossing of the Big Blue River of Missouri.

4. Encamped with the Russell company this day on Soldier Creek, Bryant writes: "We were joined to-day by nine wagons from Illinois, belonging to Mr. Reed and the Messrs. Donner, highly respectable and intelligent gentlemen, with interesting families. From this day until June 19, Miller's diary may be read in conjunction with the McKinstry diary and the Bryant journal.

5. "Wapalore" is a novel name for the Little Vermilion.

6. "Bear Creek," another novel name, is apparently the present Sandy.

7. After encamping, Bryant "counted twenty-five islands, varying in dimensions, generally from a rod to a quarter of a mile in diam-eter."

8. Miller had encamped near Ash Hollow on June 19. Next day Bryant and McKinstry had ridden ahead to Fort Laramie, so along this stretch Miller's diary is the only daily record of the Donner Party. This "Beautiful pine ridge" (southeast of Bridgeport, Ne-

braska), which evokes one of the rare personal comments by Miller, is shown by Jefferson as bordering "Ninewa C.," the present Pumpkin Creek.

9. Miller applies the name "Fremonts spring" to the present Robidoux Spring at Scotts Bluff. Without applying a name, Charles Preuss had described it, July 11, 1842, for the benefit of Fremont's report of his first expedition.

10. See George Donner's letter written from Fort Bernard the following day, reprinted in Volume II.

11. Clyman talked with Reed this night; see Introduction.

12. This camp was on Cottonwood Creek. Although J. Quinn Thornton, Edwin Bryant, and (very briefly) George McKinstry give us occasional glimpses of the Donners as they move on west of Fort Laramie, this diary is the sole daily record, however interestingly it is supplemented by the Reed letters in this volume and the Stanton letters in Volume II.

13. McKinstry arrived just as the company was getting under way on the 30th and says, "Capt Boggs just resigned." But as far along as July 4, Bryant is still calling the train Gov. Boggs's company.

14. Miller's mileages are rather hit-or-miss, but he reached Labonte Creek this day. For the "red mouns," see the Taylor diary, Note 20.

15. This is the last entry made by Miller himself. Bryant says on this day that "Mr. [William] Kirkendall, whom I expected would accompany us, having changed his destination from California to Oregon, in consequence, as I suppose, of the unfavorable representations made at Fort Bernard in reference to the first-named country, we were compelled to strengthen our party by adding to it some other person in his place. For this purpose we [the Russell pack party] remained encamped during the day, waiting for some of the rear emigrant parties to come up. None appearing during the forenoon, in the afternoon, accompanied by Brookey, I rode back some five or six miles, where I met Governor Boggs's company, and prevailed upon Mr. Hiram Miller, a member of it, to join us."

16. This first entry by James Frazier Reed brings the party to La Prele Creek. (There, next year, William Clayton also noted the natural bridge, "a tunnel from ten to twenty rods under the high rocky bluffs . . . high enough for a man to stand upright in it." This natural bridge may still be seen in Ayers Park.) The name Beaver Creek prevails among the diarists and letter-writters of 1846 who celebrated the national holiday there. With the letters printed in these two volumes should be compared Bryant's account, since the Russell party shared in the festivities before parting once and for all from their fellow travelers. J. Quinn Thornton in Rice Dunbar's company camped three or four miles farther along on the 3rd. On the 4th having the last guard, he fired his rifle and revolving pistol

at dawn, "in honor of the anniversary of the Declaration of American
Independence. The pulsations of my heart were quickened as I heard
the morning gun, and saw the banner of my country run up to the
top of the staff, in my own little city, and thought of the rejoicings
of the nation." He mentions that the Californians remained in camp
to celebrate the day, but his own party continued on. Thornton again
moved along on the 5th while the Californians recruited, late in the
afternoon passing "two companies of Oregon emigrants, the one being
led by a Mr. [James] Campbell, and the other by a Mr. Crabtree.
Two of our company had gone forward in advance of our wagons,
for the purpose of proposing a union between these two companies.
They declined receiving any new accessions."

17. The anthracite coal at Deer Creek was observed by many other
emigrants this year, including Jefferson, who on the morning of the
6th was about 28 miles ahead of Reed.

18. When Reed speaks of superior travel on the south bank of
the North Platte, he means in the vicinity of present Casper. It was
not until late 1849 that a wagon road was opened up on the north
bank all the way from the Fort Laramie area. Thornton crossed at
the "lower ford" on July 6, and camped opposite the upper ford;
no mileage is stated, but his party halted early in the afternoon
after fording the river at 11 a.m., so the fords were not far apart.

19. As seen by Charles T. Stanton's letter of July 19 reprinted
in Volume II, the encampment of July 14 was just below the "Narrows" of the Sweetwater, otherwise known as the Three Crossings,
Jefferson's "Bird Pass." The travel of the next few days as described
by Reed is made more interesting by reference to Stanton's letter.
Thornton encamped at Independence Rock on July 9, stopped $1\frac{1}{2}$
miles above Devils Gate on the 10th, moved 15 miles up the Sweetwater on the 11th, and on Sunday, July 12, "at noon encamped on
the bank of the river, near the companies of Dickinson and West,"
no mileage given. Most of the men went out buffalo hunting, he says.
On the 13th Thornton moved along another 12 miles, on the 14th
20 miles, and after resting a day, traveled an unstated distance on
the 16th. He then says on the 17th, "The little company with which
I had been traveling having left camp, I remained until Ex-Gov.
Boggs came up, about 10 o'clock, with some sixteen wagons, when
I joined his company." By this time, as we learn from Stanton,
Boggs headed a separate company, which had separated from the
others on the 12th. Stanton's letter helps materially in identifying
and locating the various companies during the ascent of the Sweetwater.

20. Thornton tells of reaching South Pass on the 18th, nooning at
the last crossing of the Sweetwater and arriving a little after sunset
"at a small stream, which takes its rise in a spring near at hand,

known as the Pacific Spring." Reed's diary, being brought up to date
after lapsing for a time, is somewhat confused, but Stanton's letter
of July 19 shows that the company made the mistake of going on to
the Dry Sandy (13½ miles farther by the Mormon roadometer in
1847) instead of stopping at Pacific Spring or on the creek below.
Like Reed, Stanton calls Pacific Spring "Green Spring."

21. See the Jefferson map for variant roads used by the 1846
emigrants in the vicinity of the Little Sandy. Reed does not mention the junction with the Greenwood Cutoff, which in 1847 was
located by the Mormons 6 miles east of the Little Sandy; in all
likelihood Reed was on that cutoff as far as the Little Sandy, and
by going down that stream on the 21st came into the road to Fort
Bridger generally used after 1847. Thornton arrived on the Little
Sandy late on the 19th. In his book he writes:

"A large number of Oregon and California emigrants encamped
at this creek, among whom I may mention the following:—Messrs.
West, Crabtree, Campbell, Boggs, Donners, and Dunbar. I had, at
one time or another, become acquainted with all of these persons in
those companies, and had traveled with them from Wokaruska, and
until subsequent divisions and subdivisions had separated us. We had
often, since our various separations, passed and repassed each other
upon the road, and had frequently encamped together by the same
water and grass, as we did now. In fact, the particular history of
my own journey is the general history of theirs. . . . the greater number of the Californians, and especially the companies in which George
Donner, Jacob Donner, James F. Reed, and William H. Eddy, and
their families traveled, here turned to the left, for the purpose of
going by way of Fort Bridges [Bridger], to meet L. W. Hastings,
who had informed them, by a letter which he wrote, and forwarded
from where the emigrant road leaves the Sweet Water, that he had
explored a new route from California, which he had found to be much
nearer and better than the old one, by the way of Fort Hall, and the
head waters of Ogden's River, and that he would remain at Fort
Bridges to give further information, and to conduct them through.

"The Californians were generally much elated, and in fine spirits,
with the prospect of a better and nearer road to the country of their
destination. Mrs. George Donner was, however, an exception. She
was gloomy, sad, and dispirited, in view of the fact, that her husband
and others could think for a moment of leaving the old road, and
confide in the statement of a man of whom they knew nothing, but
who was probably some selfish adventurer."

Thornton adds on the 20th, "The previous night having passed
away cheerfully and pleasantly, we all resumed our journey; our
California friends turning to the left, and we continuing along the
right-hand road" to the Big Sandy (where he and his fellows, includ-

ing Boggs, recruited their cattle over the 21st, preliminary to entering upon the forty-mile drive to the Green which was the distinguishing feature of the Greenwood Cutoff).

22. Reed's reference to the Bridger establishment on Green River as his "New fort," and that on Blacks fork as his "old Fort," is puzzling. I am inclined to think he got new and old forts mixed, though Joel Palmer, in the "Table of Distances" published with his journal of 1845, twice refers to "Bridger's Old Fort" on Blacks Fork. Fremont on August 16, 1843, tells of nooning "at the upper end of a large bottom, near some old houses, which had been a trading post," the past tense used even so early, and at the well-marked point about 8 miles below the mouth of the Big Sandy where the emigrant road left the Green to cross over to Blacks Fork.

John W. Gunnison, accompanying Howard Stansbury east, with Bridger as guide, alluded in his diary on September 12, 1850, east of Fort Bridger, to "Bridger's . . . fort which was formerly on Green River between the mouths of Black's & Henry's fork." Apparently Gunnison should have written Big Sandy rather than Henry's fork. When the Mormon Pioneers fell in with Bridger near the Little Sandy on June 28, 1847, Bridger advised them as to the route by saying, as William Clayton reports him, "After crossing Green River we follow down it four or five miles to the old station then cross over to a stream which heads in the mountains west." Jefferson shows the site, and Bryant refers to it on July 15, 1846, "the ruins of several log-cabins, which I have since learned were erected some years ago by traders and trappers, and have subsequently been deserted."

I conjecture that Bridger began to build on this site in August, 1841, and that his partner Henry Fraeb was killed on the Little Snake while out "making meat" for the fort builders. But how long was this site occupied? It might have seemed too exposed to Sioux incursions in view of Fraeb's fate; or if it was too dangerous to hunt in the country to the east, Bridger may have found it necessary to relocate closer to the Uinta Mountains on Blacks Fork. Yet so substantial was the construction (William B. Lorton in 1849 noted chimneys yet standing, and "a great quantity of wood" cut, evidence that someone had wintered there) that one might suppose Bridger stayed at this site till he went down to the States in the summer of 1842, only relocating his post after coming back to the mountains with his new partner, Louis Vasquez, that fall. Joseph Williams, eastbound from Oregon in the summer of 1842, reached Green River near Horse Creek, then with his companions "turned out of our intended route, and went about a southwest course, in order to avoid the Black Feet [*i.e.,* Sioux?] Indians." Thus in a few days he reached deserted "Bridger's Fort," from which he could see "mountain-tops spotted with snow." Perhaps Williams traveled south by way of upper Hams Fork, reversing William Marshall Anderson's route of 1834, which would explain an initial "southwest" course. Although Williams' context best fits the Blacks Fork site (he says nothing of coming back to the banks of the Green) the logic of the situation is all in favor of the Green River site. At the fort Williams remarked the grave of "an Indian woman, who had been killed by the Shiennes," and conceivably if not hopefully archeological investigation might benefit from the fact. It appears that on first removing his fort to Blacks Fork, Bridger established it on a butte or bluff, but in the summer of 1843 relocated it in the valley bottoms a short distance farther west; Theodore Talbot passed by in August, 1843, in time to remark this second removal.

23. J. Roderic Korns in the posthumously-published *West from Fort Bridger,* edited by myself and expressing my own views, prints the remaining entries of the Reed diary, with elaborate notes that utilize the 1847 Mormon diaries and other records. Students are referred to that work; only minimal annotation is undertaken here. On leaving Fort Bridger, Reed camped at the base of Bridger Butte.

24. Pioneer Hollow.

25. To the crossing of Sulphur Creek; see the Mathers diary, Note 18. Stanton's letter of July 19, 1846, has a final addition made at Bear River the following morning, August 3. How was this letter sent back to Fort Bridger?

26. Probably near Cache Cave, at the head of Echo Canyon.

27. In Echo Canyon, some miles below Castle Rock. So early as 1846 Jefferson used the term "Echo Defile," though Lienhard's name was Willow Canyon.

28. On the Weber River near present Echo.

29. Compare the Reed account in the *Illinois Journal,* with accompanying Note 110. This camp was at present Henefer.

30. Reed writes the diary until the 10th from the viewpoint of the company, not as a personal record for his own travels. That would be consistent with his intention that the diary should guide friends and relatives in future years.

31. As seen in the Mathers diary, Note 26, Lienhard on August 3 met Hastings en route up the Weber to leave this notice. Thornton's account of the Donner tragedy relates that Hastings' letter was found "at the first crossing of Weber river, placed in the split of a stick, in such a situation as to call their attention to it. In this letter they were informed that the road down Weber river, over which the sixty-six wagons led by Lansford W. Hastings had passed, had been found to be a very bad one, and expressing fears that their sixty-six wagons could not be gotten through the canyon leading into the valley of the Great Salt Lake, then in sight; and advising them to remain in camp until he could return to them, for the purpose of showing them a

better road than that through the canyon of Weber river which here breaks through the mountains. . . . In this letter, Hastings had indicated another road which he affirmed was much better; and by pursuing which they would avoid the canyon. Messrs. Reed, Stanton, and Pike then went forward, for the purpose of exploring the contemplated new route."

According to Thornton, Stanton and Pike accompanied Reed on the ride to overtake Hastings. Although Reed, as quoted in Note 110, says that McCutchen was the third man, this confuses McCutchen's subsequent ride to Sutter's with Stanton in quest of supplies; note that McKinstry, in his letter in the *California Star* of February 13, 1847 (see Volume II), specifically names "Messrs. Reed, Stanton and Pike" in the present connection.

32. The wagons ascended Main Canyon to camp beyond the divide at the head springs in Dixie Hollow. With Hastings and Hudspeth, Clyman had camped here on June 3.

33. What appears in records of the 1840's as Bosman or Bauchmin's creek was called by Stansbury in 1849 Beauchemin's Creek, the present East Canyon Creek. The U. S. Geological Survey's *East Canyon Creek* quadrangle, reflecting modern interest in the subject, undertakes to locate the Donner-Mormon trail through this area and on across the Wasatch, on the whole correctly, but an error is made in taking the trail down through Dixie Hollow to East Canyon Creek. As shown by the Mormon diaries of 1847 quoted by Korns, the Donners found it necessary to detour the brush-choked lower reaches of Dixie Hollow, reaching East Canyon Creek half a mile above its narrows by a ravine which debouches into the canyon bottom half a mile below Dixie Hollow. Thus far across the mountains Reed had been following Bryant's trail of July 24 as well as Clyman's trail of June 3-4 (though Clyman, for one, was able to traverse Dixie Hollow, not being burdened with wagons). Bryant turned down East Canyon to the Morgan meadows, but Reed stayed with Clyman's trail some days longer. He markedly underestimates mileages while crossing the Wasatch.

34. Actually Reed ascended East Canyon about 8 miles, this day and the next, to Little Emigration Canyon, before leaving "Basman Creek."

35. The camp was in Little Emigration Canyon. "Reeds Gap," so called because Reed had been conducted to that point by Hastings, next year was renamed by the Mormon Pioneers "Pratt's Pass," but soon became known simply as Big Mountain. Clyman's is the first recorded description.

36. We infer from Thornton's narrative that it was on this sixth day of cutting out the road that the Graves family, with their three wagons, overtook the Donners, the last addition to the company.

W. C. Graves, writing in the Healdsburg *Russian River Flag,* April 26, 1877, implies that the family overtook the Donners immediately after Reed's return over the mountains, but there are so many inaccuracies in Graves's account that we accept Thornton as a better authority. By way of confirmation, in his narrative printed in the *Pacific Rural Press,* March 25, 1871, Reed says, "The afternoon of the second day, we left the creek turning to the right in a canyon, leading to a divide. Here Mr. Graves and family overtook us." Franklin Ward Graves and his family had left St. Joseph with the last company from there; see many references in Volume II to this company, initially captained by (Fabritus?) Smith, in which Edward Trimble was killed by the Pawnees.

37. Reed's 1871 recollection was that on the evening (afternoon) of the day the Graves family came up, "the first accident that had occurred was caused by the upsetting of one of my wagons," which goes to confirm the diary entry. Thornton would have it that the accident occurred at the south shore of Great Salt Lake, and that Reed had to go fifteen miles to obtain timber for the repairs on which William H. Eddy and Samuel Shoemaker worked all night. Unless there were two such accidents, I prefer to go along with the diary.

38. Having crossed Big Mountain to Mountain Dell, and descended that canyon nearly to the present reservoir, the Donners were now again encamped preliminary to crossing Little Mountain into Emigration Canyon. Clyman and Hastings in June had ascended Parleys Canyon to Mountain Dell, .but that canyon was obviously too much for wagons in 1846 (a road through it first opened in 1850), and the Donner Party crossed the divide into the next canyon north. The Mormons, with far more manpower at their disposal, did the same in 1847; and until the 1860's Emigration Canyon was the standard approach to Salt Lake City. It would appear from Thornton that Stanton and Pike rejoined the Donner company in Mountain Dell, after a period of recuperation following the hard ride with Reed to overtake Hastings. Lienhard had left the Twenty Wells on August 14. If Stanton and Pike turned back then, they should have been able to reach Mountain Dell by the 16th in easy stages, so there is about a two-day discrepancy. Accordingly, Stanton and Pike may have returned to the camp in Little Emigration Canyon, east of the divide, and on the 16th.

39. In Emigration Canyon; see next note.

40. At its mouth in 1846 Emigration Canyon was obstructed by an abutment from the south wall now called Donner Hill. "The canyon being impracticable as a wagon way," Thornton relates, "they doubled teams and got their wagons to the top of the hill, from which there was a gradual descent into the valley." In her "Across the Plains in the Donner Party," Virginia Reed Murphy recalled in 1891

that "we reached the end of the canyon where it looked as though our wagons would have to be abandoned. It seemed impossible for the oxen to pull them up the steep hill and the bluffs beyond, but we doubled teams and the work was, at last, accomplished, almost every yoke in the train being required to pull up each wagon." Salt Lake Valley was in full view, for the Donners had reached an upper bench of Pleistocene Lake Bonneville. In 1847 the Mormon Pioneers followed the Donner route across the Wasatch without the slightest variation, except that they cut a road past this obstruction in Emigration Canyon in preference to hazarding the dangerous ascent of Donner Hill. They too emerged into the open valley by ascending the southern side of the Emigration gulch. The modern "This is the Place Monument" stands north of the gulch and does not commemorate an exact site.

41. The Jordan River, where Clyman had crossed in June and Bryant in July, four miles south of the North Temple Street ford used by some of the Harlan-Young party, and about 10½ miles south of where Lienhard (and doubtless Jefferson and Mathers) forded the river at present North Salt Lake. For a detailed discussion of these fords, see Korns, *op. cit.*, pp. 135-137, 206.

42. This junction with the Harlan-Young road was near present Magna; Reed seems to say he camped 1½ miles west of the junction. In his 1871 narrative Reed remarked: "We progressed our way and crossed the outlet of the Utah, now called Jordan, a little below the location of Salt Lake City. From this camp in a day's travel we made connection with the trail of the companies that Hastings was piloting through his cutoff. We then followed his road around the lake. . . ."

43. Reed's 18 days evidently were August 7-24. The mileages given in his diary add up to 39, rather than 30 miles. (But he would be referring to the mountain travel only, actually less than 30 miles by his consistent underestimates.) Reed repeated the figures, 18 days and 30 miles, in his *Illinois Journal* account. In his letter of February, 1847, McKinstry speaks of 30 miles having been accomplished in 16 days. By the Mormon roadometer in 1847, the true distance from the site of Henefer to the point of emergence into Salt Lake Valley was 35 miles.

44. Luke Halloran, a waif picked up at Fort Bridger, was buried at the site of Grantsville. At the same place, as recorded by Lienhard, a brother-in-law of William Fowler named John Hargrave had died on August 11, buried the following day. Reed says that Halloran "made himself known to me as a Master Mason" before his death. Thornton adds that he "gave his property, some $1500, to Mr. George Donner," and the company buried him "at the side of an emigrant who had died in the advance company." Halloran

was thus the first casualty in the Donner Party proper, having been one of their number less than four weeks.

45. The repetitive account of Halloran's burial is further evidence that Reed kept this diary spasmodically, bringing it up to date as convenience permitted.

46. The first fresh water was Burnt Spring in Skull Valley, some 20 miles along; hence Reed may have stopped at a saline spring farther north, after rounding the northern end of the Stansbury Mountains. His course was more north than west until he reached the Big Spring near Timpie.

47. Probably where Mathers encamped on August 13-14; see the Mathers diary, Note 35.

48. According to Thornton, at this camp the Donner Party "found a letter from Lansford W. Hastings, informing them that it would occupy two days and nights of hard driving to reach the next water and grass." Eliza P. Donner Houghton, though only four years old at the time, considerably elaborates upon this remark in her *The Expedition of the Donner Party and Its Tragic Fate* (Chicago, 1911), pp. 39-40.

49. The preliminary drive on August 30 was to Redlum Spring. Reed seems to recommend that emigrants should cut across the northern end of Skull Valley as does the modern highway, then rounding the Cedar Mountains by Low Pass. But there was no water on such a route; in 1846 no material improvement on the Hastings road was possible.

50. Compare Reed's rather disorganized diary entries respecting the disastrous Salt Desert crossing with Virginia E. B. Reed's letter of May 16, 1847, printed in the present work. In his 1871 narrative Reed made his fullest statement:

"We started to cross the desert traveling day and night only stopping to feed and water our teams as long as water and grass lasted. We must have made at least two-thirds of the way across when a great portion of the cattle showed signs of giving out. Here the company requested me to ride on and find the water and report. Before leaving I requested my principal teamster [Milford Elliott], that when my cattle became so exhausted that they could not proceed further with the wagons, to turn them out and drive them on the road after me until they reached the water, but the teamster misunderstanding unyoked them when they first showed symptoms of giving out, starting on with them for the water.

"I found the water about twenty miles from where I left the company and started on my return. About eleven o'clock at night [September 2], I met my teamsters with all my cattle and horses. I cautioned them particularly to keep the cattle on the road, for that as soon as they would scent the water they would break for it. I proceeded on and reached my family and wagons. Some time after leaving the man one of the horses gave out and while they were striving to get it along, the cattle scented the water and started for it. And when they started with the horses, the cattle were out of sight, they could not find them or their trail, as they told me afterward. They supposing the cattle would find water, went on to camp. The next morning they could not be found, and they never were, the Indians getting them, except one ox and one cow. Losing nine yoke of cattle here was the first of my sad misfortunes. I stayed with my family and wagons the next day, expecting every hour the return of some of my young men with water, and the information of the arrival of the cattle at the water. Owing to the mistake of the teamsters in turning the cattle out so soon, the other wagons had drove miles past mine and dropped their wagons along the road, as their cattle gave out, and some few of them reaching water with their wagons. Receiving no information and the water being nearly exhausted, in the evening [September 3] I started on foot with my family to reach the water. In the course of the night the children became exhausted. I stopped, spread a blanket and laid them down covering them with shawls. In a short time a cold hurricane commenced blowing; the children soon complained of the cold. Having four [five] dogs with us, I had them lie down with the children outside the covers. They were then kept warm. Mrs. Reed and myself sitting to the windward helped shelter them from the storm. Very soon one of the dogs jumped up and started out barking, the others following, making an attack on something approaching us. Very soon I got sight of an animal making directly for us; the dogs seizing it changed its course, and when passing I discovered it to be one of my young steers. Incautiously stating that it was mad, in a moment my wife and children started to their feet, scattering like quail, and it was some minutes before I could quiet camp; there was no more complaining of being tired or sleepy the balance of the night. We arrived about daylight [September 4] at the wagons of Jacob Donner, and the next in advance of me, whose cattle having given out, had been driven to water. Here I first learned of the loss of my cattle, it being the second day after they had started for the water. Leaving my family with Mrs. Donner, I reached the encampment. Many of the people were out hunting cattle, some of them had got their teams together and were going back into the desert for their wagons. Among them Mr. Jacob Donner, who kindly brought my family along with his own to the encampment."

Although somewhat confused, Thornton's account should be compared with the above. Thornton's dates are incorrect, but the facts as he gathered them from William H. Eddy would indicate that the desert crossing required from August 31 to September 2 for the advance contingent. Eddy with some others evidently reached the springs at Pilot Peak at 10 A.M. on September 2, after leaving his wagon 20 miles out. Reed reached the water at Pilot Peak just at dark to report that his wagons and those of the Donners were 40 miles out. After resting an hour, he turned back into the desert, accompanied for 5 miles by Eddy, who carried a bucket of water to resuscitate an ox. Thornton says that Reed "met the drivers ten miles from the spring, coming forward with the cattle. He continued on, and the drivers came into camp about midnight, having lost all of Mr. Reed's team after passing him." By this account, the Donner brothers got to water, with part of their teams, about 2 A.M. on September 3. At daylight Eddy started back, and at dawn on the 4th brought up Mrs. Reed and her children in his wagon. This same day, September 4 (by Thornton's account, the 14th; but Thornton's dates must be corrected by reference to Reed's diary), some of the company "started back with Mr. Reed and Mr. Graves, for the wagons of the Messrs. Donner and Reed: and brought them up with horses and mules, on the evening of the [5th]."

51. Reed wrote in 1871: "We remained here [at Pilot Peak] for days hunting cattle, some of the party finding all, others a portion, all having enough to haul their wagons except myself. On the next day, or day following, while I was out hunting my cattle, two Indians came to the camp, and by signs gave the company to understand that there were so many head of cattle out, corroborating the number still missing; many of the people became tender footed at the Indians coming into camp, thinking that they were spies. Wanted to get clear of them as soon as possible. My wife requested that the Indians should be detained until my return, but unfortunately before returning they had left. The next morning, in company with young Mr. [William C.] Graves—he kindly volunteering—I started in the direction the Indians had taken; after hunting this day and the following, remaining out during the night, we returned unsuccessful, not finding a trace of the cattle. I now gave up all hope of finding them and turned my attention to making arrangements for proceeding on my journey. In the desert were my eight [three] wagons; all the team remaining was an ox and a cow. There was no alternative but to leave everything but provisions, bedding and clothing. These were placed in the wagon that had been used for my family. I made a cache of everything else. Members of the company kindly furnishing team to haul the wagon to camp. I divided my provisions with those who were nearly out, and indeed some of them were in need. I had now to make arrangement for sufficient team to haul that one wagon; one of the company kindly loaned me a yoke of cattle, and with the ox and cow I had, made two yoke. We remained at this camp from first to last, if my memory is right, seven days."

According to Thornton, 36 head of working cattle were lost by the company, "and the oxen that survived were greatly injured. One of Mr. Reed's wagons was brought to camp; and two, with all they contained, were buried in the plain. George Donner lost one wagon. Kiesburg also lost a wagon." Compare Virginia Reed's letter of May 16, 1847.

52. Again compare Thornton's version for this day's travel and the next: "Having yoked some loose cows, as a team for Mr. Reed, they broke up their camp on the morning of September 16th [10th], and resumed their toilsome journey . . . . On this day they traveled six miles, encountering a very severe snow storm. About 3 o'clock P.M., they met Milton Elliot and William Graves, returning from a fruitless drive to find some cattle that had got off. They informed them that they were in the immediate vicinity of a spring, at which commenced another dry drive of forty miles. They encamped for the night, and at dawn of day of September 17th [11th], they resumed their journey, and at 4 o'clock, A.M., of the 18th [12th] they arrived at water and grass, some of their cattle having perished, and the teams which survived being in a very enfeebled condition."

Seemingly it was on this day, September 10, that Charles T. Stanton and William McCutchen left the company to ride ahead to Sutter's for supplies. Thornton says that "Messrs. Stanton and McCutcheon" departed on this mission "on the day they broke up their encampment on the Salt Lake," and George McKinstry's narration in the *California Star,* February 13, 1847, is to the same effect (see Volume II). See also the remarks by Reed in the *Illinois Journal* account.

53. This was the long drive to the springs at the Johnson Ranch. Mathers had arrived at these springs on the early morning of August 24. Reed had fallen farther and farther behind since encamping on the Weber River August 6. He was then, in effect, four days in the rear; now he trailed by nineteen days.

54. In bringing his diary up to date, Reed at first overlooked the fact that he did not reach Jefferson's "Relief Springs" till the 12th.

55. To Flowery Lake.

56. Across Jasper Pass to Mound Springs, two in number, as Reed says. Oddly, Bryant tells of an altercation in the Russell pack party at Flowery Springs on August 7; there must have been something about the place!

57. Across Spruce Mountain Ridge to the Warm Spring in Clover Valley.

58. Over the southern shoulder of the East Humboldt Mountains to Ruby Valley, encamping perhaps on Thompson Creek. Thornton says the Donner Party applied the name of the Fifty Springs to Ruby Valley; to Jefferson it was Valley of Fountains, while Reed calls

it Mineral Valley.

59. The night camp may have been about 4 miles south of Ruby Valley P. O. I do not quote Thornton's version of the daily marches after September 10, as he seems to have become confused. See the analysis by Korns.

60. The encampment was about 20 miles south of Ruby Valley P. O. Cave Creek, passed during the day, is shown by Jefferson and still so called.

61. Probably near the Davis Ranch, the last camp in Ruby Valley.

62. Across Overland Pass to Huntington Creek. Reed may have encamped where Mathers and Jefferson had on September 2.

63. Reed's name for Huntington Creek reflects its tendency to flow underground over a stretch of some 15 miles. He may have encamped where the stream first disappears, a mile south of the Sadler Ranch.

64. On the 23rd Reed probably encamped half a dozen miles south of the confluence of Huntington and Smith creeks, next day halting above the small canyon through which Huntington Creek passes to join the South Fork of the Humboldt. Mathers had camped in this vicinity on September 5.

65. In South Fork Canyon, which has an open space midway of its length.

66. Thornton says, concerning the arrival on the Humboldt, "On the [26th] they pursued their way down the canyon, and after traveling eight miles, came out into the valley of Mary's river, at night, and encamped on the bank of the stream, having struck the road leading from Fort Hall. Here some Indians came into camp and informed them by signs, that they were yet distant about two hundred miles from the sinks of that river."

67. Presumably on Susie Creek below Carlin (sometimes called Moleen) Canyon.

68. The hot springs were at present Carlin; Thornton intimates that the previous night's encampment was at that point.

69. Back to the Humboldt at Gravelly Ford. Thornton, who combines the events of the 28th and 29th, relates: "On the morning of the 2d [*sic*] they commenced passing over these hills. About 11 o'clock, an Indian, who spoke a little English, came to them, to whom they gave the name of Thursday, on account of their believing that to be the day; although at the time, they were inclined to believe that they had lost one day in their calculation of time [!] About 4 o'clock, P.M., another came to them, who also spoke a little English . . . . They traveled all that day, and at dark encamped at a spring about half way down the side of the mountain. A fire broke out in the grass, soon after the camp fires had been kindled, which would have consumed three of the wagons, but for the assistance of these two Indians. The Indians were fed and after the evening

meal they lay down by one of the fires, but rose in the night, stealing a fine shirt and a yoke of oxen from Mr. Graves."

70. On the Humboldt 8 or 9 miles east of Argenta Station.

71. Probably on the north bank of the Humboldt about midway between Battle Mountain and Argenta, somewhat west of Jefferson's and Mathers' camp of September 11; note the coincidence that Jefferson shows "Pauta Lodges" a day's journey below that camp. Thornton notes merely that the emigrants camped this night "on Ogden's river, after a hard and exhausting drive. During the night the Indians stole a horse from Mr. Graves." W. C. Graves writes in *Russian River Flag*, April 26, 1877, "we had no more trouble till we got to Gravelly Ford, on the Humboldt, where the Indians stole two of father's oxen and in two days after they stole a horse . . . ." That memory accords exactly with Reed's diary.

72. Reed encamped on October 2 on the north bank of the river about midway between Battle Mountain and Stonehouse, and on the 3rd near Stonehouse, on the south bank of the Humboldt. On the 4th, for which Reed began an entry never completed, he probably camped in the vicinity of Redhouse, after going another 10 or 15 miles. On the 5th, as he was toiling through "Pauta Pass" near Iron Point, he became embroiled with John Snyder, hired man for the Graves family, with fatal consequences for the party as a whole. It will be enough here to quote McGlashan:

"On this fifth of October, 1846, F. W. Graves was ahead, Jay Fosdick second, John Snyder third, and the team of J. F. Reed fourth. Milton Elliott was driving Reed's team. Arriving at the foot of a steep, sandy hill, the party was obliged to 'double teams,' that is, to hitch five or six yoke of oxen to one wagon. Elliott and Snyder interchanged hot words over some difficulty about the oxen. Fosdick had attached his team to Graves' and had drawn Graves' wagon up the hill. Snyder, being nettled at something Elliott had said, declared that his team could pull up alone. During the excitement Snyder made use of very bad language, and was beating his cattle over the head with his whip-stock. One account says that Reed's team and Snyder's became tangled. At all events, Snyder was very much enraged. Reed had been off hunting on horseback, and arriving at this moment, remonstrated with Snyder for beating the cattle, and at the same time offered him the assistance of his team. Snyder refused the proffered aid, and used abusive language toward both Reed and Elliott. Reed attempted to calm the enraged man. Both men were of fiery, passionate dispositions, and words began to multiply rapidly. When Reed saw that trouble was likely to occur, he said something about waiting until they got up the hill and settling this matter afterwards. Snyder evidently construed this to be a threat, and with an oath replied, 'We will settle it now.' As Snyder uttered these words, he struck Reed a blow on the head with the butt-end of his heavy whip-stock. This blow was followed in rapid succession by a second, and a third. As the third stroke descended, Mrs. Reed ran between her husband and the furious man, hoping to prevent the blow. Each time the whip-stock descended on Reed's head it cut deep gashes. He was blinded with the blood which streamed from his wounds, and dazed and stunned by the terrific force of the blows. He saw the cruel whip-stock uplifted, and knew that his wife was in danger, but had only time to cry 'John! John!' when down came the stroke full upon Mrs. Reed's head and shoulders. The next instant John Snyder was staggering, speechless and death-stricken. Reed's hunting-knife had pierced his left breast, severing the first and second ribs and entering the left lung . . . . W. C. Graves . . . caught the dying man in his arms, and in a few minutes he was carried a little way up the hill and laid upon the ground. Reed immediately regretted the act and threw the knife from him. His wife and daughters gathered about him and began to stanch the blood that flowed from the gashes on his head. He gently pushed them aside and went to the assistance of the dying man. He and Snyder had always been firm friends, and Snyder had been most active in securing a team for Reed after the latter had lost his cattle in the desert. Snyder expired in about fifteen minutes, and Reed remained by his side until the last . . . . Camp was immediately pitched, the Reed family being a little removed down the hill from the main body of emigrants. Reed felt that he had only acted in defense of his own life and in defense of the wife he adored. Nevertheless, it was evident that trouble was brewing in the main camp where Snyder's body was lying . . . . The feeling ran so high that at one time the end of a wagon-tongue was propped up with an ox-yoke by some of the emigrants with the intention of hanging Reed thereon, but calmer counsel prevailed [and he was told that he was to be banished. At first he refused to comply, but at last his wife] urged him to remember the want and destination in which they and the entire company were already participants. If he . . . would go forward, if he would reach California, he could return with provisions, and meet them on the mountains at that point on the route where they would be in greatest need. It was a fearful struggle, but finally the mother's counsels prevailed. Prior to setting out upon his gloomy journey, Mr. Reed made the company promise to care for his family."

73. Reed's letter of June 16, 1846, to his brother-in-law was originally printed in the Springfield *Sangamo Journal*, July 30, 1846, under the head, "Sports of the West," and with the introductory remark, "The following letter from a late citizen of this place, now on his way to Oregon, with his family, has been politely communicated to us for publication."

74. See Fred B. Rogers, *William Brown Ide Bear Flagger* (San Francisco, 1962), which reprints Ide's letters to the *Sangamo Journal,* written en route to California in 1845. For Reed's brother-in-law, Robert Cadden Keyes, see Index.

75. The superiority of his blooded mare, misnamed Glaucus, is said to have contributed to the dislike of Reed felt by some in the company and which weighed against him afterward.

76. The original letter is in the George Wharton James Collection, Southwest Museum, clearly written to Mary C. Keyes, though sent in care of "Mrs. M. Gillespia" at Edwardsville, Ill. It was first printed, with notes by Frances E. Watkins in *The Masterkey,* May 1944, vol. 18, p. 82.

77. For Sarah Keyes and her grave, see Index.

78. Young Virginia had a pleasant way with numbers. For "20050" read 250.

79. Bonney did not succeed in returning to Oregon. See Volume II, Index.

80. Originally printed in *Sangamo Journal,* November 5, 1846.

81. Compare Reed's diary for July 18-22.

82. Louis Vasquez and Jim Bridger had gone down to Fort Laramie in the spring, as appears elsewhere in this work. The precise date of their return to the fort has not been established. The Reed Papers include a note signed by Vasquez on July 30 authorizing "Mr. Jas. Reed to take where ever he should find three horses stolen or strayed from us," two bearing the brand BV, and all described. The document is photographically reproduced in Carroll D. Hall, ed., *Donner Miscellany,* p. 30.

83. Here the *Sangamo Journal* interjected, "this is manifestly Capt. Freemont's newly discovered route to California," Fremont's letter of January 24, 1846, having by this time gone the rounds.

84. James M. Hudspeth had primarily taken on the job of finding a better-watered way than that across the Salt Desert.

85. Bridger was correct; the Salt Desert originated in the recession of Lake Bonneville into Great Salt Lake, the waters becoming progressively more saline as the surface area diminished.

86. As in his diary Reed gives this figure of 60 wagons ahead on the Hastings Cutoff. Compare the Mathers diary, Note 18.

87. But apparently Bridger did not visit the States in the winter of 1846-1847. Perhaps Vasquez "went in," carrying this letter, and Stanton's letter of July 19-August 3 as well.

88. See the McKinstry diary, Notes 69 and 70.

89. This paragraph is a major contribution to history, for it dates the genesis of Miles Goodyear's "Fort Buenaventura" on the site of Ogden. The Connecticut-born Goodyear had come west with Marcus Whitman in 1836 as a youth of 19 and since had made himself a

name among the mountain men. In the summer of 1845 he revisited the States, and on leaving Independence in September told the editor of the *Western Expositor* that he intended "building a kind of a fort, and cultivating a portion of ground, more as an experiment than anything else, and if possible make it a sort of *half way house* between this and Oregon and California, where the companies may stop and refresh themselves, and obtain re supplies, for he expects to have the coming summer all kinds of vegetables, and plenty of Indian corn and wheat, which they may pound up or grind into flour and meal." Possibly Goodyear originally proposed to establish this "half way house" in the Bear River Valley, for the westbound Mormons in 1847 first heard of him as a man who was making a farm in that valley. It is even possible that Nicholas Carriger encountered him in the Bear River Valley on July 24 or 25, just a week before Reed wrote this letter. Now, at Fort Bridger, he was about to make a permanent location; the new stream of traffic on the Hastings Cutoff suggested to him the advantages of a site in the Valley of the Great Salt Lake, near the mouth of Weber Canyon.

Goodyear's partner, Captain Wells (or Welles, or Wills) had apparently spent some time on the Arkansas at Hardscrabble. Alexander Barclay recorded in his diary on December 21, 1845, that Wells had killed two mountain men the previous day—justifiable homicide apparently. The following summer he had gone north to Fort Laramie, and as recorded by McKinstry and Bryant (see the McKinstry diary, Note 72, where Bryant's account of his antecedents is quoted), Wells rode on to Fort Bridger with the Russell party, arriving July 16. Sometime in the late summer of 1846 Goodyear and Wells commenced their fort. Goodyear then took a pack train of dressed deerskins south to Pueblo de los Angeles, leaving Wells to look after the fort. His return from California by way of the Hastings Cutoff has been recorded in our text by John Craig. The presence of Wells at Goodyear's post attracted much interest from the Mormons after they reached the valley of the Great Salt Lake, particularly because of the garden he was raising, irrigated with a bucket. They invited him to join their community, but he did not accept. What became of him after Goodyear sold his post to the Mormons in November, 1847, remains to be learned. Goodyear himself died in the California gold fields in the fall of 1849. For fuller information, see Dale L. Morgan, "Miles Goodyear and the Founding of Ogden," *Utah Historical Quarterly,* April, July, 1953, vol. 21, pp. 195-218, 307-329.

90. What is here printed as Virginia Reed's letter of May 16, 1847, is clearly the original draft, preserved for many years among Reed's own papers until found by his daughter Patty, as described in the introductory sketch. The fair copy sent back to Illinois and printed in the Springfield *Illinois Journal,* December 16, 1847, was

reprinted by George R. Stewart in *Westways,* December, 1934, as
"A Child's Tale of the Donner Tragedy." After I called to his attention the existence of the photostatic copy of the draft original in
the Southwest Museum, Dr. Stewart printed that version in the appendix to the 1960 edition of his *Ordeal by Hunger;* he was primarily concerned, however, to render Virginia's original text, without
much regard for Reed's additions and corrections. My own concern
is to render the draft text in such a form as to enable us to comprehend what Virginia wrote originally, and also what Reed added, even
capitalization; this makes the document as printed somewhat ungainly,
but I imagine students will bear with my editorial apparatus. James
W. Keyes wrote Reed from St. Louis on March 24, 1848: "I Reced.
your letters & Virginia's they have extracts from them [been] published in many of the papers. Virginias letter was first published in
our own paper, and was copied by the N. Y. Herald, Tribune, &
several other papers, it Contained the most heart-rending account of
human suffering, that ever has taken place in this Country . . ."
(Reed Papers, Sutter's Fort Collection). Mary Keyes, to whom Virginia's letter was addressed, as shown by the version printed in 1847,
was the daughter of James W. Keyes.

91. See Reed's diary and his letter of July 31, 1846.

92. See Reed's 1871 narrative quoted in Note 50. Virginia vividly
recalled this frightening night in her article of 1891.

93. Virginia similarly wrote in 1891: "Some of the company went
back with papa and assisted him in cacheing everything that could
not be packed in one wagon. A cache was made by digging a hole
in the ground, in which a box or the bed of a wagon was placed.
Articles to be buried were packed into this box, covered with boards,
and the earth thrown in upon them, and thus they were hidden from
sight. Our provisions were divided among the company."

94. Like Reed himself, Virginia could not bring herself in 1847
to tell of Snyder's death and Reed's expulsion from the company,
though she freely discussed these matters in her 1879 correspondence
with McGlashan.

95. It is singular how Virginia refers to Stanton as "a man" and
"that man" in this letter. Did she have some hostile feeling about
him? Though Thornton says he arrived about October 1, it is not
known precisely when Stanton reached Sutter's Fort. October 15
may be an approximation, for the McGlashan papers contain a transcript of a note he wrote Sutter dated 'Monday Morning 20th Oct,"
clearly written from near Johnson's Ranch:
"Dear Sir,
"Yesterday the large mule became lame with his heavy pack. I got
Mr. Rhodes, one of the emigrants to examine him who said that his
lameness was caused by a *Sweency* [?]

"I have tried hard to get another horse but could not succeed. If I find the mule will not stand the journey, I will send it back by some of the companies and *cache* his load. . . .
P S Saw Mr McKinstry this morning who will be with you in a day or two."

It had been supposed on Thornton's authority that Stanton rejoined the Donner Party on October 19, on the third day after they commenced the ascent of the Truckee River, but the chronology will have to be restudied. It will be noted that in the opening entry of his diary, Patrick Breen says that Stanton did not get back until (it would seem) November 1, after the unsuccessful first effort to surmount Donner Pass. If this view is correct, Stanton's conduct is all the more honorable, for he must have crossed the summit after the first heavy storm. Reed tells in his *Illinois Journal* account of meeting Stanton in Bear Valley, which would have been about October 22. One would suppose that he had time to get over the pass in advance of the snowfall of October 28, though something could have happened to delay him in the ascent toward Donner Pass, and he might then have been stormbound on October 29-30.

George W. Tucker's 1879 statement in the McGlashan Papers tells of reaching Bear Valley and of Stanton's going past with the pack mules and the Indian vaqueros lent by Sutter; "that Same day J. F. Reed of the Donner party also past us." William C. Graves, writing in the *Russian River Flag,* May 3, 1877, says that the Donner company met Stanton on the Truckee: "he told us to go slow and recruit our teams, so they could pull us over the mountains, for they were very rough; that there was no danger of the snow, for others had crossed in midwinter and we could do the same; so we did as he said, and lost five days between there and the mountains, which would have put us over safely had we kept on and not taken his advice." In 1879 Graves wrote McGlashan that they met Stanton at Wadsworth where the trail came in off the Forty-Mile Desert. In no way do these recollections accord with Breen's diary. Having opened up an important question, I leave it for future disposition.

96. Reed seems to have reached Sutter's in just six days from Bear Valley, October 23-28.

97. Evidently on October 31; see Breen's diary. But on Eddy's authority Thornton writes that the party encamped upon Truckee Lake at dark on October 28 and next morning "went on within three miles of the top of the Pass, where they found the snow about five feet deep. This compelled them to return to a cabin, which was situated one mile in advance of their camp of the previous night. Here they remained in camp during the 30th. At dark their fellow-travelers, Stanton, Graves, the Donners, and some others, came up.

"On the morning of Oct. 31st the whole body again started to cross the mountain. They succeeded in getting within three miles of the top of the Pass. The snow had deepened to about ten feet. The night was bitterly cold; the wind howled through the trees, and the snow and hail descended. Finding it utterly impossible to cross, they commenced retracing their steps on the morning of November 1st, and arrived at the cabin about 4 o'clock."

98. See the Breen diary for Notes respecting these matters.

99. Virginia is now describing the unsuccessful venture of November 21-23.

100. The "snowshoe party" set out December 16 after the preparations Breen describes. Their misfortunes are more fully described elsewhere in this work.

101. On January 4, as recorded by Breen.

102. On January 8; see the Breen diary.

103. Probably Aquilla Glover.

104. Carcajous, or wolverines.

105. The Reeds and Breens alone suffered no losses.

106. A certain amount of sport was made of Eliza Williams, an old maid in Illinois but now destined for a more ample life. Apparently her suitor was Antonio Armijo, but she exercised her woman's prerogative and married someone else. Pattie Reed, by then Mrs. Martha Lewis, wrote McGlashan on April 16, 1879: "Eliza was so deaf that she could but faintly hear a loud loud voice, always so afflicted from birth. . . . [Her brother Baylis did not survive the overland journey but] Eliza did worry through, went to Mr Sinclair's with us, from there to Mr George Younts in Napa, from there to San Jose Mission, from there to San Jose, while at Mr Yount, she became acquainted with Thomas Foulmer, he accompanied her to the mission, & their, they made up their minds to have the holy knot tied. . . . when they came to San Jose they lived near us, & Father & Mother did provide for them, for years, but Father & Mother went to sleep, asleep in Heaven, & poor Eliza lived eight month, after that sad, sad day. . . . [She] was buried in the Catholic burial grounds, her husband's choice, in sight of my house." The 1860 census records at San Jose a family consisting of Thomas Fulmer, 44, born in Prussia, Elizabeth, 45, born in Virginia, and two children born in California, Virginia E., 11, and John, 9.

107. The interlineation in the draft original to "Dochter Maniel," properly McNiel, refers to a message added to the fair copy. As printed in the *Illinois Journal*, December 16, 1847, Virginia's letter concludes as follows: "Tell the girls that this is the greatest place for marrying they ever saw, and that they must come to California if they want to marry. Tell —— that —— is engaged to be married. You all think this is a joke, but I tell you 'tis the real truth. Tell Doctor —— that they doctor the funniest in this country that

he ever saw. They grease the sick all over with mantaja and kill a bienna and cut it in four pieces, and put a great piece of fat carrina on the wrist, and kill a sheep and wrap the sick up in the skin. Father is now down at St. Francisco. He is going to write when he comes back. Give my love to all.—So no more at present, my dear cousin."

George R. Stewart has spelled out the Spanish terminology in Virginia's medical report: "We may take *mantaja* as *manteca,* butter or lard; *carrina* is probably for *carne,* meat. As for *bienna,* my guess is that it is for *gallina,* hen. . . ." Stewart's further remarks about this letter, in its various versions, may be read with interest in his *Ordeal by Hunger,* 1960 edition, pp. 348-354.

108. That is, Reed was then visiting at Yerba Buena, or as it had now been renamed, San Francisco.

109. Apparently this narrative was first printed in the *Illinois State Register,* December 3, 1847. The *Sangamo Journal* on September 10, 1846, was renamed *Illinois Journal,* Whig interests. The list of those who lived and died [reprinted in Volume II] had appeared in the *Journal* September 2, followed a week later by the Breen diary, derived from the St. Louis *Reveille.*

110. Compare Reed's 1871 account quoted in Note 50.

111. See Note 43 above.

112. Compare Note 52; Stanton and McCutchen set out from the Pilot Peak area September 10.

113. See Note 72 and the discussion of "The Reed Map." Reed separated from the company east of present Golconda, above the bend of the Humboldt.

114. Note the somewhat variant figures on the face of the Reed Map. Apparently he reached the camp in Bear Valley on the afternoon of October 22, continuing on to Sutter's the following morning.

115. Reed later wrote a much fuller account of this abortive first effort to recross the Sierra, which I omit for lack of space; William McCutchen added some remarks, printed at the conclusion of Reed's, in the *Pacific Rural Press,* April 1, 1871. Both tell of getting as far as the camp of Jotham Curtis and his wife in Bear Valley. The Curtises, who had set out from Missouri in William Fowler's company and had undertaken to winter with their wagons in the high country, were badly frightened by heavy snowfalls. According to an article by Frances H. McDougall in the *Pacific Rural Press* for January 21, 1871—a story which provoked Reed and McCutchen into writing their own account of the Donner tragedy—Reed had made his meal of "wheel-grease and mustard" at the Curtis wagon, left on the mountain until it could be recovered. See also Thornton's more nearly contemporary narrative respecting the Curtises.

116. J. H. Merryman no doubt hashed up the account Reed had sent his brother-in-law; Reed went to the Pueblo de San Jose and

served there under Captain Charles M. Weber in the campaign culminating in the battle of Natividad, but he did not go south to Pueblo de los Angeles during this period when the fate of his family was in doubt.

117. There are three different versions of Eddy's journal, the one here reprinted, another in John Sinclair's statement of February, 1847, printed in Edwin Bryant's *What I Saw in California,* pp. 251-255; and a third in Thornton's *Oregon and California in 1848,* vol. 2, pp. 129-156. No effort is made here to reconcile the discrepancies.

118. Compare Reed's diary of the Second Donner Relief printed herein.

119. Reed is more outspoken about Woodworth in this letter than in any other document relating to the Donner tragedy.

120. Although Reed appears as the authority, we should be slow to accept these remarks as factual. As written, they could apply only to the Donner families.

121. The Breen family refused to go on. See the "Diaries of the Donner Relief" printed herein.

122. Such is Reed's summation of the Third Donner Relief.

123. Reprinted from the Springfield *Illinois Journal,* December 23, 1847.

DIARY OF PATRICK BREEN

1. See the Reed section, Notes 95 and 97. The second effort to cross the divide having failed, the Breens settled in at the Schallenberger cabin which had stood since 1844 at the foot of Donner Lake.

2. According to Thornton, who had his information from Eddy, on the morning of November 2, Eddy "commenced building a cabin. When finished the following day, he went into it, with Mrs. Murphy and family, and Wm. Foster and family, Nov. 3d. The snow at the place at which they were encamped, was about one foot deep. A single ox constituted the whole stock upon which the family were to winter.

"Mr. Eddy commenced hunting on the 4th, and succeeded in killing a prairie wolf, of which supper was made in the evening for all in the cabin. On the 5th he succeeded in killing an owl, of which supper was made. The Messrs. Graves, Donner, Dolan, and Brinn commenced killing their cattle. Mr. Eddy also killed his ox. On the 6th, an ox belonging to Graves starved to death. He refused to save it for meat, but upon Mr. Eddy's applying to him for it, he would not let him have it for less than $25. This, Mr. Eddy told me, he had paid the estate of the deceased Graves since getting into the settlement. Mr. Eddy spent the 7th in hunting, but returned at night with a sad and desponding heart, without game. The three following days he assisted Graves in putting up a cabin for himself and family, and Mrs. Reed and her family. The day after, they cooked some of their poor beef."

The Donner families never had got their wagons all the way to the lake, and settled in on Alder Creek. Among the Reed Papers are several items dating from this time. On November 1, at "River Trucky," W. M. Foster authorizes Millford Elliott to purchase for him or hire four work mules and one set harness and 3 yoke work cattle, for which he will be responsible on his arrival in California. Next day Jacob Donner authorizes Elliott to purchase for him six yoke of work cattle and three beeves, for which he will pay cash or goods on arrival in California. In another note, undated, Jacob Donner writes Elliott: "Please bring me five mules to pack also four low priced active ponies suitable for women & children to ride, 200 weight flour 2 bushels beans. 2 gallons salt, 3 dollars worth sugar if it can be had on reasonable terms & a cheese." These instructions are given in case he returns this winter; if he stays until spring, perhaps oxen will be better. On the verso of Donner's note is one partly illegible: ". . . but a poor orphan . . . with nothing . . . dians killed my father. . . . I will give my rifle for a pony or a mule to ride John Trudeau." Since a fourth note, signed by George Donner, is dated November 28, 1846, Jacob's second note may be of comparatively later date. This fourth note authorizes Elliott "to purchase and buy whatever pro-property he may deem necessary for my distress in the mountains for which on my arrival in Callifornia I will pay the Cash or goods or both." Food supplies are listed, also "5 pack mules and two horses —purchase or hire." See Carroll D. Hall, ed., *Donner Miscellany,* pp. 33-35, for the full texts of these notes, found in the pocket of the Miller-Reed diary.

3. Breen does not refer to the first effort made to cross the mountains after the storms subsided, but Thornton tells the tale: "On the 12th, Mr. Eddy, C. T. Stanton, Wm. Graves, Sen. [*i.e.,* Franklin Graves], Jay Fosdick, James Smith, Charles Burger, Wm. Foster, Antoine (a Spaniard), John Baptiste, Lewis, Salvadore, Augustus Spitzer, Mary Graves, Sarah Fosdick, and Milton Elliot, being the strongest of the party, started to cross the mountains on foot. Mr. Eddy, in narrating the afflicting story, said to me, that he could never forget the parting scene between himself and family; but he hoped to get in and obtain relief, and return with the means for their rescue. They started with a small piece of beef each; but they had scarcely gone within three miles of the top of the Pass, when the snow, which was soft, and about ten feet deep, compelled them again to return to the cabins, which they reached about midnight." During the next ten days Eddy spent much of his time hunting, managing to kill a

few ducks, a squirrel, and on one great occasion, a bear weighing some 800 pounds.

4. According to Thornton, on November 21 "six women and sixteen men, including Stanton and the two Indians, made another effort to cross the mountain on foot. . . . They crossed the pass on the crust of the snow. Mr. Eddy measured the snow here, and found it to be twenty-five feet deep. They encamped in a little valley on the west side of the mountain, in six feet snow. They experienced great difficulty in kindling a fire and in getting wood, in consequence of their extreme weakness. Here Mr. Stanton and the two Indian boys refused to go any further, in consequence of not being able to get along with seven mules belonging to Capt. Sutter. Fully aware of their peril, Mr. Eddy exhausted all his reasoning powers in a vain effort to induce them to proceed; urging the imminent danger of their all perishing from starvation, and offering to become responsible for the mules. He knew that Capt. Sutter would rather lose the animals, than know that his fellow-beings had perished in a foolish attempt to save them: but all persuasion was in vain. He then proposed that they should compel the Indians to go forward. This was objected to; and a good deal of angry feeling was exhibited by Mr. Eddy, and those against whose plans he vainly remonstrated. Accordingly, on the morning of the 22d, faint and dispirited, they again commenced their return to their unhappy companions in peril. They arrived, almost exhausted, at the cabins about midnight. . . ."

As Breen notes and Thornton also says, the "mountaineers" hoped to make another effort on the 26th, but the furious storm prevented. In that storm the cattle that might have seen the beleagured emigrants through the winter strayed away and were lost.

5. On this day Stanton wrote his last letter, now in the Reed Papers:

Mrs Donner   9th Dec 1846

You will please send me 1# your best tobacco.

The storm prevented us from getting over the mountains   we are now getting snow shoes ready to go on foot   I should like to get your pocket compass as the snow is so very deep & in the event of a storm it would be invaluable

Milt & Mr Graves are coming right back and either can bring it back to you

The mules are all strayed off—If any should come round your camp —let some of our Company know it the first oportunity

Yours Very Respectfully

Capt. George Donner,   C. T. Stanton
          Donners Ville.

6. Breen now notes the departure of the snowshoers, among whom Stanton would be the first to die; snowblind and accepting his fate,

on a morning to come he would remain at the campfire smoking his pipe and telling the others to go on.

7. See Virginia Reed's account in her letter of May 16, 1847.

8. In this entry Breen sums up the grim worsening in the relationships at Donner Lake. Although names were omitted when the diary was originally printed in the *California Star,* William C. Graves saw fit to omit this, with like entries, from the version of the Breen diary included in his final contribution to the *Russian River Flag,* May 17, 1877.

9. The First Donner Relief, headed by Reasin P. Tucker and Aquilla Glover. Tucker had departed St. Joseph in 1846 in the Smith company as one of the Graves family's fellow emigrants.

10. Those who set out for the settlements with the First Relief were Mrs. Reed and her children Virginia, Patty, James, and Thomas; Mrs. Keseberg and her daughter Ada; Mrs. Wolfinger; Eliza Williams; John Denton; Noah James; three of the Graves children, William, Eleanor, and Lavina; two of the Murphy children, Mary and William; the child Naomi Pike; four of the Donner children, Leanna, Elitha, George, Jr., and William Hook; and two of the Breen children, Edward and Simon. Breen gives the total as 24 but all other sources say 23. It is odd that he does not mention the departure of his own children. As Breen observes, Patty and Thomas Reed soon had to be brought back. Of those who went on, John Denton, Ada Keseberg, and William Hook would not survive the journey.

11. The snowshoers in January had been forced to the last resort, but here is the first intimation of cannibalism east of the divide.

12. Sarah Winnemucca Hopkins, granddaughter of chief Truckee, was born in 1844, too late for any independent recollection, but in her *Life Among the Piutes,* p. 13, she tells of a band of white people who perished in the mountains. "We could have saved them, only my people were afraid of them. We never knew who they were, or where they came from. So, poor things, they must have suffered fearfully, for they all starved there. The snow was too deep." At the time, as observed earlier, Truckee and two of his sons were serving with Fremont's California Battalion.

13. Reed and the Second Relief, perhaps actually a party of 11 men. See the "Diaries of the Donner Relief," Note 19.

DIARIES OF THE DONNER RELIEF

1. The original manuscript has this heading, though it will be seen that not Ritchie but R. P. Tucker kept the journal after the first ten days.

2. The Edward M. Kern collection in the Henry E. Huntington Library, known as the "Fort Sutter Papers," includes a "Pay Roll of Men employed in expedition to California Mountains under Command of Edw. M. Kern, U. S.A.," as follows:

Names	Commencement of Service.	Expiration of Service	No. of Days Service	Pay per diem	Total Amt.
†Adolph Bruheim	Jan 31	Mar 19	48	$1.50	$ 72.00
*R. S. Moutey	Jan 31	Mar 5	34	3.00	102.00
*Aquila Glover	Jan 31	Mar 14	43	3.00	129.00
*Joseph Sel	Jan 31	Mar 5	34	3.00	102.00
*Edward Cophymeyer	Jan 31	Mar 5	34	3.00	102.00
*Danl Rhodes	Jan 31	Mar 9	39	3.00	117.00
*John Rhodes	Feb 5	Mar 15	39	3.00	117.00
*R. P. Tucker	Feb 5	Mar 15	39	3.00	117.00
‡Wm. D. Ritchie	Feb 5	Feb 23	19	1.50	28.50
‡Edw. Pyles, Sr.	Feb 20	Mar 11	19	1.50	28.50
‡Edw. Pyles, Jr.	Feb 20	Mar 19	27	1.50	40.50

†Employed in butchering and assisting in carrying provisions from Johnsons to Bear V.

*Employed in carrying provisions to the Camp of the Suffering Emigrants, and bringing Twenty one Souls in to the Sacramento Valley.

‡Employed in carrying supplies to meet the above party.

In another account the name of George Tucker appears but is crossed out, 19 days services indicated. The name Curtis is also listed and crossed out, "000." "Joseph Sell" is here credited with 38 days service. Also: "Mr Tucker one Coverlid left with Mr Denton valued a $20 dollars." The George McKinstry Papers in the California State Library contain another payroll record for the First Relief, certified by Kern and totaling $1129.50.

3. Mule Springs, so known to this day, rise north of the town of Dutch Flat between Steephollow Creek and the Bear River.

4. George Tucker in 1879 described to C. F. McGlashan his experiences while waiting at Mule Springs. With some emendation, McGlashan printed this portion of Tucker's manuscript in his *History of the Donner Party,* 1880 edition, pp. 114-119.

5. Rather, destroyed by wolverines, unrelenting enemy of the relief parties in 1847.

6. It is to be hoped that Tucker did not personally have to make good on this $5 per day offer. The payroll in Note 2 indicates that $3 per day was finally approved.

7. See the Breen diary, Note 10.

8. For John Denton, see the story in the *California Star,* April 10, 1847, reprinted in Volume II, with accompanying Note 204. As appears from Note 2 above, R. P. Tucker left with him a coverlid (highly valued) in the vain hope of fending off the cold.

9. This first child who died was Ada Keseberg. Mrs. Keseberg had previously lost at the lake cabins the infant who was born on the overland journey.

10. The Second Relief, headed by James Frazier Reed. The two men met the previous day were R. S. Mootrey and Edward Coffeymeyer, "with a little beef."

11. William Thompson, who had joined Reed's party at Sonoma on February 10.

12. This was as close as Selim Woodworth ever got to Donner Lake, the stretch of trail traveled by Mathers on October 13.

13. See the entry for Sunday, February 28. William Hook, Mrs. Jacob Donner's child by a prior marriage, had given vent to his hunger, climbed a tree to reach the provisions suspended from a branch, and literally eaten himself to death. Tucker says that two others also ate to excess and had to be left behind. William G. Murphy was one of these children, but he wrote McGlashan many years later that his feet had been badly frozen, so that he could not keep up with the others. He also said that after William Hook died, he and the camp-keeper "took the biscuits and jerked beef from his pockets, and buried him just barely under the ground, near a tree which had been fired, and from around which the snow had melted." McGlashan adds (p. 156): "Those who were in the company thought Wm. G. Murphy could not possibly walk, but when all had gone, and Hook was dead, and no alternative remained but to walk or die, he did walk. It took him two days to go barefooted over the snow to Mule Springs, a journey which the others had made in one day [a mistake; see the diary]." (His sister Mary had cut William Murphy's shoes open to get them off, when his frozen feet "swelled up as if they had been scalded.") The third child remains to be identified. The camp-keeper was John Gordon, detached from Reed's party.

14. Edward M. Kern does not appear to advantage in Tucker's diary, nor in the appended remarks by John Sinclair. Tucker had Kern in mind when he wrote McGlashan in 1879 that soon after they reached Mule Springs "the Colonel from the forte arived horses and soldier to escort the party in he stuted around as big as big as the dog in the Smok hous we had et our suppe sent one of his men to

my camp to get some flour and sugar Sent it to him apart of arobe of sugar the same of flower he kept it then came down ater wards and gave me [s]trict orders not to open no more Sugar & Flowr the girls said thay were Sorry thay though thay starved long tim thay thought to backe acake to eat on the way the next day this touck the tender spot I took out knife ript open Sack flour Sugar & wat ever thay wanted I told them I was Boss ove this tab" (McGlashan Papers, Bancroft Library).

15. See McKinstry's account of the return of the First Relief from the mountains, reprinted in Volume II from the *California Star,* March 13, 1847. McKinstry provides an abstract of what he calls Glover's journal, to be compared with that printed here.

16. Apparently some public or private development involving Sinclair and Kern led the former to write out this statement.

17. Reed refers to the story in the *Pacific Rural Press,* January 21, 1871, cited in the Reed section, Note 115. Mrs. Curtis had been the source for Mrs. McDougall.

18. In part Reed's diary was written on the trail, but other parts obviously were written afterward.

19. Although he deleted that entry, Reed says here that 17 men (including Caleb, John, and Britton Greenwood?) at this time comprised his party. Those who went all the way to Donner Lake, supposed to number only ten, have usually been listed with confidence, but their identification is a stickier problem than has been supposed. Reed's diary names among his men William McCutchen, Charles L. Cady, Nicholas Clark, Charles Stone, Joseph Jondrou (Gendrou), Mathew Dofar, and John Turner. Hiram O. Miller definitely was one of the party. But Britton Greenwood is also supposed to have been along; and at Alder Creek on March 2, when Miller auctioned off personal property belonging to the estate of Jacob Donner, among the purchasers were Henry Dunn and Joseph Varo. Even if Brit Greenwood remained behind, despite Thornton's mentioning him in connection with events at the cabins after Reed arrived here, we have one name too many. Compare Carroll D. Hall, ed., *Donner Miscellany,* pp. 80-81, with its document for March 2, and note that Thornton also mentions Dunn. Perhaps there were really 11 in the party.

20. Since Reed did not fall in with Woodworth until some days later, clearly his diary was written out afterward.

21. What became known as the Starved Camp was in Summit Valley, just west of the divide. Respecting the geography, see the Mathers diary, Note 64.

22. It would seem that these events occurred on March 5, the day before the great storm set in, and two days after Reed began shepherding the 17 survivors up toward Summit Valley.

23. Thornton says that soon after the Reed party reached the first encampment west of Starved Camp after the great storm ended (apparently on March 8), "Mr. Stone and Mr. Cady, who had been left at the Mountain Camp, came up. All the men, excepting Mr. Miller and Mr. Stone, found, upon coming to the fire, that their feet were without sensation. Mr. Reed, suspecting that they were frozen, thrust his into the snow, and advised the others to do so. Some of them did it. Mr. Cady, Mr. Dunn, and Mr. Greenwood lost more or less of their toes. Some of them were crippled for life."

24. John Stark was one of the unquestionable heroes of the Donner Relief. McGlashan, p. 197, prints a biographical note. He was at this time only 20 years old, but "a powerfully built man, weighing two hundred and twenty pounds. He was sheriff of Napa County for six years, and in 1852 represented that county in the State Legislature. He died near Calistoga, in 1875, of heart disease. His death was instantaneous, and occurred while pitching hay from a wagon."

25. See Note 2. The Reed Papers in the Sutter's Fort collection also contain payroll data. The government archives at Washington must contain documents reflecting the final accounting made by Woodworth, and determined search may bring these into the light of day. It is not possible in the present work to go into all the details of the Donner Relief; the subject is well worth a special study.

26. McGlashan took a more charitable view of Clark after some correspondence with him, reflected in his book at pp. 163-169, 199-201.

27. So says Thornton. R. P. Tucker wrote McGlashan in 1879 respecting "the 2 trip" that "J. Rhods & Jack [*i.e.,* Sailor Jack or Joseph Sels] and myself and others . . . got as fair as the foot of Bearvaly then pack on back this nite comce snowing sta[r]ted went 6 miles the snow fells fast and tile we were compeled to turn back."

28. Carroll D. Hall, ed., *Donner Miscellany,* pp. 86-87. The original document is in the Reed Papers.

29. For a biographical sketch of Fallon, see Dale L. Morgan and Eleanor T. Harris, *The Rocky Mountain Journals of William Marshall Anderson* (San Marino, 1964).

30. As seen in Volume II, McKinstry forwarded Fallon's journal to the *Star* under cover of a letter of April 29, with accompanying remarks. R. P. Tucker wrote McGlashan concerning his "3 Trip": "R. P. Tucker Rodes Jack or Jo Foster [Sels] Falon Keyster Renar Succeeded in reachin the huts Death & Destruction horrible site human Bones womans Skulls Salled to get the Brains. Beter dwell in the midts of alarm than to r[em]ain in this harable Place we prospect and for the doner camps on the way we met with a fresh track on hearing of us he turn and hid behind some tres we pass on reacked the camps the dead bodies Lay around no liveing being

to to toll the tales of sorrow on my first trip we cut down alarg pine tree and Lay ther good out to sun on the trunk of this tree and thear thay lay yet excepting what Reed company Carried off we Campt thea over night & arrange our packs and left for the upper Camps & found Keis Burg enjoying his Breakfast on the human Flesh."

According to R. P. Tucker's son George, in an 1879 letter to Mc-Glashan, "The fourth relief party was Wm Fallon—John Rhodes—Reason P. Tucker,—Joseph Foster Edward Coffemire in all, 5—Wm Foster and myself went with them to Bear Valley and brough the horses back and met them there agane on their return when they brought Kesberg out."

31. After his return to the settlements, Keseberg brought suit against Edward Coffeemeyer, "for Defamation of Character. Damages $1,000." The case was heard on May 5, and a verdict in Keseberg's favor rendered—but with the significant proviso that the damages were reduced to $1, a dubious result. W. R. Grimshaw, in some notes attached to the John Rhoads dictation in the Bancroft Library, says that "when Keeseburg was on his trial before Captain Sutter the latter had the best of reasons of a personal nature for acquitting him. What those reasons were partakes too much of the nature of gossip & scandal to be detailed here. You can get them from anyone who lived at New Helvetia in those days." Keseberg's behavior in 1846-1847 was far from savory, whether or not he was guilty of murder, and not much sympathy has been wasted on him.

32. In its issue for June 12 the *California Star* corrected this statement: "In the Journal Extracts, published last week, it was stated that 'one body, supposed to be that of Mrs. Eddy, lay near the entrance,' &c., which statement we have been requested to correct, as her undisturbed remains have since been found."

33. The particular point was that if the kettles were full of human blood, Keseberg must have committed murder, for in dead bodies blood would coagulate; he could not have obtained blood from the bodies of those who died earlier. Keseberg denied the truth of this statement to McGlashan.

34. Periodically over the years, caches of coins and other valuables turned up at the Donner sites. See a photograph of such a find made in 1891, reproduced in the 1940 edition of McGlashan's book at p. xiv.

35. As appears from McKinstry's letter of April 29, 1847, reprinted in Volume II, Fallon had reached Sutter's by that date. The Reed Papers include a letter from John Sinclair to Reed, Rancho del Paso, June 23, 1847, which says in part:

"Enclosed you will find a list of articles belonging to yourself and Miss Williams in possession of Mrs Fosdick.

"Mrs. Fosdick informs me that she gave Mr. Fallon no authority to bring in any of your property she says that Fallon remarked he supposed Reed would be willing to pay as much as other people for bringing in his property and she replied she *reckoned* so and she can prove that by persons who were present— She tells me that her Mother offered you the goods when you was at the cabins and that you said you would cash them.

"It is needless for me to enumerate all that I have heard as there can be no settlement until the case is settled by law or refferees, which will make it necessary for you to come up [from Napa Valley] and at same time bring such witnesses as you think can give any evidence in the matter. . . ."

The above is printed in full in Carroll D. Hall's *Donner Miscellany,* pp. 96-97. In the same work is printed a document which would go to show that another salvage expedition after Fallon's was at least contemplated. Dated May 5, 1847, the same day the Keseberg action was litigated, the document reads:

"Know all men by these presents that it is mutually agreed by John Sinclair on the one part acting in behalf of the Heirs of Jacob and George Donner deceased and by the undersigned on the other part, that they shall proceed to the Cabins in the California Mountains where the property of said Jacob & George Donner now is (or was lately) and if the property still remains there that they shall bring away all or as much of said property as they possibly can, the property so brought away to be delivered into the hands of said John Sinclair when an equal division shall be made to the undersigned receiving one half of said property for their services and the said John Sinclair retaining the other half for the benefit of the Heirs of said Jacob & George Donner." Signers were John Rhoads, P. A. House, P. C. Stice[?] and Thomas Rhoads.